THE
HUMAN
WAY

THE HUMAN WAY

Readings in Anthropology

H. RUSSELL BERNARD

MACMILLAN PUBLISHING CO., INC.
New York
COLLIER MACMILLAN PUBLISHERS
London

Macmillan Publishing Co., Inc.
866 Third Avenue, New York, New York 10022

Collier-Macmillan Canada, Ltd.

Library of Congress Cataloging in Publication Data

Bernard, Harvey Russell, (date)   comp.
  The human way.

    Includes bibliographical references.
    1. Ethnology—Addresses, essays, lectures.
I. Title.
GN325.B447   301.2   74–4890
ISBN 0–02–308920–2

Printing: 1 2 3 4 5 6 7 8   Year: 5 6 7 8 9 0

DON ADAMS, "The Monkey and the Fish." Reprinted from *International Development Review* (October 1960) by permission of the Society for International Development.
MARSTON BATES, "On Being Human." From *Gluttons and Libertines*,
by Marston Bates. Copyright © 1967 by Marston Bates. Reprinted by
permission of Random House, Inc.
ALAN R. BEALS, "Getting There." From "Godalpur, 1958–1960" by
Alan R. Beals, in *Being an Anthropologist: Fieldwork in Eleven Cultures* edited by George D. Spindler. Copyright © 1970 by Holt, Rinehart and Winston, Inc. Reprinted by permission of Holt, Rinehart and
Winston, Inc.
DWIGHT BOLINGER, "Some Traits of Language." From *Aspects of Language* by Dwight Bolinger, © 1968, by Harcourt Brace Jovanovich,
Inc., and reprinted with their permission.

VANCE BOURJAILY, "Middle Age Meets the Kid Ghetto." Excerpted from a selection entitled "Middle Age Meets the Kid," in the book *Country Matters,* by Vance Bourjaily. Originally published in *The New York Times.* Copyright © 1973 by Vance Bourjaily. Reprinted by permission of The Dial Press.

BRENT C. BROLIN, "Chandigarh Was Planned by Experts But Something Has Gone Wrong." Reprinted by permission from *Smithsonian* (June 1972).

MERVYN CADWALLADER, "Marriage as a Wretched Institution." Copyright © 1966 by The Atlantic Monthly Company, Boston, Mass. Reprinted with permission.

JOHN B. CALHOUN, "Plight of the Ik and Kaiadilt: A Chilling Possible End for Man." Reprinted by permission from *Smithsonian* (November 1972).

CHARLOTTE GOWER CHAPMAN, "Marriage in Sicily." Reprinted from *Milocca: A Sicilian Village* by permission of Schenkman Publishing Company.

CORA DUBOIS, "Adolescence, Marriage, and Sex" and "Burial on Alor." Reprinted by permission from Cora Dubois, *The People of Alor: A Social-Psychological Study of an East Indian Island,* University of Minnesota Press, Minneapolis. © 1944 by University of Minnesota.

LAWRENCE DURRELL, "How to Buy a House." From the book *Bitter Lemons* by Lawrence Durrell. Copyright © 1957 by Lawrence Durrell. Published by E. P. Dutton & Co., Inc. and used with their permission.

MORTON H. FRIED, "A Four-Letter Word That Hurts." Copyright 1965 by Saturday Review Co. First appeared in *Saturday Review* October 2, 1965. Used with permission.

JEFF GREENFIELD, "Middle America Has Its Woodstock, Too." Copyright © 1972 by Jeff Greenfield. Reprinted by permission of The Sterling Lord Agency. First appeared in *Saturday Review* July 1, 1972.

EDWARD T. HALL, "How Different Cultures Use Space." From *The Silent Language* copyright © by Edward T. Hall. Reprinted by permission of Doubleday & Company, Inc.

MARVIN HARRIS, "Bah, Humbug!" Reprinted with permission from *Natural History* Magazine, December 1972. Copyright © The American Museum of Natural History, 1972.

MARGARET HASLUCK, "Course of the Blood Feud." From *The Unwritten Law in Albania* by Margaret Hasluck. Reprinted by permission of Cambridge University Press.

JULES HENRY, "Golden Rule Days: American Schoolrooms." From *Culture Against Man* by Jules Henry. Copyright © 1963, by Random House, Inc. Reprinted by permission of the publisher. "The Development of the Child's Personality." From "Some Cultural Determinants of Hostility in Pilaga Indian Children," *American Journal of Ortho-*

psychiatry, Vol. 10, No. 1 (January 1940). Copyright © 1940, the American Orthopsychiatric Association, Inc. Reproduced by permission.

ALLAN HOLMBERG, "The Siriono Children." From *Nomads of the Long Bow* by Allan Holmberg. Copyright © 1969 by Laura H. Holmberg as Executrix to the Estate of Allan R. Holmberg. Reprinted by permission of Doubleday & Company, Inc.

WILLIAM HOWELLS, "Culture: How We Behave." From *Back of History*, copyright © 1954, 1963 by William Howells. Reprinted by permission of Doubleday & Company, Inc. "The Nature of Religion." From *The Heathens*, copyright 1948 by William Howells. Reprinted by permission of Doubleday & Company, Inc.

CLYDE KLUCKHOHN and DOROTHEA LEIGHTON, "Ghosts and Witches." Reprinted by permission of the publishers from Clyde Kluckhohn and Dorothea Leighton, *The Navaho*. Cambridge, Mass.: Harvard University Press, Copyright, 1946, by the President and Fellows of Harvard College; renewed 1974 by Florence Kluckhohn Taylor and Dorothea Leighton.

WESTON LA BARRE, "Professor Widjojo Goes to a Koktel Parti." © 1956 by The New York Times Company. Reprinted by permission.

CHARLTON LAIRD, "The Sons of Hengist and Horsa Get Embarrassed About Grammar." From *The Miracle of Language* by Charlton Laird. Copyright 1953 by Charlton Laird, with permission of Thomas Y. Crowell Company, Inc., publisher.

RICHARD B. LEE, "Eating Christmas in the Kalahari." Reprinted with permission from *Natural History* Magazine, December 1969. Copyright © The American Museum of Natural History, 1969.

ROBERT A. LEVINE, "Sex Antagonism in Gusii Society." Reproduced by permission of the American Anthropological Association from *American Anthropologist*, Vol. 61, No. 6 (1959).

OSCAR LEWIS, "The Culture of Poverty." Copyright © 1966 by Oscar Lewis. Reprinted from *La Vida*, by Oscar Lewis, by permission of Random House, Inc.

ELLIOT LIEBOW, "A Field Experience in Retrospection." From *Tally's Corner* by Elliot Liebow, by permission of Little, Brown and Co. Copyright © 1967 by Little, Brown and Co., Inc.

JOSEPH LOPREATO, "How Would You Like to Be a Peasant?" Reproduced by permission of the Society for Applied Anthropology from *Human Organization*, Vol. 24, No. 4 (Winter 1965).

JUDITH MARTIN, "There She Is . . . Miss America." From *The Washington Post* (September 14, 1969). © *The Washington Post*. Reprinted by permission.

PETER MATTHIESSEN, "Under the Mountain Wall." From *Under the Mountain Wall* by Peter Matthiessen. Copyright © 1962 by Peter Matthiessen. Reprinted by permission of The Viking Press, Inc.

JESSICA MITFORD, "The Funeral Transaction." From *The American Way of Death* by Jessica Mitford. Copyright © 1963 by Jessica Mitford. Reprinted by permission of Simon & Schuster, Inc.

CHARLES C. MOSKOS, JR., "Why Men Fight." Published by permission of Transaction, Inc., from *Transaction* Volume 7. Copyright © 1969 by Transaction, Inc.

DAVID PILBEAM, "The Fashionable View of Man as a Naked Ape Is: 1) An Insult to Apes 2) Simplistic 3) Male Oriented 4) Rubbish." © 1972 by The New York Times Company. Reprinted by permission.

HORTENSE POWDERMAKER, "Stranger and Friend." Reprinted from *Stranger and Friend, The Way of an Anthropologist,* by Hortense Powdermaker. By permission of W. W. Norton & Company, Inc. Copyright © 1966 by Hortense Powdermaker. "The Man Who Knocked at the Wrong Woman's Door." From *Copper Town* by Hortense Powdermaker. Copyright © 1962 by Hortense Powdermaker. By permission of Harper & Row, Publishers, Inc.

JESUS SALINAS, "On the Clan of Anthropologists." Translated by H. Russell Bernard. Used with permission of the author and translator.

IRWIN SANDERS, "Religion and the Greek Peasants." Reprinted by permission of the publishers from Irwin T. Sanders, *Rainbow in the Rock: The People of Rural Greece*. Cambridge, Mass.: Harvard University Press, Coypright, 1962, by the President and Fellows of Harvard College.

LYLE SAUNDERS, "Healing Ways." Chapter IV of *Cultural Difference and Medical Care* by Lyle Saunders, © 1954 by Russell Sage Foundation, New York. Reprinted by permission of Basic Books, Inc., Publishers.

DAVID M. SCHNEIDER, "Abortion and Depopulation on a Pacific Island." Case 8 in *Health, Culture, and Community: Case Studies of Public Reactions to Health Programs,* edited by Benjamin D. Paul, with the collaboration of Walter B. Miller, © 1955 by Russell Sage Foundation, New York. Reprinted by permission of Basic Books, Inc., Publishers.

SCHOLASTIC MAGAZINES, INC., "Language Conflicts." Reprinted by permission from *Senior Scholastic,* © 1965 by Scholastic Magazines, Inc.

COLIN M. TURNBULL, "The Giver of the Law." From *The Forest People* by Colin M. Turnbull. Copyright © 1961, by Colin M. Turnbull. Reprinted by permission of Simon & Schuster, Inc.

ROBERT WAUCHOPE, "Reminiscences of a Field Trip." Reprinted by permission of the Society for American Archaeology from *American Antiquity,* Vol. 35, No. 5, Part 2, 1966.

ROSALIE WAX, "The Warrior Dropouts." Published by permission of Transaction, Inc., from *Transaction* Volume 4. Copyright © 1967 by Transaction, Inc.

MARGERY WOLF, "Lim-a-Pou: A Wife and a Sister." From Margery Wolf, *The House of Lim: A Study of a Chinese Family,* © 1968. Reprinted by permission of Prentice-Hall, Inc., Englewood Cliffs, New Jersey.

Martha Wolfenstein, "French Parents Take Their Children to the Park." From *Childhood in Contemporary Culture,* edited by Margaret Mead (1955). Reprinted by permission of The University of Chicago Press.

Francis E. Wylie, "Pilgrims Elude a Pilgrim Hunter." Reprinted by permission from *Smithsonian* (October 1971).

PREFACE

This book was compiled for undergraduate students and their instructors to read and enjoy. It grows out of my experience in teaching the introductory anthropology course steadily for nine years. The readings were selected to meet two criteria simultaneously: 1) they had to be innately interesting to the general reader; and 2) they had to be of real anthropological value within the traditional concerns of the discipline. The following data led me to select these criteria.

1. About 300 Ph.D.s were awarded in anthropology in 1971–1972. It takes an average of seven years beyond the B.A. to get a doctorate in anthropology, so the 1972 crop began sprouting between 1965 and 1966. They took their introductory course between 1962 and 1966. During that time at least 75,000 people a year took introductory anthropology. Because my classes hold 125 students each, on average I have to teach about two semesters before my courses become the foothold to a professional degree for one student. Bad odds, but one does have an obligation to provide the majors in the department with a solid foothold.

2. In 1962–1963 there were 746 bachelor's degrees awarded in anthropology. In 1966 there were 1,503. By 1973 there were over 5,000. At that rate, even if I put my energies into training the upper division majors, I'd still only be sending one out of seventeen on to the ultimate degree. Still terrible odds, but one does have an obligation to the profession and to science. Meanwhile, sixteen out of seventeen anthropology majors become homemakers, insurance repre-

sentatives, career military personnel, capitalists, and ski bums, among other things.

These facts have caused me to consider the purpose of introductory anthropology. I feel that anthropology is exciting and, at its best, fun to study. It is an excellent component of a general education. Furthermore, I believe that the rare anthropology major is not shortchanged by a breezy and fun introduction to his or her career. Quite the contrary.

I have organized the material very traditionally, according to the standard rubrics of ethnography. Section 1 reviews the general field of anthropology and begins with a charming piece on being human by Martson Bates. It sets the irreverent tone of anthropology in general, and puts the reader in the proper mood for the book. Then there follows a series of papers dealing with what anthropology is, how it is done, and who does it. One article, by Sr. Jesús Salinas, is printed here for the first time. It is a rare view of the tribe of anthropologists, written by one of the "natives" studied by anthropologists. I have also included in this section papers on the nature of culture and on the biosocial concept of race, two of the cornerstones of modern anthropological thought.

The other sections deal with language, economics, politics and law, the life cycle, religion, and culture change (including applied anthropology). I have specifically avoided articles dealing with the intricacies of kinship systems. Kinship is one of the most basic areas of human custom and is treated in several articles in the various sections. However, I have not found articles on kinship per se that meet the criterion of being innately interesting to the general reader. I think it will be clear throughout the volume, however, how important kinship is in the rationalization of human behavior. No attempt was made to treat American society and culture separately. Instead I assume that anthropology has long since come of age; the study of American culture is just another part of good traditional anthropology. However, I purposely juxtaposed pieces on American culture with corresponding pieces about non-Western peoples whenever possible. Different ideas about adolescence and beauty are seen in the descriptions of the Miss America pageant and the Alorese tooth-blackening ceremony. Customs concerning death, burial, and treatment of the aged are similarly juxtaposed. Therefore, the one area that gets more than its fair share of coverage is culture (and subcultures) in the United States.

Finally, no attempt is made to separate "social problems" from other aspects of ethnography. West Virginia snake-handling fundamentalists are a problem to the authorities who want to stop the sect; Custer was a problem for the Sioux; black children are a problem for white racist school teachers in the United States and vice versa; making the family budget balance during rampant inflation is a problem for most Americans; and finding scarce game during a drought is a problem for the Kalahari Bushmen. This book assumes that social problems are not the unique possession of "civilized" societies. They are simply one part of culture, and culture is what this book is about.

My debts are many. Carole Bernard and Kathy Palakoff read through the selections to offset my having lost touch with what nonanthropologists consider good reading. Their advice and counsel were invaluable. Ms. Palakoff suggested the title. John Lozier read the preface and introduction and offered sound collegial advice. Carol Wallace typed the manuscript; and Ken Scott of Macmillan has offered sound editorial advice all along. My thanks to all.

H. R. B.

CONTENTS

4 ECONOMICS 129

5 POLITICS AND LAW 172

6 RELIGION 219

7 THE LIFE CYCLE 252

8 APPLIED ANTHROPOLOGY 348

THE
HUMAN
WAY

INTRODUCTION

Anthropology is the study of human beings as biological and social animals through time and space. Anthropologists are interested in understanding human *anatomy* and how it got that way during the past 75 million years or so since the first monkey-like creatures, or early primates, appeared on earth. Anthropologists are also interested in human *behavior* and how it got that way during the past five million years or so since the first human-like animals, or Australopithecines, appeared. We are interested in the similarities and differences in the physical and social make-up of human beings today—all 3½ billion of them in all the nooks and crannies of this planet.

To be interested in all these things is a tall order, and it is not surprising that most anthropologists wind up specializing in one or two very specific areas of the study of people, such as blood groups, prehistoric cultures of the New World, kinship systems of Africa, and so on. What is surprising is that it took so long for scientists to develop all these interests and the skills needed to pursue them. There is no doubt that human beings have always been the most curious and fascinating object of study to other human beings. Philosophers, historians, and theologians have discussed the nature of the human beast for thousands of years. The application of the scientific method to the study of human creatures is relatively new.

Science began by looking at the stars, the furthest things in our universe. When science came down to earth it addressed itself to the nature of inanimate matter in the study of physics and chemistry. It was not until the eighteenth and nineteenth centuries that economics, political science, and sociology developed. Then, at the end of the nineteenth century, psychology and anthropology began in the first feeble scientific attempts to understand the human mind and the totality of the human condition. No doubt, 100 years from now (maybe even 10) our current efforts will appear feeble.

1

There seem to be two reasons for the general lateness of social science. First, a person is a very complicated thing to study. Science depends on measurement; but how do you measure the difference between a Christian and a Buddhist? How do you measure the way in which people learn to be, say, Hopi Indians or Italian Americans so that you can tell precisely what is unique and what is the same about the two learning experiences? A few generations ago there were no tools for measuring—no matter how inadequately—the behavior, the thinking, the values of human beings. Now that we've started, we see how thoroughly unsophisticated we are.

The second reason for the lateness of social science is that it's scary. The study of human anatomy, for example, serves to point out very painfully how weak we are. We don't run or swim or fly worth a darn; we have no claws or teeth to speak of; we have poor vision, poor lungs, terribly fragile sacroiliacs, and we don't live very long. We pride ourselves on overcoming these difficulties with logic and reason. It is undeniable that we have the best brains of any animal on earth right now. But we use our logical capacity to make wars as a way of demonstrating how strong we are. We poison ourselves with chemicals to show how well we can manufacture food. Somehow, the more we study about people the more we find out that our reason and logic are not total compensation for the physical puniness with which we live.

In addition to flashy exposés of our physical weakness, anthropology has not been kind to some cherished myths of Western civilization. During the last few decades anthropologists have marshalled impressive evidence that: 1) there are no primitive languages; all people speak highly complex tongues, with rigorous grammars at least as subtle as English; 2) there are not now, and there have never been, any "pure" races of people; 3) there are no human populations biologically superior to any other, either in physical structure or in mental capacities. As far as we can tell, all human groups have their share of idiots and geniuses; 4) the idea that economic growth can go on indefinitely is a fairly recent disease. For 99 per cent of all human history, primitive peoples lived in cooperation with their environment rather than as predators on it.

The common element in all these findings is that they challenge the traditional thinking of Western civilization. And that's scary.

It would be wrong to give the impression that anthropology is, or has ever been, free of these biases. In fact, many scholars now concede that anthropology was the handmaiden of Western colonialism and imperialism. The information collected by anthropologists was used by colonial administrators to more effectively exploit native populations around the world. To the extent that American Indians are colonized peoples, the same is still true in this country. However, it is safe to say that an awareness of ethical principles has recently become a major focus in anthropology. So things are changing.

With these changes, however, some things remain constant. Anthropology is still the study of humans, characterized by an enthusiastic interest in all the biological and social forms of this animal, in all time and throughout the world. On the biological side there is one major field, physical anthropology. Physical anthropologists are zoologists who happen to specialize in people. Paleozoologists study the bones and teeth of fossil creatures in order to piece together the evolution of some modern species. Some physical anthropologists study the paleozoology of *Homo sapiens*. However, because people are cultural animals (they use tools to survive instead of relying on their bodies), physical anthropologists have to take this into account. For example, it is probably no accident that 600,000 years ago the major transition from ape-man (Australopithecus) to almost-man (*Homo erectus*) was accompanied by the first taming of fire. The basic rule of population dynamics is the principle of adaptive radiation. This means that critters fill up their environment as fast as they can until the environment won't take any more of them. Fire allowed people to move from their original Eden in the tropics of East Africa and to occupy the northern hemisphere where glaciers had previously kept them out. As people moved into China and Europe men hunted the cold-adapted animals of the ice age, like the woolly mammoth. People became cold adapted, too. Not surprisingly, human jaws began to shrink and their teeth got daintier. (Cooking food makes tough teeth unnecessary.)

At the same time, the human cranium began to fill out, the forehead became more rounded (making more room for brains), and the brain became brainier. What happened to the human brain is very much like what we do to light bulbs in order to make them brighter. By winding up the wire into small circles, we get about one-half yard of filament into a two inch lamp. In brains this process is called "convolution."

Taming and making fire is a cultural invention; it led to a series of physical changes that made people more people-like. Among those changes was a more powerful cerebrum, which led to more cultural inventions, and so on. This is called the *biocultural feedback effect* in evolution. It doesn't matter to paleozoologists who study elephants, but physical anthropologists have to worry about it. (We will return to this concept of biocultural feedback at the end of this chapter.)

Some physical anthropologists are interested in reconstructing human social evolution. They study non-human primates (apes and monkeys) in the field, watching them eat and sleep, fight and make love, searching for clues to the way we might once have been. They are also interested in culture because what they find tells us about the early pre-human condition and the physical, social, and psychological prerequisites for becoming human.

Finally, there are physical anthropologists who study neither old bones nor apes, but *Homo sapiens*. They describe the physical variation in this species, but more importantly they study the physical and cultural factors that cause those variations. For example, it is probable that people started out black. Melanin, a darkening agent in the skin, is a fine shield against ultraviolet sun rays, which are dangerous in the tropical latitudes where people were spawned. As the human moved northward, black skin might not have been very useful. The same ultraviolet rays stimulate the manufacture of vitamin D in the body and in northern latitudes lighter skin (less melanin) would have been an advantage.

Consider another physical factor in population variation called the *Bergmann effect*. We notice that, by-and-large, animals are round and short in the arctic, long and skinny at the equator. People sometimes exhibit this trait, too. Diet does not appear to be the cause of this body-shape phenomenon. Young Eskimos who migrate to Seattle and do not eat blubber continue to grow up with the classical short and round shape of Eskimo peoples.

The geometric shape that has the ratio of the greatest mass and the least surface area is a sphere. A long, thin plank has the most surface area and the least mass. A large body mass generates heat and a low surface area prevents the heat from escaping. The reverse is true of tall, thin people. Retention of body heat is obviously an advantage in the arctic, whereas loss of heat (a cooling effect) is just as obviously an advantage in the tropics. Cooking food *does not cause* teeth to become smaller; cold climate *does not cause* people to become short and round. But these environmental conditions constitute the circumstances under which genetic mutations will be advantageous or disadvantageous.

Cultural factors are also important in population differentiation. One reason why everyone in the United States is not brown is because white and black people do not breed randomly. They sometimes *mate* rather cavalierly, but they are very careful with whom they make babies. The perpetuation of current racial differences is thus mostly a cultural phenomenon.

This brings us to the other main branch of anthropology. Social or cultural anthropology is divided into three major fields: ethnography, linguistics, and archaeology. Ethnography is a descriptive science rather than an explanatory one. It tries to describe in detail how people learn to be what they are, how they live out their lives, and how they perpetuate their society by teaching young members to become adults. Ethnographers study the education, economics, politics, religion, art, folklore, games, marriage, and other areas of custom in societies around the world. This is done mostly by living with a people for at least a year or 18 months, learning to speak their native language, and listening a lot. Ethnography is based on the principle that no one knows one's own culture completely, but that a culture can be more or less understood from the knowledge of different people in a society. In other words, an ethnographer learns about another culture by participating in it, speaking its language, and piecing together from its members a picture of the totality. This may seem a little "unscientific" because it relies very heavily on the intuition of the scientist rather than on more concrete investigative devices, such as surveys, statistics, polls, and scales. But this is one of the distinctive features of ethnography.

It is an "intuitive science" because it *makes the observer the instrument of analysis*. If a chemist wants to test a liquid to see if it is acid or alkaline, he might dip a piece of litmus paper in it. If it turns blue, it is an acid; red, it is an alkaline. Ethnographers have only their experience, training, perception, and intuition to use, and no litmus paper. This does not mean that ethnography is unsystematic. Like any science, it requires enormous amounts of time devoted to notetaking, sorting, filing, and cross-checking of information. In other words, the *procedure* is "scientific" and the *analysis* is "artistic." This is one reason why ethnographers (like me) enjoy their work so much. Ethnography is the foundation of anthropology. It provides the basic data from which formulation of general laws of human behavior is attempted.

Language is the mirror of culture and we need to understand how people learn to speak and how they come to internalize their culture. We need to know how language affects other parts of culture and *vice versa* if we are to gain an understanding of what culture is. Linguistics is the study of language. It is true that most linguists speak more than one language, but that is only coincidental because linguistics is certainly not the study of languages, but of the fundamental properties of human communication.

Anthropological linguists are rather "hard science ethnographers" because the field of linguistics has achieved the greatest degree of formalization. This is because the data of linguistics are relatively easy to record. Even if a language has no writing system, it is a fairly simple trick to make up one. Then, we can record real, natural utterances by the thousands, take them home and study them at our leisure to see what grammatical rules and other cultural influences are operating in people's speech. Naturally, the tape recorder has proven very valuable because it records even the tone of voice and lets us get at things like emotional qualities of speech, as well as at the formal grammar. Now, with videotape, we can even record facial expressions, body movement, and other nuances that help us analyze even more fully the psychological and cultural content of language. We find, for example, that "accent" is a major factor in how people perceive one another. Many native speakers of English in the southwestern United States are also bilingual speakers of Spanish. Both their English and their Spanish are distinctive. Non-Spanish-speaking Americans often refer to bilinguals as "disadvantaged" because they have a Spanish accent. Any sensible person would say that it is the poor monolingual American who suffers from speaking only one language. But because jobs and housing and medical services are denied to people on the basis of an accent, they are seen as "disadvantaged."

The study of anthropological linguistics may include how people stand and gesture when they talk to one another. I once witnessed an American businessman in Mexico City negotiating the importation of glass lamps to a New York store. The Mexican businessman should have been advised to avoid prolonged direct eye contact during the negotiations; it makes most Americans uncomfortable and distrusting. The American should have stood about twice as close as he normally does in conversation; Americans tend to place great distance between themselves in talking but this is seen as a sign of distrust in most Mediterranean cultures.

Anthropological linguistics also addresses itself to how people categorize the things in their world. This is the study of *linguistic taxonomies*. Most Americans would classify animals into two major categories, wild and domestic, and then go on dividing from there. In the desert region of Mexico known as the Mezquital, the Otomi people divide the world of animals into "hot" and "cold" or "day" and "night" creatures, in addition to their domestic or wild status. Eskimos, as everyone knows, have many words for various kinds of snow, which speakers of English do not distinguish. On the other hand, most American men distinguish more kinds of motor vehicles (hatchback, club-cab, sedan, convertible, GT, hardtop, mid-size, and so on) than any other population in the world.

How people categorize the things in their world and the linguistic labels they hang on those things tell us a lot about the culture and thinking patterns of a people. More important, comparative studies of taxonomies promise to tell us something about the thinking of people in general. Recent work, for example, indicates that people everywhere use about five levels of categories to classify even the most complex sets of items, including animals, diseases, foods, colors, plants, machines, and so on. Professor George Miller, a social psychologist, found that people remember about seven, plus or minus two (5–9), things at a time, like a row of numbers, for instance. Recently we have learned that English speakers, at least, will give complex directions in 7 ± 2 steps, across town or across a continent. Unless they are written down, complicated food recipes are told in 7 ± 2 steps. These findings have led Peter Killworth and me to look at how many *people* are used by an individual in relating to his world. Not surprisingly, we find that people, in general, have about 7 ± 2 friends, contacts, and so on in the various spheres of activity in which they interact: family, business, social life. One thing leads to another in the study of what it means to be human.

Archaeology is the reconstruction of cultures that are no longer living. Archaeologists are interested in the religion, economics, politics, marriage customs, games, and other things that ethnographers study. But archaeologists can't ask people about those things (the people are all dead), so they have to reconstruct them from the material stuff the people left behind. An archaeologist might discover the fact that Aztecs used a 260 day calendar. However, it's a sure bet that most of the six million people in the Aztec Confederacy in 1520 A.D. knew how long their years was. Thus, archaeologists are the cultural anthropologists of the past. They give anthropology its time dimension. From all this, it is fair to say that cultural anthropology (ethnography, linguistic anthropology, and archaeology) is the science of finding out what people already know or used to know. No one in any culture (even in the smallest hunting band) knows his or her total culture. But people know enough of their total culture to get along, and they certainly know a common core of it. Taken together, all the things that people know about a culture *is* the culture.

A culture is more than this, however. If you took all the parts of a motor and laid them out on a table, it would be impossible to predict the properties of the finished product just by gazing at the parts. You would have to know how they fit together. Professor John Keosian, a molecular biologist, has spent a lifetime studying how inorganic chemicals produce lifelike substances. He concluded that it is pointless to define life, to attempt a minimal distinction between living and nonliving things. "There are only different levels of organization of matter," he says. "If you knew all the properties of sodium and all the properties of chlorine, you still wouldn't be able to predict that sodium chloride would taste salty. And as things get more complicated than a salt molecule, your ability to predict their properties from their parts gets worse and worse."

A human being is a good deal more complicated than a salt molecule; and a culture is more complicated than a single human being. This is the concept of the *superorganic*. A person is organic and the carrier of culture; so if culture is more than the knowledge of all the people who carry it, then it is *super*organic. We might reasonably ask: "If culture is a real thing, with a life of its own, then how come we can't see it or touch it?" The superorganic view answers this question by pointing to things like gravity; you know it's there but you can't touch it. The atom can be seen now that we have electron microscopes, but long before man could see or split one he knew it was there. The reason we know culture is real—that it's *there*—is because it has impact on us. Sometimes it stands up and kicks us. Consider these two statements: 1) "Wars are hell and I wish we didn't have to fight them"; and 2) "I know 460 horsepower is more than I need, but I have just as much right as anyone else to own a big car. After all, they make them and if I don't buy it someone else will." These are examples of cultural impact. If people die and choke in spite of the fact that they *say* they know better, then something must be bigger than individual thought. But this does not mean that people do not understand the superorganic nature of their own culture. To say otherwise, I would have to insist that the anthropologist is the only one who ever knows a culture. This would run counter to everything I've learned in the past ten years of active field work in Greece, Mexico, and the United States. Perhaps it was just luck, but every time I found out something really important about the cultures I have studied, it was because someone told me.

This makes anthropology as a science very different from, say, geology. If a geologist finds a crack in the earth, he "discovers" it. If he can figure out its significance in the history of the earth, he writes a paper and publishes it. If it is a good piece of figuring and discovering, he will be rewarded by the university or oil company where he works. Improvements in rank, salary, and prestige result, but the geologist never has to thank the crack in the earth for letting him discover it. By contrast, anthropologists are beholden to their data. Coming to grips with this is a little like admitting that Columbus didn't "discover" America. After all, there were about 25 million people in the New World when Columbus landed, and they *all* knew America was here.

If cultural anthropology finds out what people already know, then what good is it? Its value lies in piecing together the millions of bits of information known by different people in a society so that we may understand how human groups are put together. From the point of view of pure research, this is enough. We study stars billions of miles away because we're curious about them. We study strange insects and fishes at the bottom of the deepest ocean because we're curious about them. We have no idea what use these studies will be in the search for a cancer cure or a way to feed us all. But we do these studies anyway, because we are curious.

We are most curious about ourselves and we study ourselves to satisfy this curiosity. Sometimes the work can have immediate practical value. Imagine a social survey commissioned to draw a map of all the houses of prostitution in a city. The city might spend $20,000 on the survey and some people would be very angry about it. After all, many taxi drivers could point out most of them to you for a $20 ride around the city. But if the survey is initiated because the city is developing a campaign against VD, then things are a bit different. Then we need to know what many cab drivers know, as well as what many patrons, call-girls, streetwalkers, and madames know. We would need a composite picture of the *total culture* or subculture of prostitution in order to solve the social aspects of the problem of VD epidemiology. And the information would need to be accurate, checked, reliable, not simply the folk wisdom of one informant in the society.

This brings us to the notion of society and culture. All

people live in a *society*. The first and most important function of any society is to perpetuate itself. After all, no one lives forever; hardly anyone manages even 100 years. So societies have to have ways to keep themselves going longer than the lifetime of anyone. This is mostly because human beings, like other animals, continually produce new human beings. It would hardly be fair for one generation of humans to cut off the next generation from inheriting the society (even though it sometimes seems that they would like to). Fair or not, it can't be done; making the transition as painless and as efficient as possible requires that people be raised in a society. In other words, people are *socialized*. The old teach their young to be just like them; and to the extent that human beings are ornery, and never turn out exactly the way they're supposed to, social change takes place between generations. Nevertheless, it is apparent that societies tend toward self-perpetuation.

Among baboons, ants, dolphins, and other social animals, the mechanism for doing this is probably genetic. No ant needs to be taught how to be a drone. Baboons learn a lot about being acceptable baboons, but there is a limit to how much they can learn and the limit is very much lower than that for humans. In humans, the mechanism for learning how to be human is *culture*. Because there are many ways to be human, there are many different *cultures*. Culture is what gives people a sense of right and wrong (though what is right in one culture can be totally wrong in another, and vice versa). Culture is not just ideas. It is behavior and the stuff that results from behavior. The idea that it would be nice to have a clay pot for carrying water is a cultural idea. The idea that the pot should have some designs on it that show what the rain god looks like is a cultural idea. The moulding of clay to make the pot and the painting of the designs are cultural behaviors. The pot is a cultural thing. I can't think of any ideas or behaviors or things that are thought or done or made by humans that are not cultural. But it is obvious that there are many ways to do things. *Culture* is the human way of coping with the environment and of perpetuating the social groups in which people live (and without which they would not survive). But *cultures* are all the ways that people have figured out how to do this.

Differences in cultures are related to the physical environment in some respects: it is no wonder that Eskimos invented snow goggles and African Bushmen did not. But things are not always so simple. Eskimos use exactly the same form of kinship system as most Americans. In general, an emphasis on the nuclear family (father, mother, and unmarried children) shows up among the most technologically primitive and the most technologically complex people of the world. The reasons are very different, however. In current United States society we de-emphasized the grand-family idea (which was the norm before 1900) as life became impersonal. We have schools to educate us, churches to give us salvation, a welfare office to take care of our poor, a social security administration to take care of our elderly. All these bureaus, offices, administrations, schools, and churches are just buildings. Some of them are not even that, but names for a complex of buildings spread out across the land. Primitive society handles these tasks in the family. Eskimos live in an environment that does not support large families and thus we find that the nuclear family handles all the educational, religious, economic, and political needs of each Eskimo.

The differences in custom are the feast of anthropology. Anthropologists study these differences, without passing judgment on their value. Eskimo marriage rules are not "better than" or "worse than" anyone else's. They are different from ours and we seek to learn more about what it means to be human—just human—by studying the many ways people do just that.

The abstinence from moral judgment on the customs and habits of a people is called *cultural relativism*. This concept is very powerful but it is also a double-edged sword. It could be argued that it was part of German culture to exterminate Jews between 1939 and 1945. It could be argued that it was part of Aztec culture to cut out peoples' hearts every day to feed their sun god. Because very few Aztecs liked the idea of having their own hearts torn out, they used those of other people, whom they would capture in regular war raids. In our own society we have been at war or preparing for war since about 1940. Thus it could be argued that war is just another part of American culture, neither right nor wrong. There are many people who would find all or some of these examples unacceptable candidates for a relativistic attitude. Anthropology does not seek to shake anyone's faith so much that one gives up all notions of morality forever. Rather the study of how different people solve problems common to all people shows us that our own way is not always the best or the only correct way. We question, but we seek to do this without becoming moral vegetables.

The concept of culture is the foundation of anthropology and we keep adding new insights to our understanding of how it works. Linguists have shown us how we learn our culture by learning our language. Archaeologists have shown us that culture is accumulative and accelerative: the more it grows, the faster it grows. The Early Paleolithic period (Old Stone Age), for example, lasted about 1½ million years. During that time our ape-brained ancestors learned to make stone axes. The next period (Middle Paleolithic) lasted only about a half million years and man learned to make nicer looking axes and to chip neat, sharp flakes off large rocks. The next period (Upper Paleolithic) lasted only about 100,000 years. During that time people learned a lot more. Special stone tools with special shapes were invented to whittle down bone and wood. Needles were used toward the end of the period to make the first tailored clothing. The bow and arrow were invented and man became a superb hunter. During all these eons human social life was getting more complicated, too. By the time our species got the bow and arrow we had figured out how to hunt in groups, trap mammoths in swamps where they could be safely slaughtered, run herds of animals off cliffs, and so on. We don't know how Upper Paleolithic man divided up all this bounty, but it's a sure thing that economic rules for distribution had to be developed.

When we learned to cultivate our food instead of chasing it down, a revolution was started that is still going on. The Neolithic period (New Stone Age) lasted only a few thousand years. And now we make up technological ages every day: the computer age, the atomic age, the industrial age—all kinds of "ages," tripping over one another. That is what archaeologists mean when they tell us that culture is accumulative and accelerative.

Another example of how interrelated all the parts of anthropology are comes from some recent experiments in "linguistic archaeology." At Washington State University, Henry Irwin and I collected two tons of obsidian (volcanic glass rock). We put together two groups of 17 male students each and invited them to learn to make primitive stone tools. Guy Muto, a gifted flint knapper (stone tool maker), gave lessons to both groups. In one group, however, he explained everything he did very carefully: how to hit the rock, what angle to give it, how to hold it and direct the waves of percussion, and so on. In the second group he used *no verbal communication* at all. Then we measured how well people learned to make the same stone tools with and without verbal teaching.

Our basic finding was that no significant difference in learning was observed until tools known as Levallois-type were attempted. In making the early stone tools, primitive man (Australopithecus) banged at rocks and took off chips; what was left (the core-tool) was the finished product. If a nice sharp chip happened to fall off in the process, no doubt early man used it for something. But the main purpose of earliest stone tool making was to get a core-tool out of a big piece of rock.

About 600,000 years ago some people (*Homo erectus*) began using the large flakes and throwing away the cores. This was a rather difficult task for those without verbal instruction. They couldn't get nice big flakes to come off the cores, which could then be chipped and worked into nice flat-sided tools. The real change, however, came with the Levallois tools. About 100,000 years ago the first *Homo sapiens,* or Neanderthals, began mass producing flake tools. They prepared a core to look like a tortoise shell; then they would carefully hit the core with another rock and take off long, thin, razor-sharp blades. In this way, about 40 feet of razor edge could be had from a three or four pound rock. All they had to do was carry the core around, and when the blade got dull they chipped off another with one swipe.

No one in the group without verbal instruction could manage this Levallois trick. But many in the group *with* verbal instruction began doing quite well at it by the time we ran out of rock and the experiment ended. The implications are rather clear: the origins of modern human speech may be linked to tool-making capabilities and primitive speech may have emerged no earlier than 100,000 years ago. We are still a long way from solving this riddle; but anthropological linguists, archaeologists, and human anatomists are all involved in it. And they are all interested in the role of culture on the development of humans.

Of all the characteristics of culture, perhaps the most important is that it *is* the environment. This is not an easy thing to digest. It is relatively common to say that culture is the human way of coping with the environment: wearing clothes instead of growing fur, building airplanes instead of growing wings. That part is easy because we are accustomed to thinking about the environment in terms of air, mountains, plants, bacteria, and so on. The hard part is to imagine that our culture *is* the physical environment to which we adapt both biologically and socially. This is the biocultural feedback mechanism I spoke of earlier. Human evolution in general may be seen in terms of this peculiar mechanism. Basically, it works like this: Among those animals who use culture to survive, the more sophisticated their cultural capability, the more likely their survival. Thus, culture (once started) placed a premium on mutations that led to increased cultural capacity. A good example of this is the relationship between language and tool-using. Biological mutations, which make increased communications possible, led to more sophisticated cultural techniques for tool-making, which had increased survival benefits. Here are two more examples:

1. Sickle-cell anemia is a hereditary disorder that can be a killer. It affects black people generally, although many related kinds of disorders are also found among whites, especially those of Mediterranean origin. In the heterozygous condition (where the gene has been inherited from only one parent), sickle-cell is harmless, except at high altitudes. On the other hand, the heterozygous condition appears to give people immunity to malaria. But if two people with the trait (not the disease) marry, then they each have one gene for normal hemoglobins (red blood cells), and one for sickle-cell hemoglobins, like this: $A B \times A B$, where $A =$ sickle-cell and $B =$ normal. This means that, in this marriage at least, the chances are one out of four that a child will be AA (in which case it will probably die of anemia before puberty), one out of four that it will be BB (in which case it might die of malaria), and two out of four that it will be AB. One out of four with a deadly disease is a high price to pay for immunity to malaria. But that is what happened to certain groups of black Africans no more than 8,000 years ago.

The important part of this case is that, prior to 6,000 B.C., the people in central Africa did not have sickle-cell trait or anemia. They did not have malaria, either. When they began clearing the dense forests for agriculture, they opened up areas where stagnant pools formed, which attracted the mosquito, that brought the malaria. Agricultural techniques are part of culture. Human culture created the circumstances that in turn resulted in the biological changes we call sickle-cell trait. Humans are the creatures of culture, as well as its creator.

The sickle-cell story is an example of physical evolution in response to cultural conditions.

2. An example of our need to evolve socially in response to such conditions is environmental pollution. Each of us feels that it is our right to acquire material wealth in great abundance if we can. Every 5,000 pound automobile uses up a lot of energy. Coal is burned to extract steel, oil is consumed to run the auto plants, and more oil is used up running the car itself. All along the line, each operation uses up resources and pollutes the atmosphere, but it has been very difficult for us to give up

those big cars. Now it appears that we will either change our living habits and become less wasteful and more careful with our resources, or we will be faced with the same thing that all creatures face when they do not adapt to their changing environment.

1 CULTURE IS HUMAN

The fact that human beings all eat, sleep, eliminate digestive waste, and reproduce sexually, says nothing about what it means to be human. After all, cattle do all these things too. On the other hand, I can't think of a single biological function that is performed in the same way by all peoples of the world, and this says a lot about what makes us different from other animals. Mexican Indians eat with tortillas; Japanese eat with chopsticks; Bushmen eat with their fingers; and Americans manage to use a variety of instruments called silverware.

Besides the differences in behavior among human groups for solving the same biological problem, there is another factor that makes people unique in the animal world. They all believe that their way of doing things is the "natural" way. Once my wife and I had some Otomi friends to our house in Mexico for dinner. They were not uncomfortable with knives and forks, but they couldn't help remark on what a waste silverware is. "Isn't it better to eat your utensils when you finish using them, than to work so hard at keeping them clean?" The logic of that question is inescapable; but then so is every people's logic for doing things the "natural" way.

The first thing we need to understand, then, is what it means to be natural as a human being. The first of the four articles in this section is by Marston Bates, a human ecologist. He shows that the effect of culture on behavior in humans is so overwhelming that it is impossible to describe humans in purely biological terms. Humans blush when they are ashamed. They get ulcers because of things they think about. They get out of breath when they are late for appointments, even when they haven't been running.

None of these things happens to apes (although you can make them get ulcers by cooping them up and depriving them of a constant food supply), and it is tempting to

16

try to understand why by comparing apes and humans biologically. As Bates shows, though, "anatomy and physiology tell us nothing about shame, pride, or modesty."

The second selection is by William Howells, who explores the concept of culture further. He observes that apes can and do make tools; they can teach their young new modes of behavior; and they can "make and handle abstractions to a significant degree."

As a physical anthropologist, Howells wonders about the difference between the capabilities of apes and humans in handling abstractions. He concludes that human culture is rooted in our ability to *accumulate abstractions* and to use *symbols* (words) to dredge them up when we need them. We owe a lot of our humanity to the apes; but "culture is only human," says Howells.

A third point of view on culture comes from Vance Bourjaily, a journalist. He is not concerned with the biological foundations of human behavior. Rather, he tries to understand what a culture contains and how a group of people with a particular culture can be defined. He tackled this problem by studying the youth counterculture of an American city. He sensed that understanding the culture of youth was of vital importance to the middle-aged population of a rapidly changing society. "Kids always win . . . they outlive us," says Bourjaily. In his study he found all the prerequisites of a culture in the youth society. It had a history and a beginning; art, music, and language of its own; and a way to recruit and socialize new members on the right (or "natural") way to behave.

The last article in this section is by Morton Fried, a cultural anthropologist who deals with the concept of race. Is *race* a biological term or a cultural one? Fried concludes (with many other anthropologists) that racial classification is nonsense when applied to humans. Of course, no one can deny that there are obvious physical differences among populations of the world. But culture is so important in human populations that most "racial types" are anything but biological in origin. In 1970, for example, the U.S. Census had a question on "race." Each citizen was asked to check whether he or she was "White," "Black or Negro," "Indian," "Japanese," "Korean," "Hawaiian," "Chinese," "Filipino," or "other." Skin color, national origin, geographic location of residence, and language were equally considered to be racial types! Fried asks "Why is it so hard to give up this miserable little four-letter word that of all four-letter words has done the most damage?" One answer is that "the word 'race' expresses a certain kind of unresolved social conflict that thrives on divisions and invidious distinctions." Another answer is that we still have a lot to learn before we can untangle the biological and cultural sides of being human.

■ ON BEING HUMAN

Marston Bates

Every schoolday morning our son Glenn comes to the bedroom at a quarter to seven with cups of coffee. Nancy, obviously, has done a good job of raising our children—the oldest at home has the alarm clock, and they all take a certain amount of responsibility for keeping their parents in line. The coffee routine has now passed on through all four of them; and when Glenn goes away I don't know what we will do. Look after ourselves, I suppose.

I switch on the light and automatically look at my watch to check on Glenn's timing—we are all slaves of that damned clock. School, office, lecture, railway, dentist. They say it all started with the monastery bells of the Middle Ages; but however it got started, Time now permeates every aspect of our civilization. The slavery starts at an early age: the schools, whatever else they do, manage to instill an acute dread of being tardy in most children. A few rebellious people manage to be tardy for most of their lives, despite the pressures; but we hardly regard them as models of conduct.

Anyway, I try to make some bright crack as I check on Glenn's timing, but it usually falls flat because neither of us feels very chipper before dawn. I reach for a cigarette—a deplorable habit, but again I am a slave —and start the slow process of pulling myself together to face the world for another day.

I have been sleeping on a bed. This seems perfectly natural to me. But if we take "natural" to mean doing what most people do, it is rather odd behavior. My guess would be that perhaps a quarter of the people of the world sleep on beds. I suspect that the commonest sleeping arrangement is matting that can be rolled up and stowed during the day—which is certainly practical from the point of view of space utilization. In warm climates the most practical sleeping arrangement is the hammock—an invention of the American Indians. It is easily taken down if the space is needed; it is portable; it isolates the sleeper from creeping things on the ground; and it provides maximum ventilation. It takes getting used to; but so do most things.

The paraphernalia involved in Western sleeping become more peculiar when looked at in detail: springs, mattresses, sheets, blankets, pillows, pillowcases. Beds have a long history in the Graeco-Roman and Western worlds, but this total accumulation must be rather modern. Much of it I find puzzling. Our bed, for instance, has springs; but my wife has put a bedboard over them. Why not just have a board to start with? And then there are all of the rules for making up a bed, for covering it, for airing it. You could write a whole book about beds, and I suspect someone has.

Habitually I sleep naked. This seems to be rather aberrant behavior in our culture—or in most others. To be sure, I keep a dressing gown close at hand, just in case the house should catch on fire. But it appears that most men in the United States nowadays sleep either in pajamas (a word and custom of Hindu origin) or in underclothes (a particularly common habit with college students). A sociologist might study this, to see whether there is any relation between night clothing and geographical region, or median income, or level of education. I remember reading in the Kinsey report on the human male that nudity was an upper-class characteristic, which made me feel smug for a while.

Women, in my limited experience, cling to nightgowns, though they can sometimes be persuaded to take them off. Nightshirts for men became rare about a generation ago; I know a few people who still wear them—eccentrics, I suppose. It is curious how fashion penetrates even into the privacy of the bedroom. It may be, of course, that more women now wear pajamas than wear nightgowns—my figures on the subject are not really statistically significant.

I left myself smoking a cigarette and drinking a cup of coffee. I wish I could break that cigarette habit. Do you suppose anyone starts the morning in bed with a cigar or a pipe? It doesn't seem right, somehow. As for coffee—in England it would be tea—and mostly in the United States in a private home many people find it an absolute necessity to start the day with a cup of coffee.

Finally I get courage enough to crawl out from under the blanket into the world—or at least into the bathroom. Civilization does have advantages. I brush my teeth and exercise my gums just as my dentist has told me to—what a lot of trouble those teeth cause us! Then I shave. This is an ancient practice among some of the so-called "white" races which, along with the Australian blackfellows, are the only peoples with enough facial hair to bother with. It is said that the ancient Egyptians shaved off all body hair, but with us nowadays men limit the shaving process to the face. Our women shave their legs and their armpits, as I am reminded when I find my razor out of place. I cut myself, and I think that my wife will scold. She can't understand why, after some forty years of daily shaving, I haven't learned better. I don't understand either.

My morning routine has become quite fixed over the years: teeth, shave, shower. One summer at a conference I lived for a while in a dormitory and discovered that most of the people there took their baths either in the afternoon or evening. This came as a surprise—I had thought that taking a bath first thing in the morning was one of those basic laws of nature. I had realized, though, that men can be sharply divided into two groups: those that bathe before they shave and those that bathe after. The bath-first group believe that the preliminary soaping of the face helps soften the beard; the bath-afterward people (where I belong) find an economy of effort in using the shower to wash the shaving soap off their faces. But the subject of bath timing is apparently much more complicated than this.

Then I get dressed. What a long cultural history lies behind each action here! The males in our society wear "arctic type" fitted garments, an invention of the barbaric tribes of prehistoric northern Europe. Trousers, neatly preserved by the acid waters, have been dug up from Danish peat bogs. These trousers are convenient in cold weather, as any woman can tell you. The tropical draped garment, which carries over into the dress of our females, is more comfortable in hot weather. But comfort is a minor consideration in our clothing habits.

Each morning I have to face the problem of what to wear. I have lived much of my life in the tropics, and I hate the feeling of a tie around my neck and of leather shoes encasing my feet. But a professor is supposed to wear shoes, tie and coat. He is far less subject to convention than, say, a banker or a physician is; but there are limits if he doesn't want to be considered a crackpot. I want to play my role well enough to be accepted by the society in which I live, so most often (on days when I am due to lecture) I put on a tie and try to look respectable even though I feel like a fraud. My aim, as I phrase it to myself, is to be "a reasonable facsimile of a proper professor." But I don't know that I succeed very well.

Breakfast. "Glenn, you *must* finish your cereal." Eating soon after you get up is another of those fundamental laws of nature in the United States. In other parts of the world the fundamental laws of nature differ, but they are equally inexorable, whatever their form. Cereal, milk—whoever first had the idea of getting food by squeezing the udder of a cow or goat?—eggs, toast, fruit juice. In the South, grits come with the eggs automatically; at some line in Kentucky and Virginia these give way to hash-browned potatoes. To the west, grits disappear somewhere in Texas.

Thus in the matter of breakfast we have cultural diversity, geographical diversity, individual diversity. We conform with the common usage of our group in when we eat, what we eat, how we eat it. Sometimes, too, we diverge. I almost wrote "rebel" but such a strong word hardly seems appropriate for breakfast—though a child's reaction may be a real enough rebellion.

Quite unintentionally I have got into a curious situation in this breakfast matter. I have never been much given to eating, especially the first thing in the morning, and I solved the breakfast problem some years ago by the simple expedient of breaking two raw eggs into a glass of orange juice and drinking the mixture. The needed nutrients are present, with no time spent over the stove, no frying pan to clean—only a glass to rinse out. This seems to me eminently sensible. The rest of the household accepts my behavior, though no one has ever made any move to imitate.

For years I didn't have the courage to order this breakfast in a restaurant. Finally a friend who knew of my home habits persuaded me to try it: he pointed out that restaurants were supposed to serve people's needs, and why should I be afraid of what the waitress would think. This first try was in the French Quarter of New Orleans, and no eyebrows were raised. But when I gave the same order in cafés along the highway driving north, I met incredulity and reluctance. It turned out to be all right if I asked to have the eggs beaten in the juice—I suppose because everyone knows about eggnogs. I still haven't had the courage to order anything except an ordinary breakfast in the dining room of a proper hotel.

Such is the force of opinion governing human conduct even in a trivial detail. My conduct, at least. Then I stop and wonder whether I am peculiar. I suppose the average waitress in the average middle-class restaurant would definitely say "yes." On the waterfront they are used to the idea of raw eggs in beer, but they might think the orange juice odd. So whether I am peculiar or not depends on where I am, which opens up some large questions.

Everyone, really, is peculiar. Any biologist, used to studying the behavior of animals, becomes puzzled when he turns to man—and he is forced to the conclusion that the human animal as a species is peculiar. How did we get this way? And what does it mean?

We could say that human actions are never to be understood in purely biological terms. Like other animals, we have to eat—we need proteins, fats, carbohydrates, assorted vitamins and minerals. There is nothing unusual about these food requirements or about the way the human digestive system works. The process of metabolism with man, as with other animals, results in the accumulation of waste products which must be got rid of. The wastes take the form of urine and feces. The inner workings, then, are biological; but the outward actions, the modes of behavior, are something else again. Feces is just another word for shit—but see the problem?

I broke my leg a couple of years ago and learned many things in the slow process of recovery. The hospital immobilized me in traction and I remember, on one of the first mornings, that a nurse came in and asked "Have you had a B.M. yet?"

I was puzzled for a moment because they had been doing all sorts of odd things to me, and then asked her wonderingly, "But why on earth would they give me a basal metabolism?"

It turned out, of course, that B.M. meant "bowel movement." Somehow I had got through life without learning that particular circumlocution and it struck me as very odd—one of the many compromises with reality that have developed in the nursing situation. Because of our animal nature, we produce shit more or less regularly, but we dislike to admit this openly and we cannot talk about it with any equanimity. We would much rather pretend there was no such thing—stopping off in a "rest room" when the need arises—but in a hospital situation we are forced to be somewhat more direct.

Obviously I am skirting over a whole series of somewhat different problems here. There is the problem of action, of behavior; the problem of symbols, of words; the problem of relations between the sexes (I would have been able to talk much more directly with a male orderly); the problem of dealing with new situations (I eventually learned to cope both with bedpans and with nursing vocabulary). Yet all of these are but aspects, really, of the general human problem of being natural.

What does it mean, to be "natural"? Maybe it is natural for man to hide himself when excreting. Then maybe it is natural not only to hide the fact in the bushes, but also to gloss over the action with a deceptive kind of vocabulary. In many parts of the world the idea of decent and indecent actions is entangled with the use of decent and indecent words. One could argue that it is natural for man to treat actions and words as equivalent—at least it seems to be easy enough to start a fight by calling someone a bad name. If excretion, though unfortunately necessary, is naturally bad, one can see how the word for it naturally becomes bad too. But this still leaves puzzles.

"Natural" clearly means quite a number of different things, so that, when we start to talk about it, we can easily become lost in semantic problems. I checked the unabridged Oxford English Dictionary and found eighteen main definitions for "natural," each with a number of subheadings. For our present purposes, however, we can reduce these to three general ideas, which can be most readily distinguished in terms of their opposites. We can use "natural" as distinguished from "supernatural," "artificial" and "unnatural."

Natural and supernatural need concern us little. Our scientific civilization assumes that the world is orderly and not subject to capricious intervention and control by spirits. There are many cultures in which spirits are just as "real" as sharks or leopards—and a great deal more dangerous and more difficult to cope with. But in theory at least we treat the events of everyday life as the consequence of natural, rather than supernatural, forces.

Artificial is an easy word in some ways, more difficult in others. Essentially it means man-made. This is clear in the case of artifacts. An artificial rose is made from wax, glass, paper or what have you, in imitation of nature. Yet, if we stop to think about it, the "natural" rose growing in our garden is also man-made—the product of selection, hybridization and cultivation by man, and unlike anything that occurs in nature without human intervention. We recognize this rather vaguely when we talk about artificial hybrids or artificial selection, but we are, in general, reluctant to face the extent to which our environment has been altered by our own actions—the extent to which, in this sense, it is artificial.

If we use artificial to cover anything made or altered by man, the word really loses much of its usefulness. There is nothing natural left in the environments that most of us live in. To escape from an artificial world we have to go to the north woods of Canada, the forests of the upper Amazon, or the southwestern deserts. So much for the environment. But there is nothing natural left in human behavior, either: it is all governed or modified in varying degree by culture, tradition, opinion. We can hardly talk about artificial manners, for instance, because all manners are artificial; there is no natural man.

There may be a gain in the use of artificial in this very broad sense because we begin to see the extent to which human actions are the consequence of the human condition. We begin to see the hazards of trying to determine what is natural for man by studying apes or monkeys or white rats.

But if everything about man is artificial, if nothing is natural, does this mean that all human actions are unnatural? Clearly not, because we have shifted to another meaning of natural. Unnatural carries the idea of abnormal, unusual, strange. This doesn't help much: you can get into as much trouble with normal and abnormal as with natural and unnatural. We are involved with the cultural context in which all people live: what is unusual for some may be commonplace for others. For us it is unnatural to eat worms; for the Chinese, unnatural to drink milk. Sometimes I am driven to think that calling anything unnatural merely means that the speaker does not approve of it.

All of which sheds little light on the human problem of being natural. In the case of supernatural, most of us have no alternative to being natural during life, whatever may happen afterward. The sorcerers and magicians in our midst may think they escape this kind of naturalness, but the rest of us have come to view their claims dubiously. In the case of artificial, there seems to be no escape from artificiality into naturalness. Only in the case of natural versus unnatural do we have an apparent choice—which boils down to the question of whether or not to act in accord with the usual, the normal, of our particular culture, our way of life. We are faced with the problem of conformity, about which we in the West at least have lately become self-conscious.

One could argue that natural behavior is that usual to, or conforming with, human nature—but for that one needs a fairly definite concept of human nature. The anthropologists, with their descriptions of cultural relativism, and the psychologists, with their emphasis on individual learning and experience, have shown us that this is not easy. One comes to sympathize with the existentialist position that there is no such thing as human nature, that each man makes himself.

But if it is difficult to determine human nature, one can at least discuss the human condition, most easily in physical terms. Man is a mammal and a primate, which immediately defines many characteristics. He cannot spend his whole life swimming, like a dolphin; nor browse on grass, like a cow; nor scramble up a tree trunk unaided, like a squirrel or like some of his monkey relatives. He has an upright posture, with appropriately modified feet, legs and trunk, which makes him unique among the primates. His hands and arms, not needed for walking, are free for other functions, thus allowing him to develop his great ability at manipulating things. There are limits though: I have often wished, in situations such as cocktail parties, that I had a prehensile tail so that I could manage my drink, my canapé and my cigarette at the same time. A spider monkey would have no trouble.

Man has binocular vision, which enables him to judge distance well; and he can discriminate form and color. Many animals, however, have keener vision. Man's hearing is moderately good, but his sense of smell is quite poor. One could go on with such a list and describe the anatomical and physiological traits of the human animal with some accuracy, and in so doing one aspect of the human condition would be described. But how little this helps us in understanding ourselves! No matter how much care we devote to the study of the anatomy of the brain, we learn nothing about why "shit" is an indecent word for a necessary action; nothing about why men wear trousers and women skirts in our culture; nothing about food habits or sex habits. Anatomy and physiology tell us nothing about shame, pride or modesty.

Our problem turns on the mind rather than the body: but how do we dissect the mind? It doesn't help much to say that body and mind are not separate entities, but simply different aspects of the physical organism. Maybe we should shift terms and talk, not about mind, but about self-consciousness or awareness. But we are still bogged down in words. How our awareness compares with that of a chimpanzee, a monkey or a dog, we do not know. Certainly we can find comparable expressions of emotions in animals and men, as Charles Darwin showed long ago. Perhaps from this we can infer comparable emotions, but it is difficult to find out about this because we cannot carry on discussions with other animals.

Certainly is is difficult to separate human actions, emotions and attitudes from the human habit of talking. It would be interesting to know how all of this got started. Did those ape-men living in South Africa a half a million years ago "talk" in some way comparable with ours? Did they listen to the advice of a wise old chief, and did they try to be faithful to their mates? Had they developed special ideas about food, sex and excretion—in other words, did they have cultural taboos? Which I suppose is asking how human they were. Their brains were only a little larger than those of modern chimpanzees: a cranial capacity of 450–550 cc., compared with the 350–450 for the chimp and with 1200–1500 for modern man. But it is hard to know what this means in terms of behavior.

These Australopithecines—as the South African apemen are properly called—were at least human enough to commit murder. Raymond Dart, in his book *Adventures with the Missing Link*, remarks on the jaw of an adolescent "which had been bashed in by a formidable blow from the front and delivered with great accuracy just to the left of the point of the jaw." Nothing of this sort happens in the case of squabbles among apes and monkeys, though they may be mean enough to each other when cooped up together in a zoo.

We have here direct evidence of a kind of behavior on the part of our remote evolutionary ancestors, though with no clue as to the meaning of the behavior; but even this much is rare. For the most part we have only bones and tools made of materials likely to survive—which tell us nothing about sex habits, or even skin color or body hair. We have, in short, considerable evidence to help us in reconstructing the evolution of the human skeleton, but almost none to help us reconstruct the history of human behavior. Yet our striking peculiarities are in behavior, not in skeleton. We can get ideas about the possible background by watching living monkeys and apes; but man is so different that these inferences must be interpreted with great caution. For the most part we can only speculate about the history of human behavior, bolstering our speculations with whatever evidence we can find. This is no road to certainty; but speculation often is the impetus for scientific investigation, and it can be illuminating.

To the outstanding peculiarity of man is the great control of custom, of culture, over behavior. This is obvious enough in the case of such things as food, sex and excretion, but it is far more pervasive. We can't even get out of breath "naturally." If we are late for an appointment we may tend to exaggerate our breathlessness to show how hard we were trying. On the other hand, people of my age try to suppress their panting, trying to hide the deterioration of age—or of too much smoking.

The effect of culture on behavior is not limited to actions; it influences all physiology in many ways. This shows up in the psychosomatic diseases—ulcers, dermatitis, asthma and a host of little-understood effects of "mind" on "body." This relationship is especially irritating when you know that a particular worry is causing a distressing physical effect like dermatitis—yet you can't escape the worry. Here is where psychotherapy or drugs, benign or otherwise, come in.

Then there is the curious human trait of blushing, whereby thoughts influence peripheral blood circulation. Here again we run into the perplexing problem of consciousness: you can't stop yourself from blushing by deciding not to. The possible origin and meaning of blushing fascinated Darwin, but neither he nor anyone else seems to have arrived at a satisfactory explanation of the phenomenon.

There is also the opposite and equally little understood process of influence of conscious thought on inner physiology, as in the exercises of Yoga. Apparently there is little a man can't do to his body if he puts his mind to it.

The human habit of hiding physiology brings up the corresponding habit of hiding anatomy. This of course depends on the development of clothing—a subject that fascinates me and that I want to explore in some detail later in this book. It would be interesting to know how the idea of covering parts of the body got started, but we shall probably never have direct evidence. It is quite likely that clothing started, not as protection against weather, nor as a consequence of a dawning sense of modesty, but rather as one aspect of the general human tendency to tamper with appearance. The list of things that different peoples do to their bodies is both curious and impressive: cutting hair; chipping teeth; painting, tattooing and scarring skin; deforming the infant skull or feet; circumcising the penis; cutting or enlarging the clitoris; cutting holes in ears or nose to hang things from; draping objects around the neck or waist or arms or ankles. The motive among Ubangi women for adorning themselves with ridiculous lip plugs is no different from the motive of Western women who use make-up and hair curlers—or from that of men who endure haircuts, shaves and button-down-collar shirts.

Clothing probably derives from the habit of hanging things around the neck or waist, or perhaps from the habit of painting or scarring the skin. The advantage of an extra and artificial skin in bad weather would then be a later and accidental discovery. The concealing function of clothing is surely a secondary development and even in our society it is difficult to decide whether modesty or display is more important in the design of clothes: witness the bikinis, and the street-corner boys with their tight jeans.

I have not been able to think of any animal except man that ornaments itself by picking up additions for skin, fur or feathers. There is no argument about man's being a peculiar creature. But there is also no argument—among biologists at least—about his being an animal. The animal heritage is clear enough in anatomy and physiology—in the form of bones and muscles and guts; in the need for breathing and eating and excreting and copulating. But what of our heritage in behavior?

Human behavior has long formed the subject matter of a series of special sciences: psychology, anthropology, sociology, economics; probably history and political science should be added to the list. I can claim no special training in any of these subjects—though I once flunked a course in sociology. I am a biologist, and my special field as a research scientist has been mosquitoes and the diseases they transmit. But I am also a human being, and I have long been interested in watching other people and in trying to gain some understanding of myself. Somewhere, early, I came to feel that the behavior of the peoples of the Western world gave them no patent on the right way of living—no monopoly on either the satisfactions or the miseries available to our species.

Thus both the peculiarities of man as a species and the diversity in his ways of life fascinate me. It seems to me that diversity in itself is good; that there is no single "right way" for all people.

■ CULTURE: HOW WE BEHAVE

William Howells

It ought to be plain by now that man, in his physical and social nature, is very much at home among the Primates. If he did not do certain other things which mark him off from his relatives, this book would be finished here. But he does: almost every action we take, all day long, is something that apes, the brightest of the other animals, cannot do. For man is a creature with culture.

I am not indulging in a piece of outrageous snobbery, hoping that the gorillas will not find out what I have said. I am not trying to say we have better breeding than they, or more appreciation of the Finer Things; for culture, in this proper sense, is something much broader, and all men live by it, even though some have more than others. It consists, simply, in all the inventions, and all the conventions, ever made by humanity. Culture is what it takes to be human.

Without it, we would simply be another kind of animal, a kind of ape, living like the other kinds in small groups, true societies, but culture-less societies. Every band, or society, of chimpanzees behaves in the same way, in its manner of eating, sleeping in nests, traveling around, and in its noisy social intercourse. This is all characteristic of chimpanzes, and it is determined by their general nature and capabilities. The case of man is different. Every human society has an added stock of behavior, which overlies, and modifies, the other, and it is this added stock that is called culture. Furthermore, this overlay is never identically the same for two different societies. Why? Because it is not inborn and never becomes inbred. It is not in itself biological; it is "inherited," which is important, but it is inherited like property, not like blue eyes. Culture is all those things that are *not* inherited biologically.

Instead, culture consists of everything that has ever been accepted as a way of doing or thinking, and so taught by one person to another. Because that is how it is passed on, and—this is vital—that is how it can change and grow so readily. It is the entire knowledge, and patterning of behavior, which human beings have, and of course it must be taught and learned for the very reason that it is not inborn. The teaching and learning can be perfectly direct, like arithmetic in school, or it can be so subtle, as in adopting attitudes from parents and friends, as to be quite unconscious and unrealized. That does not matter; man is the only animal capable of both teaching and learning this mass of conventional patterns. As any psychologist will tell you, animals react to stimulus according to their nature and needs, and also according to their experience or conditioning (Pavlov's famous dogs drooled at the dinner bell as well as at dinner). So also do we, but we alone have this extra, socially shared screen between us and our actions. And of course since we alone can teach and learn culture, we alone can invent or create it effectively. Once started, however simply, there is no end to its complexity.

Let us take some simple examples from what would be a very simple human culture. A digging stick of a particular kind, for digging up wild vegetables for food, is culture. So is using a skin for keeping warm. So is the idea of appointing a war chief for the group, or the idea of marriage. Now apes might give the impression of having or using these things. They will use sticks readily in captivity, given sticks and something interesting to use them for. You may have seen a young orang in the zoo rapturously using a gunny sack for a blanket. As you know, many Primates will defer to a dominant animal and take their cue from him. And gibbons pair off permanently for mating. But there is distinction. Different gibbon societies have no choice in the matter; their kind of mating is all the same because it is entirely controlled by biology instead of biology plus convention; it is in their natures. That is why their monogamy cannot be compared with human monogamy, and why their mating is not marriage. So with dominance and leadership. As for sticks, chimpanzees can use them in ways of their own devising, and even fashion them; in fact, fads of stick-using, particularly for mischief, may sweep through a captive chimp colony. But this actually happens at random. It is not created, maintained, handed on and understood, as a regular prop of chimpanzee life.

To men, however, such things can be handled not only as objects but as ideas. A digging stick is not just a stick you happen to have around. It is a *digging* stick for digging *vegetables*. You are welcome to chastise your wife with it, but if you do, you are beating her with the *digging stick*. Furthermore, the important thing is not so much the stick as the pattern for the stick. It is a pattern of behavior. The social group possesses it; we know one uses a digging stick for vegetables, and we know what the best kind of such stick is. This known pattern, which breeds digging sticks, is the actual culture item. The same for a skin robe, or a war chief, or a form of marriage. Man is able to maintain these ideas, to change them, and to add to them. So I do not feel rash in saying that there is, in a way, less difference between Buckingham Palace and a cave with a fire near the entrance than there is between a cave with a fire near the entrance and a cave in which nobody can make a fire.

BRAINS AND THEIR USES

How does it happen that men can handle culture and apes cannot? Because of greater brain power, certainly. We have brains larger by about three times than the great apes, and that is a huge difference. We all have the same general pattern of the cerebrum, the outer layer, which takes care of the senses, of control of the muscles, and of higher processes. Sight and hearing, an itch in the scalp, a command to the toes to wiggle, each has its special part. Around such special parts there are other areas of the brain, more general, in which things seen and heard in the past are stored up, or special patterns of toe-wiggling kept; in still more general parts of these association areas, wider connections between such specific odds and ends can be handled. It is a little like going from the mail room busily dealing with incoming and outgoing stuff all through office hours, past the executive offices to the quieter research laboratory, which can take the resources of the business and come up with new ideas and ways of doing things. The association areas are already large in the higher Primates, and it is in these parts of the brain that the great human expansion has principally taken place.

Sad to say, this kind of thing is most difficult to study, and we still know all too little about the brain at work and at play. However, chimpanzees at work and at play do give us some idea about the end product, and about the elements of intelligence which underlie our capacity for culture, the chimps in particular showing us where they fall down and where we rise above them. As Yerkes said, we must be grateful for the existence of chimpanzees, who make fine, generally enthusiastic laboratory animals, and who are so like us: we know they hear about the same sounds, and that they see in the same terms, with full color and stereoscopic vision. Like us also, they are poor at smelling and good at handling. Only in apes can we find a usable smaller-brained near-facsimile of humanity.

You can hardly find more delightful reading than what has been written on the doings of chimps, from anecdotes about chimps living in the house to their report cards in the most carefully designed tests. I regretfully leave all this to other books, and confine myself to remarks on the results. Chimps are masterly imitators, both of one another and of human beings, being able to observe and copy whole patterns of action with the greatest of ease. Thus do they learn our own low habits, smoking and spitting. Köhler saw an anthropoid victim of the Tom Sawyer motif: the chimp absorbedly watched a workman painting the enclosure and, when the man temporarily went off and left his paintpot, the chimp at once fell to and painted a large rock in the yard, and did, what is more, a Grade A job.

Therefore they can be trained at all sorts of things, particularly those at which they would be naturally adept, as long as they are interested or can be bribed. The idea occurred to Köhler that the animals might do their own housekeeping, and he set one of them to picking up the banana peels in the yard at close of day. The chimp took a basket and went at it like a demon janitor the first time, but found it all too much like work in the next day or so, and after four or five days he could not be prevailed upon to go from one skin to the next by cajolery, threats or brute force.

Chimpanzees remember well, recognizing people or apes after long periods, and also remembering the solutions to puzzles without difficulty. Because of all this information, Yerkes did not like to have them considered incapable of culture. He noted that when the colony was founded at Orange Park, Florida (now known as Yerkes Laboratories of Primate Biology), the pioneer chimpanzees were shown how to work the drinking fountains, and through the years ape has aped ape, and no further instruction of new generations has been necessary.

But all of the above manifests what chimps can do naturally and well, the sort of thing in which they merely excel various other mammals, who do similar things well also. It does not reveal them at the height of their mental abilities, or show where their shortcomings lie. This is what the more rigorous problems are made to test. Now, typical animal learning is done by trial and error: a rat in a maze tries again and again, gradually having his right moves reinforced by success and his wrong moves checked more and more by failure, until his successful runs become more numerous and at last he makes no mistakes. This is a simple kind of learning and problem-solving, and is practically thinking with the muscles, or with the muscle-controlling part of the brain; it is like the thought, or lack of it, which we use to get us home from the bus stop after ten years of doing the same thing.

But consider a problem, an old one though a good one, which has repeatedly been put to chimpanzees. The bait, a banana, is hung well out of reach, in fact where the ape can reach it only by bringing over two boxes, which are provided, and by stacking one on the other to climb upon. Now trial-and-error solution would not solve this, without the intervention of earthquakes, since the only approach would be jumping up toward the bait repeatedly from underneath it until exhaustion or frustration ended matters. That is all a dog could or would do. This is a hard problem for chimpanzees, but most can solve it. And it demonstrates, many claim, an advance in mental processes from trial-and-error work to insight, which means fitting possible activities to the situation in the imagination, not in actuality. It means, obviously, using parts of the brain less closely related to muscle activity proper.

See how a chimpanzee would make an ideal solution of this problem. He might begin with a few jumps, for size, which he would at once observe to be unfruitful, or unbananaful. This, rather than sheer muscular failure, would stop his jumping. He might not even try a jump. There might follow evidence of continued attention to the fruit, or there might be a long period before anything else was tried. However, the moment would arrive when the ape's experience with boxes would suggest using one, and he would reveal the fact that this was a truly mental solution by the directness with which he would try to carry it out; there would, in other words, be nothing random about his actions, but rather a perfectly transparent awareness of what he was doing. Discovery that the height was still not enough has been known to cause an immediate tantrum, showing even more positively that the solution was all there in the head, with the picture of success. Going on to the use of the other box would be a repetition of what had already been done, in similar, clear-cut steps.

ABSTRACTIONS AND SYMBOLS

This is a sound example of what an ape can do in many such tests, quite unapproached by other animals except monkeys. The chimpanzee's eyes *see* the situation, just as a dog's do. (They see it more completely, as to color and depth, which is certainly important.) But the chimp himself grasps more of it, because his brain is capable of applying more things to it. Notice that he does not respond, in ordinary mammal fashion, directly to what he sees by endless jumping, or simply as a result of experience or training, like going to ring a bell for which he will be given the food as a reward. Instead, he is also using, with varying degrees of consciousness, some abstract elements of the situation: the actually unjumpable gap between him and the banana, and the movability of the box, and the property the box has of serving to fill the gap; he is also at the same time a little bit conscious of himself at work, so to speak, so that he hits the ceiling figuratively when he fails to reach it in reality, contrary to his expectations on using the first box.

Thus the apes can make and handle abstractions to a significant degree. They show it in other kinds of tests perhaps more distinctly, as in grasping the principle that the middle box or door is the right one to choose, no matter how many there are. They also seem to be superior in recognizing objects in a photograph, that is to say in a black-and-white, two-dimensional representation, which would be meaningless to a cat or a dog.

But it is apparent that ape abstraction is done with the brakes partly on: their obvious cleverness is the result largely of their particularly high ability to learn and memorize through the senses, which is an ordinary mammalian mental process. Take this problem: a chimpanzee is allowed to see food being put into one of a series of different boxes, and then led away, perhaps into another room where this is done again, or into a series of such rooms. After a lapse of time he is turned loose to find the food. This test shows how good chimp memory is, but it also shows that an ape will depend, whenever he can, on the position of the right box, rather than on any of its other properties, and this links him with other animals which respond similarly (providing, of course, that they are working from memory, without smelling the food itself). He does very well with his sight and memory, but he is largely doing what a bloodhound does with scent. If the boxes have been shuffled around after he has seen them, the ape is all too likely to try the one standing in the same place in the room, whereas we would immediately see that someone had switched the round box covered with shiny red paper and the square one covered with green baize. It seems obvious to us to remember the color, and also those other somewhat abstract qualities of shape and texture. We can thus promptly learn to solve such tests, if the solution involves any shiny box or any round box. Chimps can too, but with more reluctance compared to using clues of space.

Therefore apes can deal in abstractions, especially if they are closely related to concrete problems. But accumulating abstractions and juggling them around—abstract thinking—is a much harder job, and here we have an advantage. We can keep tabs on our ideas, or abstractions, by using symbols to represent them, especially words. We are adept at using such symbols; the apes are very poor, even if they excel other animals. Without something to stand for an idea or abstraction, it is difficult to carry the idea around and apply it elsewhere, and impossible, of course, to give it to anyone else.

For example, a chimp is able with training to recognize colors, and to use them as clues to a problem, such as this: show him a colored patch, either red or green; red is a signal to press one button, green the other button. This is simple, when the ape can take the color as a direct cue. But make him wait a short while: he sees the red, and he recognizes it, but he must somehow bear in mind the simple fact of a color, and then apply it to something that has nothing to do with color in itself; it must be remembered simply as a fact. This is easy for us: we can just say "red" to ourselves, consciously or unconsciously. But it is a tough problem for a chimp and it is clearly near the limit of his capacity to use symbols at all. Otherwise this capacity is limited to symbols relating to position and space, something of which other animals are also capable.

Frankly, we must remain vague about such important matters at the moment, because our most persevering psychologists are still only in the fringes of the jungle of the brain and how it works. But we have to try to describe man's ability to use culture nonetheless. It is clear that we make and use symbols freely, that apes give signs of being barely able to do this, and that our advantage is our much larger brain. It is also apparent that these things—abstractions, and symbols of them—crowd into the area between something we experience and our reaction to that something, and so govern our behavior, and make it "human" or "un-animal." Only because of our ability in these things are we able to invent, to keep and to be governed by the patterns of behavior that make up culture. Finally, only because we are social animals can culture exist as it does, the property of an integrated group of animals, affecting them in common and being maintained by them generation after generation.

So it is clear that we get our human quality from natural, animal sources. We would be nowhere without the hands and eyes of the higher Primates. We could not have culture, a social thing, unless we were one of the social Primates. Nor could we have culture if we had not expanded the cerebrum of the already large hominoid brain or, in practical terms, become able to deal with abstractions and symbols far beyond that place in the road, which barely points the direction, at which a chimpanzee gives up and turns back. We came by these things through straightforward evolution, in continuous descent from our simpler Primate forebears, but in us their working jointly gives us culture, something new in nature.

CULTURE IS ONLY HUMAN

Culture was obviously gradual, not sudden. It had a beginning, perhaps being present even among the higher Primates, depending on how you look at it. I have been emphasizing the lack of culture, in the sense of definite social traditions differing from group to group, in such animals as chimpanzees. Nevertheless Japanese students of the free-living macaque of their own islands have found distinct differences in the pattern of behavior of different bands of monkeys, in such things as the degree of dominance of the females by the males; and they have also observed the spread of a custom, by introducing a new and unfamiliar food to them, and seeing some animals learn to eat it and teach its use to others. Such a structure of social habits looks as though it were waiting only for the more advanced mental capabilities I have been describing—the use of abstractions and symbols—to develop at once the kind of social heritage that constitutes the culture of a particular human group.

As it is, however, there is a great gap between ourselves—living men—

and any kind of living ape or monkey, and we can only make suppositions as to the steps in the gradual process of change. We know from their skulls that men living in the remote past were more primitive than we, and that they had more primitive cultures. But we can judge very little from this. We cannot test these men as we can apes, to see what their actual capacity for culture was like.

Culture has continuously grown. From the very beginning, man has used it to solve his problems and make his life easier. This also emphasizes its special nature: it is a new, largely mental way of reacting to the environment. It is radically different from the old system of changing body form, or native abilities, in response to natural selection, and thus remaining closely bound to nature. Culture is a way of departing from nature, of putting a protective layer between man and nature, whether in concrete things like clothes and houses or in less conscious inventions like social customs and religious beliefs, which make for more efficient and happier living. The tip of the wedge was perhaps things like the use of clubs, fire and language. Just what they were in detail it would not be safe to say, but it is certain they had the characteristics of culture, and served to improve the state of man, making him more powerful (weapons), broadening his diet (cooking), and so on.

From such a point as this, of course, culture has expanded enormously, becoming an ever fatter cushion between man and his environment. But now see what happens: the bigger it gets, the more culture itself *becomes* the environment. Culture is not to be thought of as a stock of clever ideas out of which we are continually making selections for our own benefit or delight. On the contrary. Man invented culture, and culture promptly took charge of man. We do what culture tells us to, whether we quite know it or not.

In the first place, people have never been very much aware that there was such a thing as culture. It goes back before history; it has seemingly always been there; they take it for granted. It actually grew up out of the sum of inventions and adjustments they happened to make, and it could not have followed exactly the same course for two different societies. So no two societies have the same culture. And each one thinks its own is the obvious and natural way of doing things. This is not simple preference; it is because human societies, unlike animal societies, are based on their own cultures and cannot continue to exist, as human societies, without those particular cultures that have continuously sustained them.

Why must a society have that particular culture? Because a society has to be a group of individuals, and the individual grows up as the prisoner of his culture. He could not possibly escape it. A human being is no longer born simply as a social animal, like a chimpanzee; he is born into a complicated world he did not make, among a particular set of people he did not choose. Culture is practically his whole environment; culture lets him breathe as he sees fit, but it even tells him what to eat, and how. He becomes a cultured creature of necessity, and of necessity his culture is that of his own society—how could it be that of any other?

I am satisfied you would not be seen dead dressed for the street as a

Hungarian peasant, or a Tibetan monk, or even in the clothes of your own great-grandfather. Why should you object to appearing in such a fashion? You would be as warmly or as comfortably dressed. But do not be confused; you were right the first time. It is not natural, and there are good reasons why. A culture contains far more than any individual could possibly reinvent, or satisfactorily revise, and it forms a consistent whole. An individual needs all of it, not bits and pieces, and he cannot live outside of it in any conspicuous way.

■ MIDDLE AGE MEETS THE KID GHETTO

Vance Bourjaily

I do not pretend to know how many elements it takes to make a culture, but it seems to me quite clear that many such elements do exist already in the kid ghettos. I can do no more than list and comment briefly, inadequate by training and particular capacity to expound details, many of which have already been noticed and analyzed quite expertly. But perhaps I can strike a sum; perhaps the list will show something like a whole. It will be an eclectic culture, if it does show one; but what new culture could be anything but eclectic with the world the age it is?

A culture, to begin with, has an origin, some condition that presses it to develop. This one begins, it seems to me, with the incompatibility of being young, well-fed and high-spirited in a stalemated world. The dreariness of the cold war and of nuclear power politics produced an extraordinarily boring 25-year period. The response of growing up in it and trying to turn to an alternate culture seems to me far less a manifestation of atomic fear, the cause so often given, than one of simply needing an outlet for zest, and warmth, and creativity—a relief from grinding dullness.

A culture must have a history. The history of this one might begin in the middle nineteen-fifties, with what was called the Beat Generation. The marking off of American age groups into generations is too often an advertising copywriter's exercise, but I think one can recognize times when an age group, engaged with or finishing its education, began to see and feel in a new way. The Beats seem to me to have made the first such break since I was old enough to notice. They were engaged by their own present rather than (as we were) crippled by nostalgia for their fathers' pasts.

A culture must have a nationality, and, tentatively, this one does. I saw it when traveling, I thought: the American, Canadian, British,

French, German, Scandinavian members of the alternate culture seemed to have trust in and recognition of one another in a way that went beyond merely being the same age. I thought them more confident of one another than of the older citizens in their respective countries of origin. And though it was probably less true of other (former?) nationalities, the Americans had the ethnic similarity of being nothing in particular—they were the melt from what had been a melting pot.

A culture should have its own language, perhaps, but it may not need to. I thought it probable that here in America the alternate culture had not yet developed much beyond having its own slang.

A culture has its own art forms. The development of its own music by American youth is too obvious to do more than note, but there is one point to be made about it, in comparison to the swing music I danced to, which is rather overlooked. Swing was played and arranged by men 10 or 15 years older than we were, men who had been the young jazz musicians of an earlier decade. Today's musicians are the kids themselves.

To go with art forms: the poetry of rock lyrics has been cited often, and there is a great flow of poetry not tied to music, and a great interest in writing it, reading it and hearing it read. I am not aware of much fiction yet from the alternate culture, except in the work, perhaps, of Richard Brautigan; I am aware, of course, of a strong taste for fantasy, somewhat confounding to a writer like myself (though, let me acknowledge, somewhat liberating, too). Brought up on television, which was their baby sitter but which failed to grow up with them, their preference for film seems logical enough; beyond that I don't think I can comment on what is happening in the visual arts. Perhaps they are satisfied by what half a century of continuous innovation has already established.

The alternate culture produces great quantities of its own handicrafts —work in leather, for example. If a lot of it looks like stuff we did as boys in camp, still young craftsmen are developing self-taught on Mifflin Street as they haven't in the world for a long time. It is not dilettante or hobbyist's work: they produce garments their community needs, bypassing mass production.

In fact, since a culture needs its own approach to production and economics, Mifflin Street has one, and I was surprised to learn how well-developed it is. Easy enough to see in the cooperative food-growing on rural communes, its metropolitan application depends on understanding how to work the established system. Let me quote the proprietor of a record store:

"First, music is a necessity for us. When I started selling records, I discounted as much as I could, not to get volume but to share the difference between wholesale and retail with people who had a real need for an overpriced product. That made some of the straight record stores in town start discounting to meet my prices, so I became a wholesaler. Now the straight stores can get records from my wholesale operation cheaper, too, so a lot of them have started buying from me. There are still profits, and we're using them to develop our own musical groups, and the musician's union is delighted. We'll soon be able to make our own records, with our own groups, which will bring the price down even more. Eventually," he said, "we'll have our own studio."

I asked how that would be different from consumer cooperatives of the past. "They all get too big," he said, and the implication was that in the alternate culture each community, like each individual, should do its own thing—making and distributing locally, and not for profit, in its own, idiosyncratic way.

The nonprofit spirit is very strong in what they themselves call freak-owned businesses. I know of a youngster who has a health-food store who is setting up his own competitor 8 or 10 blocks away because, says the first, he's making more money than he needs. This approach to doing business earns a certain amount of harassment, too; they are often searched, not always with warrants, and, as a matter of fact, sometimes get trashed.

Personal finances are less tidy. Students are still supported by the customary scholarships and checks from home. The street people, cut off from these, don't need much. They often work as waitresses, cab drivers, construction laborers, and share what they earn. Now, in a time of unemployment, they are likely to be the first fired; a good many draw unemployment checks. Others deal in pot. Others in worse. Some steal, even from one another. A culture has its own weak, its own betrayers, its homegrown rip-off artists and flim-flam men.

The windows of the Mifflin Street Cooperative, a grocery, were ply-wood at the time I went in, but I wasn't thinking about economics at the time. I was thinking that a culture has its own cuisine, and if that is too elegant a word to be appropriate, nevertheless the alternate culture has a very distinct approach to food. I was given a "guerrila cookie," made with whole grain; it was good. They favor organic foods, various health foods, abhor processing, and are faddish about eating in a way I grew up associating with rather elderly people. It cuts considerably across the image of healthy, young all-consuming appetites requiring mountains of hamburger and pizza; it has, in fact, considerably more self-denial in it, whatever its nutritional merits, than we generally want to credit our young with.

The alternate culture, in fact, is not self-indulgent. It has its own ethic: a reverence for life, for example, in all its forms—they have seen so many of those forms destroyed, not on the frontier scale of shooting a hawk because it's a hawk but on the scale of technological society: the wiping out of whole species through careless use of pesticides and other pollutants.

Self-realization would seem to be another part of the ethic, and while I can't offer specifications, there is a great deal of religious curiosity. To seek personal fame seems to them a curious aberration; and to want more money than one needs, another. Their only non-negotiable demand is for personal freedom, their own and everyone's, which makes them poor material, I should think, for disciplined political action.

A culture, once it exists, must develop a system of education—education, that is, in the culture itself. There is, near Mifflin Street, a free school. If it follows the pattern of the free universities I have seen in other communities, then it offers courses created to fit the particular demands of students, taught by whoever is willing and feels able to teach the particular subject matter. What is perhaps more characteristic are the attacks on the present educational system—the direct one which criticizes its relevance, and the indirect attack of nonparticipation. "Dropout" is an honorable term in the alternate culture and that leads me to another explanation: many of the street people came originally to be students at Wisconsin, dropped out, and were now criticized locally as outsiders. The point was that they weren't outsiders to Mifflin Street, only to the university they'd decided was no longer relevant. Mifflin Street was no less an institution than the other place, and they had created it themselves.

The alternate culture has not begun, as far as I could learn, to develop its own system of law, but I would guess it may have to. It expects the courts of the country in which it is growing to treat it with routine unfairness. In the case, for example, of an underground newspaper editor who refused to testify about the A.M.R.C. bombing before a Wisconsin grand jury, and a newsman protecting his sources, they were far less surprised than I at the judge's remark in convicting the editor of contempt: "Something has to give. What has to give is the First Amendment. . . ."

Some of the other attributes of the alternate culture need only be itemized. They have their own ritual celebrations: rock festivals. Their own game: Frisbie. Older heroes: Vonnegut, Ginsberg, the Beatles, Buckminster Fuller. Stimulant: marijuana.

There is, of course, a near parallel between the way marijuana functions for them and the way illegal alcohol functioned in unifying their grandparents as they fought for and won the cultural revisions of the twenties. It was not hard to imagine the move for legalization of pot growing and becoming politically respectable, as Mifflin Street grew older and voted more consistently—just as the repeal movement did when I was 12 or 14.

And, of course, the alternate culture has, as any culture must, its enemies: most adults, their Government, their police. It is some of them I would hope to persuade by writing this; I have tried before, in talks at Midwest service clubs and women's clubs, going back four years now. There are always some who will listen, sometimes one or two who will agree, and it is they to whom I feel I owe an explanation. I owe it because I understand and even sometimes share their irritation, anger and despair—despair because, of course, kids always win. Unless we kill them. They outlive us.

I have never been able to make this explanation so fully before. It has taken a long time for me to learn and acknowledge my own conclusion. Here is how I learned it:

It was 10 days since I'd left Madison—a serious occasion at which I found myself speaking to a group who were 15, 16 and 17, and saying to them:

"You're good people. You're good people. You're a special part of the best American generation I've ever seen or ever hope to see. I am impressed with the quality of your thought, the courage of your actions, and astonished at how young you have learned to value kindness. . . ."

Where did they learn it? Not from you and me, Dusty; Mifflin Street.

That night I sat up late, in the dark, with a drink in my hand, looking out the bedroom window through the warm, moist fall air, a trouble light staring back at me through the mist from the next farm half a mile down the road, and thought of Mifflin Street again, and thought: Couldn't we just try loving them?

It didn't matter much if they loved us back or not.

They were so beautiful, with their funny hair and curly beards, the boys elegantly scruffy, the hostile girls lovely and young for all their grimness, and they were trying to make something.

I didn't want what they were trying to make destroyed.

I had been, earlier this year, in two of the places where the world hurt worst: Biafra and Greece. I had not been to the others, the Middle East and Southeast Asia, but my imagination told me the same grief was there, the irreparable grief of people who have made a culture and seen it destroyed. They may live on physically, as American Indians do, but there is nothing left to belong to, nothing to be in the world that matters to you, unless you agree to join or rejoin the destroying culture on its own terms.

In a way, those who gave their vision and energy, the strength of their youth, to building the alternate culture might be doing something more radical, perhaps equally courageous, certainly more joyful, than the New Left extremists. The latter, when they answered social injustice with violence, knew the consequences of being caught, understood their risk and were presumably willing to take it. But there were no known consequences of trying to create a new culture, unless you wanted to think in terms as broad as the early history of Christianity.

■ A FOUR LETTER WORD
THAT HURTS

Morton H. Fried

Taking the great white race away from today's racists is like taking candy from a baby. There are sure to be shrieks and howls of outrage. But it will be very hard to take away this piece of candy, because, to drop the metaphor, nothing is harder to expunge than an idea. The white race is not a real, hard fact of nature; it is an idea.

In 1959 a young anthropologist named Philip Newman walked into the very remote village of Miruma in the upper Asaro Valley of New Guinea to make a field study of the Gururumba. It was late that first afternoon when it began to dawn upon his native hosts that he had made no move to leave. Finally a man of some rank plucked up his courage and said, "How long will you stay, red man?"

Most people are probably amused, but a few will be puzzled and chagrined to know that what passes in our own culture as a member of the great white race is considered red by some New Guineans. But when did anyone ever really see a *white* white man? Most so-called white men are turned by wind, rain, and certain kinds of lotion to various shades of brown, although they would probably prefer to be thought bronze. Even the stay-in who shuns the sun and despises cosmetics would rarely be able to be considered white in terms of the minimal standards set on television by our leading laundry detergents. His color would likely be a shade of the pink that is a basic tint for all Caucasoids. (That, like "Caucasian," is another foolish word in the service of this concept of race. The Caucasus region, as far as we know, played no significant role in human evolution and certainly was not the cradle of any significant human variety.)

Actually, even the generalization about pink as a basic skin tint has to be explained and qualified. In some people the tint of the skin is in substantial measure the result of chemical coloring matter in the epidermis; in others there is no such coloring matter, or very little, and tinting then depends on many factors, including the color of the blood in the tiny capillaries of the dermis. Statistically, there is a continuous grading of human skin color from light to dark. There are no sharp breaks, no breaks at all. Since nobody is really white and since color is a trait that varies without significant interruption, I think the most sensible statement that can be made on the subject is that there is no white race. To make this just as true and outrageous as I can, let me immediately add that there never *was* a white race.

While at it, I might as well go on to deny the existence of a red race, although noting that if there was such a thing as the white race it would be at least esthetically more correct to call it the red race. Also, there is not now and never has been either a black race or a yellow race.

To deny that there are differences between individuals and between populations is ridiculous. The New Guineans spotted Dr. Newman as an off-beat intruder as soon as they clapped eyes on him. Of course, they were noticing other things as well and some of those other things certainly helped to make the distinctions sharper. After all, Newman was relatively clean, he had clothes on, and, furthermore, he didn't carry himself at all like a Gururumba—that is to say like a human being. I was spotted as an alien the first time I showed up in the small city of Ch'uhsien, in Anhwei province, China, back in 1947. Even after more than a year in that place, there was no question about my standing out as a strange physical type. During the hot summer, peasants who had never seen anything like me before were particularly fascinated by my arms protruding from my short-sleeved shirt, and I almost had to stop patronizing the local bath house. I am not a hirsute fellow for someone of my type, but in Ch'uhsien I looked like a shaggy dog, and farmers deftly plucked my hairs and escaped with souvenirs. Another time, a charming young lady of three scrambled into my lap when I offered to tell her a story; she looked into my eyes just as I began and leaped off with a scream. It was some time before I saw her again, and in the interval I learned that in this area the worst, bloodthirsty, child-eating demons can be identified by their blue eyes.

Individual differences are obvious, even to a child. Unfortunately, race is not to be confused with such differences, though almost everybody sees them and some people act toward others on the basis of them. I say "unfortunately," because the confusion seems so deeply embedded as to make anyone despair of rooting it out.

Most laymen of my acquaintance, whether tolerant or bigoted, are frankly puzzled when they are told that race is an idea. It seems to them that it is something very real that they experience every day; one might as well deny the existence of different makes and models of automobiles. The answer to that analogy is easy: cars don't breed. Apart from what the kids conjure up by raiding automobile graveyards, and putting the parts together to get a monster, there are no real intergrades in machinery of this kind. To get a car you manufacture parts and put them together. To get our kind of biological organism you start with two fully formed specimens, one of each sex, and if they are attracted to each other, they may replicate. Their replication can never be more than approximate as far as either of them, the parents, is concerned, because, as we so well know, each contributes only and exactly one-half of the genetic material to the offspring. We also know that some of the genetic material each transmits may not be apparent in his or her own makeup, so that it is fully possible for a child to be completely legimate without resembling either side of the family, although he may remind a very old aunt of her grandfather.

The phenomenon of genetic inheritance is completely neutral with regard to race and racial formation. Given a high degree of isolation, different populations might develop to the point of being clearly distinguishable while they remained capable of producing fertile hybrids. There would, however, be few if any hybrids because of geographical isolation, and the result would be a neat and consistent system.

Much too neat and consistent for man. Never in the history of this globe has there been any species with so little *sitzfleisch*. Even during the middle of the Pleistocene, way down in the Lower Paleolithic, 300,000 or more years ago, our ancestors were continent-hoppers. That is the only reasonable interpretation of the fact that very similar remains of the middle Pleistocene fossil *Homo erectus* are found in Africa, Europe, and Asia. Since that time movement has accelerated and now there is no major region of this planet without its human population, even if it is a small, artificially maintained, nonreproductive population of scientists in Antarctica.

The mobility so characteristic of our genus, Homo, has unavoidable implications, for where man moves, man mates. (Antarctica, devoid of indigenous population, is perhaps the only exception.) This is not a recent phenomenon, but has been going on for one or two million years, or longer than the period since man became recognizable. We know of this mobility not only from evidence of the spread of our genus and species throughout the world, but also because the fossils of man collected from one locality and representing a single relatively synchronic population sometimes show extraordinary variation among themselves. Some years ago a population was found in Tabun Cave, near Mt. Carmel, in Israel. The physical anthropologists Ashley Montagu and C. Loring Brace describe it as "showing every possible combination of the features of Neanderthal with those of modern man." At Chouk'outien, a limestone quarry not too far from Peking, in a cave that was naturally open toward the close of the Pleistocene geological period, about 20,000 years ago, there lived a population of diverse physical types. While some physical anthropologists minimize them, those who have actually pored over the remains describe differences as great as those separating modern Chinese from Eskimos on one hand and Melanesians on the other. All of this, of course, without any direct evidence of the skin color of the fossils concerned. We never have found fossilized human skin and therefore can speak of the skin colors of our ancestors of tens of thousands of years ago only through extrapolation, by assuming continuity, and by assuming the applicability of such zoological rules as Gloger's, which was developed to explain the distribution of differently pigmented birds and mammals.

The evidence that our Pleistocene ancestors got around goes beyond their own physical remains and includes exotic shells, stones, and other materials in strange places which these objects could have reached only by being passed from hand to hand or being carried great distances. If our ancestors moved about that much, they also spread their genes, to put it euphemistically. Incidentally, they could have accomplished this spreading of genes whether they reacted to alien populations peacefully or hostilely; wars, including those in our own time, have always been a major means of speeding up hybridization.

Even phrasing the matter this way, and allowing for a goodly amount of gene flow between existing racial populations through hundreds of thousands of years of evolution, the resulting image of race is incredibly wrong, a fantasy with hardly any connection to reality. What is wrong is our way of creating and relying upon archetypes. Just as we persist in thinking that there is a typical American town (rarely our own), a typical American middle-class housewife (never our wife), a typical American male ("not me!"), so we think of races in terms of typical, archetypical, individuals who probably do not exist. When it is pointed out that there are hundreds of thousands or millions of living people who fall between the classified races, the frequently heard rejoinder is that this is so now, but it is a sign of our decadent times. Those fond of arguing this way usually go on to assert that it was not so in the past, that the races were formerly discrete.

In a startlingly large number of views, including those shared by informed and tolerant people, there was a time when there was a pure white race, a pure black race, etc., etc., depending upon how many races they recognize. There is not a shred of scientifically respectable evidence to support such a view. Whatever evidence we have contradicts it. In addition to the evidence of Chouk'outien and Tabun mentioned above, there are many other fossils whose morphological characteristics, primitivity to one side, are not in keeping with those of the present inhabitants of the same region.

Part of the explanation of the layman's belief in pure ancestral races is to be found in the intellectually lazy trait of stereotyping which is applied not only to man's ancestry but to landscape and climate through time as well. Few parts of the world today look quite the way they did 15,000 years ago, much less 150,000 years ago. Yet I have found it a commonplace among students that they visualize the world of ages ago as it appears today. The Sahara is always a great desert, the Rockies a great mountain chain, and England separated from France by the Channel. Sometimes I ask a class, after we have talked about the famous Java fossil *Pithecanthropus erectus,* how the devil do they suppose he ever got there, Java being an island? Usually the students are dumbfounded by the question, until they are relieved to discover that Java wasn't always cut off from the Asian mainland. Given their initial attitudes and lack of information, it is not surprising that so many people imagine a beautiful Nordic Cro-Magnon, archetypical White, ranging a great Wagnerian forest looking for bestial Neanderthalers to exterminate.

Once again, there is no evidence whatsoever to support the lurid nightmare of genocide that early *Homo sapiens* is supposed to have wreaked upon the bumbling and grotesque Neanderthals. None either for William Golding's literary view of the extirpation of primitive innocence and goodness. The interpretation that in my view does least damage to the evidence is that which recognizes the differences between contemporary forms of so-called Neanderthals and other fossil *Homo sapiens* of 25,000 to 100,000 years ago to have been very little more or no greater than those between two variant populations of our own century. Furthermore, the same evidence indicates that the Neanderthals did not vanish suddenly but probably were slowly submerged in the populations that surrounded them, so that their genetic materials form part of our own inheritance today.

Then, it may be asked, where did the story come from that tells of the struggle of these populations and the extinction of one? It is a relatively fresh tale, actually invented in the nineteenth century, for before that time there was no suspicion of such creatures as Neanderthals. The nineteenth century, however, discovered the fossils of what has been called "Darwin's first witness." After some debate, the fossil remains were accepted as some primitive precursor of man and then chopped off the family tree. The model for this imaginary genealogical pruning was easily come by in a century that had witnessed the hunting and killing of native populations like game beasts, as in Tasmania, in the Malay peninsula, and elsewhere. Such episodes and continuation of slavery and the slave trade made genocide as real a phenomenon as the demand for laissez-faire and the Acts of Combination. It was precisely in this crucible that modern racism was born and to which most of our twentieth-century mythology about race can be traced.

In the vocabulary of the layman the word "race" is a nonsense term, one without a fixed, reliable meaning, and, as Alice pointed out to Humpty Dumpty, the use of words with idiosyncratic meanings is not conducive to communication. Yet I am sure that many who read these words will think that it is the writer who is twisting meaning and destroying a useful, common-sense concept. Far from it. One of the most respected and highly regarded volumes to have yet been published in the field of physical anthropology is *Human Biology*, by four British scientists, Harrison, Weiner, Tanner, and Barnicot (Oxford University Press, 1964). These distinguished authors jointly eschewed the word "race" on the ground that it was poorly defined even in zoology, *i.e.*, when applied to animals other than man, and because of its history of misunderstanding, confusion, and worse, when applied to humans.

Similar views have been held for some time and are familiar in the professional literature. Ashley Montagu, for example, has been in the vanguard of the movement to drop the concept of human race on scientific grounds for twenty-five years. His most recent work on the subject is a collation of critical essays from many specialists, *The Concept of Race* (Free Press, 1964). Frank B. Livingstone, a physical anthropologist at the University of Michigan, has spoken out "On the Non-existence of Human Races" (*Current Anthropology*, 3:3, 1962). In the subsequent debate, opinions divided rather along generational lines. The older scientists preferred to cling to the concept of race while freely complaining about its shortcomings. The younger scientists showed impatience with the concept and wished to drop it and get on with important work that the concept obstructed.

Quite specifically, there are many things wrong with the concept of race. As generally employed, it is sometimes based on biological characteristics but sometimes on cultural features, and when it is based on biological traits the traits in question usually have the most obscure genetic backgrounds. The use of cultural criteria is best exemplified in such untenable racial constructs as the "Anglo-Saxon race," or the "German race" or the "Jewish race." Under no scientifically uttered definition known to me can these aggregates be called races. The first is a linguistic designation pertaining to the Germanic dialects or languages spoken by the people who about 1,500 years ago invaded the British Isles from what is now Schleswig-Holstein and the adjacent portion of Denmark. The invaders were in no significant way physically distinct from their neighbors who spoke other languages, and in any case they mated and blended with the indigenous population they encountered. Even their language was substantially altered by diffusion so that today a reference to English as an Anglo-Saxon language is quaint and less than correct. As for the hyperbolic extension of the designation to some of the people who live in England and the United States, it is meaningless in racial terms— just as meaningless as extending the term to cover a nation of hetero- geneous orgin and flexible boundaries, such as Germany or France or Italy or any other country. As for the moribund concept of a "Jewish race," this is simply funny, considering the extraordinary diversity of the physical types that have embraced this religion, and the large number that have relinquished it and entered other faiths.

The use of cultural criteria to identify individuals with racial cate- gories does not stop with nationality, language, or religion. Such traits as posture, facial expression, musical tastes, and even modes of dress have been used to sort people into spurious racial groups. But even when biological criteria have been used, they have rarely been employed in a scientifically defensible way. One of the first questions to arise, for exam- ple, is what kind of criteria shall be used to sort people into racial cate- gories. Following immediately upon this is another query: how many criteria should be used? With regard to the first, science is still in con- flict. The new physical anthropologists whose overriding concern is to unravel the many remaining mysteries in human evolution and to under- stand the role that heredity will play in continuing and future evolution are impatient with any but strictly genetic characters, preferably those that can be linked to relatively few gene loci. They prefer the rapidly mounting blood factors, not only the ABO, Rh, MNS, and other well- known series, but such things as Duffy, Henshaw, Hunter, Kell, and Kidd (limited distribution blood groups named for the first person found to have carried them). Such work has one consistent by-product: the re- sultant classifications tend to cross-cut and obliterate conventional racial lines so that such constructs as the white race disappear as useful taxo- nomic units.

Some scientists argue that a classification based on only one criterion is not a very useful instrument. On the other hand, the more criteria that are added, the more abstract the racial construct becomes as fewer indi- viduals can be discovered with all the necessary characteristics and more individuals are found to be in between. The end result is that the typical person is completely atypical; if race makes sense, so does this.

That racial classification is really nonsense can be demonstrated with ease merely by comparing some of the most usual conceptions of white and Negro. What degree of black African ancestry establishes a person as a Negro? Is 51 per cent or 50.1 per cent or some other slight statistical preponderance necessary? The question is ridiculous; we have no means of discriminating quantities of inherited materials in percentage terms. In that case can we turn to ancestry and legislate that anyone with a Negro parent is a Negro? Simple, but totally ineffective and inapplicable: how was the racial identity of each parent established? It is precisely at this point that anthropologists raise the question of assigning specific individuals to racial categories. At best, a racial category is a statistical abstraction based upon certain frequencies of genetic characters observed in small samples of much larger populations. A frequency of genetic characters is something that can be displayed by a population, but it cannot be displayed by an individual, any more than one voter can represent the proportion of votes cast by his party.

The great fallacy of racial classification is revealed by reflecting on popular applications in real situations. Some of our outstanding "Negro" citizens have almost no phenotypic resemblance to the stereotyped "Negro." It requires their acts of self-identification to place them. Simultaneously, tens of thousands of persons of slightly darker skin color, broader nasal wings, more everted lips, less straight hair, etc., are considered as "white" without question, in the South as well as the North, and in all socioeconomic strata. Conversely, some of our best known and noisiest Southern politicians undoubtedly have some "Negro" genes in their makeup.

Why is it so hard to give up this miserable little four-letter word that of all four-letter words has done the most damage? This is a good question for a scientific linguist or a semanticist. After all, the word refers to nothing more than a transitory statistical abstraction. But the question can also be put to an anthropologist. His answer might be, and mine is, that the word "race" expresses a certain kind of unresolved social conflict that thrives on divisions and invidious distinctions. It can thrive in the total absence of genetic differences in a single homogeneous population of common ancestry. That is the case, for example, with the relations between the Japanese and that portion of themselves they know as the Eta.

In a truly great society it may be that the kinds of fear and rivalry that generate racism will be overcome. This can be done without the kind of millenarian reform that would be necessary to banish all conflict, for only certain kinds of hostilities generate racism although any kind can be channeled into an already raging racial bigotry. Great areas of the earth's surface have been totally devoid of racism for long periods of time and such a situation may return again, although under altered circumstances. If and when it does, the word "race" may drop from our vocabulary and scholars will desperately scrutinize our remains and the remains of our civilization, trying to discover what we were so disturbed about.

2
FIELD WORK

There are three kinds of scientific work: experimental, theoretical, and natural. Natural scientists and experimentalists describe what they see, and theoreticians try to understand what it all means. Any individual scientist, of course, can do all three kinds of work; but the difference is very important in anthropology because experiments are pretty much out of the question.

Natural scientists, like biologists, oceanographers, geologists, and anthropologists, go to where the data is, describe it, and try to understand it. Most natural scientists, however, can also *create* data. An oceanographer can study waves by building a wave-making machine. A geologist can study erosion by building an apparatus that duplicates effects of wind and water on rock. Biologists can study reproductive processes in certain animals by implanting sperm in eggs and watching what happens through an electron microscope. But anthropologists have got to settle for trying to understand how things like cultures got to be the way they are without experimenting. They observe; but because the things they observe are people like themselves, they also participate in what they observe.

Even if you stand on the edge of a ceremony and just watch, the very act of watching (and the fact that the people know you are there) constitutes some participation. Balancing participation and observation is an art and a skill that each anthropologist learns on the job. We can gain insight into the skill through the reflections of some first-class anthropologists on the process of field work.

In the next three selections, some very talented anthropologists share their experiences with us. In the fourth selection we see the other side of the coin. One of the "natives" shares with us his own feelings and the feelings of his countrymen on what it is like to be studied by primitive creatures like anthropologists. Both sides are vitally important if we are to learn how to study people constructively. Finally, in this section, we see some of the issues faced by archaeologists in their attempts to understand the nature of culture. Their fieldwork problems are different from those of cultural anthropologists. There is no way around the fact that archaeology is done by disturbing somebody's house, garbage dump, or grave. This creates some special ethical responsibilities, especially to the descendants of the population being studied.

■ GETTING THERE

Alan R. Beals

In 1952, when I was living near Bangalore in the village of Namhalli, I used to buy *bidis* (cigarettes) across the street in Sab Jan's store. When I made my purchases, we often exchanged homely bits of advice and rural wisdom. One of Sab Jan's contributions to this educational effort was: "The Hindus believe that there are many roads to Heaven, we [Muslims and Christians] know that there is only one straight road." For a time, I agreed with Sab Jan. Surely there is one right way to do everything, and surely one of the troubles with Hindus is an insufficient concern with the true truth, the straight and narrow, and the one and only.

On the other side of the coin, one of the troubles with those brought up within the Judeo-Christian religious traditions is an overconcern with the shortest distance, the right way and the absolute truth. When I came to Namhalli, I believed that all modernizing or urbanizing communities would tend to move through a series of regular and predictible changes. The family would become smaller, there would be more dependence upon a cash economy, there would be more kinds of jobs, and so on. Assuming the existence of a single straight road to urbanization, I was concerned with the channels of communication and other forces moving the village of Namhalli onward and upward.

After I had lived in Namhalli for several months, my relatively enormous height won me a place on the village volleyball team. As a member of the team and in various other capacities as well, I became familiar with many of the villages surrounding Namhalli. All of these villages, particularly those which had volleyball teams, were modern, but they were all different. In some villages families were becoming smaller; in some villages they were becoming larger. Some had become totally dependent upon cash; others still bartered goods for grain. In some there had been a multiplication of occupations; others had become more and more specialized. After I had returned to the United States and had begun to consider my experience in Namhalli, I realized that nothing was more important for an understanding of rural India than an understanding of the differences I had noticed between neighboring villages.

It was this idea, crystallized out of earlier experience, which formed the basis for the study of Gopalpur that my wife Constance and I would carry out between September 1958 and March 1960. For this, my second fieldtrip and Constance's first, I wanted to work in Gulbarga District in Northern Mysore State. The region was 100 miles away from the nearest modern city and, having been until recently a part of the kingdom of Hyderabad, it had been little influenced by the modern world. Here, in a traditional region unafflicted by rapid change, it should be possible to obtain an accurate picture of the kinds of differences and similarities normally existing between villages. To make my research proposal concrete, I planned to compare irrigated (rice agriculture) villages with unirrigated (millet agriculture) villages. Since the question of the difference between irrigated and unirrigated agriculture had been much agitated in the literature of anthropology, it was possible to produce a list of references emphasizing the theoretical importance of the research problem. The proposal appealed to the National Science Foundation and I was given an $11,000 research grant.

A former student arranged an appointment for me as Honorary Visiting Reader at Osmania University in Hyderabad. This elite connection with Osmania University was of great importance in securing visas and in arranging for assistance from influential persons in Gulbarga District. On the other hand, it is difficult for people to help you when they do not understand what you are doing, and we were largely unsuccessful in convincing important people in Hyderabad and Gulbarga that there was any value whatsoever in studying small villages. It was generally expected that we would obtain a large cool house, fill it with servants, and sit on the veranda drinking cool drinks and considering the servant problem, tropical diseases, and the unbearable heat. One distinguished member of the nobility of Old Hyderabad became incensed with us when she learned that Constance had failed to bring badminton rackets from the United States.

In Gulbarga, the English-speaking intellectual elite was so tiny that our desire to live elsewhere than in town provoked anger and frustration. A wealthy landlord ordered us to live in his village and threatened to retaliate if we failed to do so. The local missionaries warned us that we would soon die of malaria and other diseases. Government officials wondered what we could possibly be studying that they did not already know about: "Just tell me what you want to know, and I'll answer all your questions." Constance, who had been suffering from some kind of mild illness, began to feel worse and worse. The doctor in Gulbarga examined her. She was suffering from homesickness. Serious consequences might result if I subjected a delicate foreign lady to harsh conditions.

All the same, Constance did not seem to be exceptionally sick. Perhaps she was only suffering from "culture shock." We decided to go ahead and find a village. We obtained letters to the local officials of Yadgiri, one of the few irrigated regions in Gulbarga District. Soon we had established ourselves in the mosquito-filled Traveller's Bungalow at Yadgiri. Constance was quarreling with the caretakers in a vain attempt to get good food at reasonable prices, and I was conducting involved negotiations with the local government official (Tahsildar). The Tahsildar felt that Yadgiri Tahsil would be unhealthy for us. In fact, the Assistant Commissioner had just recently died of malaria. I pointed out that my wife was ill, that we could not simply wander from place to place, and that Yadgiri Tahsil seemed ideal for my purposes.

The Tahsildar had a letter from the Commissioner. He would have to find us a village. We waited. It seemed that our affairs were not of very high priority. Repeatedly I made the dusty walk to the Tahsildar's office to find out why the jeep had not come as promised. Each day something had come up and the jeep had been sent elsewhere. When the jeep finally came, it took us to Minaspur.

Minaspur is a large village containing thousands of people. Just outside the village is an attractive bungalow located on the shores of a deep and beautiful lake. Below the lake stretch thousands of acres of irrigated rice land. The family that owned the land and the village would make us comfortable. Like Rama and Sita in the forest, Constance and I would enjoy the utmost delights. I turned to the Tahsildar and to the wealthy, powerful, hospitable landlords of Minaspur: "What a pity that I speak Kanarese and the people of Minaspur speak Telegu; what a pity that the American Government has ordered me to study a small village instead of a large one."

We returned in glum silence to Yadgiri. After several days of impatient waiting, I managed to track down the Tahsildar: "Never mind bringing the jeep, we shall go out on the bus and find a village." I had put the Tahsildar in an impossible position. He could not allow a distinguished visitor to ride a bus like a common peasant; on the other hand, he knew of no place to take me. "We have found the perfect village for you"; said the Tahsildar, "the jeep will come by at 9:00 tomorrow." For several days the jeep failed to appear and I had difficulty tracking down the Tahsildar. One day at noon, the jeep appeared. The Gauda[1] of Gopalpur was in the back seat.

Gopalpur seemed perfect. It filled the specifications I had given the Tahsildar. It had irrigated land, it was some distance from the road, it contained less than 500 people, it was close to an unirrigated village, and everyone spoke Kanarese. Besides this, Gopalpur was only 2 miles from a large village containing a dispensary. In the Gauda's garden was a vacant house that he would be glad to lend us. In our present state of mind the garden seemed perfect. It was fenced, which would keep people from bothering us. There was an outdoor sitting room shaded by sacred nim trees. There was a shallow irrigation well filled with clear water. A stream flowed across one edge of the garden.

---

[1] A kind of headman.

SURVIVAL

In 1952, on the way to India, I asked a distinguished British anthropologist to tell me his secret of success in doing fieldwork. His response was "Never accept free housing and always carry a supply of marmalade." To Gopalpur we brought stoves, cooking utensils, typewriters, and other equipment we were sure would not be available. Our plan was to live totally without servants, depending upon locally available food supplies and vitamin tablets. As soon as we had arrived in the garden house, I unpacked our equipment and began getting the stove ready to boil water. The Gauda, his servants, and some twenty important persons from the village gathered around to watch the lighting of the primus stove and to give me such helpful advice as they could. With an air of great coolness, I began assembling the parts. Accustomed to carrying out the business of living in complete privacy, the steady flow of advice soon broke my nerve. My hands began to tremble, my face flushed, and the stove became more and more obdurate. After hours of tinkering, the stove came to life. With an air of confidence, Kanamma (Mrs. Connie) seized a pan and went to the creek to obtain water. With a quick glance at the other ladies to see what they were doing, she dug a shallow hole in the sand, waited for the dust to settle and began to scoop water into her pan. Somehow, the water trickled away between her fingers and the little water that reached the pan turned out to be full of dirt. A seven-year-old child came over and filled Kanamma's pan.

In a surprisingly short time, we were painfully aware that we had achieved an almost legendary reputation for incompetence. We could not get water, we could not make fire. We seemed totally unable to get food or prepare it properly once we had it. Already exhausted by such simple tasks as getting water, Kanamma was in no shape to scrounge around for foodstuffs or to endure the routines of cookery that involved six to eight hours of hard work on the part of highly skilled local women.

Within a few days, we were begging the Gauda to find us a servant. The Gauda greeted our request with consternation. Servants were hard to find and he was reluctant to part with any of his own. Besides he felt responsible for the well-being of the people in the village and he was well aware of the fact that Europeans customarily beat and kicked their servants. On the other hand, there was Tamma. Although Tamma was supposedly working for the Gauda, he was lazy and insolent. Lately he had been caught helping himself to tamarind from the Gauda's tree.

The Gauda told us to pay Tamma 18 to 20 rupees per month (less than $5) and to keep him working day and night so he could not sneak off and sleep with his wife. At odd times throughout the day, the Gauda would appear in the garden: "Where is Tamma? Why is he not working?" Actually, Tamma was working: At 9:00, he had gone 2 miles away to the village of Yelher to buy some meat for lunch. He had arrived at that village at 9:30 and stopped at a relative's house to rest. The relatives had urged him to stay and eat. People had gathered about him and interviewed him concerning the behavior of the strange foreigners in

Gopalpur. The missionaries had sent for him, given him some tea, and a package of jello to give to us. By 12:30, the Sabaru (plural[2] of Sahib, meaning distinguished foreigner) was storming about the house demanding to be fed. Tamma returned to face the combined wrath of the Kanamma, the Sabaru, and the Gauda. The great people are always scolding their servants for no particular reason. Servants are the people who understand the business of being servants, the great people do not understand the problem and their advice is not to be listened to. Tamma had faced indignation all of his life. He weathered the storm gravely and quietly.

In time, Tamma and Kanamma developed a kind of secret language. Tamma's free spirit appealed to Kanamma. She raised his pay beyond 20 rupees. The Gauda and others remonstrated with the Sabaru. The Sabaru refused to discuss the matter with Kanamma. The Sabaru refused to kick or beat Tamma. It was felt that the Sabaru lacked the force and dignity required to maintain a smoothly running household. Still with Tamma's aid, Kanamma managed to obtain small quantities of meat and vegetables. There was almost always a pot of something vaguely resembling lamb stew simmering on the primus stove and there was usually rice to go with it. Later, Kanamma discovered the Bombay Store and the market in Yadgiri and there were weekly trips to obtain carrots, potatoes, and the inevitable marmalade.

But Kanamma was still sick. Almost every day she had a slight temperature which the Sabaru assured her was psychological. Gathering together her failing strength, Kanamma took Tamma in town and walked the 2 miles to the bus stop. An obliging conductor, in defiance of government regulations against overcrowding, allowed Kanamma and Tamma to squeeze onto the bus. For thirty minutes while the bus negotiated the seemingly interminable trip to Yadgiri, Kanamma, and Tamma endured bone-wracking misery. From the bus station, they walked a mile to the hospital. At the hospital was an attractive young woman doctor who had been trained in the United States. There seemed to be a good chance that she could diagnose the mysterious tropical illness that had baffled doctors in Hyderabad and Gulbarga. "You are pregnant," said the lady doctor. "Impossible," said Kanamma reposing complete faith in the marvels of modern contraceptive techniques. Tests were performed. Again, the tedious trip to Yadgiri was repeated. Kanamma had been pregnant for four months. In fact, the worst part of her pregnancy was over. A few vitamin tablets would cure her illness completely. Kanamma announced the news to the old ladies of Gopalpur. "Of course," they said, "we noticed right away."

FRIENDS AND ENEMIES

In 1952, the Sabaru was a poverty stricken student. Seeing his youth and helplessness, the "educated class" in Namhalli, composed as it was

[2] The plural form is always used in respectful address.

of young men the Sabaru's age, had welcomed him and taught him about their village. They were able to practice their English and to learn many things about urban life. People around Bangalore were familiar with Europeans and, by and large, they liked them. In Gopalpur, things were different. People had seen few foreigners. Those they had seen, they had seen as members of an under class in the city of Bombay. In Bombay, the light-skinned Marathi and Gujerati speakers referred to people from Mysore as black people. They were considered unwelcome immigrants subject to violence and oppression. Only a few years ago, the Government of India had invaded Hyderabad State and made Gulbarga district a part of Mysore. People in Gopalpur felt like a conquered people.

The Sabaru was a foreigner, a Redman, a Bombay person. He spoke Kanarese like an official of the new and not yet accepted Government of Mysore. The foreigners had already taken most of the wealth of India. Perhaps the Sabaru had come back for something the English forgot when they left. Perhaps the Sabaru would drop an atomic bomb on the village. He might even carry the village to America on an airplane. He might conscript people for the American army. He might steal and eat young children as the missionaries apparently did. Perhaps he intended to level the village and construct a landing field for the American invaders.

Isolated in the garden house, the activities of Sabaru and Kanamma seemed more and more mysterious. The Sabaru, having read somewhere that you should start fieldwork by mapping the village and taking a census, began striding up and down the village streets measuring and taking notes. People came up to ask him what he was doing. When he replied, they shook their heads sadly, "He can't talk our language." The Sabaru became sullen and irritable. Back at the garden house, Kanamma flared out angrily at the Gauda. She was tired of his constant advice about how to cook, how to keep house, and how to dress. Relationships with the Gauda began to be strained.

After a month or two in the garden house, word came that the Commissioner himself was coming to find out if we were comfortable. Minor government officials invaded the village. The Village Level Worker, a stranger to the village, appeared and set everyone to work without pay digging drainage ditches, smoothing the streets, and generally creating an appearance of vast and successful village development activities. The Commissioner came. He interviewed us. He was satisfied. The government had done its part.

Next week, the Gauda came to the garden house. He was sorry, but we would have to leave. It was time to store the harvested grain in the garden house. The Sabaru refused to leave. The Gauda's cattle broke into the garden and ate the Sabaru's vegetables. The Sabaru threatened to write an angry letter to the Commissioner. There was hard bargaining. A house might become available if the Sabaru agreed to fire Tamma and hire Tamma's disagreeable cousin instead. The Gauda filled one room with grain. Sabaru and Kanamma defended the remaining room. We would have to leave the village. Tamma told the Sabaru that there were indeed plenty of empty houses. The Sabaru offered to pay rent. People said, "In Bombay, you Red people make us pay 100 rupees a month for houses no bigger than a packing crate." The Sabaru offered 10 rupees.

There was a large house in the center of the village. It was dark and old. The ceiling was beginning to rot and there was a steady rain of twigs, scorpions, mud, and carbon from old fires. There were rat holes in the floor large enough to accommodate a large cat. The owner of the house was an old woman who lived just outside the front door in a small hut with her one surviving teenage son. The other six children had died. Thus, the house had acquired its reputation and fallen empty.

Tamma and his friends, the Shepherd, and the Confidence Man began to clean up the house. Lime for whitewash had to be brought from a town 25 miles away. While Sabaru and Kanamma fought off the nameless horrors of the decaying house, Tamma and his friends disappeared for days on end collecting the materials required to make the house livable. Neighbor ladies brought in samples of their cookery. A crowd of people who had ignored us while we lived protected in the garden appeared to request shirts and other gifts. Missionaries generally had old clothing to distribute and people felt dishonored if their requests were refused. They demanded their rights. Tempers flared. We said we were poor. We said we did not have any old clothing. Finally, we drove everyone out and locked the door.

For an outrageous sum, the Confidence Man brought special wear-resistant mud and spread it on the floor. The Sabaru obtained some Wafarin rat poison from a supplier in Poona. The rats died in their holes filling the house with the odor of their decay. The Confidence Man rented a cart and brought special clay to spread on the roof and render it proof against the rain. The day Kanamma returned from the hospital with her baby, the monsoon would strike, and, as water spouted from the roof, we would discover the true value of his labors. The landlady insisted on tying her buffalo in our living room. All night long we could hear it chewing, moaning, and stamping its feet. Kanamma drove the buffalo outside while the landlady wept and expostulated.

We offered to buy milk from the landlady. She was delighted and sold us several buckets of water before we angrily cancelled her contract. Tamma installed himself in our kitchen where he was frequently visited by the Shepherd and the Confidence Man. The landlady visited daily to complain about her husband who had taken a second wife and was living on the opposite side of the village. At times, the husband would appear and attempt to remove grain from its hiding place in our living room. He and the landlady would scream at each other. He would accuse her of killing her children. She would burst into tears. Later, Kanamma would comfort her and listen once again to her tale of woe.

Another neighbor, an elegent lady dressed in silk and bedecked with jewelry, brought milk for Kanamma and little gifts of food, usually flat cakes of unleavened bread heaped with a fiery mixture of spinach and chili. In the evening, Tamma would spirit the food away to his family.

We discovered that Kanamma's friend was the mistress of a number of important people. She had a husband who lived in another village. Sometimes he would appear, loaded with marihuana, and beg her to return to him.

As we bought salt in the village store and as we carried out our widening search for eggs and milk, we gradually began to acquire friends and supporters. Although nobody profited very much from our presence, a large number of people were beginning to see us as a valuable resource. They became friendly. Even their relatives became friendly, so that when the Sabaru went out into the fields of ripening grain, people began to call to him and to offer him the delicacies of the fields. There were sugar-filled stalks of cane, strange and inedible fruits pressed upon the Sabaru by smiling children, there was fresh-roasted grain. The Sabaru began to have special friends out in the fields. There was Little Brother who smiled at him and explained the mechanics of his agriculture. Little Brother took the Sabaru 4 miles away to his distant field and prepared a lavish portion of roasted grain and brown sugar. He told the Sabaru how people in the village were trying to kill himself and his brothers. He told how they had attacked his house and how his older brother had killed one of the attackers and been sent away to jail. The Sabaru discovered that the Farmer caste was divided between two hostile families and that each family had claimed a life and was daily threatening to take another. The Saltmaker caste, of which Tamma was a member, was similarly divided, and so was the Shepherd caste. The rival groups were divided into two factions that daily threatened to split the village. In time, it was discovered that most of our friends were in a single faction.

The enemy faction, "the partners," were engaged in collectively farming some land belonging to the Gauda. Each year the Gauda auctioned this land to one of the factions and their competitive bidding was a delight to the Gauda. When the Sabaru approached the fields belonging to the partners, they waved him away. When the Sabaru attempted to take pictures, they covered their heads with their blankets. Sometimes, they told him to leave the village. The leaders of the enemy faction were the "Thug," the "Crook," and Tamma's relative, the "Untouchable." We believed that these men were allied with the Gauda against us.

The Untouchable's chief goal in life appeared to be to secure Tamma's job for his younger brother. The Untouchable and the Crook plotted endlessly to bring this about. Sometimes, they would welcome the Sabaru to their houses and gradually bring the conversation around to the absolute necessity of firing Tamma. Eventually, the Crook and the Thug gave Tamma a good drubbing with their staffs. The Sabaru brought a policeman into the village and had everyone sign a paper promising that there would be no further violence.

The enmity of the partners was upsetting. It did not square with the mystical notion of "establishing rapport." To me, this meant being on friendly terms with everybody. Certainly, getting involved in local disputes was a poor way to do fieldwork, yet we had become involved before we knew what was happening and there now seemed no way out. Sometimes, particularly when there was a festival, even the partners would become friendly. They would invite the Sabaru to their houses, feed him, and give him pancakelike festival delicacies to take home. "At last," we would say to ourselves, "the magic of anthropology is working and rapport is established." A few days later, a new-found friend would begin demanding a shirt in the most offensive manner possible and the dream of rapport would collapse.

In Namhalli, I had been surrounded by a protective ring of educated people. They were prepared to treat me as an equal and to establish the kind of friendship most valued by Americans. Such egalitarian relationships were virtually unknown in Gopalpur. The Sabaru was a person of high status, and his great wealth and power could never be forgotten. On the other hand, a kind of mutual respect developed and, while relationships were not always warm and friendly, they were always close and intense. In retrospect, the ideal rapport that I thought I had had in Namhalli seemed shallow and impersonal. The continual three-cornered duel among the Sabaru, Tamma, and the Untouchable was close and personal. We learned each other's weak spots and we set clever little traps for each other. There would be a time when we missed our enemies almost as much as we missed our friends. Somehow we became involved in Gopalpur in a way that had been impossible in Namhalli.

In Gopalpur, people had come to forget that we were honored guests and had come to treat us in much the way that they treated each other. This kind of treatment carries real dangers. Being involved, we had to choose sides in village quarrels. In 1952, I had refused to play a role in disputes. I had stood unmoved when the village women tearfully begged me to intervene to prevent violence. I had watched children playing in the forbidden milkweeds and said nothing to their mothers. In Namhalli, I was an audience, a dispassionate observer. In Gopalpur everything was different. I was in the center of village conflicts. When I saw children tormenting a calf, I scolded them and sent them packing.

Somehow it seemed that from the very beginning people in Gopalpur were unwilling to let us play a dispassionate role. They were unaccustomed to strangers and they would not let us remain strangers. We began our fieldwork as people always do, cast in the role of child or idiot. At first, proper behavior was not expected from us. Later, as we learned about the village, we were subjected to social sanctions that we at first interpreted as disrespect. When we failed to behave properly, people told us what they thought of us. This applied with special force to our treatment of our baby, Robin. She was not to be allowed to cry; she was not to eat foods regarded as dangerous; and she had to have a rather costly naming ceremony. We were forced to become properly behaving human beings.

Except under extraordinary circumstances, there will always be a kind of clear plastic film separating the fieldworker from the rest of the community. The fieldworker does not fully understand the motives of others, he may in fact come to display a kind of paranoia arising in the fact that he knows that he is a center of attention, but is not sure why.

The fieldworker who behaves like a mechanical man, who treats others as subjects, or who coldly calculates the degree of friendship to be extended in each case, is going to appear less than human. People will be puzzled and dismayed by his behavior. Certain kinds of information are available to the dispassionate observer. He is not likely to make enemies or to become involved in disputes. On the other hand, he may have a considerable impact simply because his behavior is impossible to understand or predict. Perhaps the ideal fieldworker would be a person who learned to behave in a natural and predictible manner, involved but not strongly involved. For our part, we came to feel at home in Gopalpur. Even today we can remember each friend and each enemy as well as we remember our friends and enemies at home. We were a part of the community, and we shall never forget it.

■ A FIELD EXPERIENCE IN RETROSPECTION

Elliot Liebow

BACKGROUND

When I came to the Child Rearing Study Project on January 1, 1962, this NIMH-supported study of "Child Rearing Practices Among Low Income Families in the District of Columbia" was well into its third year. My job was to collect field material on low-income adult males to complement the data already secured through family interviews.

From the very beginning I felt comfortable with the prospect of working with lower-class Negroes. I was born and raised in Washington, D.C. My father and mother were both Jewish immigrants from Eastern Europe—my mother from Latvia, my father from Russia. My father was a grocer and we lived in rooms above or behind the various stores which he operated. All were in predominantly Negro neighborhoods.

School and playground were white, but all of our customers and most of the neighbors were Negroes. Among them and their children I had many acquaintances, several playmates and a few friends. The color line, retraced daily at school and playground and home, was always there; but so were my day-by-day contacts with Negro men, women and children in the store, on the street, and occasionally in their houses; watching a crap game in Sam's place; witnessing the Devil being exorcised from a woman writhing on the floor of a storefront church from my seat in the back row; shooting crap for pennies in a dark hallway; sitting with Benton on the curb, poking aimlessly at debris, waiting for something interesting to happen. It was not until I was seventeen and enlisted in the Marine Corps that I began to move in an almost exclusively white world.

PREPARING FOR THE FIELD

I spent the first week in familiarizing myself with the project and with the work that had already been done. I had several informal discussions with Dr. Hylan Lewis, the director of the project, and gradually gained a feeling for the kind of material that was wanted. Importantly, he laid down no hard-and-fast ground rules on the assumption that the job could best be done if I were free to feel my way around for a few weeks and discover for myself the techniques that were most congenial to me. His one prescription was that the work be securely anchored in the purposes of the project, remembering, too, that "Everything is grist for our mill." As I think back on this now, I see a clear connection between his instructions and his fondness for the quotation, "The scientific method is doing one's darndest with his brains, no holds barred."

Having partially digested the project literature, I told the director that I was ready to get started. He suggested a neighborhood that might be "a good place to get your feet wet." His instructions were: "Go out there and make like an anthropologist."

"Out there" was not at all like the Indian village of Winisk on Hudson Bay in which I had done field work. I was not at all sure how one "makes like an anthropologist" in this kind of "out there." Somewhat wistfully, perhaps, I thought how much neater things would be if anthropologists, as they had done in the early thirties, limited themselves to the study of "wholes," a tribe, a village, or some other social unit with distinct boundaries and small enough to be encompassed in its entirety by direct observation.

When I thought about just what I was going to do, I kept in mind the job Richard Slobodin had done for the Child Rearing Study in the summer of 1960.[1] As part of the effort to get at community as well as family influences in child rearing, the director had assigned Slobodin to "make like an anthropologist" in a one-block enclave in northwest Washington. It seemed to me that I could use his work as a model and, in the course of a year, produce several such studies, each covering a strategic part of the world of the low-income male. I thought of doing a neighborhood study, then moving on, say, to a construction laborers' union, then a bootleg joint, and perhaps rounding these out with a series of genealogies and life histories. I was going to give myself about a month or so of poking around town, getting the feel of things, before committing myself to any firm plan of action.

[1] Richard Slobodin, " 'Upton Square': A Field Report and Commentary."

IN THE FIELD

In taking up the director's suggestion that this would be "a good place to get your feet wet," I went in so deep that I was completely submerged and my plan to do three or four separate studies, each with its own neat, clean boundaries, dropped forever out of sight. My initial excursions into the street—to poke around, get the feel of things, and to lay out the lines of my field work—seldom carried me more than a block or two from the corner where I started. From the very first weeks or even days, I found myself in the middle of things; the principle lines of my field work were laid out, almost without my being aware of it. For the next year or so, and intermittently thereafter, my base of operations was the corner Carry-out across the street from my starting point.

The first time out, I had gone less than one short block when I noticed a commotion up the street. A man—Detective Wesley, I learned later—was dragging a kicking, screaming woman to a police call box. A small crowd had gathered on each of the four corners to watch. I approached two men and asked what the woman had done. Both were uncertain. The younger of the two said that he had heard two stories and proceeded to tell me both of them, concluding with the observation that he had known Detective Wesley for six or seven years and that he was "nobody to fool with."

I said that sometimes being a cop seems to do something to a man. This led to a discussion of policemen and each of us contributed personal experiences or anecdotes on the subject. After ten or fifteen minutes of this, the older man said goodbye and walked off. The younger man stayed on. Across the street from where we were standing was the Downtown Cafe. I suggested that we go in and have some coffee and he agreed. As we walked across the street he asked if I was a policeman. I told him no and explained that I was working on a study of family life in the city. There was no more discussion about who I was or why I was there. We sat at the bar for several hours talking over coffee.

I had not accomplished what I set out to do, but this was only the first day. And, anyway, when I wrote up this experience that evening, I felt that it presented a fairly good picture of this young man and that most of the material was to the point. Tomorrow, I decided, I would go back to my original plan—nothing had been lost.

But tomorrow never came. At nine the next morning, I headed down the same street. Four men were standing in a group in front of the Carry-out.

> Three were winos, in their forties—all marked with old scars on face and neck, dressed shabbily, but sober. The fourth was a man of thirty-two or thirty-three, who looked as if he had just stepped out of a slick magazine advertisement. . . . One of the winos had a month-old puppy stuck in the front of his overcoat. Only the dog's head was exposed.
>
> The group approached me and one of the older men said, "Isn't he a nice puppy?" I said yes, and began patting the dog. "He just bought him,"

one man said. "I wanted the female, too, to breed them," said the man holding the dog, "but that woman, she sold the female to her friend."

The puppy was whining. "Maybe it's hungry," said the older man, "let's get him some hamburger." "No man, he'll get worms from that stuff," said one of the others. I suggested milk and we all went into the Carry-out. I asked the waitress for a half pint of milk. The man asked for a saucer. "You can't feed him here," the waitress said, "the Health Department would close us up." She gave us a paper plate and the milk (paid for by me). We took the dog into a hallway next door. Everybody was pleased at how eagerly the puppy drank.

A man who had been in the Carry-out joined us in the hallway. "That's a shepherd, isn't he? Just what I want for my little boy." I said, "I wish I could get one for my little girl, but she's allergic to all animals, dust, and lots of things." "It's better that way," said one of the winos. "She'll outgrow it. But man, if you don't have that until you're full grown—man, look out." "Yes, that's right," the newcomer agreed. "I know a woman who got allergies after she was grown and she got bronica asthma with it."

The dog finished the milk. The owner put him back in his overcoat and I shook hands all around with the winos. We split up three ways. The winos went up the street, the well-dressed man down the street, and the newcomer —who turned out to be Tally Jackson—and I went into the Carry-out.

For more than four hours Tally and I lounged around in the Carry-out, talking, drinking coffee, watching people come in and go out, watching other hangers-on as they bantered with the waitresses, horsed around among themselves, or danced to the jukebox. Everyone knew Tally and some frequently sought out his attention. Tally sometimes participated in the banter but we were generally left undisturbed when we were talking. When I left at two o'clock, Tally and I were addressing each other by first names ("Elliot" was strange to him and we settled for "Ellix") and I was able to address the two waitresses by their first names without feeling uncomfortable. I had also learned to identify several other men by their first names or nicknames, had gotten hints on personal relationships, and had a biographical sketch (part of it untrue I learned later) of Tally.

Back on the street, I ended up at the Downtown Cafe, this time by way of the morning's now very drunk owner of the puppy, who was standing near the entrance. The puppy was our bond and we talked about him with an enthusiasm that perhaps neither of us felt. Later, the well-dressed man who had also been part of the puppy episode came in and joined me at the bar. Then, still drinking beer at the bar stool, I met two other men in quick succession. The first man had to leave shortly for his night-shift busboy job at the restaurant. The other was a surly man in his middle thirties who initiated the contact by taking the stool next to me and asking what kind of work I did, adding that he had seen me around the day before, watching Detective Wesley drag that woman across the street.

I told him briefly what my job was.

"Well, if you hang around here you'll see it all. Anything can happen and it does happen here. It can get rough and you can get your head knocked in. You'll be okay though, if you know one or two of the right people."

"That's good to know," I told him, guessing (and hoping) that he was one of the "right people." He left me with the impression that he was being friendly and, in a left-handed sort of way, was offering me his protection.

By the end of the second day I had met nine men, learned the names of several more, and spent many hours in close public association with several men, at least two of whom were well known. And perhaps most important of all, in my own mind I had partly sloughed off that feeling of being a stranger and achieved that minimum sense of "belonging" which alone permits an ease of manner and mind so essential in building personal relationships.

Over the next three or four weeks, I made several excursions into other neighborhoods and followed up at the Downtown Cafe and the Carry-out shop on an irregular basis, getting to know some of the people better and many others for the first time. Frequently I ate breakfast and lunch at the Carry-out and began putting occasional dimes in the juke-box and in the pinball machine. Ted Moore, who worked at a liquor store nearby and whom I had first met in the Carry-out while he was waiting for the store to open, regularly alternated with me in buying coffee and doughnuts in the morning. At the Downtown Cafe the man who told me that I'd be okay if I knew "one or two of the right people" publicly identified me as his friend. ("Sure I know him," he told another man in my presence. "We had a long talk the other day. He's my friend and he's okay, man, he's okay. At first I thought he was a cop, but he's no cop. He's okay.")

All in all, I felt I was making steady progress. There was still plenty of suspicion and mistrust, however. At least two men who hung around the Carry-out—one of them the local numbers man—had seen me dozens of times in close quarters, but they kept their distance and I kept mine. Once, accidentally, I caught the numbers man's eye as I walked in. We held the stare for three or four seconds and I nodded slightly but he wouldn't let go. I went on about my business, determined that I wasn't going to be stared down next time and that he'd get no more nods from me unless he nodded first. As it turned out, I didn't have long to wait.

One mid-February day, I walked into the Carry-out.

. . . Tally was having a cup of coffee. "Look here," he said. "Where is this place?" Tally took out a sheet of paper from an envelope and handed it to me. It was a summons to appear as a witness for the defense in the case of the United States versus Lonny Reginald Small. A faint stamp indicated that Tally was to report to the United States District Court for the District of Columbia at 3rd and Pennsylvania Avenue, Northwest, at ten o'clock this morning. I read off the address. It was then 9:40. I suggested that Tally take a cab, but when Tally said he didn't have the money I offered to drive him down. He quickly accepted. On the way, Tally explained that Lonny was a friend of his. Lonny was being tried for murdering his wife last summer. "Lonny is a nice guy," he said. "He's one hundred percent."

Thus began a three-week odyssey into the world of Lonny Small, a young man of twenty-six who, according to the jury's subsequent verdict of "not guilty," had choked his wife to death accidentally. Upon his acquittal, Lonny was rearrested in the courthouse for a violation of probation (on a previous grand larceny conviction) in another jurisdiction. He waived extradition, was given a hearing, was released on an appearance bond, and after another hearing he was again placed on probation.

Almost imperceptibly, my association with Tally, and through him with Lonny, was projecting me into the role of a principal actor in Lonny's life. By being with Tally through the trial, I found that first Tally, then Lonny, were looking to me for leadership and, as in the question of waiving extradition, for decision making. Court officials, apparently taking their cues from Lonny, began looking to me as his spokesman.

The follow-up of Lonny, which took most of my time for at least the next two weeks, carried me into dozens of places and into contact with scores of people. Throughout this period I stayed in close touch with the project director, getting clearance for and weighing the possible consequences of my growing involvement with the authorities. I went to three different jails during this time, sat through one murder trial and two hearings in judges' chambers, testifying at one of them. I went to bondsmen's offices, to the United States Employment Service, to the Blessed Martin de Porres Hostel (for homeless men) and into several private homes. I met policemen, judges, lawyers, bondsmen, probation officers, and one of Lonny's former employers. I talked with his friends and at least one enemy, his mother-in-law, whose daughter he had killed. I met in council several times with various members of his extended family (who accepted me, through Tally, as Lonny's friend, no questions asked) in their houses, and drove around with them to the houses of other members of the family trying to raise money for Lonny's bond.

Meanwhile, back at the Carry-out, where Tally and I were meeting regularly at night and where I tried to stop in during the day whenever possible, people I had never seen, or others I had seen but never spoken to, began coming up to me and asking, "Is Lonny out yet?" or "Did you raise his bail yet?" or simply, "How's it going?" Bumdoodle, the numbers man, one of those who had not known Lonny, was especially solicitous of Lonny's welfare. He, too, began calling me by my first name and, although I kept no record of it, I think it was at this time that he dropped all subterfuge in taking numbers in my presence and soon began taking bets from me.

By the middle of March, Tally and I were close friends ("up tight") and I was to let him know if I wanted or needed "anything, anytime." By April, the number of men whom I had come to know fairly well and their acceptance of me had reached the point at which I was free to go to the rooms or apartments where they lived or hung out, at almost any time, needing neither an excuse nor an explanation for doing so. Like other friends, I was there to pass the time, to hang around, to find out "what's happening."

I switched my day around to coincide with the day worker's leisure hours: from four in the afternoon until late at night, according to what was going on. Alone, or with one, two or half a dozen others, I went to poolrooms, to bars, or to somebody's room or apartment. Much of the time we just hung around the Carry-out, playing the pinball machine or standing on the corner watching the world go by. Regularly at five, I met my five "drinking buddies" when they came off from work and we went into a hallway for an hour or so of good drinking and easy talk.

Friday afternoon to Sunday night was especially exciting and productive. I'd go to Nancy's "place" (apartment) where, at almost any hour, one could get liquor, listen to music, or engage in conversation. Or perhaps seven or eight of us would buy some beer and whiskey and go up to Tonk's apartment near the Carry-out where he lived with his wife. Occasionally, I'd pair up with one or two men and go to a party, a movie, or a crap game, which might be in almost any part of town. Sunday afternoon was an especially good time to pick up news or happenings of the preceding forty-eight hours. People were generally rested up from the night before, relaxed, and ready to fill one another in on events which involved the police, breakups of husband-wife relations and bed-and-board arrangements, drink-stimulated brawls, sex adventures, and parties they had witnessed, heard about, or participated in over Friday and Saturday.

By April most people seemed to be taking it for granted that I belonged in the area. At least two men did not trust me or like me, but by then I was too strongly entrenched for them to challenge successfully my right to be there, even had they chosen to do so. New people moved into the area and I found myself being regarded as an old-timer, sometimes being asked to corroborate events which predated my arrival.

Throughout this period, my field observations were focused on individuals: what they said, what they did, and the contexts in which they said them or did them. I sought them out and was sought out by them.

My field notes contain a record of what I saw when I looked at Tally, Richard, Sea Cat and the others. I have only a small notion—and one that I myself consider suspect—of what they saw when they looked at me.

Some things, however, are very clear. They saw, first of all, a white man. In my opinion, this brute fact of color, as they understood it in their experience and as I understood it in mine, irrevocably and absolutely relegated me to the status of outsider. I am not certain, but I have a hunch that they were more continuously aware of the color difference than I was. When four of us sat around a kitchen table, for example, I saw three Negroes; each of them saw two Negroes and a white man.

Sometimes, when the word "nigger" was being used easily and conversationally or when, standing on the corner with several men, one would have a few words with a white passerby and call him a "white mother-fucker," I used to play with the idea that maybe I wasn't as much of an outsider as I thought. Other events, and later readings of the field materials, have disabused me of this particular touch of vanity.

Whenever the fact of my being white was openly introduced, it pointed up the distance between me and the other person, even when the intent of introducing it was, I believe, to narrow that distance.

> . . . All of us left Tally's room together. Tally grabbed my arm and pulled me aside near the storefront church and said, "I want to talk to you." With no further introduction, he looked me straight in the eye and started talking.
>
> "I'm a liar. I been lying to you all along now and I want to set it straight, even if it means we can't be friends no more. I only lied to you about one thing. Everything else I told you is gospel truth but I did lie about one thing and that makes me a liar. I know that some white people think that if you catch a man in a lie one time you can't never trust him after that. And even if you feel that way about it I still got to tell you. You remember when you first come around here, I told you. . . . Well, that was a lie. . . . I didn't think nothing of it at first, but then you and me started going around together and when we started getting real tight, my conscience started whomping me. I kept looking for a place to tell you but it never seemed right. Then tonight . . . I knew this was the right time. I knew you were going to find out and I didn't want you to find out from somebody else. . . ."

Once I was with Richard in his hometown. It was his first visit in five years. We arrived in the middle of the night and had to leave before daybreak because Richard was wanted by the local police. We were in his grandmother's house. Besides Richard, there were his grandmother, his aunt, and two unrelated men, both long-time friends of Richard.

The group was discussing the possibility of Richard's coming home to stay and weighing the probable consequences. In the middle of the discussion, Richard interrupted and nodded at me. "Now Ellix here is white, as you can see, but he's one of my best friends. Him and me are real tight. You can say anything you want, right to his face. He's real nice." "Well," said his Aunt Pearl, "I always did say there are some nice white people."

Whether or not there is more to these citations than "Some of my best friends are . . ." or "Yes, but you're different," the wall between us remained, or better, the chain-link fence, since despite the barriers we were able to look at each other, walk alongside each other, talk and occasionally touch fingers. When two people stand up close to the fence on either side, without touching it, they can look through the interstices and forget that they are looking through a fence.

The disadvantage of being white was offset in part by the fact that, as an outsider, I was not a competitor. Thus, in the matter of skin color, I saw myself nowhere in the spectrum of black- to light-skinned (or "bright"); I was completely out of it, with no vested interest. It could be that this made it possible for some people to speak freely to me about skin color.

> "You know, I'm the darkest one in my family. All my aunts, uncles, every-body is light-skinned and they were all down on me, except my grandmother. . . . She'd do anything for me, maybe because she saw everyone else against me. . . . All the time I was coming up, I kept hoping somebody would have a baby darker than me."

Looking at me, however, the people I came to know in the area probably saw more than a "white male adult." They saw or knew many other things as well, any one of which relegated me to outside status. Those with whom I was in regular contact knew, for example, that I was with them because it was my job to be with them, and they knew, according to their individual comprehension and my ability to communicate, just what my job was. They knew that I lived outside the area. They knew that I was a college graduate, or at least they associated an advanced education with the work I was doing. Moreover, it was apparent, certainly to me, that I was not fluent in their language. Thus, I was an outsider not only because of race, but also because of occupation, education, residence, and speech. The fact that I was Jewish came up only twice. Once, a man who worked but did not live in the area threw some Yiddish expressions at me because "I thought you looked Jewish." The other time was when I met a soldier in a local bootleg joint. We had been talking for some ten minutes or so when he asked me whether I was "Eyetalian." I told him I was Jewish. "That's just as good," he said. "I'm glad you're not white."

The fact that I was married and a father, and that I was bigger than average size—6'1", 185 pounds—probably didn't matter much, except as they entered incidentally into my personal relationship with one or another individual. Since the people I spent most of my time with ranged in age from twenty to the middle forties, I would guess that my age (thirty-seven) was not significant in itself.

On several different counts I was an outsider but I also was a participant in a full sense of the word. The people I was observing knew that I was observing them, yet they allowed me to participate in their activities and take part in their lives to a degree that continues to surprise me. Some "exploited" me, not as an outsider but rather as one who, as a rule, had more resources than they did. When one of them came up with the resources—money or a car, for example—he too was "exploited" in the same way. I usually tried to limit money or other favors to what I thought each would have gotten from another friend had he the same resources as I. I tried to meet requests as best I could without becoming conspicuous. I was not always on the giving end and learned somewhat too slowly to accept food or let myself be treated to drinks even though I knew this would work a hardship on the giver.

When in the field, I participated as fully and as whole-mindedly as I could, limited only by my own sense of personal and professional propriety and by what I assumed to be the boundaries of acceptable behavior as seen by those I was with.[2]

Occasionally, when I wanted to record a physical description of say, a neighborhood, an apartment, or a social event, I tried to be an observer only. In practice, I found it impossible to keep all traces of participation out of a straight observer role.

One Saturday night, with my observer role clearly in mind, I went to a dance at the Capitol Arena where more than a thousand people were jammed together. I was the only white male, this was my first time at such an event, the music was so foreign to me that I picked out the wrong beat, and I was unable to identify several of the band instruments. I was, willy-nilly, an observer. But here are a few lines excerpted from the field observation:

> It was very hot, it was very noisy, it was very smelly, and it was all very exciting. It was impossible to remain simply an observer in a place like this, even for someone as phlegmatic as I. It was only a few minutes after Jackie Wilson started singing that I discovered that the noise wasn't nearly loud enough, the heat wasn't nearly hot enough, and the odor from more than a thousand closely packed people was not really strong enough at all. Like everyone else, I wanted more of everything.

Almost from the beginning, I adopted the dress and something of the speech of the people with whom I was in most frequent contact, as best I could without looking silly or feeling uncomfortable. I came close in dress (in warm weather, tee or sport shirt and khakis or other slacks) with almost no effort at all. My vocabulary and diction changed, but not radically. Cursing and using ungrammatical constructions at times— though they came easily—did not make any of my adaptations confusable with the speech of the street. Thus, while remaining conspicuous in speech and perhaps in dress, I had dulled some of the characteristics of my background. I probably made myself more accessible to others, and certainly more acceptable to myself. This last point was forcefully brought

---

[2] From the outset, I had decided that I would never shoot crap, pool, or play cards for money, or bet money in any way (numbers excepted, since playing numbers is safely impersonal), and would meticulously avoid the slightest suspicion of a personal involvement with any woman. These self-imposed restrictions to some extent did underline my marginality. My explanation that I couldn't afford to chance a fight or bad feelings because of my job was usually accepted and I was generally excused from participating in these activities rather than excluded from them.

home to me one evening when, on my way to a professional meeting, I stopped off at the Carry-out in a suit and tie. My loss of ease made me clearly aware that the change in dress, speech, and general carriage was as important for its effect on me as it was for its effect on others.

In retrospect, it seems as if the degree to which one becomes a participant is as much a matter of perceiving oneself as a participant as it is of being accepted as a participant by others.

■ STRANGER AND FRIEND

Hortense Powdermaker

As I wandered through the Hollywood maze, I saw myself as an objective scientist, and took pride in a Jovian detachment. Now, with hindsight, I know the situation was quite different.

As I left Hollywood after a year and drove past a sign marking the boundaries of Los Angeles, I burst into song, as is my habit when feeling joy. But even that reaction did not make me realize how deeply I had hated the place. When leaving other field sites, I have usually been both glad and sorry—glad to depart because I have been tired and fed-up; sorry to leave my friends and life in the field. Except for the Hollywood situation, I have never been joyous on leaving, nor have I hated a society I studied. Although it might be difficult, there is no reason why an anthropologist could not study a society he hated, so long as he was aware of his feelings at the time, and was able to cope with them. But my rage was bottled up, and never fully conscious.

I happen to be a person of strong feelings, and it might have been predicted from the previous conditioning of my personality that I would feel rage in Hollywood. The plunge into the labor movement had been a rebellion from authority in the family and against the subjugation of unorganized workers by employers. Nor was it irrelevant that World War II, in which we fought a totalitarian concept of man, had just ended before I went to Hollywood, or that I had always been (and still am) concerned with the moral problem of freedom. I had, also, always been hostile to a way of life in which the accumulation of wealth was the primary motive. My identifications had long been with scientists and artists, and I have never seen any real ideological or temperamental incompatibility between them.

But I played it cool, as today's jargon would express it. I pretended a role of amused detachment. I knew, of course, that the fraudulence of the human relations, the treatment of people as property, the debasement of taste, and the whole dehumanization which occurred in the making of most movies were foreign to my values. But instead of letting my deep feelings spill over into rage, I felt superior. I now wonder what would have happened if the men at the top of the power hierarchy had been accessible to me. It is possible that I might have acquired a feeling of compassion that would have allowed me to get inside their roles and then detach myself, as I had done with white planters in Mississippi. Or I might have seen that the behavior of the front office did not necessarily spring wholly from malice, but could be the all-too-frequent denegation of the talented by the untalented.

My role as a field worker was also affected by the fact that the Hollywood study attracted more attention than anything I had ever done. Colleagues and people outside the academic world were intrigued by the idea of an anthropologist studying Hollywood. Unfortunately, I, too, became intrigued with playing a role and doing something unusual. In no other field work had this happened. I had merely followed my interests and my profession: any other role-playing was secondary and incidental.

Given my personality, it was inevitable that I should be on the side of the artists in their struggle against the power of the front office, and this attitude was not detrimental to the study of the artists. Through my identification with them, I was able to get inside their roles, then detach myself and see them with considerable objectivity. The best parts of the book on Hollywood are the chapters on directors and actors, precisely because I was openly and consciously identified with them.

It had not taken me long to learn that the director was the key person and belonged to movie-making in an organic sense. Even without actually seeing directors at work, I was able to understand their creative excitement in interviews and to be sympathetic with their frustrations. The chapter on directors gives far more data on the creative ones than their number warranted. But they were the key to understanding the translation of a fantasy into a film. Furthermore, the relationship between director and actors is natural, i.e. indispensable for the making of the film, and not imposed by the financial power structure.

I quickly understood a basic fact about actors: that acting is a way of life for them. I saw them as human beings with the kind of personality whose needs were best met by acting. Whether the script and directors were good or bad, the actor usually did the best he could and thus maintained his integrity as an artist. Acting was essential to his being fully alive. This I could understand. Field work, writing, teaching are among the ways in which I feel alive.

Then, too, I saw actors, regardless of their success or wealth, as an underprivileged group; many of them knew they were looked down upon by other members of the Hollywood hierarchy. In the chapter, "Actors are People,"[1] I discussed their resentments to the seven-year contract, by which they were legally owned by the studio for that people, and to camera man, producer, director, and front office. The talented artists were

[1] Hortense Powdermaker, *Hollywood, The Dream Factory* (Boston: Little, Brown & Co., 1960).

being treated as synthetic products of publicity and make-up departments, deeply sincere about their work, and I related to them easily. Naturally, I met and interviewed many actors without much ability, who were of interest only as they represented certain types. But they intrigued me, too. The actor's personality was new to me and I was constantly trying to understand him.

I think, too, that I was not immune to the charm and "glamor" of some of the actors. I remember interviewing a handsome well-known actor, as we lunched beside a pool. I wondered if any observer would call that work! However, the interview did produce good data, as did similar ones.

My relationship with writers, however, was quite different from that with directors and actors. Although closer by temperament and profession to the writers than to any other group in Hollywood, I failed to identify with them or to get inside their roles. The producer-writer relationship was not functional in the social structure as was that of director-actor. As I interviewed producers and writers and read the files on the arbitration of screen credits, the cliché of the writer being the producer's lead pencil seemed, and was, only too true. I was *indignant* at the writers for getting into this position and *horrified* when I found gifted writers (whose work before coming to Hollywood had been literature) working on admittedly mediocre scripts and taking them *seriously*. But was this any different from the actor taking his role in a mediocre film with seriousness? Obviously not. For both it was a way of preserving some measure of self-respect. But at the time I did not see this. I wrote that the writers had become "soft," that they sacrificed their integrity as artists for monetary rewards. To a large extent, this may have been a true value judgment, i.e. for those who were artists and who possessed integrity. But indignation limited my understanding.

I duly listened as the writers told me of the compensations they enjoyed: for the first time they were free of debt, able to buy pretty clothes for their wives, save money for the education of their children, and, in general, live in upper-class comfort. All this left me "cold"; I wrote, "the creative person who functions as such has to make some sacrifices."[2]

Many of the writers not only experienced a prosperity unknown before coming to Hollywood, but also enjoyed, for the first time, participation in an occupational group. Writing is generally a lonely condition. But in Hollywood writers were with each other in the studio dining room and at conferences and, away from the studio, they had a lively social life among themselves; some were also active in the Screen Writers' Guild. Although "a producer's lead pencil," they enjoyed having an essential role in a multi-million-dollar industry and knowing that the film on which they worked reached a world-wide audience. Writers, gifted or not, talked quite honestly about the advantages of Hollywood for them. But I scornfully thought of the gifted ones as moral prostitutes and labeled many of their ideas about the advantages of Hollywood as rationalizations. The fact that most writers, left, center, and right politically, accepted the system, received

2 *Ibid.*, p. 136.

satisfaction from it, and even defended it, primarily because of financial rewards, or for the glamor of being part of Hollywood (though they also lampooned it), put them beyond the pale for me—not a favorable situation for understanding. I could not step outside their roles for objective analysis because I had never been inside them.

I was (and am) a writer. Writing is a way of life for me. The writers had let me down, because they had not come up to my expectations of professional integrity. Yet, I had understood and objectively studied white Mississippians whose standards of behavior towards Negroes certainly lacked integrity and were far different from mine. Why were my reactions to the Hollywood writers and to the white Mississippians (both members of my own race and culture) so different? The behavior of each cut clearly across my strongly held values. But in Mississippi, I knew quite consciously that I might have behaved like the white people if I had lived there all my life. I was glad that this had not been the case, and felt compassion for the whites. This was in sharp contrast to my "holier-than-thou" attitude towards the Hollywood writers.

In looking back upon the Hollywood field work, I think I was unconsciously threatened by the writers. Perhaps I had wanted to become one of them but would not admit it. Unconscious envy usually underlies a "holier-than-thou" attitude. It was inevitable that I should be involved with the writers, since I regarded myself as one. The problem, however, was not in my involvement, but that I was unaware of its real nature. If I had been more aware, I might have been able to objectify the situation and to have studied it with more detachment.

In other field experiences I knew when I was involved. When I met a would-be lynching gang on a road in Mississippi, my involvement and wanting to save the Negro were so open that I had an anxious and sleepless night. But the next day I was able to get outside the situation and take notes. In Lesu I was quite aware of my personal involvement when my friend, Pulong, was critically ill; I took notes on my feelings, as well as on the ill woman, her husband and her relatives. Conscious involvements are not a handicap for the social scientist. Unconscious ones are always dangerous.

After the manuscript of the book was completed and accepted by the publisher, he suggested that I insert more comparisons with primitive societies. I had used only a few which were pertinent. I resisted the suggestion, arguing that I did not think more such comparisons were relevant. Then, against my better judgment, I accepted and implemented the publisher's suggestion, inserting many analogies with primitive societies which now seem out of place and weakening to the book. The profuse use of analogies was a gimmick, designed to make the book more popular rather than meaningful, and not too different from the gimmicks used in movie scripts. The possibility of popularity was not unpleasant. I had submitted to the Front Office!

My "holier-than-thou" attitude in Hollywood should have put me on guard, but, unfortunately, did not. I thought that objectivity was obtained by having as good a stratified sample as the situation permitted, allowing respondents to speak freely about their behavior and attitudes without any expression of my values, and recording as exactly as possible what they said. All these are necessary techniques, but do not insure a field worker's psychological mobility to step in and out of the roles of peoples with different value systems.

Is it possible for anyone—artist, social scientist, or reporter—to write both meaningfully and with objective detachment about Hollywood? Lillian Ross's superb reporting of the making of *The Red Badge of Courage* is the most objective writing I know on Hollywood.[3] In a sense she was doing for one picture what I had tried to do earlier for the social structure as a whole. Her success as a participant observer in following the making of an atypical film over a period of two years could be the envy of any field worker. She observed the interplay between John Huston, a fascinating and gifted director-writer, Gottfried Reinhardt, an intelligent, cynical producer, and Dore Schary, intelligent and optimistic, in charge of the studio's production. She caught and portrayed well their creative excitement, frustrations, and compromises. The description of their relations with the front-office executives is much less detailed and more second-hand, although penetrating. Powerful Louis B. Mayer did not want to make the picture, but the still more powerful Nicholas M. Schenk in the New York office of Loew's, Inc., supported Dore Schary so that the latter would learn by making a mistake, i.e. making a picture that would be a financial flop. But objective as her report was, reviewers referred to its subjects as "victims" and wrote that she would not be welcome in Hollywood again.

Viewing my Hollywood field work in retrospect, I think it succeeded to a considerable degree in describing the social structure in which movies were made and the manner in which this structure influenced their quality, form, and content. My point of view as a humanist and my concern with the human and social costs of movie making gave meaning and strength to the book. Identification with artists enabled me to understand and present their roles, their frustrations, and their occasional victories in a factory producing fantasies. Many readers praised the book for its portrayal of the artists' position in the United States. But I think of what the book might have been if some of my involvements had not been hidden, if I had possessed the psychological mobility and the sociological opportunity to enter and understand all the contending groups, if my value system had not so aggressively dominated the whole study, if I had known more humility and compassion.

3 Lillian Ross, "Picture" in her *Reporting* (New York: Simon & Schuster, 1964). First published as, "Onward and Upward with The Arts" in *The New Yorker*, May 24th, 31st, June 7th, 14th, 21st, 1952.

■ ON THE CLAN OF ANTHROPOLOGISTS

Jesús Salinas

EDITOR'S NOTE

This article, by Sr. Jesús Salinas Pedraza, an Otomi school teacher of Ixmiquilpan, Hidalgo, in Mexico, is a rare view of anthropologists by one of the "natives." Sr. Salinas was the first person with whom I worked in the Otomi region in 1962 and we have since become close friends. In June 1967, I returned to the Mezquital Valley with a group of graduate students who were enrolled in a course on field methods in cultural anthropology. The course ran for five summers and sixty students completed it. They spent a week in the town of Ixmiquilpan, one of the cultural centers of Otomi country and the heart of the Mezquital desert region about 100 miles north of Mexico City. In Ixmiquilpan the students received instruction on techniques, local landmarks, and other basics. Then they were sent individually to villages for seven weeks to do field work. One of the course directors visited each student once a week to check on his or her progress. Finally, the students spent a week back in Ixmiquilpan discussing their common experiences.

In 1972, a year after the field school ended, Salinas wrote down some of his observations of the anthropologists who had invaded his homeland.

In 1967, a group of white, bearded men came out of the north again. They were descendants of the clan of anthropologists, which I believed had disappeared from the face of the earth. Between 1962 and 1966 I didn't see anything of them, but it is certain that they were preparing another invasion with a greater number of people. Alternatively, they could have been the survivors of the clan migrating south to free themselves from the attacks of other nomadic groups. By 1967 they had achieved a higher degree of civilization and they returned as sedentary peoples to the Mezquital. They brought with them such items as sleeping bags, portable stoves, and gasoline lanterns. And they had obviously entered a new cultural era marked by the growth of long hair. They also smoked a great deal, a primitive custom that made them look like furnaces. They walked about with restless eyes, trying to take it all in. They stayed in Ixmiquilpan for a week and then they left for the villages where they would stay for the remainder of the summer. This was a group to fatten the ranks of the anthropology clan, and they tried out their remarkable and superficial theories on the lives of the people of my country in the Mezquital.

One of them went to a community called Dextho, where I was working as a school teacher. The teacher always has a room in the schoolhouse in which to sleep; we were able to give the student anthropologist a similar room and ensconce him in the village.

In Dextho the annual festival is celebrated on the 29th of June. But in this particular year it had been postponed and it was celebrated on the 29th of July. It was the festival of St. Paul, St. Peter, and All Saints. It is the custom to celebrate the patron saint or saints of a place for eight days, during which time the participants are offered much food and drink.

The most important food is the traditional *mole,* which is made from large chilies, peanuts, chocolate, cumin, pepper, cloves, walnuts, and cinnamon. Chicken, cooked separately, is mixed with the sauce. We, that is the anthropologist and I, were invited to eat at the fiesta. We were brought over to the kitchen that had been improvised next to the church; it was called the "town kitchen" and everybody in the pueblo and all of the invited guests from the outside eat on this site. My friend, interested in knowing all the foods that people eat around here during fiestas, was in a great rush to get going. I hadn't even gotten out of bed when he came to say, "Let's go. It's time to eat breakfast."

We arrived at the kitchen, which was 200 meters to the south of the school. Those who had the responsibility of serving us seemed excited at having the honor to serve for the first time in the history of the fiesta, a North American visitor. All of those cooking, men and women, stared at my friend and looked him over as if he were an exhibition piece. We finished eating but they would not let us leave. Instead they served us beer and, of course, the sweet pulque. They served my colleague by the liter. They wanted to see him lose his equilibrium, but he was as strong as an oak tree and he didn't even move. About every hour and a half there was another meal, and thus we passed eight days during that fiesta.

The last day of the festival includes the change of *mayordomos,* those who are responsible for putting on the festival. The old ones leave office and the new ones enter and they exchange gifts. Those who are leaving office are sent off with music and given necklaces of fruit, bread, and flowers. They are also given cakes, and in the cake there is a paper with a name of the next *mayordomo* written on it. Even without being *mayordomos* we received our share. To the member of the anthropology clan they gave a basket filled with cakes, wine, cookies, and chocolates. After the meal he said that he was quite happy because during that week he had learned a lot about life in the local area. Whenever I invited him to eat with me he insisted that everything was delicious; of course, what he made for himself was totally different. In fact, he didn't know how to cook what he had. For example, when he "cooked" rice he didn't let it cook, and then, to finish the destruction completely, he would throw in cans of fish. After his meals, he gave whatever was left over to the dogs, which was natural enough. But he fed the dogs out of the same plate from which he was eating, which was the same pot in which he had cooked it!

Undoubtedly, he brought this custom with him from his house. But one must understand that where he comes from they bathe their animals, they groom them, and they watch after them in a completely different way than in the Mezquital. Here, from birth to death, nobody ever bathes a dog and as a result the animals are loaded with parasites. He must have known this, but he couldn't change his ways. Custom and habit interfered with common sense.

I used to visit houses with the anthropologist in Dextho. We were making our accustomed visits one evening when we were invited to have supper. We chatted with the family about the recently installed irrigation system in the area. We were discussing the increased production that resulted from the new system, and the head of the household asked us to stay and eat some of the new crop of string beans. We eagerly accepted the invitation and when we were served we began chatting around the table.

The anthropologist asked us many questions about the meal and we answered each question in turn. It happened that he inquired about the Otomi word for the string beans that we were eating and I told him that it was written "x++" and pronounced like the English letter *h,* plus a very long vowel like the *u* in "put." Then he asked about the plant from which this comes and I told him it was "s̈i," which is pronounced like the word "she" plus "x++." A little while later, in discussing this, he had occasion to refer to this plant but instead of pronouncing it "she huu," he pronounced it inside out—"huu-she," which is the word in Otomi for pubic hair. The family, on hearing what my indelicate friend had said, remained close-mouthed. Nobody would even comment on what had happened, because in Otomi this word is never mentioned in front of women and children.

Finally, at the end of the summer and after a great struggle, the Otomis were able to impede the progress of the anthropology clan in dominating the Mezquital and we bid them farewell. With our offerings of *mole,* flowers, and wine, they left for a period of eleven months. Perhaps these offerings of departure aroused the desire in other members of their clan to receive similar treatment; in any case, 1968 brought another group of adventurers in search of truth. Once again, one of them, abandoned by the rest of his group, landed in Dextho.

It was the second year since the installation of the new irrigation system, and most of the people were out in the fields planting. Immediately after he arrived the anthropologist asked me why there were no people around in the village, and I told him they were out working their plots of ground. He looked around, but he couldn't see anybody because the schoolhouse is surrounded by large mezquite trees. Wanting to orient him to the area and to put him in contact with the local people, I pointed him in the direction he should walk and told him to go chat with the people he found along his way. I told him the people here in this village speak a lot of Spanish and he, having just returned from 2 years in Peru, also spoke Spanish.

Off he went. Imagine my surprise when he came running back to the school a few minutes later. He said excitedly, "Professor! I was frightened by an animal. It chased me. I'm feeling faint and my head hurts!" He was in a cold sweat and completely pale. He said, "I'm going to take an aspirin and lie down; I am feeling rather sick. While the animal was chasing me I ran a lot and I got lost!"

I was dismayed to find that an animal had frightened him so badly, and I tried to learn the name of this dangerous beast. I thought it must have been a coyote, or at least a rattlesnake. But he was so out of breath from running that he couldn't tell me what it was. I went immediately to the place where I thought it must have happened and when I arrived I found a group of women practically dying of laughter. They said to me, "You'd better watch out, professor, or the pigs will get you too." A feeble oaf of a pig had frightened my friend, who had been abandoned by his tribe in the desert. The animal was just scared at the sight of someone he had never seen, and so he bolted. But the poor creature couldn't attack a mouse, much less an American.

Thus, the days passed. We walked about in the mountains together, and sometimes we would see a rabbit or a roadrunner. During the early evening we would see the natives going out into the desert after work, with their shotguns over their shoulders in search of one of these creatures for their supper, if they should be lucky in their hunt. Our friend longed to have one of these weapons. It seemed strange to him to see people carrying around these examples of the earliest forms of firearms ever made. It was even stranger to him because these were not antiques but "made in Ixmiquilpan." He learned to use this weapon and bought his own. He was especially interested in the powder horn, which is made from the horn of an ox. A hunter must carry a powder horn in order to load these weapons. It is the most ordinary thing imaginable, but these anthropologists have a great desire to possess what they call "curious objects." The day after he purchased his gun he went to the slaughter house in Ixmiquilpan very early in the morning to buy a horn. They didn't give him a horn; they gave him a dozen!

Arriving back in the village, he rolled up his sleeves and began to make this thing that he wanted so badly. Some young men in the village, interested in seeing that he got his complete set of hunting equipment, had promised to help him with the powder horn if he would bring the raw material. The horn has to be hollow in order for the powder to get through it, but the end is solid. In order to pierce the end, the tip is cut off and a heavy needle is used to bore through the bone. The needle is heated in a fire until it is red hot and it is pushed into the horn. The anthropologist had tried it, but the needle he used was too thin and he wasn't getting anywhere.

At suppertime we went back to the house of the family that used to feed us. (As a teacher, I was also a stranger in the village and we both had to have a local family provide us with meals.) When we arrived the whole family had gotten together from the village; altogether they consisted of eighteen people. A few minutes before supper was served, someone asked about the horn that we had brought with us. We told them what had happened and immediately they took out a big, thick needle and when it got red hot one of the boys there drilled it into the horn. The anthropologist came close to the action to see how it was done, took one smell of that burning horn, and fainted because he had not yet eaten and was not used to the smell. As soon as he came to his senses, he staggered back to his room in the schoolhouse. We explained to him later that many people drink *pulque* as a medicine for fright—a good prescription for someone who is scared by a pig.

He had terrible luck; even the mice scared him. One day when I decided to visit him in his room he told me excitedly that during the night he heard noises in the closet where he kept his food. I told him that it was just a little "raton" or mouse. On hearing the word *raton,* he became excited and surprised, even incredulous, at the possibility that there might be mice in his room. He looked frightened enough to run and he asked me if I was absolutely certain of what I had said. I said, "Yes," but that there was nothing to be worried about and I told him that if he wanted we would look for the creature together. He said, "Yes. Let's look for it, but let me go and load the rifle." I left him loading the gun while I looked for the animal.

The first bag I lifted was the one in which he kept bread and a mouse ran out. It escaped by running right through my friend's legs; the rifle didn't do him a bit of good because these field mice are about the size of walnuts. When he saw the tiny creature (which could have literally run up the barrel of his gun), he began to laugh with all his might. Later we were talking and he told me he had been afraid of the word *raton* because in his country he had seen vicious rats as big as cats. In this area, the "ratones" weigh about four ounces, and it was strange to see somebody prepared to call in air strikes against such harmless creatures.

Another time we had an anthropologist visit us in the village of Espiritu. He was a huge man and he could hardly fit through the door in his room at the schoolhouse. He was always smiling and easygoing. Everybody in the village remembers him well and holds him in high esteem because he organized a trip for the school children to Mexico City for a day. He was deathly afraid of snakes and held the primitive belief that keeping a rope on the floor would keep snakes from bothering him. In fact, that's exactly what he did. He brought three meters of rope and laid it on the floor beside his bed every night. I wondered whether this was actually believed to be a defense against snakes or if it was part of these primitive people's religion.

I should say that many of the difficulties experienced by members of the anthropology tribe from the north also occur to the local Mexican variety. They have no idea of the animals in our region, possibly because Mestizos rarely trust what Indians have to say. It doesn't occur to them to ask natives about things they don't understand. This would help explain why people from Mexico City also suffer shock when they find themselves in a strange environment. Furthermore, in the indigenous areas there is the additional problem of a language barrier, even for Mexicans. But for anthropologists, this is where classroom lessons have to be translated into real work; this is where "living with people" becomes a must. The most important thing, it seems to me, is for students of other peoples to remain humble. That is, that they should understand that their scientific training doesn't make them any better than the people they are studying. They should not look at poverty as something beneath them—which is unfortunately what happened when we were visited by a woman anthropologist from Mexico City.

She arrived in the Valley with personal servants, thinking that in this way she could demonstrate her position in the social hierarchy. This is the worst way to try to gain real prestige in this environment. To the contrary, she was seen by the natives in a way that I cannot delicately describe here. I can only salute her teachers who managed to understand the situation and would not accept this young girl with her servants. The servants were an example of this student's political influence, but such influence should not be a part of education. All it does is create obstacles to comprehension by the student. If doing without servants is suffering, then I guess one must be prepared to suffer in order to do anthropology.

A year later in the same village, we had a married couple who were nicknamed "the sacred family" because their names were Joseph and Mary; because my name is Jesús the people of the village would say, "There go Jesús, Mary, and Joseph," whenever we walked together. But it was nice to know that the tribe of anthropologists was achieving some sort of social integration and encouraging marriage.

One of the most amazing things occurred in Orizabita, my home village. One year there arrived an utterly enormous anthropologist, larger than we had ever seen. He drove a cream-colored automobile. This gentleman won the nickname "El Prado." This is the name of a brand of cigarettes that advertises itself as being "extra long," and because our friend was so tall he was secretly "rebaptized" by the members of the village with this new name.

He was invited by the members of the village to participate in the regional basketball championship that we have every year during the regional fiesta. The tournament is participated in by teams representing the various communities in the region. This enormous member of the anthropology tribe was asked to participate because of his size. However, on the matter of speed he was extremely slow. The important thing is that the public had a good time watching this poor man who had lots of height and very little agility. Now, whenever the boys in my village play basketball anywhere, the spectators ask about the "athlete who would take second place to a tortoise."

Finally, I should mention the most fearless anthropologist of them all. The first day after he arrived in the village he got up and went outside at about six o'clock in the morning. His first experience was with a prickly pear plant. He must have been one of the more primitive members of his clan because he had no sense of fear with regard to this plant. I recall that I got up and looked outside and saw him cutting the fruit from the plant without protecting his hands. I supposed that this was a true example of his valor and so I asked him, "Aren't you troubled by the thorns?" He answered me, "Well, they are a bit rough." After that, of course, he was pulling thorns out of his hands all day—not an easy job, as anyone familiar with the *nopal* plant knows.

The next day, knowing how dangerous it would be for him to explore alone, I introduced him to his first teacher, who would orient him to the dangers of the desert cactus. Slowly he came to know the flora and fauna of the region. If it had not been for his master it is likely that this primitive anthropologist would have walked into the mouth of a coyote. His inseparable guide and teacher, a boy of seven, bravely prevented this from happening.

By some miracle, no doubt brought upon him by his ancestors, he was able to get through his period in the region and return to his own land. The truth is that he hardly ever ate; he just drank coffee and smoked cigarettes in the morning. At midday he ate a few tortillas with soup and coffee. He didn't eat meat, which surprised me because these primitives are carnivores. He was a man of indestructible faith in the study of anthropology, who bore up under these difficult conditions to return to his group, and to his priests, and to his gods with his head held high. Even though he was tortured by thorns, he had accomplished the mission they had charged him with.

The priests who guided these groups year after year were four in number. They directed the invasion of the Mezquital in a majesterial manner. The first priest-anthropologist was among the most primitive; he was always walking out among the Mezquite trees through the desert. The environment was his deadly enemy. He insisted on wearing sandals. It was a very foolish thing to do, especially for someone new to the desert. Not knowing how to walk in the desert, he was forever picking cactus thorns out of his toes.

Another was large and bald, with a great mustache. He was very polite and always called me "teacher." The other two were dressed like cowboys. Perhaps they thought they might settle in the desert and became pastoralists instead of nomads. The last year they came was 1971. It was a year that will live in the pages of our history. The Mezquital Valley has now regained its liberty and independence from this group of nomadic invaders. The priests and the remaining survivors of the clan seem to have left the native population of the desert to live in peace. Now we live in tranquility without strangers in our midst. All of them who were here have gone following the North Star, which seems to be their guide.

■ REMINISCENCES OF A FIELD TRIP

Robert Wauchope

The rural inhabitants of northern Georgia were among the most hospitable people, in their own way, I have ever met. Many a freezing night I warmed body and soul at their cabin fireplaces and listened to some of the finest folk music and tallest tales I have ever heard; for me, a stranger and flatlander, to be invited into their homes meant more to me than one who does not know these people can imagine. For when you approach a mountain house for the first time, in north Georgia, the man on the front porch is likely to disappear quickly, the womenfolk hide, and the hounds begin to bay. Once they become your friends, however, their concern for you can become downright embarrassing. I frequently unloaded my pickup truck in Athens or Atlanta after a winter drive down from the hills, and found, perched on top of piles of pottery bags, in plain sight of anyone who wanted to see, a half-gallon fruit jar of highly illegal, home-grown corn whiskey which some anonymous benefactor had felt I would need during the long cold ride home.

The famed "water boy" of WPA projects was a mere figurehead in north Georgia winter field work. Each man kept his own jug behind some nearby tree or bush, and about every half-hour, all day long during the bitter months on the windswept bottomlands, each workman would disappear for a moment, emerge wiping his mouth with the back of his hand, warm himself at the fire, and then, refueled so to speak, go back to his digging. I learned how to roll a Ford through the worst mudholes, taught by experts: the men who loaded their own old Model A's with moonshine and outran the sheriff across the lonely red clay roads almost every night of the week—less for profit, I always thought, than for sport.

It was often the independent small farmer who was quickest to give us permission to dig on his land. Many larger operators and absentee land-owners were equally generous and interested in our work, but a few were suspicious, afraid, or simply uncooperative, and one or two deliberately tried to hold us up for money long after our excavations had begun. Although we were protected by written permits, nevertheless we were determined to leave only good will behind us everywhere, and more than once we filled our trenches and moved out rather than give the farmer any excuse for complaint. The infuriating belief we met everywhere was that we were really digging for gold. I do not know how many times crafty individuals tried to trick us into "reading" petroglyphs for them, on the pretense that they could read most of it but wanted us to fill in a few passages! Here is a typical entry in my log, for January 18, 1939:

A man from Ball Ground walked all the way out to the dig to tell me about some Indian signs on the other side of the river. He said that he would take me to see them if we could slip off without anyone seeing us. I explained that we are not hunting gold and if we went anywhere it would have to be openly. We drove across the river and after devious wanderings parked the car. We walked a mile through the woods down the river. My guide looked back across his shoulder repeatedly and talked in a hushed voice. The petroglyphs turned out to be grooves caused by weathering and by roots growing along the surface of some big boulders. He then wanted to take me to another spot to see Indian signs on trees and rocks showing where the gold was buried: the rocks we had just looked at "pointed to them." Declined.

On February 13, 1939, my diary records the following, which was about par for the course that winter:

To begin with, we found the 1½-ton truck absolutely dead. We transferred to the station wagon and drove to Mr. H.'s house for the permit which he had signed, but nobody was at home. We returned to Ball Ground and Mr. B. swore that he had personally seen the permit signed, so we took a chance and drove to work without it. On arriving at the Settingdown Creek site, which we thought was Mr. H.'s property, we were told that it belonged to Mr. F. in Ball Ground and that Mr. H.'s site was farther upriver, so we walked back to the road, climbed in the station wagon, and before going fifty yards we stalled in a terrible mudhole. Dug out with shovels and immediately bogged down again fifty feet farther on and had to repeat the performance. Then we parked the vehicle and walked two miles down into the river valley carrying all our tools and equipment. We finally found the site but it was almost noon before we got dirt moving. Neither Myers nor I had brought lunch with us, for we had intended to return to Ball Ground, so we worked all day long without a bite to eat. During most of the afternoon we had to listen to an old man who tagged about telling us how much gold the Indians had buried and how unlikely we were to find it at this place. In desperation to get away from him, Myers and I walked out in the middle of a big field and dug a very small hole with a trowel, and out of a possible two hundred acres our little six-inch hole hit a skeleton only a foot below the surface. We decided life was not too black after all.

Three days later, February 16, 1939:

The road to the site we found yesterday was very bad after two days of rain so we took the 1½-ton truck; it is unwieldy and skids, but it has the power to pull out of almost anything. Nine miles out of Canton, after turning into the field road that goes down into the bottoms, we had a puncture, and then found that our spare tire was also flat and we had no pump. So we unloaded all the tools and surveying instruments and walked the remaining mile and a half to work. Started an exploratory trench and several test pits; found two burials. Mr. W. came to see the work and carried me back to Canton with the spare tire; I bought some patching, repaired the tire, and then Mr. W. took me back as far as our stranded truck. Returned to Ball Ground at night and worked until after midnight on another WPA unit cost analysis. We found to our great alarm that the average cost per unit for our project had risen two ten-thousandths of a dollar! To bed, dead.

And now to show that troubles could mount on all fronts, I quote the next two entries two days later. Here is February 18:

After work I drove to Atlanta and met with the Atlanta members of the Executive Committee of the Society for Georgia Archaeology at the home of Mr. X. He gave a fine short report on the work of the survey and then the committee spent the rest of the evening giving me hell for not keeping more publicity in the papers, and for not calling on or writing to each of them regularly to keep them in touch with the work. Mr. Z. of the Associated Press was there and put in the word that if I would only give him an article he would see that it went out over AP. They all kept referring to such trifling omissions in my work that I felt too disgusted to reply.

About two months ago while working at Sandtown, I took an Associated Press feature writer, at his own request, to the excavation and spent the entire day explaining everything to him and pointing out items of human interest that I thought he'd like to work into his story. Instead of using anything that I showed him or anything that he actually saw, he wrote me two days later asking me to furnish him with data supporting the following heading which he had decided on for his story: "First Gunmen or Gangsters in America were the Roving Hill or Mountain Indian Tribes Who Preyed on the More Peaceful Indian Tribes Habitating Swamps." [This is a direct quote.]

And then the next day's entry, Sunday, February 9:

The Executive Committee of the Society and a great many guests, which it had invited, came up to Cherokee County to inspect our work. First I showed them our maps and field records, in which they displayed little interest. Then we spent several hours at the excavation at Ball Ground, and they were enthusiastic. Since the weather had been clear for several days I took them to our dig at the other site, for the road to it is the best around here. After leaving the highway, I had them park their cars and transfer to our vehicles so their own cars would not be scratched or muddy. Before going very far, about half the crowd decided they would not go any further and we had to take them back. The others went down into the valley with me and I showed them what we had done; they were wonderful sports all the way in and out. I brought my group out safe and sound, but the group in Mr. W.'s car stalled in the mud twice. I think that those who accompanied us all the way now realize some of the difficulties we contend with in the field. Mrs. Y. of the Executive Committee was appointed to write up the excavation for the paper. [She never did, but twelve days later Mr. X. telephoned from Atlanta to complain about the continued lack of publicity.]

Personnel problems with WPA labor were constant, for along with the deserving cases there was always assigned to us the usual quota of alcoholics and bums. For several weeks our regular practice every morning before driving off to work in Fulton County was to lock our "timekeeper" in his rented room to let him sleep off the previous night's binge. By evening when we returned, he had almost invariably left by a window and was well on his way with another spree. Our principal "engineer" disappeared so often and for such long periods we finally asked that he be transferred; he retaliated by bringing charges against us in Atlanta, where the foreman and I had to appear at a formal hearing to defend ourselves against accusations of having forced our workmen to cross a river repeatedly in an unsafe, overloaded boat, and of requiring the men to work in trenches deeper than regulations permitted. Then the new engineer assigned to us ran up fifty-two dollars in unpaid rent and food bills before we got rid of him.

The matter of complaints reminds me of a letter one of our workmen wrote directly to President Roosevelt. The White House referred it to the Works Progress Administration, which sent it to the Gainesville office, which forwarded the letter back to me. Here it is verbatim:

September 15, 1939

Dear Mr. Franklin D-Rosey Bell

Dea Dea Mr. President of USA

I am Wrighting you in the name of our Dear Lord and Saviour Jesus christ a most noble President I Honor our Dear Lord and Saviour Jesus Christ for a great Roaler lik you—the WPA transfered me [name deleted] to Archaeological Survor that is a digging Up Ded peple and I am a Precher And dont bleav in digging up the ded hit is aginst my Righes Bleaf Wish you would help me to git off from diging Up the dead your to greater Precedent tan to make me Dig them up Aginst the Word of Jesus from you Sinseare Friend [name deleted] to Franklin D. Rosey the Worlds reatest Presedent. I worked with them 3 days before I new I was digging them Up They told me we were hunting pots don't think Hard of me for wrighting you I need your help the rist don cear for me I will starve if you dont Help me to git off from digging Up the Ded.

your Best Friend [name deleted]

We received many letters from treasure hunters, mystics, and assorted cranks. One such letter that I kept begins:

Athens Ga Feb. 24—1940

Prof. Wauchope
Dept of American Indian Archaeology
University of Ga

Dear Sir:

The bible states that "*We spend our years as a tale that is told.*" Here is a true tale of which only the frame is fiction. *All nations* of the globe will be *interested* because it *encircles* the *earth two opposite ways* with Mt Ararat as cradle base. This is a super undertaking and would *cost a plenty,* yet if handled properly with Govt. aid and an adequate reserve of part of the profits be a timely addition to the coffers of the Dept of Indian Affairs to spend *directly* on the Indian Reservations also to aid and Indian *Archaeological Field Research* in America. We owe these pioneer "Skraelings" of Lief Erickson and "Indians" of Columbus a great debt. World wide public interest in this Historical human trek assure profits if the picture is technically executed. *Enthusiasm knows no defeat.*

The author enclosed a manuscript which read as follows:

Amerikas "Ark-aic" Asiatic Archaeology

White man!! Your God and our "Great Spirit" the "Ancient of Days" are *one and the same.* Many many moons "before the morning stars sang together and the earth was still void and without form and the waters covered the face of the great deep," before this O!! pale face had "The Great Spirit" preordained that the eyes of the Red Man look to the "Rising Sun" as his heritage, the day Noah let Japeth out of the ARK on dry ground on ASIATIC ARARAT mountain in "Ark-Aic" ARMENIA. We the reddish yellow MONGOLIC sons of Japeth took our ancient Eastern trek across Turkestan Steps, through Siberia to Kamtchatka and across Behering Straits to Alaska, the Artic and Greenland to the Atlantic shores, thence down the Appalachians and the Rockies to Panama and Central America thence down the Andean back bone to the South American tip of Patagonia. At that same moon NOAH release Shen on Armenian soil, he setting his "PALE FACE" towards the setting sun over the Caspian Sea in the Caucasus Mtns with his *coveteous eyes* westward to Europe, whence from thou comest O!! pale face, to our eastern American shores from the East as a *"sickly east wind"* to blast, dispossess and banish we proud Red Men. White man, we art the *first section* of this colossal Eastern bound Continental Mongol folk train, whilst thou art the pale West bound Caucassian *second section* from the reverse side of the earth. We are originally from a common earthly also Heavenly Father, yet thou hast not treated us as breathren. Thy ways are divergent from our ways as the East is from the West though our bloods blended in the Patriarch Noah. White man!! thou art greedy and avaricious, thou preacheth but dost not practice the "Golden Rule" but art *ruled by gold.* Thou stole our lands and depleted without cause our buffalo herds and put us *in slavery to thee* on land of our forefathers priority. We were the first and only *true* conservationists of Wild Life never taking more game than for necessity or frugal food needs. Thou wast overbearing intemperate and envious of the Red Man cheating us out of our virile health with vicous "fire water" and wild disapations. Thou was conceited because *wealthy* and enlightened because *"much learning had made thee mad."* Well may thou now in these latter days repent of thy evils and say to thy Maker to show thee ways and means to get forgiveness for thy COVETOUS-NESS of the former things of thy proud, but poor RED NEIGHBORS. Thou hast at the "eleventh hour" shown a broken and contrite spirit in many ways to recompense and reimburse thy red "blood brother." Thou hast inaugurated Indian Archaeology and museums to preserve and perpetuate their ancient cultures and *exalted antiquity*. You are our early enemy but we are your late friends. We have at last buried the hatchet in the soil of an area big enough for us both. We are now true *"blood brothers"* but formerly for a time and season our "eyes were dull" and we could not be friends we thought, and you thought. We now O!! White Father and Red Men of our America SALUTE THEE "but not as those about to die" but rather as those of increasing fecundity looking forward to the fond hope set before us by our great White Chief whose physical body has "known sorrow and been acquainted with grief" but whose *mind burns bright* as the EAGLE'S.

One more letter, which I shall not quote in its entirety because it goes on much longer than the manuscript quoted above, begins:

> May 24, 1940
> Santa Cruz, Calif.

Dear Professor:

Enclosed is a picture which I hope I may be able to persuade you, with the help of the description attached, is a really genuine, honest-to-goodness likeness of a young lady who lived during the latter part of the Ice Age, about 20,000 years ago. I should know because I have drawn it myself from the young lady in person, and she was my wife!

However it is really quite simple. I happen to possess very strong dreams intuitions. I have seen many of our hairy ancestors in my dreams, of various types, and some, like the enclosed, clearly enough that I can draw them. Nearly everyone has the falling dreams that come down to us from the long ages that our forbears found refuge from their enemies on the cliffs (they never lived in trees) and often fell off; but it appears that I dream of many other scenes and incidents as well.

I believe that my dream pictures should be accorded a proper place in our human family album because they came to me while I was studying the scientific revelations of the Bible. . . .

In spite of the malcontents, the gold hunters, the grifters, the mystics, and the cranks, I look back on my stay in Georgia as rich in friendships. Lest I have given too black a picture, let me cite a few instances that stand out brightly in my memory. Late one afternoon in April 1939, near dusk, I was reconnoitering the rolling terrain along Mountain Creek in DeKalb County. I had picked up a few artifacts at one place, when a farmer about fifty years old came out and talked to me and invited me to his house, where I sat on the floor (he had no chairs) and talked with him about this and that for almost two hours. Just before I left, to my astonishment he went to the back of his house and brought out a box of a great many very beautiful flint and chert projectile points and told me to take my pick of them for the University. I gingerly picked out three or four, but he impatiently selected about three dozen of the best specimens and insisted that I take them. He said that he had declined to give them to a great many private collectors, but as he had been financially unable to go to college himself, and he was afraid that his children would not be able to go either, he would like to give these relics to the University if in a small way he would be contributing something to education.

In a small village up in Gordon County the following summer, when I looked up a property owner to ask permission to dig on his land, I was told at the front door that he was dying. I murmured abject apologies and was leaving hastily when a weak voice called from an adjoining room and demanded to see me. The old man insisted that I explain what I was doing there, then he had me lean over close to him, and mustered his failing strength to whisper detailed instructions as to which part of his farm we could dig, which land we could walk on, and what we were to do with the earth and rocks removed. He asked me to promise to stick to these directions, and then he gave me permission to work also in a cave on the property. He told his wife, and sent word to some of the tenant's boys to guide us to the cave and show us around the farm. The next morning he was dead, and a few days later his widow called us and gave us the written permission he had promised.

Twenty years afterward, when my wife and two children and I stopped to ask questions of a young farmer in Forsyth County, he left his tractor, got out the pickup truck, and spent the rest of the day driving us around the farm to spots where he had found arrowheads and pottery, then urged us to stay for supper. Georgia hospitality, I was glad to see, had not diminished with the younger generation.

I think that of all our many experiences in Georgia, perhaps the most interesting was that which involved some Indian fakes, a stone mason who lived near Atlanta, and the widely heralded "Virginia Dare" stones at Brenau College. I cannot resist prolonging this introduction with a brief résumé of the story, for I doubt that I shall ever have opportunity to tell it elsewhere. As will be seen later in this report, there is an ancient quarry and workshop in DeKalb County only about 4 miles south of Decatur, near Atlanta. Here the Indians used to quarry blocks of rather coarse chlorite schist and fashion them into bowls. I suspect that these authentic stone vessels inspired a series of schemes involving falsifications of Indian relics in this area, in Atlanta, and then far afield. In 1938 a Mr. Foarde showed me a stone effigy bowl, which he stated had been discovered by a Mr. William Eberhart, who was said to have a lease to quarry stone on or near Little Mountain. At another time, an antique dealer in Atlanta attempted to interest me in a similar bowl allegedly found in a cave near Atlanta. I did not pursue either matter further, for the effigy bowls were not authentic. Later, the Atlanta *Georgian* newspaper of December 21, 1938, carried a feature story about a cave discovered near Atlanta, where several rows of those stone effigy bowls were said to have been standing around the walls. The persons giving the information to the paper were most mysterious about the entire matter, and secretive concerning the cave's location. It seemed likely that all three of these situations were in some way linked, so I asked my field foreman, without revealing his connection with the survey, to make the acquaintance of Mr. William Eberhart. As a result of this investigation, we decided that it would be definitely unrewarding to look further into these so-called Indian relics.

It was not until some time later that the much publicized "Virginia Dare" stones began to appear. Sponsored by Brenau College, the discoveries attracted national attention. My interest in the case was stimulated when it became known that the person who had discovered almost all the stones, in various places across the southeast from Virginia to North and South Carolina and finally over Georgia to a cave near Atlanta, was none other than an Atlanta stone mason named William Eberhart.

In 1940 Brenau College called a conference to consider the authenticity of the Virginia Dare stones. By then I had moved to the University of North Carolinia at Chapel Hill, but I attended the conference and brought to the attention of the group the sequence of events involving dubious Indian stone bowls, Virginia Dare stones, and William Eberhart. At the conference my warnings, together with other skeptical opinions expressed by some of my archaeological colleagues, were largely ignored. No less an authority than Professor Samuel Eliot Morison of Harvard stated for the press that he believed most, if not all, of the stones were authentic. A few months later, it was reported that William Eberhart, embroiled in a financial disagreement with Brenau College, confessed that he manufactured Virginia Dare stones. Brenau College officials immediately announced this, but maintained belief that at least some of the Dare stones were authentic.

Another thing that I should like to mention here is the astonishing change that the Georgia landscape underwent in the twenty years from 1938 to 1958. This was brought most forcibly to my attention during the two summers that my wife, my daughter, and my son and I tried to revisit certain sites to get new surface collections to supplement those we already had or to replace some that had been lost. Even though I had the most detailed directions and had visited these sites myself, in most cases we had great difficulty in finding them again; more often we failed entirely.

The first rule of site survey is to record one's sites in purely geographic terms and locate them on a detailed topographic map, so that they can be found again regardless of what man does to the landscape. This we had of course done, but everyone knows that in vast rural areas one also needs considerable help from directions based on landmarks of a more transitory nature. I had expected that in twenty years a few old things might have changed, a footpath here or a fence there, perhaps a new highway cutting across my old familiar roads. But I was unprepared for the wholesale changes that had taken place; archaeologically speaking, we were lost most of the time.

The old roads were almost all gone, or so improved as to be unrecognizable. New bridges spanned the rivers and creeks, with new approaches from different routes. But most confusing of all, small streams had dried up—simply disappeared—and what were once vast acreages in corn or cotton had been abandoned to jungles of giant weeds, towering 10 feet high and interlaced with almost impenetrable branches and spiny vines, or their once deeply plowed surfaces now hard-packed green meadow. Presumably this was "soil bank" land, under government contract no longer cultivated. As long as these lands remain uncultivated, the Indian sites on them will be as unrecognizable as those today covered by the huge artificial lakes. Thus our survey of the 'thirties served another purpose: it located sites that might never again have been discovered. A good example is the rich Lithonia site (Da-1) on the once cultivated summit of a hill high over Yellow River in DeKalb County. When Mr. W. Julian Thomas took me to this site in 1938, the hill slopes were seamed with gulleys, exposing scores of quartz crystals and Early to Middle Woodland potsherds. In the middle of the plowed red clay at the top of the hill was a distinct area of black earth that could be seen as one approached the summit. On top, in this plowed earth, were thousands of potsherds, hammer stones, chipped stone implements, quartz crystals, and projectile points. I have seldom been more impressed with a site, and I remembered (or thought I remembered) almost every detail of its appearance and the surrounding topography. I took minutely detailed notes on how to reach it. In 1958, when I took my wife and children to this place to show them what a really rich surface collection could be, the surrounding roads had so changed that first of all I had difficulty locating even the group of hills, then I climbed three of these before deciding, with considerable doubt, which ones I had visited twenty years before. The slopes were overgrown in tall pine, and by the sheerest chance I found a quartz crystal on a footpath that led up through the woods to an old lumber mill. That was our only clue that we were on the right track. When we reached what I calculated must be the site of the ancient village, half the area was in pine, the other half was meadow. Not a potsherd was in sight; I broke off a heavy dead branch and gouged a hole into a slight terrace in the meadow slopes, and in a matter of seconds the sherds began to appear, but after several hours of hunting and scratching in this fashion we got a few handfuls of artifacts rather than the bagfuls I had come prepared to carry away. If this rich and apparently pure Woodland site is ever excavated—and it should be— it will be due to the fact, I am sure, that our survey once recorded its location, unless, as seems unlikely, it should some day be cultivated again.

Or take the Thomas Site (Fo-4) on the Chattahoochee River west of Suwanee in Forsyth County. When Mr. Thomas showed me this site in 1938 I wanted to start digging it then and there. River floods year after year had exposed masses of potsherds, burned clay floors, refuse pits, and restorable vessels. In mind's eye I can picture it exactly as it looked then. In 1958 I wanted to show this beauty to my long-suffering family, who by now must have become disenchanted with Georgia archaeology; this site, I knew, would cure that. We drove out of Suwanee, Georgia, on a street I remembered clearly and, on the basis of my old notes, turned left at a fork. We followed this road 0.4 mile past a house on the right side and at the next fork turned right; we were soon (to my considerable surprise and pleasure) crossing a bridge over the river, just as my old field notes said we would. We drove part way up the hill on the west side of the Chattahoochee, parked, and I walked confidently upstream to look for the mound. Everything was as it should have been; true, the bridge was new and the road wider, and what had once been cornfields was now part meadow, part scrubby woods, but I had come to expect such changes. Half a day later, having walked the river banks for miles, clambered up and down the deeply eroded sand bluffs along the water's edge, and fought our way through jungles of vines, poison ivy, willow, and underbrush, and paced the hot meadow hundreds of yards back and forth in near 100° temperature, we gave up. We found one small sandy mound, holes in which yielded, if I remember correctly, three miserable potsherds. Luckily we had left a jug of cool water and a bottle of martinis in the car.

Fall and early winter is the season for archaeology in northern Georgia and the Piedmont south. Crops are harvested, the ground is not yet frozen, mornings, the weather is likely to be bright, and clay roads are still not hazardous. Labor is more available; everyone is not fretting over making a good crop. Last summer's cotton fields, now dark brown but still flecked here and there with white, sweep in slow curves along the contours of the rolling terrain, and one can walk through them briskly, scanning several rows on each side, while the projectile points and potsherds lie on little pedestals of earth as if on display. Skimpy, shoulder-high, buff-colored stubble corn has replaced the tall green stalks under which, in summer, you could walk for hours without seeing the outside world. The endless miles of grazing land, brown and yellow, are dotted black or brown with herds of beef cattle, and partitioned by easel-shaped groves of brown and red oaks, bright gums, and green pines. The air is brisk; one tends to overestimate his capacity to walk to the next horizon, but the once deeply plowed fields are now firm underfoot, easy to traverse, and one need not fear the rattlesnakes. There are few threats. The great ropes of poison ivy on steep river banks are deceivingly stripped of their telltale leaves and seem to be innocent roots placed there for your climbing convenience. One must beware of eating rabbits that were trapped or shot wild in the riverbottoms. What appear to be firm banks along the little swamps that bar your way from one slope to another may actually be hip-deep soft mud, and if you miss your footing and stumble in the ice-cold streams you must build a fire against what you had just before considered a delightfully bracing wind.

Unfortunately, archaeological schedules do not always follow the appropriate seasons and latitudes. We worked in all environments and in all climates. We lived in a drafty log cabin on the banks of the ice-covered Nacoochee River during the subzero blizzard of 1939, sleeping nights in our long underwear under mountains of quilts, and mornings, by lamp light, washing in ice water. We sacked down on the freezing bottomlands of the Chattahoochee with our boots almost smoking in our campfire, and subsisted for months on a steady diet of sausage, pork, chittlins, sweet potatoes, and collard greens from the nearest farmhouse. We sweltered in 110° summer scorchers as far south as Blakely, and even up in Bartow County we would spend our summer lunch hour lying naked in the closest cooling stream, seeking some respite from the merciless sun. It seemed that winters we were always scraping ice from our windshields in the frigid mountains, and summers we were forever slogging through the steaming swamps of the lower Savannah. But from Atlanta to the sea, from No Business Creek to Shake Rag, from Between and Social Circle to Box Ankle and Settingdown Creek Georgia was for me a wonderful experience that I shall always cherish with deep affection.

▪ PILGRIMS ELUDE A PILGRIM-HUNTER

Francis E. Wylie

"Maybe there never were any Pilgrims. Maybe the *Mayflower* story is just a legend."

Dr. James Deetz was expressing in his wry way the frustration of months of digging during the hot Massachusetts summer without finding any traces of the first settlers. In fact, Deetz has recovered thousands or artifacts from the rich trash heaps of the last three centuries, but nothing that can be positively identified with the 50 years before.

Last July Deetz and a group of student volunteers were at a site in the center of Plymouth, just behind a shoe store which occupies a house built in the early 18th century. The site probably marked the northern side of the Pilgrims' first village. Deetz thought there was just a chance the diggers would uncover evidence of the log stockade built around the village. Post holes, perhaps. A volunteer dug the soil from around the rotted stumps of three cedar posts.

"Could this be it?"

"If it is, we still have to find some proof," said Deetz, following the archaeologist's rule to be skeptical about anything he turns up. "Cedar lasts a long time, but these could have been the posts of a lady's clothesline 50 years ago."

The question was answered in a few days. In further digging the bottom of the posts was reached, and beneath one of them was a fragment of Mocha pottery.

"At the very earliest, 1790," Deetz said. "We can't tell how old the posts are, but we can be sure the Pilgrims didn't put them there."

A few days later the diggers gave up and shoveled back the dirt they had so carefully sifted. They had found Indian arrowheads, possibly contemporary with the Pilgrims. They were able to piece together much of a fragile Whieldon ware teapot, which could be dated to 1760, and they glued together 36 pieces of a handsome English agateware bowl of the same date. Shattered chamber pots were harvested in abundance, particularly creamware ones of about 1800. In fact, the excavation produced a remarkable cross section of New England culture, from clay pipes and pewter spoons to modern alarm clock remnants. But no Pilgrim artifacts.

Nonetheless, the cross section is important to Deetz, one of the leaders of a new breed of investigators who are as much anthropologists as archaeologists. While archaeologists have always sought to make inferences from what they find, their work in the past has tended to be merely descriptive. Deetz and other practitioners of what is sometimes called the New Archaeology would like, through rigorous scientific method, to develop unifying theory and basic laws explaining the behavior of Man in all ages.

A pioneer of this approach, Deetz did not start out as an archaeologist. He wanted to be a doctor until, at Harvard university, he failed chemistry and switched to anthropology. After his sophomore year, he went to South Dakota for a summer of salvage archaeology, digging Indian sites which were about to be covered by dammed-up water.

It was during a subsequent trip to South Dakota that Deetz made a remarkable find: While digging, he saw something brown and shiny gleaming in the dirt. "Hey, what's this?" he yelled, and colleagues gathered around him. He carefully brushed away the soil and unearthed his own polished shoe. He again returned to that state for his doctoral thesis work. By rigorous computer analysis of potshards from an Arikara Indian site, he demonstrated three distinct cultural phases between 1700 and 1780. He showed how, under the impact of trade in guns and horses and of the white man's smallpox, a stable society quickly altered to one of great mobility and small units.

He became a professor at the University of California at Santa Barbara, but summer fieldwork brought him back to New England. He recalls that he set out in 1965 in a Ford station wagon with his wife, eight children, one babysitter and 140 reptiles and amphibians. A consignment of 16 cats—two mothers and their litters—had been flown ahead, as well as cages containing additional lizards, including a three-foot iguana.

All went well in the station wagon until, after a 900-mile day, they discovered that a king snake had escaped and eaten 30 lizards. "He looked like a Christmas stocking," says Deetz.

In contrast to the unstratified and exuberant chaos of Deetz's mobile household, his precise archaeological method was sharpened in the summers of 1965 and 1966. Without digging so much as a spoonful of dirt, Deetz and a Harvard student, Edwin Dethlefsen, studied the carvings in over 20,000 tombstones in southern New England cemeteries. They traced the evolution of a grim death's head motif into a relatively cheerful cherub, correlating the change with the transition from stern Calvinistic doctrine to a theology in which the Resurrection played a more conspicuous part. His "archaeological" inferences could in turn be confirmed by written records of the time, serving to prove the validity of the archaeological method. His most exciting moment was "sitting in a Concord cemetery and suddenly realizing that all those gravestones made sense."

By 1967, Deetz had decided he was a New Englander, not a Californian. He resigned from Santa Barbara, driven also by the failure of the protest movement there. He had been on a faculty-student committee which organized the first protest march on the state capitol after the firing of Clark Kerr. A television network collected a group of bearded, wild-looking kids and made pictures of them pouring out of the dormitories. They appeared on national television as well as the 5,000 soberly dressed and legitimate protestors marching on Sacramento. "I decided to give it up," says Deetz, "because one, it doesn't do any good, and two, no matter how hard you try they're going to mess you up."

In answer to activists, who say his archaeology is an escape from the important things in the world, Deetz replies: "That's a lot of nonsense. We can't have social change until we understand what we are, and we can't understand that until we understand where we come from. More than any other generation, the kids today are interested in history, and what we are doing is to help them understand the past."

Deetz became professor of anthropology at Brown University and assistant director of the Plimouth Plantation at Plymouth, Massachusetts. A re-creation of the original Pilgrim village, Plimouth Plantation was organized principally by a serious amateur archaeologist and successful businessman, Henry Hornblower II. In addition to the village, the organization built the ocean-going *Mayflower II* and has sponsored archaeological research into the colonial past. Authenticity was a key word in the venture, and Deetz was looked to as a scholar who could help provide it.

POTTERY AND BARNS BUT NO TURKEY BONES

At 41, Jim Deetz is exuberant and animated. His blond curly hair is shaggy, and he wears snug, belled trousers on his lean hips, like the young people with whom he works. Wherever he goes, he is surrounded by admiring youngsters who dig for days on end without pay and without college credit, in a common acceptance with Deetz of modest scholarly goals.

"No one really knows what the Pilgrims were like," he says. "There are valuable written records, to be sure, and some of the furniture and weapons have survived. But in more than three centuries a lot of legend and folklore have accumulated, and no one knows how much of it is true.

"Through digging in the ground where they lived we believe we can learn a great deal more—not only about the Pilgrims but about the evolution of American society and culture since then."

Thus far, some 100,000 pieces of colonial pottery and other artifacts have been uncovered, but no momentous conclusions have yet been reached. There is evidence that while the Pilgrims were all equal to begin with, Plymouth society was distinctly stratified by 1700. And Deetz observes that in spite of the Thanksgiving tradition no turkey bones have been found.

A year ago Plimouth Plantation and the National Park Service sponsored a major Deetz excavation at the site of a tavern on Great Island in Wellfleet Harbor on Cape Cod, where whalers apparently made their headquarters between 1690 and 1740.

In midsummer this year another Deetz crew started digging in Marshfield, a dozen miles north of Plymouth, for debris left by Edward Winslow, a *Mayflower* passenger who settled there about 1635 and later served as governor of the colony, as did his son Josiah.

In 1941, Henry Hornblower conducted an excavation on the Winslow lands and found the foundation of a house built in about 1650. Two years ago two amateurs did some digging in the same general area. They wouldn't reveal where, which is the sort of thing that makes an archaeologist climb a wall, but Deetz saw some of their finds and, he says, "They were getting some real jazzy stuff."

So he decided to make a try at the Hornblower site. The dig's director was Geoffrey Moran, a history teacher at Bradford Junior College. The crew varied from day to day, but there were some regulars, including Barbara Haines, a rosy-cheeked blond from Pembroke College, who has been attracted to archaeology ever since she took a course under Deetz at Brown. (There were about 500 in the class—quite large for Brown but proof of his popularity. "I would always sit in one of the front rows because I didn't want to miss anything," Barbara remembers. "He has a habit of making comments aside, almost to himself, in a low voice— like 'I guess I'd better try that sentence again. I confused everyone.' The next year I went back to visit the class and he said, 'Hey, what are you doing here?' He remembered me as a person.")

The early days of digging for the Winslow house were not very rewarding. There were small mounds of crumbled brick—"soft as peanut butter," as Deetz put it, and obviously very old. There were some small pieces of black glazed ware commonly used in 17th-century England but rarely found in America. As the string-marked squares were extended and the excavation deepened, prospects became more promising.

Some 18 inches below the surface dark bands of earth began to show against the yellow sand and clay. They looked as though they marked the foundations of buildings. Stones large enough to serve as foundations are not native to this shore area of Marshfield and would have had to be carted from elsewhere. Since such stones would have a value, they could have been dug from the original trenches and used for the foundations of new structures. Topsoil would wash into the trenches, accounting for the dark bands.

The diggers followed one band for 80 feet, where it turned a precise right angle—clearly the corner of a building. If three other corners could be found the complete dimensions would be established. But 80 feet!

"We believe the Pilgrims may have had houses 30 or 40 feet long, built in three bays about ten feet square," explained Deetz. "There is evidence of such houses, although previously Pilgrim homes were supposed to be much smaller. A building 80 feet long would have to be a barn. And we believe there were such barns—funny looking buildings, long and low."

The excavation was extended in other directions, and after a few days Deetz came back for an inspection. Moran handed him an odd assortment of objects taken from a new hole—some rusted wire nails, a corroded brass cotter pin and a curious little glass tube about an inch long, containing a clear fluid.

"What in the hell is that?" exclaimed Deetz. They finally determined that is was the bubble chamber from a carpenter's level, the wooden frame of which had rotted away. Wire nails, cotter pin and such an artifact certainly didn't belong to the Pilgrims, even though they were found at a depth in the soil indicating the right age.

Further digging failed to reveal the other corners of the building or anything else of special value, and in another week the site was abandoned. But there were other projects to undertake; the exuberant Deetz was not discouraged. He and his band would continue their search elsewhere for remains of the Pilgrims. And meanwhile, he continues to perfect his analytical methods and to seek broad anthropological conclusions from those artifacts they do dig up.

Digging, of course, is only the beginning of the job. Every shard and scrap from an excavation is carefully numbered, showing the exact position of discovery. Bags of material are taken back to the Plimouth Plantation laboratory for careful study. Students work for hours and days trying to fit together jagged pieces of pottery, often gluing together recognizable and even beautiful reconstructions of the original ware. The bore of every clay pipestem fragment, of which there are bushels, is measured. (Between 1590 and 1800 the bore became $\frac{1}{64}$ of an inch smaller every 30 years and pipestems serve as reliable indicators of the age of associated artifacts.)

However productive of theory his research may prove to be, it is very productive of artifacts and students. Plimouth Plantation now has one of the largest collections of 17th-century artifacts, surpassed, perhaps, only by that at Jamestown, Virginia. And the students who have worked with Deetz now number in the hundreds. On Friday nights they are likely to gather at his house to celebrate the end of a week's work. The house is a big gray Victorian summer place a half-mile from Plimouth Plantation.

Some of the college students who spend the day in gray Pilgrim garb, as inhabitants of Plimouth Plantation, show up in the quaint costumes of the 1971 youth culture. A record player blares with Bluegrass music, the staple in the Deetz household. When it stops, Deetz yells, "Where's the music? It's too damned quiet here." Traffic to the kitchen increases, where a makeshift bar offers everything from milk to Scotch. Tomorrow is Saturday and artifacts can wait.

3

LANGUAGE

If we were forced to name one single trait that marks humans off from the other primates, it would have to be language. Language is the mirror of culture. Through language we know what others are thinking; and it is this complex communication that makes culture possible. Many animals have fairly sophisticated systems of communication. Gibbons use a series of screeches to report danger, food sources, and other things. Bees, orienting themselves to the sun in particular ways, dance with movements that tell other bees exactly where new sources of pollen are to be found. But none of this is language in the human sense, because it is unproductive or uncreative. Only human language is creative; human beings say new things to one another every day and they understand each other.

Pick up a book. Choose any sentence at least as long as this one. If you tried to find just that sentence in any other book, you would probably spend the rest of your life searching without success. Human languages are composed of a finite number of words, operated upon by a finite (but very large) number of rules on how to string them together. The curious thing is that this system produces an infinite number of grammatical sentences. Because of this property, human culture is abstract and the abstractions accumulate in the minds of all the members of a culture. Writing allows cultures to accumulate more thoughts than the culture's members can keep in their heads. This is why language or speech is an information *creating* device, whereas writing is an information *retrieval* device.

The thoughts and culture of a people are locked in their language. And the secret of any creative language is its grammar. Knowing just what a grammar is, however, is not as easy as it might seem.

Imagine an immortal monkey, sitting at an unbreakable typewriter, pounding away randomly and churning out an infinite length of paper filled with words and gibberish.

93

Given an infinite amount of time, the creature will produce all the grammatical sentences in a language (in fact, in all languages) and all the nonsense as well. Thus, such a monkey constitutes a grammar of all languages, but a very inadequate one. A grammar is a series of rules about speech that produces *all and only* the grammatical sentences of a language.

Meaning is very important in grammar. We do not say "jealous oboes climb hauntingly around on thrifty aardvarks." *Some* of the traditional grammatical rules of English (put adjectives before nouns, follow all transitive verbs with objects, and so on) would permit such a sentence. But *all* the grammatical rules, taken together, forbid it, so we would not expect to hear it.

The study of human language is the search for the fundamental characteristics of culture. In the first three selections, Dwight Bolinger and Charlton Laird describe the basic properties of human language and speech. But there is more to language than just words and grammars. As Edward Hall shows in his article, people use space and time in different ways; it effects their speech and other behavior and must be considered part of the language of any people.

In the fourth article we see what happens when language becomes a political affair. There are many current examples of attempts to legislate how people should speak, and they all have one thing in common: they are dismal failures. The French Academy, for example, tried desperately to stop *le hot dog, le weekend,* and *le cowboy* from entering the French vocabulary. Removing those words from French today would be like removing *village* or *bureau* from English. In Greece, children learn a special, formal language that is used only in university lectures and in certain court proceedings. No one ever uses it in ordinary conversation, not even university professors.

These examples are trivial, however, compared to political attempts to suppress whole languages entirely. What happens in such cases is the subject of the last article in this section.

■ SOME TRAITS OF LANGUAGE

Dwight Bolinger

One estimate puts the number of languages in active use in the world today somewhere between three and four thousand. Another makes it five thousand or more. The latter is probably closer to the truth, for many languages are spoken by only a few hundred persons, and many areas of the world are still not fully surveyed. In one subdistrict of New Guinea, for example, there are sixteen languages spoken by an average of fewer than a thousand persons each[1] Also, it is impossible to be exact, for no one knows just what constitutes "one language." Danish and Norwegian have a high degree of mutual intelligibility; this makes them almost by definition dialects of a single language. Do we count them as two? Cantonese and Mandarin, in spite of both being "Chinese," are about as dissimilar as Portuguese and Italian. Do we count mainland Chinese as one language? To be scientific we have to ignore politics and forget that Denmark and Norway have separate flags and mainland China one. But even then, since differences are quantitative, we would have to know how much to allow before graduating X from "a dialect of Y" to "a language, distinct from Y."

However that may be, the number of different languages is formidable and is quite awesome if we include the tongues once spoken but now dead. Languages are like people: for all their underlying similarities, great numbers mean great variety. Variety confronts us with this question: Do we know enough about languages to be able to describe language? Can we penetrate the differences to arrive at the samenesses underneath?

The more languages we study—and previously unexplored ones give up their secrets each year by the score—the more the answer seems to be *yes*. Learning a new language is always in some measure repeating an old experience. Variety may be enormous but similarities abound, and one can even attempt a definition, perhaps something like "Human language is a system of vocal-auditory communication using conventional signs composed of arbitrary patterned sound units and assembled according to set rules, interacting with the experiences of its users." However we word it—and obviously no one-sentence definition will ever be adequate—there is enough homogeneity to make some sort of definition possible. Languages are alike because people are alike in their capacities for communicating in a uniquely human way.

[1] Richard Loving and Jack Bass, "Languages of the Amanab Sub-district," report published by the Department of Information and Extension Services, Territory of Papua and New Guinea, Port Moresby, April, 1964.

LANGUAGE IS PATTERNED BEHAVIOR

Our five-hundred-year romance with printer's ink tempts us to forget that a language can disappear without leaving a trace when its last speaker dies and that this is still true of the majority of the world's languages in spite of the spread of presses and tape recorders. Written records and tape recordings are embodiments of language, but language itself is a way of acting. Our habit of viewing it as a *thing* is probably unavoidable, even for the linguist, but in a sense it is false.

What is somewhat thing-like, in that it persists through time and from speaker to speaker, is the system that underlies the behavior. This is what makes language so special. Breathing, grasping, and crying are also ways of acting, but we come already equipped to do them. Language is *skilled* behavior and has to be learned. Probably as the child acquires it the system is engraved somehow on the brain, and if we had the means to make it visible we could "read" it. For the present all we can see is the way people act, and linguists are useful precisely because, not being able to look into the brain, we need specialists to study the behavior and infer the system.

THE MEDIUM OF LANGUAGE IS SOUND

All languages use the same channel for sending and receiving: the vibrations of the atmosphere. All set the vibrations going in the same way, by the activity of the speech organs. And all organize the vibrations in essentially the same way, into small units of sound that can be combined and recombined in distinctive ways. Except for the last, human communication is the same as that of most other warm-blooded creatures that move on the earth's surface: the most effective way of reaching another member of one's kind seems to be through disturbances of the air that envelops us.

Paradoxically, what sets human speech apart also sets it above dependence on any particular medium: the capacity for intricate organization. The science of phonetics, whose domain is the sounds of speech, is to linguistics what numismatics is to finance: it makes no difference to a financial transaction what alloys are used in a coin, and it makes no difference to the brain what bits of substance are used as triggers for language—they could be pebbles graded for color or size, or, if we had a dog's olfactory sense, a scheme of discriminated smells. The choice of sound is part of our pre-human heritage, probably for good reason. We do not have to look at or touch the signaler to catch the signal, and we do not depend on wind direction as with smell—nor, as with smell, are we unable to turn it off once it is emitted.[2]

2 Thomas A. Sebeok, "Coding in the Evolution of Signaling Behavior," *Behavioral Science* 7.435 (1962).

Language is sound in the same sense that a given house is wood. We can conceive of other materials, but it is as if the only tools we had were woodworking ones. If we learn a language we must learn to produce sounds. We are unable to use any other medium except as an incidental help. So part of the description of language must read as if the sound that entered into the organization of language were as indispensable as the organization itself.

SOUND IS EMBEDDED IN GESTURE

If language is an activity, we cannot say that it stops short at the boundaries of *speech* activity, for human actions are not so easily compartmentalized. It is true that we can communicate over the telephone, which seems to prove that everything is carried by the sound voice wave; but we can also communicate pretty efficiently in writing, and we know that writing leaves out a great deal—intonation, for example. No communication is quite so effective as face-to-face communication, for some part of the communicative act is always contained in the expression and posture of the communcators. We call this *gesture*.

Not all gestures are equally important to language. Three kinds can be distinguished: *instinctive, semiotic,* and *paralinguistic.* The third is closest to language proper.

Instinctive gestures are automatic reactions to a stimulus. They are not learned. Dodging a blow, widening the eyes in astonishment, leaning forward to catch a sound, bowing in submission, smiling with pleasure, and others of the kind either are instincts or are based on instinct in such a way that, like the flight of a young bird, it takes no more than a slight parental or social push to set them going. Of course all such gestures give information to anyone observing them, and this is soon noted by the one performing the gesture, who then puts it on as a disguise: he smiles to please rather than to show pleasure, bows when he would rather hurl insults, and weeps when he feels no pain. In the long run all gestures acquire a social significance and take on local modifications, which is one reason why members of one culture behave awkwardly when transplanted to another.

Whereas instinctive gestures tell something—true or false—about the person making them, *semiotic* gestures are free to mean anything. They are not like distinctive sounds, because they do have their own meanings (semaphoric signs, which are just ways of signaling the alphabet, are not included here); they are more like words or even whole sentences. Thus a waving hand means "good-bye," both hands held palm up and outstretched with shoulders raised means "I don't know," the thumb and forefinger held close together means "small"—that is, these are the meanings in our culture. Being arbitrary, semiotic gestures are are not the same everywhere. In some places the gesture for "come here" is to hold out the hand cupped palm up with the fingers beckoning; in other places it is the same except that the hand is cupped palm down, and to an outsider it may appear to be a greeting rather than a summons. Semiotic gestures are independent of language. Cooperation between the two is only incidental—a "come-hither" gesture accompanied by a sign reading *Stop, look, and listen.*

Paralinguistic gestures are not really an independent class but a subclass of instinctive gestures, more or less systematized, much as intonation was perhaps systematized out of a set of instinctive cries and calls. They cooperate with sound as part of a larger communicative act. In the following utterance,

$$\text{You } _{\text{don't}} \quad {}^{\text{mea}}{}_{\text{n}} {}_{\text{it.}}$$

everything else can remain the same, yet with one's head held slightly forward, eyes widened, and mouth left open after the last word, the result is a question ("You surely don't mean it, do you"?), while with head erect, eyes not widened, and mouth closed afterward, it is a confident assertion. Facial gestures are sometimes the only way to tell a question from a statement.

Gestures of the hands and head are used to reinforce the syllables on which the accent falls. A person too far away to hear a speaker can often tell what syllables he is emphasizing by the way he hammers with his fist or jabs downward with his jaw. How closely the two are related can be shown by a simple test: reversing the movement of the head, going up instead of down on each accent, in a sentence like *I wíll nót dó it.* It is hard to manage on the first attempt.

At the outer fringes of the system we call language is a scattering of gestural effects on speech, more curious than important. The [m] of *ho-hum* and the [p] of *yep* and *nope* come from closing the mouth as a gesture of completion: "He was the last juror and quite unconsciously smacked his lips as he finished the oath."[3] Certain gestures get tangled with sets of words and serve as a kind of semantic cohesive. The kinship of *vicious, venomous, vituperative, violent, vehement, vindictive, vitriolic, vile* (and indirectly *vital, vigorous, vim*) is helped by the suggestion of a snarl in the initial [v]. Similarly there is a suggestion of lip-smacking in the last syllable of *delicious, voluptuous, salacious, luscious* that results in a new slang alteration or coinage every now and then—*scrumptious* in the early 1800's, *galuptious* about 1850, *crematious* in the 1940's, the trade name *Stillicious* at about the same time, *scruptillicious* in teen-age talk in the 1960's.[4]

[3] Raymond Postgate, *Verdict of Twelve* (New York: Simon and Schuster, Pocket Books, 1946), p. 70.
[4] *Boulder Camera* (Boulder, Colorado), June 10, 1963.

LANGUAGE IS LARGELY ARBITRARY

It is exceptional to find words as alike as *meow* in English and *miaou* in French. Identical meanings in different languages are almost never expressed by the same combination of sounds (the fact that the same *spellings* are often encountered is another matter). If there were a real connection between the sound of a word and its meaning, a person who did not know the language would be able to guess the word if he knew the meaning and guess the meaning if he heard the word. This almost never happens, even with words that imitate sounds: *to caw* in English is *croasser* in French; *to giggle* in English is *kichern* in German. Elsewhere it does not happen at all. *Square* and *box-shaped* mean the same but have no resemblance in sound.

Arbitrariness comes from having to code a whole universe of meanings. The main problem with such vast quantities is to find not resemblances but differences, to make a given combination of sounds sufficiently unlike every other combination so that no two will be mistaken for each other. It is more important to make *wheat* and *barley* sound different than to use the names to express a family relationship as a botanist might do. Our brain can associate them if the need arises more easily than it can help us if we hear one when the other was intended.

Syntax is no less arbitrary than words. Take the order of elements. *Ground parched corn* has *first* been parched and *then* ground—the syntactic rule calls for reversing the order in which the events occur. Often the same meanings can be conveyed by quite different sequences of elements which may themselves be the same or different: *nonsensical*, which contains a prefix and a suffix, means the same as *senseless*, which has only a suffix; *more handsome* and *handsomer* are mere variants. Here and there one detects a hint of kinship between form and function—in *He came in and sat down* the phrases are in the same sequence as the actions; but other syntactic devices quickly override it: *He sat down after he came in.*

The most rigidly arbitrary level of language is that of the distinctive units of sound by which we can distinguish between *skin* and *skim* or *spare* and *scare* the moment we hear the words. It was noted earlier that the very choice of sound itself for this purpose was, while practical, not at all necessary to the system built up from it. And once it was determined that sound was to be the medium, the particular sounds did not matter so long as they could be told apart. What distinguishes *skin* from *skim* is the sound of [n] versus the sound of [m], but could just as well be [b] versus [g]—there is nothing in the nature of skin that decrees it shall be called *skin* and not *skib*. The only "natural" fact is that human beings are limited by their speech organs to certain dimensions of sound —we do not, for example, normally make the sound that would result from turning the tip of the tongue all the way back to the soft palate; it is too hard to reach. But given the sets of sounds we *can* make (not identical, of course, from one language to another, but highly similar), arbitrariness frees us to combine them at will—the combinations do not have to match anything in nature, and their number is therefore unlimited.

Arbitrariness is the rule throughout the central part of language, the part that codes sounds into words, words into phrases, and phrases into sentences. To use computer terminology, language is *digital*, not *analog:* its units function by being either present or absent, not by being present in varying degrees. If a man is asked how many feet tall a friend is and answers *six,* he gives a digital answer; for a lower height he will no longer say *six.* If words were coded analogically he might, to express "six," take half of the word *twelve,* say *twe.* We actually do communicate analogically in situations like this, not using words but holding up our hands to the desired height; the height of the hand is "analogous" to the height of the person.

But the digital island floats on an analog sea. If one is tired, the feebleness of the voice will show how tired one is—degrees of sound correspond to degrees of fatigue. If one is angry and not controlling oneself, the loudness of the voice will tell how angry. And wrapped around everything that is spoken is a layer of intonation which in many languages comprises an analog system that is highly formalized; for example, varying degrees of finality can be expressed by deeper and deeper lowering of the pitch at the end of an utterance.

It would not be surprising if now and then a bit of the analog sea washed over the digital island. There seems to be a connection, transcending individual languages, between the sounds of the vowels produced with the tongue high in the mouth and to the front, especially [i] (the vowel sound in *wee, teeny*), and the meaning of "smallness," while those with tongue low suggest "largeness." The size of the mouth cavity—[i] has the smallest opening of all—is matched with the meaning. We *chip* a small piece but *chop* a large one; a *slip* is smaller than a *slab* and a *nib* is smaller than a *knob.* Examples crop up spontaneously—"A *freep* is a baby *frope,*" said a popular entertainer in a game of Scrabble—or in modifications of existing words, for example *least* with an exaggeratedly high [i], or the following:

> "That's about the price I had in mind," said Joe Peel. "Eight to ten thousand, but of course, it would depend on the place. I might even go a *leetle* higher."[5]

But mostly the digital island stays pretty dry.

LANGUAGES ARE SIMILARLY STRUCTURED

The average learner of a foreign language is surprised and annoyed when the new language does not express things in the same way as the

[5] Frank Gruber, *The Silver Jackass* (New York: Penguin Books, 1947), p. 45.

old. The average linguist, after years of struggling with differences between languages, is more surprised at similarities. But at bottom the naive learner is right: there are differences in detail, but in broad outline languages are put together in similar ways. A study on universals in language reached these conclusions about syntax:

1. All languages use nominal phrases and verbal phrases, corresponding to the two major classes of noun and verb, and in all of them the number of nouns far exceeds the number of verbs. One can be fairly sure that a noun in one language translates a noun in another.
2. All languages have modifiers of these two classes, corresponding to adjectives and adverbs.
3. All languages have ways of turning verbal phrases into nounal phrases (*He went*—I know *that he went*).
4. All languages have ways of making adjective-like phrases out of other kinds of phrases (*The man went*—The man *who went*).
5. All languages have ways of turning sentences into interrogatives, negatives, and commands.
6. All languages show at least two forms of interaction between verbal and nominal, typically "intransitive" (the verbal is involved with only one nominal, as in *Boys play*) and "transitive" (the verbal is involved with two nominals, as in *Boys like girls*).[6]

A more recent study views nouns as the one category of syntax that can be assumed for all languages, with the other elements being defined (differently, from language to language) by how they combine with nouns.[7]

One of the promising developments of transformational-generative grammar is the hypothesis that all languages are fundamentally alike in their "deep grammar," an underlying domain of universal grammatical relationships and universal semantic features, and different only on the surface, in the more or less accidental paths along which inner forms link themselves and make their way to the top. One is reminded of what is so often said about sexual behavior—that it can be modified by social restrictions but never seriously changed. If the hypothesis is true then our bent for language is as much a part of us as our mating instincts and our hunger drives.

[6] Paraphrased from Samuel E. Martin's review of J. H. Greenberg (ed.), "Universals of Language," *Harvard Educational Review* 34.353–55 (1964).
[7] John Lyons, "Towards a 'Notional' Theory of the 'Parts of Speech,'" *Journal of Linguistics* 2.209–36 (1966).

■ THE SONS OF HENGIST AND HORSA GET EMBARRASSED ABOUT GRAMMAR

Charlton Laird

English grammar, like other phenomena of this world, must have grown through some prolonged, almost infinitely complex evolution. That, we must assume. But if modern notions of English grammar are so new that most users of the language have never heard them whispered, the changes in our thinking about grammar must have been so violent as to be described as nothing short of revolution. They are revolutionary, not to say, in some quarters, pyrotechnic. Let us try to find out how this revolution came about. Or rather, let us first try to find out how we acquired a grammatical statement, which we accepted as English grammar, and which was so remote from English that it did not contain some of the most elementary principles. When we know that we should know why we had to have a twentieth-century grammatical revolution. Let us start with English in the earliest forms we have it, with Anglo-Saxon.

Hengist and Horsa, and their sons after them, were intelligent and somewhat subtle people. They knew how to kill their enemies, and even how to kill each other; they knew how to steal land, cattle, and other people's wives; they knew how to keep the faith even though they lost their heads as the penalty; and they knew also how to do what they had promised not to do and yet do it so cleverly that they could not be accused of breaking their word. We know these facts about them, because these are among the facts which interest many people, and they were recorded. The sons of Hengist and Horsa must have known, also, how to use grammar. Otherwise they could not have made themselves understood. But if they had any abstract curiosity about the nature of grammar, when it was right or wrong, good or bad, precise or slovenly, their chroniclers did not record the fact. As far as we know, the Anglo-Saxons just talked their grammar, and did not talk *about* it. And why should they? Latin grammar was theirs to study—the few, that is, who supported learned pretensions—but nothing learned was written in Anglo-Saxon. Not until Alfred's time, just before A.D. 900, was there much practical writing in the native tongue, and then only as a war emergency. Then, before Englishmen had developed enough leisure to become self-conscious about their grammar, the Normans arrived, made French the official language, and reduced English to a vulgar speech. Only among very sophisticated people is the language of swineherds and woodchoppers a subject for serious study, and the descendants of Hengist and Horsa were some time becoming sophisticated.

But the time came. In the fifteenth century, and especially in the sixteenth century, Englishmen became self-conscious about their language.

They recognized that their native tongue was an obscure dialect, not much removed from the speech of barbarians, nothing to be compared with Latin. Latin was not only the speech of the Holy Roman Empire, but assuredly the language of the Lord God, of Christ, of the Holy Ghost, of all the angels and devils, and of the Virgin Mary, even though the Virgin, being a woman, presumably could not read and might therefore get her declensions wrong. Nor was Anglo-Saxon—and later Middle English—anything to be compared with French or Italian, which had many words like Latin, and in any event were the languages of relatively sophisticated peoples. But by the fifteenth century all this was changing, at least somewhat.

Chaucer had lived and died, and had left behind him a body of poetry of very high order, and a school of imitators who were trying to be little Chaucers. Chaucer, if he was not quite a national poet, had become a national hero. He had proved that the English language was a good language, good enough for great poetry. Accordingly, Englishmen began worrying and started to do something about grammar. If English was to be an important language, it surely needed a grammar. But where were they to get one? Not even Chaucer seemed to have grammar, at least nothing like the teachings of the Latin grammar schools. If Chaucer wanted to rhyme the past participle of *find* with *bounden,* he spelled it *y-founden,* and if he did not want the extra syllable, he left off the *y-.* If he wanted to rhyme it with *hounde,* he spelled it *founde,* but if he wanted to rhyme it with *ground,* he spelled it *found.* Was this inflection? And he would make plurals with either *n* or *s.* What kind of grammar was that?

Very well, if Englishmen needed a grammar, they would get one. By the sixteenth century the revival of classical studies, which we know both as the Renaissance and as Humanism, was in full cry. Everybody who was anybody at all knew how to get information—one went to the classics after it. Especially, everybody knew that the Greeks had been famous students of grammar. The Romans had made use of this excellent Greek grammar, and had elaborated it with Latin. Furthermore, this grammar was taught to every schoolboy. Quite naturally, scholars assumed that Latin grammar was not merely Latin grammar, but that it was grammar itself. They borrowed it and made the most of it.

Not that they could make much, since Latin grammar was the grammar of an inflected language, and English had by now become mainly a distributive language. That is, the two languages were radically different in the etymological sense of that word, different down to the roots. But the scholars did not consider such problems, and as a matter of course they did not go to the English language itself, study a piece of ordinary prose, and ask themselves, what is it that gives the prose meaning? No. The world was as yet too young in science for that, and the study of grammar must be, at least to a degree, scientific. They went to Aristotle and Pliny for their physical and biological science, and even more they went to Greek and Latin grammar books for their syntax. For which, after all, there was good reason. Pliny may have been bad zoology, but the Roman grammars, as grammars of classical Latin, were excellent. Apparently no one stopped to ask whether or not the principles embodied in these grammars applied to a language descended from Anglo-Saxon. That, they assumed.

Accordingly, the Humanist grammarians took out their Latin textbooks, and searched in them for rules which would apply to English. They found some, made up examples in English to fit the rules, and these became the basis of what has become our traditional grammar. They did not find as much as they might have liked. Obviously, there were many splended agreements which could be expressed in Latin endings for which there were no English equivalents. That was a pity. But what should one expect? Latin was the great language of all time—unless Greek, being more elaborately declined than Latin, had this honor—and should one expect to find English, a tongue but lately derived from barbarism, possessed of all the grammar that Latin had? Of course not. But the grammarians were happy to find that some of the rules applied, and no doubt they hoped that in time the language would become purified so that more would apply. Meanwhile, anything which came to their attention and which was not accounted for by a Latin rule, they assumed was either bad grammar or no grammar at all. Most English grammar never came to their attention.

CRUSADER FROM CONNECTICUT

With variations, this veneration and repetition of Latin rules continued. The Humanist grammar books were modest works, but their descendants did not remain modest. They grew, they elaborated, they became even more authoritarian, and they continued to be written on the basis that grammar was Latin grammar. Grammarians, disputing the rules of English grammar, lost their tempers but not their love of Latin. Thus Noah Webster, publishing a new grammar book in 1807, could write, "Since the days of Wallis, who published a Grammar of the English Language, in Latin, in the reign of Charles II, from which Johnson and Lowth borrowed most of their rules, little improvement has been made in English Grammar." He goes on to say that many of Lowth's criticisms were "extremely erroneous"—Lowth's was long the standard grammar book. When the Lowth work was superseded, it was replaced by Murray's *English Grammar*. Lindley Murray, "the father of English Grammar," Webster dismisses as follows: "Murray, not having mounted to the original sources of information, and professing only to select and arrange the rules and criticisms of preceding writers, has furnished little or nothing new."

Noah Webster was a very downright sort of Yankee, given to dismissing people who disagreed with him, and few men have been able to commit and print so many errors in solemn places as he did. Yet Noah Webster, in spite of his bad temper and his occasional bad judgment, was a very great man. He often had the wit to recognize a good suggestion when he saw it; he had the courage to think with his own head; and he had the stubbornness to fight for his beliefs in the face of ridicule, indifference, and poverty. He was a born crusader and his love was language. He managed to live, in considerable part, on the returns from his spelling book; he gained fame from his dictionary. Meanwhile, but little attention has been given his *A Philosophical and Practical Grammar of the English Language,* in many ways a more original book than either of the others.

For Webster was original. His detractors sometimes mentioned his monumental conceit, and even doubted his sanity, but none of them, so far as now appears, ever accused him of being conventional. And in grammar he had reason to believe himself the voice of the new truth, for he had happened upon a remarkable and neglected volume by one Horne Tooke, and he apparently conceived that in his crusade for truth in language the line of battle formed where Noah Webster and Horne Tooke defied the world.

Horne Tooke was the assumed name of John Horne, vicar by profession, politician by practice, and philologist by avocation. He was the author of *Epea Pteroenta,* or *Diversions of Purley,* perhaps the most original and suggestive statement by an Englishman on the whole subject of language prior to the nineteenth century. It came to the attention of few people. Had not Tooke been tried for high treason and changed his cognomen for shame? Had he not been convicted of libel? Had he not been excluded from Parliament? And was it not extremely improbable that any such person—a liberal, a believer in the Bill of Rights, and a supporter of the American Revolution—would have anything important to say about philology, even though he had been only accused, not convicted, of high treason? No doubt many British students of language reasoned in this way, and in any event, if they looked into the *Diversions of Purley* they would have found there no adequate respect for the grammatical rules of Latin. For whatever reason, they pretty much ignored the book.

Not so, Webster. *The Diversions* was republished in Philadelphia, and Webster saw it in 1787, shortly after he had published a conventional grammar as Part II of his *Grammatical Institute.* In Tooke he discovered that the accepted parts of speech were all wrong, that the accepted verbs were not the verbs of the English language, that the rules in the grammar books were not the rules of English at all. He discovered further that to understand English grammar the scholar should not go to Latin, but to Anglo-Saxon (which Webster called Saxon), and devise the grammar of English from the English language. He set himself to learn Anglo-Saxon, and twenty years later he produced his grammar book.

In the preface, he gives credit for his ideas to Tooke, and goes on to explain why he had written the book, as follows:

I have long expected that some English scholar would attempt to reduce these [Tooke's] discoveries to practical use, by framing a system of rules to illustrate the construction of sentences, upon the genuine principles of the language. Being hitherto disappointed, and seeing nothing issue from the press but new compilations of old rules, and fresh editions of the same errors, I have at length undertaken to construct a Grammar, upon what my own researches into the ancient English, or Saxon language, with various extensive reading in modern books, have proved, to my full satisfaction, to be its only legitimate principles, and established usages.

Nor was Tooke's influence restricted to Webster's grammar. It is all over Webster's dictionary; Tooke may have altered the whole course of Webster's life, but that is another story, not to be told here.

Tooke had not been immune to error. Webster was not immune to adopting Tooke's errors, or augmenting them with errors of his own. For instance, he thought the article *the* developed from an Anglo-Saxon relative, and that the relative *since* grew from the verb *see*. The resulting grammatical statement was what he himself would probably have called "extremely erroneous" if it had been written by somebody else. Yet Webster's *Grammar* was a remarkable work. If we know what English grammar is, then Webster did not, but he made great strides in the direction in which English grammar and our understanding of English grammar have recently gone.

Lately there have been important changes which presage more changes, but the fact remains that almost a century and a half after Webster wrote his grammar, most books in use and most courses being taught in schools are still founded upon a grammar very much like that in the books by Lowth and Murray. And if Webster was not always right when he described our grammar, he was certainly right when he said that Lowth and Murray were wrong. If he did not appreciate the importance of a shift from an inflected to a distributive language, he did have an inkling of this shift and of its import. Most American textbooks on the subject do not betray an inkling.

■ GRAMMAR IS NOT A PIGEONHOLE DESK

Charlton Laird

People who think the conventional grammar makes sense usually do so because they are not examining the grammar at all. They are doing one, and usually all, of the following:

(1) They restrict examination of language to sentences made up to fit rules, and they do not examine these sentences further than to notice that

they do fit. This of course is nonsense. If grammar will not explain ordinary prose—to say nothing of sentences made up *not* to fit the rules —there is something wrong with the grammatical rules.

(2) They expect to save any rule which gets into trouble by assuming, in any example which will not fit it, that additional words or a different order is "understood." The sentence is accordingly changed so that it does fit. Let us see how this works. Since I have recommended taking a sentence at random from a book, I will take one from a book which happens to be lying on the table. It is Josephine Tey's *The Daughter of Time* (New York; Macmillan, 1952), opened to page 80. Running my eye down the page—since I am now looking for an example, not trying to explain any piece of prose—I find that one character says "Oh!" unexpectedly, and the hero asks, "What was the 'Oh' for?" Let us endeavor to parse this last sentence. *What* is an interrogative pronoun, subject of the sentence. *Was* is the verb. *Oh* is the complement. What is *for?* The *New International Dictionary*, second edition, which embodies a good compendium of conventional but relatively liberal grammatical opinion, gives *for* as a conjunction or a preposition. (Lest I be accused of treating dictionaries unkindly—and I am very far from wishing to do so—let me say once for all that I am citing dictionaries partly for my own convenience, and partly because the makers of widely used dictionaries have generally been more liberal than the makers of widely used grammars.) But *for* in this sentence cannot be a conjunction; it has nothing to join. It cannot be a preposition; it has no object.

Obviously, *for* must be something. Accordingly a conventional grammarian would be likely to start by changing the sentence to another which is "understood." He might substitute "What was the 'Oh' intended for?" *Intended* can modify *oh,* and if *for* can be an adverb, it can modify the past participle *intended.* This is possible, for although the *New International* does not enter *for* as an adverb, doubtless some other authority does so. Or the grammarian could change the sentence to "For what was the 'Oh' intended?" *For* has now become a preposition. Other additions are possible, for instance, "For what remark which you suppressed was the 'Oh' intended to substitute?" and "What does the 'Oh' stand for?" The conventional grammarian also changes the order, although, if order is the basis of English grammar, one wonders what right he has to change it. He might say that the sentence is understood to be "For what was the 'Oh'?" No one would talk such nonsense, but let us pass that. Is *for what* the subject? Obviously not, for whatever a *for what* is, it is not and was not an *Oh.* Nor does the sentence improve if we try to make *for what* the complement and *Oh* the subject. Can *for what* be a modifier of *is?* Surely not; it does not qualify the is-ness of *is.* Unless *is* means *serves, substitutes,* or something else it does not mean, *for what* can scarcely modify it.

This sort of grammatical juggling might warrant several comments, but here are two obvious ones. First, these additions of words and changes of structure are not "understood." If they are understood, how are we to know which of the various possibilities we are to understand?

I suspect that Miss Tey would have been outraged were we to suggest that she had meant any of these words or structures to be understood in place of the words and structure she used.

Now for a second comment. If we are to discuss the grammar of this sentence, we must discuss the sentence as it is. Obviously it has grammar. It was written by a reputable writer; it is put into the mouth of a presumably well-educated man and one who is highly intelligent; the man is at the moment discussing a subject seriously. Certainly Miss Tey thought the sentence had grammar when she wrote it. Any competent reader of English would know at once what the sentence was intended to mean. Therefore, Miss Tey is right; the sentence has grammar, and any grammatical statement which will not account for "What was the 'Oh' for?" without changing it in any particular is an inadequate statement. Our grammatical rules, not Miss Tey's grammar, are at fault.

(3) The people who defend conventional grammar are not concerned with understanding the grammar, but with putting words into pigeonholes. This is a harmless diversion, but it has little to do with English grammar, particularly since there are no pigeonholes into which grammatical concepts in English can be assorted so as to form anything like a classification. On what basis does the conventionally accepted grammar classify words? Not on form. Most of the so-called parts of speech have no connection with form, and those which do have some have not much. Adverbs end in -ly, but *fast* and *well* are adverbs (unless you call them verbs, modifiers, or adjectives, which of course they can be) and *homely* and *family* are supposedly not adverbs, although they end in -ly. Neither does traditional grammar classify words on meaning. Supposedly nouns are determined on meaning, and within limits, the division is valid, but the presence of nouns determined by meaning among other pigeonholed objects determined on other bases only confuses the classification. And last, the conventional grammarians do not use function as a means of classification, although this is the most commonly supposed basis. Most of the supposed functions do not exist, and those that do, do not fit the categories.

For instance, where does the verb in the following sentence begin and end? *You'd better start doing something about getting the tire blown up. You* is the subject. *Had* (contracted to *'d*) is part of the verb, but part of what verb: *had start, had doing, had start doing?* None of these makes any sense. Unless the verb includes *better* the sentence has no meaning, and yet no conventional grammarian can admit, and no conventional authority I have consulted does admit, that *better* in this sense can be part of a verb. (Just in case anyone should suggest that this sentence is not "good grammar," notice E. B. White's "I better get them today" [*One Man's Meat*, p. 261]. I assume that most modern writers would agree that if *better* as a verb is good enough for White it is good enough for them.) Is the verb *better start doing?* This still has no meaning. *Had better start doing something* has meaning, but not the meaning of the sentence. Clearly the verb must include *doing something about;* it must also include *getting,* and *blown up* if the words in the sentence are to have their meanings. *The tire,* by all conventional statements, is a noun with its article and presumably is a complement. But observe what happens if we remove it: *You'd better start doing something about getting blown up.* Can we say that even a noun is not somehow involved in the verb if the entire meaning of the verb changes when the noun is removed? Pretty clearly we have one idea which develops all the way from *had* to *blown up;* it cannot be broken up into little chunks which can be filed in pigeonholes unless we are willing to ignore the meanings of words and the whole meaning of the sentence.

But perhaps this sentence is exceptional. Suppose we try *Grandma was peeling apples by the window.* This is certainly a simple, ordinary sentence which should fit conventional rules if any sentence will. The conventional statement would be as follows: *Grandma* is a noun, subject of the verb; *was peeling* is a verb made up of present participle *peeling* and auxiliary *was; apples* is a noun, direct object of *peeling; by the window* is an adverbial prepositional phrase, made up of the preposition *by,* which introduces the object of the preposition, *window,* modified by the article *the,* and the whole prepositional phrase modifies the verb, *was peeling.* This sounds objective, learned, even final. But does it make much sense? *By the window* is said to modify *was peeling,* but it must also modify *grandma* and *apples.* They must all have been by the window or grandma could not have been peeling the apples. But to say this is heresy, for *grandma* and *apples* are both nouns, and modifiers of nouns are adjectives, not adverbs. That is, it is completely impossible to decide whether *by the window* is an adjective or an adverb. It is a modifier, but pretty clearly it modifies the whole sentence. Now for *apples;* it is said to be the direct object, because it receives the action of the verb. But it also determines the action of the verb. Remove it, and the action becomes quite different: *Grandma was peeling by the window.* Grandma has now become scrofulitic, or perhaps ecdysiastic.

GRAMMAR IS SLIPPERY STUFF

Grammar is somewhat like a freshly caught fish. Take it in your hand to wash it in the stream; two wriggles, and it is gone. So with grammar, and I speak as one who has gone through the chastening experience of asking himself quite soberly what our grammar is. I have tried to divest myself of old grammatical prejudices beaten into me at an early age, and acquired later with the profligate expenditure of midnight electricity. I have at times thought I had drawn from the deceptive grammatical waters a fine, trim, grammatical fact. I grasped him firmly by the tail, and meant only to clean him up a bit. Two flips, and he was gone.

And thus, in all humility, I point out that we have not as yet described our grammar. Grammatical concepts are not easy to deal with. Grammatical phenomena are numerous, varied, and bafflingly shifty. Part of our trouble is that we have no precedent. Except English, Chinese is the only great distributive language, and the Chinese seem to have done no more than we to understand distributive grammar. At least, if there is any adequate Chinese analysis of language it has gained no currency in this country to provide students of English with anything like a pilot job. Apparently, if we are to understand our language we shall have to think, and observe, and argue our way through the exploration ourselves.

We have a start. In fact, we have an excellent start. All grammarians now concede—even those who still think as though Latin grammar is the basis of grammar—that the grammar of any language must be derived from the language itself. All grammarians now concede that the source of English grammar is to be sought in Anglo-Saxon, and in the changes which the English language has undergone since Anglo-Saxon days. They all concede that in studying language we must take account of both written and oral language, and that of the two, oral language is probably the more significant, although the more difficult to deal with.

■ HOW DIFFERENT CULTURES USE SPACE

Edward T. Hall

Several years ago a magazine published a map of the United States as the average New Yorker sees it. The details of New York were quite clear and the suburbs to the north were also accurately shown. Hollywood appeared in some detail while the space in between New York and Hollywood was almost a total blank. Places like Phoenix, Albuquerque, the Grand Canyon, and Taos, New Mexico, were all crowded into a hopeless jumble. It was easy to see that the average New Yorker knew little and cared less for what went on in the rest of the country. To the geographer the map was a distortion of the worst kind. Yet to the student of culture it was surprisingly accurate. It showed the informal images that many people have of the rest of the country.

As a graduate student I lived in New York, and my landlord was a first-generation American of European extraction who had lived in New York all his life. At the end of the academic year as I was leaving, the landlord came down to watch me load my car. When I said goodby, he remarked, "Well, one of these Sunday afternoons I put my family in the car and we drive out to New Mexico and see you."

The map and the landlord's comment illustrate how Americans treat space as highly personalized. We visualize the relationship between places we know by personal experience. Places which we haven't been to and with which we are not personally identified tend to remain confused.

Traditionally American space begins with "a place." It is one of the oldest sets, comparable to, but not quite the same as, the Spanish *lugar*. The reader will have no difficulty thinking up ways in which place is used: "He found a place in her heart," "He has a place in the mountains," "I am tired of this place," and so on. Those who have children know how difficult it is to get across to them the whole concept of place —like Washington, or Boston, or Philadelphia, and so on. An American child requires between six and seven years before he has begun to master the basic concepts of place. Our culture provides for a great variety of places, including different classes of places.

Contrasted with the Middle East, our system is characterized by fine gradations as one moves from one space category to the next. In the world of the Arab there are villages and cities. That is about all. Most non-nomadic Arabs think of themselves as villagers. The actual villages are of varying population, from a few families up to several thousands.

The smallest place category in the United States is not covered by a term like hamlet, village, or town. It is immediately recognizable as a territorial entity, nevertheless, because such places are always named. They are areas with no recognizable center where a number of families live—like Dogpatch of the funny papers.

Our Dogpatches present the basic American pattern in uncomplicated form. They have scattered residences with no concentration of buildings in one spot. Like time, place with us is diffused, so that you never quite know where its center is. Beyond this the naming of place categories begins with the "crossroads store" or "corner" and continues with the "small shopping center," the "county seat," the "small town," "large town," "metropolitan center," "city," and "metropolis." Like much of the rest of our culture, including the social ranking system, there are no clear gradations as one moves from one category to the next. The "points" are of varying sizes, and there are no linguistic cues indicating the size of the place we are talking about. The United States, New Mexico, Albuquerque, Pecos are all said the same way and used the same way in sentences. The child who is learning the language has no way of distinguishing one space category from another by listening to others talk.

The miracle is that children eventually are able to sort out and pin down the different space terms from the meager cues provided by others. Try telling a five-year-old the difference between where you live in the suburbs and the town where your wife goes to shop. It will be a frustrating task, since the child, at that age, only comprehends where *he* lives. His room, his house, his place at the table are the places that are learned early.

The reason most Americans have difficulty in school with geography or geometry stems from the fact that space as an informal cultural system is different from space as it is technically elaborated by classroom geography and mathematics. It must be said in fairness to ourselves that other cultures have similar problems. Only the very perceptive adult realizes that there is anything really difficult for the child to learn about space. In reality, he has to take what is literally a spatial blur and isolate the significant points that adults talk about. Sometimes adults are unnecessarily impatient with children because they don't catch on. People do not realize that the child has heard older people talking about different places and is trying to figure out, from what he hears, the difference between this place and that. In this regard it should be pointed out that the first clues which suggest to children that one thing is different from another come from shifts in tone of voice which direct attention in very subtle but important ways. Speaking a fully developed language as we do, it is hard to remember that there was a time when we could not speak at all and when the whole communicative process was carried on by means of variations in the voice tone. This early language is lost to consciousness and functions out of awareness, so that we tend to forget the very great role it plays in the learning process.

To continue our analysis of the way a child learns about space, let us turn to his conception of a road. At first a road is whatever he happens to be driving on. This doesn't mean that he can't tell when you take a wrong turn. He can, and often will even correct a mistake which is made. It only means that he has not yet broken the road down into its components and that he makes the distinction between this road and that road in just the same way that he learns to distinguish between the phoneme *d* and the phoneme *b* in initial position in the spoken language.

Using roads for cross-cultural contrast, the reader will recall that Paris, being an old city as well as a French city, has a street-naming system that puzzles most Americans. Street names shift as one progresses. Take Rue St.-Honoré, for example, which becomes Rue du Faubourg St.-Honoré, Avenue des Ternes, and Avenue du Roule. A child growing up in Paris, however, has no more difficulty learning his system than one of our children learning ours. We teach ours to watch the intersections and the directions and that when something happens—that is, when there is a change of course at one of these points—you can expect the name to change. In Paris the child learns that as he passes certain landmarks— like buildings that are well known, or statues—the name of the street changes.

It is interesting and informative to watch very young children as they learn their culture. They quickly pick up the fact that we have names for some things and not for others. First, they identify the whole object or the set—a room, for instance; then they begin to fixate on certain other discrete objects like books, ashtrays, letter openers, tables, and pencils. By so doing they accomplish two things. First, they find out how far down the scale they have to go in identifying things. Second, they learn what are the isolates and patterns for handling space and object nomenclature. First children are often better subjects than second children, because, having learned the hard way, the first one will teach the second one without involving the parents.

The child will ask, "What's this?" pointing to a pencil. You reply, "A pencil." The child is not satisfied and says, "No, this," pointing to the shaft of the pencil and making clear that she meant the shaft. So you say, "Oh, that's the shaft of the pencil." Then the child moves her finger one quarter inch and says, "What's this?" and you say, "The shaft." This process is repeated and you say, "That's still the shaft; and this is the shaft, and this is the shaft. It's all the shaft of the pencil. This is the shaft, this is the point, and this is the eraser, and this is the little tin thing that holds the eraser on." Then she may point to the eraser, and you discover that she is still trying to find out where the dividing lines are. She manages to worm out the fact that the eraser has a top and sides but no more. She also learns that there is no way to tell the difference between one side and the next and that no labels are pinned on parts of the point, even though distinctions are made between the lead and the rest of the pencil. She may glean from this that materials make a difference some of the time and some of the time they do not. Areas where things begin and end are apt to be important, while the points in between are often ignored.

The significance of all this would undoubtedly have escaped me if it hadn't been for an experience on the atoll of Truk. In a rather detailed series of studies in technology I had progressed to the point of having to obtain the nomenclature of the canoe and the wooden food bowl. At this point it was necessary for me to go through what children go through—that is, point to various parts after I thought I had the pattern and ask if I had the name right. As I soon discovered, their system of carving up microspace was radically different from our own. The Trukese treat open spaces, without dividing lines (as we know them), as completely distinct. Each area has a name. On the other hand, they have not developed a nomenclature for the edges of objects as elaborately as Westerners have done. The reader has only to think of rims and cups and the number of different ways in which these can be referred to. There is the rim itself. It can be square or round or elliptical in cross section; straight, flared, or curved inward; plain or decorated, and wavy or straight. This doesn't mean that the Trukese don't elaborate rims. They do; it just means that we have ways of talking about what we do and not as many ways of talking about what happens to an open area as they do. The Trukese separate parts which we think of as being "built in" to the object.

A certain decoration or carving at either end of a canoe-shaped food bowl is thought of as being separate or distinct from the rim in which it has been carved. It has an essence of its own. Along the keel of the canoe the carving, called the *chunefatch,* has characteristics with which it endows the canoe. The canoe is one thing, the chunefatch something else. Open spaces without obvious markers on the side of the bowl have names. Such distinctions in the dividing up of space make the settling of land claims unbelievably complicated in these islands. Trees, for instance, are considered separate from the soil out of which they grow. One man may own the trees, another the soil below.

Benjamin Whorf, describing how Hopi concepts of space are reflected in the language, mentions the absence of terms for interior three-dimensional spaces, such as words for room, chamber, hall, passage, interior, cell, crypt, cellar, attic, loft, and vault. This does not alter the fact that the Hopi have multi-room dwellings and even use the rooms for special purposes such as storage, grinding corn, and the like.

Whorf also notes the fact that it is impossible for the Hopi to add a possessive pronoun to the word for room and that in the Hopi scheme of things a room in the strict sense of the word is not a noun and does not act like a noun.

Since there is a wealth of data on how strongly the Hopi feel about holding onto things which are theirs, one has to rule out the possessive factor in Whorf's references to their inability to say "my room." It's just that their language is different. One might be led to assume by this that the Hopi would then lack a sense of territoriality. Again, nothing could be farther from the truth. They just use and conceive of space differently. We work from points and along lines. They apparently do not. While seemingly inconsequential, these differences caused innumerable headaches to the white supervisers who used to run the Hopi reservation in the first part of this century.

I will never forget driving over to one of the villages at the end of a mesa and discovering that someone was building a house in the middle of the road. It later developed that the culprit (in my eyes) was a man I had known for some time. I said, "Paul, why are you building your house in the middle of the road? There are lots of good places on either side of the road. This way people have to knock the bottoms out of their cars driving around on the rocks to get to the village." His reply was short and to the point: "I know, but it's my right." He did have a right to a certain area laid down long before there was a road. The fact that the road had been used for many years meant nothing to him. Use and disuse of space in our terms had nothing to do with his ideas of possession.

SPACE AS A FACTOR IN CULTURE CONTACT

Whenever an American moves overseas, he suffers from a condition known as "culture shock." Culture shock is simply a removal or distortion of many of the familiar cues one encounters at home and the substitution for them of other cues which are strange. A good deal of what occurs in the organization and use of space provides important leads as to the specific cues responsible for culture shock.

The Latin house is often built around a patio that is next to the sidewalk but hidden from outsiders behind a wall. It is not easy to describe the degree to which small architectural differences such as this affect outsiders. American Point Four technicians living in Latin America used to complain that they felt "left out" of things, that they were "shut off." Others kept wondering what was going on "behind those walls." In the United States, on the other hand, propinquity is the basis of a good many relationships. To us the neighbor is actually quite close. Being a neighbor endows one with certain rights and privileges, also responsibilities. You can borrow things, including food and drink, but you also have to take your neighbor to the hospital in an emergency. In this regard he has almost as much claim on you as a cousin. For these and other reasons the American tries to pick his neighborhood carefully, because he knows that he is going to be thrown into intimate contact with people. We do not understand why it is that when we live next to people abroad the sharing of adjacent space does not always conform to our own pattern. In France and England, for instance, the relations between neighbors are apt to be cooler than in the United States. Mere propinquity does not tie people together. In England neighbor children do not play as they do in our neighborhoods. When they do play, arrangements are sometimes made a month in advance, as though they were coming from the other side of town!

Another example has to do with the arrangement of offices. In this case one notices great contrast between ourselves and the French. Part of our over-all pattern in the United States is to take a given amount of space and divide it up equally. When a new person is added in an office, almost everyone will move his desk so that the newcomer will have his share of the space. This may mean moving from positions that have been occupied for a long time and away from favorite views from the window. The point is that the office force will make its own adjustments voluntarily. In fact, it is a signal that they have acknowledged the presence of the new person when they start rearranging the furniture. Until this has happened, the boss can be sure that the new person has not been integrated into the group.

Given a large enough room, Americans will distribute themselves around the walls, leaving the center open for group activities such as conferences. That is, the center belongs to the group and is often marked off by a table or some object placed there both to use and save the space. Lacking a conference table, members will move their chairs away from their desks to form a "huddle" in the middle. The pattern of moving from one's place to huddle is symbolized in our language by such expressions as, "I had to take a new position on that point," or "The position of the office on this point is . . ."

The French, by contrast, do not make way for each other in the unspoken, taken-for-granted way that we do. They do not divide up the space with a new colleague. Instead they may grudgingly give him a small desk in a dark corner looking toward the wall. This action speaks eloquently to Americans who have found themselves working for the French. We feel that not to "make a place" accents status differences. If the rearrangement which says, "Now we admit you to the group, and you are going to stay," fails to take place, Americans are likely to feel perilously insecure. In French offices the key figure is the man in the middle, who has his fingers on everything so that all runs smoothly.

There is a centralized control. The French educational system runs from the middle, so that all students all over France take the same class at the same time.

It has already been mentioned that ordering is an important element in American patterns. As a general rule, whenever services are involved we feel that people should queue up in order of arrival. This reflects the basic equalitarianism of our culture. In cultures where a class system or its remnants exist, such ordinality may not exist. That is, where society assigns rank for certain purposes, or wherever ranking is involved, the handling of space will reflect this.

To us it is regarded as a democratic virtue for people to be served without reference to the rank they hold in their occupational group. The rich and poor alike are accorded equal opportunity to buy and be waited upon in the order of arrival. In a line at the theater Mrs. Gotrocks is no better than anyone else. However, apart from the English, whose queueing patterns we share, many Europeans are likely to look upon standing in line as a violation of their individuality. I am reminded of a Pole who reacted this way. He characterized Americans as sheep, and the mere thought of such passiveness was likely to set him off crashing into a line at whatever point he pleased. Such people can't stand the idea of being held down by group conformity as if they were an automaton. Americans watching the Pole thought he was "pushy." He didn't bother to hide the fact that he thought we were much too subdued. He used to say, "What does it matter if there is a little confusion and some people get served before others?"

FORMAL SPACE PATTERNS

Depending upon the culture in question, the formal patterning of space can take on varying degrees of importance and complexity. In America, for example, no one direction takes precedence over another except in a technical or utilitarian sense. In other cultures one quickly discovers that some directions are sacred or preferred. Navajo doors must face east, the mosques of the Moslems must be oriented toward Mecca, the sacred rivers of India flow south. Americans pay attention to direction in a technical sense, but formally and informally they have no preference. Since our space is largely laid out by technical people, houses, towns, and main arteries are usually oriented according to one of the points of the compass. The same applies to roads and main highways when the topography allows, as it does in the flat expanses of Indiana and Kansas. This technical patterning allows us to locate places by co-ordinates (a point on the line). "He lives at 1321 K Street, N.W." tells us that he lives in the northwest part of town in the thirteenth block west of the line dividing the town into east-west halves and eleven blocks north of the line dividing the town into north-south halves, on the left side of the street, about one quarter of the way up the block.

In the country we will say, "Go out of town ten miles west on Highway 66 until you get to the first paved road turning north. Turn right on that road and go seven miles. It's the second farm on your left. You can't miss it."

Our concept of space makes use of the edges of things. If there aren't any edges, we make them by creating artificial lines (five miles west and two miles north). Space is treated in terms of a co-ordinate system. In contrast, the Japanese and many other people work within areas. They name "spaces" and distinguish between one space and the next or parts of a space. To us a space is empty—one gets into it by intersecting it with lines.

A technical pattern which may have grown out of an informal base is that of position value or ranking. We have canonized the idea of the positional value in almost every aspect of our lives, so much so that even children four years old are fully aware of its implications and are apt to fight with each other as to who will be first.

In addition to positional value, the American pattern emphasizes equality and standardization of the segments which are used for measuring space or into which space is divided, be it a ruler or a suburban subdivision. We like our components to be standard and equal. American city blocks tend to have uniform dimensions whereas towns in many other parts of the world are laid out with unequal blocks. This suggests that it was no accident that mass production, made possible by the standardization of parts, had its origins in the United States. There are those who would argue that there are compelling technological reasons for both mass production and parts standardization. However, an examination of actual practice indicates that Europeans have produced automobiles in the past—and very good ones too—in which the cylinders were all of different sizes. The difference in dimensions was not great, of course, a matter of a very few thousandths of an inch. This, however, was enough to cause the car to make noise and use too much oil if it was repaired by an American mechanic unfamiliar with the European patterns that lack the uniformity isolate.

Japan, too, has a passion for uniformity, though it is somewhat different from ours. All mats (*tatami*) on the floors of Japanese houses and all windows, doors, and panels are usually of identical dimensions in a given district. In newspaper advertisements of houses for sale or rent the dimensions are usually given in terms of the number of mats of a specific area. Despite this example of uniformity, the Japanese differ from us in a way which can have considerable economic results. In one case, for example, they manufactured a very large order of electronics parts according to rigid specifications which they were quite able to meet. When the product arrived in the United States, it was discovered that there were differences between various batches of these parts. The customer subsequently discovered that while the whole internal process of manufacture had been controlled the Japanese had failed to standardize their gauges! It is no accident that in the United States there is a Bureau of Standards. Much of the success of this country's technical skill and productivity, which we are trying to pass on to other nations, rests on these and similar unstated patterns.

HOW SPACE COMMUNICATES

Spatial changes give a tone to a communciation, accent it, and at times even override the spoken word. The flow and shift of distance between people as they interact with each other is part and parcel of the communication process. The normal conversational distance between strangers illustrates how important are the dynamics of space interaction. If a person gets too close, the reaction is instantaneous and automatic—the other person backs up. And if he gets too close again, back we go again. I have observed an American backing up the entire length of a long corridor while a foreigner whom he considers pushy tries to catch up with him. This scene has been enacted thousands and thousands of times—one person trying to increase the distance in order to be at ease, while the other tries to decrease it for the same reason, neither one being aware of what was going on. We have here an example of the tremendous depth to which culture can condition behavior.

One thing that does confuse us and gets in the way of understanding cultural differences is that there are times in our own culture when people are either distant or pushy in their use of space. We, therefore, simply associate the foreigner with the familiar; namely those people who have acted in such a way that our attention was drawn to their actions. The error is in jumping to the conclusion that the foreigner feels the same way the American does even though his overt acts are identical.

This was all suddenly brought into focus one time when I had the good fortune to be visited by a very distinguished and learned man who had been for many years a top-ranking diplomat representing a foreign country. After meeting him a number of times, I had become impressed with his extraordinary sensitivity to the small details of behavior that are so significant in the interaction process. Dr. X. was interested in some of the work several of us were doing at the time and asked permission to attend one of my lectures. He came to the front of the class at the end of the lecture to talk over a number of points made in the preceding hour. While talking he became quite involved in the implications of the lecture as well as what he was saying. We started out facing each other and as he talked I became dimly aware that he was standing a little too close and that I was beginning to back up. Fortunately I was able to suppress my first impulse and remain stationary because there was nothing to communicate aggression in his behavior except the conversational distance. His voice was eager, his manner intent, the set of his body communicated only interest and eagerness to talk. It also came to me in a flash that someone who had been so successful in the old school of diplomacy could not possibly let himself communicate something offensive to the other person outside of his highly trained awareness.

By experimenting I was able to observe that as I moved away slightly, there was an assorted shift in the pattern of interaction. He had more trouble expressing himself. If I shifted to where I felt comfortable (about twenty-one inches), he looked somewhat puzzled and hurt, almost as though he were saying: "Why is he acting that way? Here I am doing everything I can to talk to him in a friendly manner and he suddenly withdraws. Have I done anything wrong? Said something that I shouldn't?" Having ascertained that distance had a direct effect on his conversation, I stood my ground, letting him set the distance.

Not only is a vocal message qualified by the handling of distance, but the substance of a conversation can often demand special handling of space. There are certain things which are difficult to talk about unless one is within the proper conversational zone.

Not long ago I received a present of some seeds and chemicals along with the information that if I planted the seeds the chemicals would make them grow. Knowing little about hydroponics except that the plants should be suspended above the fluid in which chemicals are dissolved, I set out to find a suitable flowerpot. At every flower shop I was met with incredulity and forced to go through a routine involving a detailed explanation of just what it was I wanted and how hydroponics worked.

My ignorance of both hydroponics and florist shops made me feel somewhat ill at ease, so that I did not communicate in the manner that I use when I am speaking on a familiar subject in a familiar setting. The role that distance plays in a communication situation was brought home to me when I entered a shop in which the floor was filled with benches spaced at about twenty-inch intervals. On the other side of the benches was the female proprietor of the shop. As I entered, she craned her neck as though to reach over the benches, raised her voice slightly to bring it up to the proper level, and said, "What was it you wanted?" I tried once. "What I'm looking for is a *hydroponic* flowerpot." "What kind of flowerpot?" still with the neck craned. At this point I found myself climbing over benches in an effort to close up the space. It was simply impossible for me to talk about such a subject in a setting of this sort at a distance of fifteen feet. It wasn't until I got to within three feet that I was able to speak wih some degree of comfort.

Another example is one that will be familiar to millions of civilians who served in the Army during World War II. The Army, in its need to get technical about matters that are usually handled informally, made a mistake in the regulations on distance required for reporting to a superior officer. Everyone knows that the relationship between officers and men has certain elements which require distance and impersonality. This applied to officers of different ranks when they were in command relationship to each other. Instructions for reporting to a superior officer were that the junior officer was to proceed up to a point three paces in front of the officer's desk, stop, salute, and state his rank, his name, and his business: "Lieutenant X, reporting as ordered, sir." Now, what cultural norms does this procedure violate, and what does it communicate? It violates the conventions for the use of space. The distance is too great, by at least two feet, and does not fit the situation. The normal speaking distance for business matters, where impersonality is involved at the beginning of the conversation, is five and a half to eight feet. The distance required by the army regulations borders on the edge of what we would call "far." It evokes an automatic response to shout. This detracts from the respect which is supposed to be shown to the superior officer. There are, of course, many subjects which it is almost impossible to talk about at this distance, and individual army officers recognize this by putting soldiers and junior officers at ease, asking them to sit down or permitting them to come closer. However, the first impression was that the Army was doing things the hard way.

For Americans the following shifts in the voice are associated with specific ranges of distances:

1. *Very close* (3 in. to 6 in.).   Soft whisper; top secret.
2. *Close* (8 in. to 12 in.).   Audible whisper; very confidential.
3. *Near* (12 in. to 20 in.).   Indoors, soft voice; outdoors, full voice; confidential.
4. *Neutral* (20 in. to 36 in.).   Soft voice, low volume; personal subject matter.
5. *Neutral* (4½ ft. to 5 ft.).   Full voice; information of non-personal matter.
6. *Public Distance* (5½ ft. to 8 ft.).   Full voice with slight overloudness; public information for others to hear.
7. *Across the room* (8 ft. to 20 ft.).   Loud voice; talking to a group.
8. *Stretching the limits of distance.*   20 ft. to 24 ft. indoors; up to 100 ft. outdoors; hailing distance, departures.

In Latin America the interaction distance is much less than it is in the United States. Indeed, people cannot talk comfortably with one another unless they are very close to the distance that evokes either sexual or hostile feelings in the North American. The result is that when they move close, we withdraw and back away. As a consequence, they think we are distant or cold, withdrawn and unfriendly. We, on the other hand, are constantly accusing them of breathing down our necks, crowding us, and spraying our faces.

Americans who have spent some time in Latin America without learning these space considerations make other adaptations, like barricading themselves behind their desks, using chairs and typewriter tables to keep the Latin American at what is to us a comfortable distance. The result is that the Latin American may even climb over the obstacles until he has achieved a distance at which he can comfortably talk.

■ LANGUAGE CONFLICTS

In India, government efforts to implement a constitutional provision to replace English with Hindi as the nation's official language resulted in widespread rioting in February. More than 50 persons were killed, hundreds more were injured and some 1,000 arrested.

In Belgium, parliament approved a plan to redistribute legislative seats in accordance with actual population. But the new voting arrangement would mean a gain in representation for the Flemish-speaking regions at the expense of French-speaking regions threatening once more to heat up a long simmering feud between the two language groups in Belgium.

In Canada, an interim report by a Royal Commission declared that the conflict between French and English languages and cultures in Canada poses "a grave danger to the future of Canada and all Canadians." Discontent in predominantly French-speaking Quebec has already spawned a separatist movement advocating Quebec's secession from the Canadian confederation.

The conflicts that divide mankind come in seemingly infinite varieties: territorial disputes, economic clashes, political differences—to name a few that come readily to mind. These conflicts are likely to be expressed through a torrent of words, sometimes of the printable kind and sometimes not. Often the disputes are centered in language itself. Even a glance at the news items above should be enough to show how languages differences can create tensions between people and even arouse them to violence.

That language differences tend to promote misunderstanding is hardly a surprise. How can men hope to fully understand one another if they are even fighting over language—their most basic tool of communication?

Poets tell us that lovers can "communicate" with nary a word being said. They may gaze deeply into each other's eyes in a romantic version of the eyeball-to-eyeball confrontation. But for most other people at most other times, staring alone will not suffice. People-to-people communication ordinarily requires sounds, symbols, or gestures. It requires language in the most basic sense—that is, human speech in either its spoken or written forms.

Those who think deep thoughts about languages (they go under the name of linguists) agree that there have been human languages almost as long as there have been people. Even the most primitive tribes in the most isolated regions of the world have developed their own spoken languages, although they may not have put them in writing.

Professor Mario Pei, a noted linguist at Columbia University, reports that scholars have counted at least 2,798 spoken languages. As an educated guess, linguists estimate that perhaps 3,000 to 4,000 distinguishable languages are extant today (not counting dialects, or spoken variations of the same language).

Variety, indeed, is the spice of language. "Few things in this world are more varied or more individualistic than human speech," observes *The Christian Science Monitor*'s managing editor Joseph G. Harrison, who has written extensively on linguistic subjects. "There are [languages] which boom like the sea, tingle like a bell, click like castanets. Others rise and fall in a never-ending rhythm, still others flow as placidly as whipped cream.

"Some are made up of short, sharp monosyllables, while others are compounded of words which go on and on through a dozen syllables . . . . But, despite such variety, most languages seem to do just what they are meant to do: enable men to communicate with one another."

And a good thing, too. For much of human activity depends on cooperation between two or more people. As the Roman orator and statesman Cicero observed, lo, those many years ago: "It is reason and speech that unite men to one another; there is nothing else in which we differ so entirely from the brute creation."

But by the same token, people who don't speak the same language would tend to be disunited because of their inability to communicate with one another easily. The problems have become increasingly acute in light of modern political developments.

By now, most parts of the world that are reasonably pleasant for human habitation have been divided into major political units. Nations are the primary example, of course. The sharp dividing lines that appear on a political map, however, may be deceptive. What may appear as a single political unit may contain many *cultural units*. And languages do not necessarily conform to arbitrary political boundaries.

Americans are often surprised to hear of the problems of such multilingual political units because one language is so overwhelmingly dominant in the U.S. Despite variations in twangs, drawls, or slurs, the vast majority of Americans speak English and can make themselves understood in all parts of this country (well, that is to say, almost always).

Not so in a nation such as India. There, census figures record some 850 different languages and major dialects. Little wonder, then, that a Hindu proverb should observe "Language changes every 18 to 20 miles."

Are language variations the result of regional disunity? Or is disunity a product of language differences? That's like asking whether the chicken or the egg came first. Certainly there are countries which manage to get along peacefully with different languages. Switzerland, with its three official languages (German, French, and Italian) is a notable example. Yet even Switzerland has had its internal strife in the past—including a brief civil war as late as 1847.

The point is that language differences *do* promote regional disunity, which in turn fosters language variations, and round and round it goes. How can a nation such as India hope to break this language-disunity cycle?

The Indian constitution of 1950 sought to tackle the problem in stages. First it sought to reduce the number of languages to manageable proportions by officially recognizing only 14 major Indian languages plus English. Then it specified that after a 15-year adjustment period Hindi would stand as India's sole official language.

The plan sounded reasonable enough in 1950. Hindi is the most common language in India (spoken by an estimated 190,000,000 persons out of India's 441,631,000). And non-Hindi-speaking Indians were given time to acquire new linguistic skills. In the meantime, all parliamentary business was conducted in English, the language most Indian political leaders understood.

But reality proved to be somewhat more difficult than theory. Hindi speakers may be the most numerous language group in India but they still add up to only about 40 per cent of the total population. Languages spoken in most of southern India—including Tamil, Telugu, and Kanarese—hardly bear any relationship to Hindi.

Furthermore, it was probably too much to expect that non-Hindi-speaking Indians would rush out in droves for language lessons. It's not entirely a matter of a lazy, can't-be-bothered attitude. Hindi, like most languages, is tricky; those who know say that it takes some three years of fairly intensive study for a non-Hindi-speaking person to acquire an adequate grasp of that language. Many persons probably have enough trouble mastering the language of their birth—let alone a strange tongue.

Thus, the move to declare Hindi the official language of India stirred deep-seated fears among India's non-Hindi-speaking population. They believed that Hindi speakers would henceforth enjoy a "cultural advantage" that could be translated into political dominance by the northern Hindi-speaking regions. Even the knowledge that a law had been passed in 1963 specifying that English would be retained as an "associate language" for at least 10 more years was not enough to hold back violence.

If English is still the most serviceable language in India's political circles, why not simply retain it indefinitely? The reason: national pride. As India's Prime Minister Lal Bahadur Shastri (himself a Hindi speaker) declared: The retention of the language of India's former colonial rulers would be "deeply humiliating." The continued use of English would serve as a constant reminder of a colonial past—something that many in India would just as soon forget, or at least minimize.

The phenomenon of language as an expression of nationalistic sentiments is by no means unique to India. For example, the revival of Gaelic in Ireland was in large measure a deliberate attempt to symbolize Irish independence from English domination. Similarly, Indonesians wasted little time after independence in abandoning the language of their former Dutch colonial rulers—even though this virtually required the creation of a new language (Bahasa Indonesia) to replace Dutch.

Sometimes the problem is even more sticky. Consider the language problems in Africa. Most of that continent was divided up in the 19th century by the European colonial powers with little regard for the tribal, cultural, and language divisions then existing in Africa. During decades of colonial rule, European languages became dominant in the colonial administration, commerce, and education systems.

Then, the post-World War II march of independence in Africa saw the withdrawal of European powers from control over much of their former African territories. But the political boundaries drawn during the colonial era remained.

For instance, the Federation of Nigeria in West Africa, a former British territory, emerged as a single independent nation in 1960. In reality, however, the Nigerian Federation encompassed more than 200 ethnic groupings in four major language divisions: Hausa and Fulani in the north, Ibo in the southeastern region, and Yoruba in the southwestern region.

Leaders of the Nigerian Federation come from various parts of the country and speak different native tongues. The one language that most of them have in common is English (many of them are British trained or graduates of British universities). The upshot is that the Nigerian government must continue to conduct its official business in English if its leaders are going to talk to each other—whatever this does or does not do for Nigerian national pride. Similar situations exist in many other new African nations that were once colonies of European powers.

A somewhat different case is that of Gambia, a former British colony that became independent in February this year. This tiny country is surrounded by a former French colony, Senegal—and a 1963 U.N. report recommended a merger between the two. So far, such a merger seems unlikely. A major obstacle is the difference in language and culture—a difference not of African orgin but introduced by the British and the French.

Why does language so often serve as a focal point for nationalistic sentiments? Ralph Waldo Emerson, the 19th-century American author, once commented: "We infer the spirit of the nation in great measure from the language, which is a sort of monument to which each forcible individual in a course of many hundreds of years has contributed a stone."

Putting it less metaphorically, language often reflects the historic evolution and development peculiar to a specific region or society. The language that a person uses, and the way he uses it, sometimes serves as a badge of identity in setting him apart from other people. The search for "one's identity" (the old question of "Who am I and where do I fit in?") seems to be a favorite avocation of human beings, either individually or collectively as a nation.

On the reverse of the coin, variations in languages point up most sharply the differences of people in different regions. English, for example, is the common language shared (sometimes grudgingly so, it seems) by the people of Britain and the United States, among others. Yet, British English and American English have diverged sufficiently in vocabularly and syntax for transatlantic misunderstandings to arise. As playwright Oscar Wilde once quipped: "The Americans and British have everything in common except language." Or as Professor Henry Higgins, the hero of the musical play *My Fair Lady,* says about the English language, "In America they haven't used it for years." (Americans, of course, would say "*in* years"!)

Problems created by language differences are not just a matter of pride and prejudice. In a multilingual society, there are also practical considerations to take into account.

In theory, most nations like to think of themselves as "big enough" in spirit to encompass a variety of cultures and languages. This seems to be true even in places where conformity is not necessarily regarded as a sin. In the Soviet Union, for instance, Russian is the dominant language and is increasingly used by non-Russian-speaking minority groups there as their "second language." Yet the Soviet constitution guarantees minority cultures the right of preserving their own languages. Indeed, the Soviet government has helped to develop alphabets for some of the minority languages that previously had no written language.

In practice, however, communications in a multilingual society tend to get unwieldy. Every government announcement or directive may have to be translated into many languages in order to get the message across to all the nation's citizens. Most modern governments are sufficiently bogged down in paper work in just *one* language.

Moreover, people who speak the same language, like birds of a feather, tend to flock together—whether the flocking is political, social, or economic. Despite frequent denials of "language discrimination," the language barrier can be formidable.

A sample of such a situation is presently found in Canada, a nation with a bicultural, bilingual (English and French) heritage. Though both English and French are officially recognized as national languages, the fact remains that English-speaking Canadians make up about two thirds of Canada's population of some 20,000,000, and that English is the dominant language in nine of the ten Canadian provinces. Most of Canada's French-speaking population is concentrated in one province: Quebec.

Relatively few English-speaking Canadians bother to learn French. And three of four French Canadians in Quebec "do not know a word of English," according to a Canadian government commission.

French Canadians claim that, for all practical purposes, they have been relegated to the status of a disadvantaged cultural minority. They contend that they have a harder time finding jobs, even in Quebec, because Canada's businesses and industries are operated mostly by English-speaking people. They further argue that French Canadians can never get equal weight in Canadian politics—simply because the French speakers will always find themselves outnumbered on the Canadian national scene.

Discontent among French Canadians has resulted in separatist movements in Quebec. A small but vocal minority has called for Quebec's outright secession from the Canadian confederation. More moderate spokesmen have recommended giving Quebec a larger measure of autonomy *within* the national confederation. Whatever the eventual outcome, a Canadian Royal Commission studying biculturalism has declared that disunity between Canada's two language groups has now resulted in "the greatest crisis in Canada's history."

A similar bicultural problem has plagued Belgium. As recently as in 1963, a law was passed setting up a "linguistic frontier" dividing Belgium into two language areas. This line cuts across the country just south of Brussels, the Belgian capital. North of the dividing line, the official language is Flemish (which closely resembles Dutch). South of the "frontier," the official language is a dialect of French know as Walloon. Brussels itself was declared bilingual—a sort of linguistic "neutral ground."

In a given region of Belgium, all official business is transacted in the official language of that region. Schools in the north, for example, are conducted in Flemish (with the "second language," Walloon, made a required course for all students). Schools in the south of Belgium do it just the other way around.

Relations between Flemings and Walloons has often been far from idyllic in Belgium's 135-year history as an independent nation. For many years, the two groups faced each other in a kind of standoff, since the Walloon population almost exactly matched the Flemish population. But higher Flemish birth rates in more recent times have upset the balance, gradually shifting the proportion in favor of the Flemings. Today, Flemish speakers make up approximately 55 per cent of Belgium's 9,221,000 population.

This gradual emergence of distinguishable majority and minority groups could deepen the rift between Flemings and Walloons. Some observers fear, for example, that the Belgian parliament's recent proposal to redistribute legislative seats in line with actual population (which would increase the Flemish representation because of the growing Flemish population) would only perpetuate the bitterness between Belgium's two major language groups.

Beyond the questions of language differences and their effects on national unity, what about the effect of language differences on international cooperation? In our world of "shrinking distances" and "accelerating history," the peace of the globe could rest to a critical degree on an understandable dialogue between nations.

Ideally, there should be one language understood by everyone everywhere. But with so many languages to choose from, who's going to say which one should be designated "a world language"? If a single nation such as India cannot agree on one national language, how can anyone expect the whole world to agree on one international language?

Still, some languages do have greater international influence than others. The speakers of those languages are sometimes convinced that the influence is due to the inherent superiority of the language. Linguists tend to agree, however, that this "superiority" is largely a delusion of grandeur.

According to *The Christian Science Monitor*'s editor Joseph Harrison, there are three basic reasons (or combinations thereof) for the spread of a language across the globe:

1. Cultural dominations, as in the case of ancient Greece.
2. Military conquests, as exemplified by the ancient Roman Empire.
3. Economic pre-eminence, as in the cases of modern Britain or the United States.

Different languages have served as the world's "prestige languages" at different times. For centuries, French was *the* international language of diplomacy, a legacy from the days when the dazzling royal court of France was unabashedly imitated throughout Europe. To this day, there remains a lingering sentiment among some (notably Frenchmen) that people who do not speak French have somehow been bypassed in the march of civilization.

Such sentiments notwithstanding, French has come under vigorous challenge from English in this century. Today, English ranks second only to Mandarin (North Chinese) in the number of people claiming it as their native tongue. It is the everyday language of about 300,000,000 people in the British Isles, the U.S., Canada, Australia, New Zealand, and elsewhere. English is an official language or is widely used in countries from Africa to Asia. And in many—if not most—non-English-speaking areas, it has probably become the most frequently studied foreign language. Part of the spread of English is due to the impact left by a globe-circling British Empire. Part of it is also due to the power and influence of English-speaking nations in the modern world.

For all its virtues as well as faults (some foreigners are not reluctant to recount at length the difficulties and inconsistencies in English), many linguists describe English as the language most likely to become a universal language some day. If so, that day is not yet in the foreseeable future. In the meantime, international languages remain a system of compromises.

This compromise might take the form of whittling down the "working international languages" to a manageable number. The United Nations rescognizes five official languages—English, French, Russian, Spanish, and Chinese—selected on the basis of number of speakers, political influence of the language groups, and other such factors. To operate smoothly, U.N. translators must do their jobs well (many of them are amazingly proficient, indeed). Still, any system relying on translations has inherent drawbacks. The subtleties in any language are frequently lost in the translation process. For example, French, German, and other languages have two verbs for "to know," distinguishing between degrees of thoroughness in knowledge. English, on the other hand, is richer than most languages in groups of words having the same basic meaning but a wide range of emotional overtones—such as resolute, tenacious, stubborn, dogged, obstinate, and pig-headed.

Another compromise system that has been tried, with limited success, is the creation of a new "universal" language based on a combination of existing languages. Some 600 such "universal" languages have been proposed. Almost as many have been abandoned as unrealistic.

Among the more successful of such efforts are Esperanto (a combination language intended for general use) and Interlingua (intended primarily as a language for scientific reports and communications). Both of them, however, are based on root words common to all European languages—which, of course, is no great help to those who don't speak European tongues. Besides, artificial languages have an unfortunate tendency to end up as a strange language to everyone, thus pleasing hardly anyone.

It may be that mankind has been condemned to an endless problem with languages in the tradition of the Tower of Babel. Yet, an observation made by English philosopher John Locke some 300 years ago is worth recalling: "We should have a great many fewer disputes in the world." Locke said, "if words were taken for what they are, the signs of ideas only, and not for things themselves." This may be an idea that deserves to be understood—in any language.

ECONOMICS

An economy is a system for producing, distributing, and consuming goods and services in an orderly fashion. All societies have such systems, although not all societies use money as the foundation of their economies. The most important thing about money is that you can count it. Capital, credit, risk, profit, savings, and other basic concepts are easy to deal with in our economy precisely because they are countable.

When we try to apply these basic concepts of economics to non-western and non-money societies, however, we run into trouble. We find that family organization, sex role behavior, and other non-quantifiable aspects of social life are influential in how things are produced, distributed, and consumed.

By studying the non-monetary aspects of primitive and peasant economies, we gain insight into the workings of our own economy. For example, we may pretend that our corporations are egalitarian, but everyone knows that nepotism (favoritism showed to relatives) is the natural order of things. Marrying the boss' daughter, or being the boss' son gets you to the top quicker. Moral issues aside, it is not yet culturally acceptable for a woman to become a corporation executive by marrying the boss' son. No one has yet measured the monetary effect on profits of nepotism vs. egalitarianism, and male vs. female corporate leadership. But these kinds of things *are* important in understanding how our economy works.

Here is another example. *Bribery* is considered almost a dirty word in this economy. In many other cultures it carries no such emotional overtones. I once returned from a field trip and submitted my expense vouchers to my university comptroller to account for the money I'd spent from the National Science Foundation. Out of kindness to the comptroller, I avoided accounting for about $200. When he insisted that I account for every penny, I listed my expenses for "graft and bribery," and the $200 showed up. Ultimately, I had to call it "special respondent fees" or some such nonsense. But the comptroller would have thought nothing of slipping the headwaiter at a fancy restaurant a few dollars for special service. Economic behavior is just more complicated than the stuff you can count.

The five articles in this section help to illuminate this. The first two, by Richard Lee and Marvin Harris, compare gift giving among Kalahari Bushmen and Americans. Lee tried to repay the Bushmen for their hospitality to him during a field trip by slaughtering a huge ox and throwing a feast. He was shattered when his good-will gesture was ridiculed. Later he learned how ridicule of gifts functions in the Bushman economy to keep people from feeling superior to one another. By contrast, gift giving at Christmas in our own culture helps to strengthen our feelings of superiority toward one another. In Harris' article "Bah, Humbug!" we see how little Americans really "give" at gift time.

The next two articles are about peasant economies. Lawrence Durrell describes the process of buying a house on Cyprus. We follow him through the delicate negotiations and we see how personal interactions affect face-to-face bargaining. The monetary cost of the house is not the only consideration. There is an etiquette to bargaining, and each culture defines the etiquette differently.

Many people feel that peasant life is rather carefree, easygoing, and lacking in stress. As Joseph Lopreato shows, this is a romantic myth. His article "How Would You Like to Be a Peasant?" shows that rural poverty in a money economy is translated into psychological and social stress, "social insignificance, subordination, and contemptibility." Given the social and economic conditions of peasant life, he concludes, it is no wonder that people around the world have left the countryside for the city.

Oscar Lewis followed a group of rural peasants to the city to see how they adjusted. After twenty years of work, studying the life of urban poor in Mexico, India, the U.S. mainland, Puerto Rico, and Cuba, Lewis concluded that economic poverty gave rise to a cultural system of its own. In the final selection, Lewis describes this culture, showing how worldwide patterns of behavior among urban poor can be traced to their common experience of degradation through poverty. Lewis was severely criticized because his work sometimes reads as if he were glorifying poverty and the cultural values that go along with it. For example, Lewis says, "Middle-class people . . . tend to concentrate on the negative aspects of the culture of poverty. They attach a minus sign to such traits as present-time orientation and readiness to indulge impulses. . . . The positive aspects of these traits must not be overlooked." Lewis failed to acknowledge that credit-card buying is equally indicative of an inability to deny impulse gratification in the middle-class. But Lewis was not a romantic about poverty. He concluded that the culture of the urban poor is superficial and emotionally destructive. "There is in [the culture of poverty] much pathos, suffering and emptiness . . . its pervading mistrust magnifies individual helplessness and isolation."

■ EATING CHRISTMAS IN THE KALAHARI

Richard Borshay Lee

The !Kung Bushmen's knowledge of Christmas is thirdhand. The London Missionary Society brought the holiday to the southern Tswana tribes in the early nineteenth century. Later, native catechists spread the idea far and wide among the Bantu-speaking pastoralists, even in the remotest corners of the Kalahari Desert. The Bushmen's idea of the Christmas story, stripped to its essentials, is "praise the birth of white man's god-chief"; what keeps their interest in the holiday high is the Tswana-Herero custom of slaughtering an ox for his Bushmen neighbors as an annual goodwill gesture. Since the 1930's, part of the Bushmen's annual round of activities has included a December congregation at the cattle posts for trading, marriage brokering, and several days of trance-dance feasting at which the local Tswana headman is host.

As a social anthropologist working with !Kung Bushmen, I found that the Christmas ox custom suited my purposes. I had come to the Kalahari to study the hunting and gathering subsistence economy of the !Kung, and to establish this it was essential not to provide them with food, share my own food, or interfere in any way with their food-gathering activities.

EDITOR'S NOTE: The !Kung and other Bushmen speak click languages. In the story, three different clicks are used:
1 The dental click (/), as in /ai/ai, /ontah, and /gaugo. The click is sometimes written in English as tsk-tsk.
2 The alveopalatal click (!), as in Ben!a and !Kung.
3 The lateral click (//), as in //gom. Clicks function as consonants; a word may have more than one, as in /n!au.

While liberal handouts of tobacco and medical supplies were appreciated, they were scarcely adequate to erase the glaring disparity in wealth between the anthropologist, who maintained a two-month inventory of canned goods, and the Bushmen, who rarely had a day's supply of food on hand. My approach, while paying off in terms of data, left me open to frequent accusations of stinginess and hardheartedness. By their lights, I was a miser.

The Christmas ox was to be my way of saying thank you for the cooperation of the past year; and since it was to be our last Christmas in the field, I determined to slaughter the largest, meatiest ox that money could buy, insuring that the feast and trance dance would be a success.

Through December I kept my eyes open at the wells as the cattle were brought down for watering. Several animals were offered, but none had quite the grossness that I had in mind. Then, ten days before the holiday, a Herero friend led an ox of astonishing size and mass up to our camp. It was solid black, stood five feet high at the shoulder, had a five-foot span of horns, and must have weighed 1,200 pounds on the hoof. Food consumption calculations are my specialty, and I quickly figured that bones and viscera aside, there was enough meat—at least four pounds —for every man, woman, and child of the 150 Bushmen in the vicinity of /ai/ai who were expected at the feast.

Having found the right animal at last, I paid the Herero £20 ($56) and asked him to keep the beast with his herd until Christmas day. The next morning word spread among the people that the big solid black one was the ox chosen by /ontah (my Bushman name; it means roughly, "whitey") for the Christmas feast. That afternoon I received the first delegation. Ben!a, an outspoken sixty-year-old mother of five, came to the point slowly.

"Where were you planning to eat Christmas?"

"Right here at /ai/ai," I replied.

"Alone or with others?"

"I expect to invite all the people to eat Christmas with me."

"Eat what?"

"I have purchased Yehave's black ox, and I am going to slaughter and cook it."

"That's what we were told at the well but refused to believe it until we heard it from yourself."

"Well, it's the black one," I replied expansively, although wondering what she was driving at.

"Oh, no!" Ben!a groaned, turning to her group. "They were right." Turning back to me she asked, "Do you expect us to eat that bag of bones?"

"Bag of bones! It's the biggest ox at /ai/ai."

"Big, yes, but old. And thin. Everybody knows there's no meat on that old ox. What did you expect us to eat off it, the horns?

Everybody chuckled at Ben!a's one-liner as they walked away, but all I could manage was a weak grin.

That evening it was the turn of the young men. They came to sit at our evening fire. /gaugo, about my age, spoke to me man-to-man.

"/ontah, you have always been square with us," he lied. "What has happened to change your heart? That sack of guts and bones of Yehave's will hardly feed one camp let alone all the Bushmen around /ai/ai." And he proceeded to enumerate the seven camps in the /ai/ai vicinity, family by family. "Perhaps you have forgotten that we are not few, but many. Or are you too blind to tell the difference between a proper cow and an old wreck? That ox is thin to the point of death."

"Look, you guys," I retorted "that is a beautiful animal, and I'm sure you will eat it with pleasure at Christmas."

"Of course we will eat it; it's food. But it won't fill us up to the point where we will have enough strength to dance. We will eat and go home to bed with stomachs rumbling."

That night as we turned in, I asked my wife, Nancy: "What did you think of the black ox?"

"It looked enormous to me. Why?"

"Well, about eight different people have told me I got gypped; that the ox is nothing but bones."

"What's the angle?" Nancy asked. "Did they have a better one to sell?"

"No, they just said that it was going to be a grim Christmas because there won't be enough meat to go around. Maybe I'll get an independent judge to look at the beast in the morning."

Bright and early, Halingisi, a Tswana cattle owner, appeared at our camp. But before I could ask him to give me his opinion on Yehave's black ox, he gave me the eye signal that indicated a confidential chat. We left the camp and sat down.

"/ontah, I'm surprised at you: you've lived here for three years and still haven't learned anything about cattle."

"But what else can a person do but choose the biggest, strongest animal one can find?" I retorted.

"Look, just because an animal is big doesn't mean that it has plenty of meat on it. The black one was a beauty when it was younger, but now it is thin to the point of death."

"Well I've already bought it. What can I do at this stage?"

"Bought it already? I thought you were just considering it. Well, you'll have to kill it and serve it, I suppose. But don't expect much of a dance to follow."

My spirits dropped rapidly. I could believe that Ben!a and /gaugo just might be putting me on about the black ox, but Halingisi seemed to be an impartial critic. I went around that day feeling as though I had bought a lemon of a used car.

In the afternoon it was Tomazo's turn. Tomazo is a fine hunter, a top trance performer (see "The Trance Cure of the !Kung Bushmen," *Natural History,* November, 1967), and one of my most reliable informants. He approached the subject of the Christmas cow as part of my continuing Bushmen education.

"My friend, the way it is with us Bushmen," he began, "is that we love meat. And even more than that, we love fat. When we hunt we always search for the fat ones, the ones dripping with layers of white fat: fat that turns into a clear, thick oil in the cooking pot, fat that slides down your gullet, fills your stomach and gives you a roaring diarrhea," he rhapsodized.

"So, feeling as we do," he continued, "it gives us pain to be served such a scrawny thing as Yehave's black ox. It is big, yes, and no doubt its giant bones are good for soup, but fat is what we really crave and so we will eat Christmas this year with a heavy heart."

The prospect of a gloomy Christmas now had me worried, so I asked Tomazo what I could do about it.

"Look for a fat one, a young one . . . smaller, but fat. Fat enough to make us //gom ('evacuate the bowels'), then we will be happy."

My suspicions were aroused when Tomazo said that he happened to know of a young, fat, barren cow that the owner was willing to part with. Was Toma working on commission, I wondered? But I dispelled this unworthy thought when we approached the Herero owner of the cow in question and found that he had decided not to sell.

The scrawny wreck of a Christmas ox now became the talk of the /ai/ai water hole and was the first news told to the outlying groups as they began to come in from the bush for the feast. What finally convinced me that real trouble might be brewing was the visit from u!au, an old conservative with a reputation for fierceness. His nickname meant spear and referred to an incident thirty years ago in which he had speared a man to death. He had an intense manner; fixing me with his eyes, he said in clipped tones:

"I have only just heard about the black ox today, or else I would have come here earlier. /ontah, do you honestly think you can serve meat like that to people and avoid a fight?" He paused, letting the implications sink in. "I don't mean fight you, /ontah; you are a white man. I mean a fight between Bushmen. There are many fierce ones here, and with such a small quantity of meat to distribute, how can you give everybody a fair share? Someone is sure to accuse another of taking too much or hogging all the choice pieces. Then you will see what happens when some go hungry while others eat."

The possibility of at least a serious argument struck me as all too real. I had witnessed the tension that surrounds the distribution of meat from a kudu of gemsbok kill, and had documented many arguments that sprang up from a real or imagined slight in meat distribution. The owners of a kill may spend up to two hours arranging and rearranging the piles of meat under the gaze of a circle of recipients before handing them out. And I also knew that the Christmas feast at /ai/ai would be bringing together groups that had feuded in the past.

Convinced now of the gravity of the situation, I went in earnest to search for a second cow; but all my inquiries failed to turn one up.

The Christmas feast was evidently going to be a disaster, and the incessant complaints about the meagerness of the ox had already taken the fun out of it for me. Moreover, I was getting bored with the wisecracks, and after losing my temper a few times, I resolved to serve the beast anyway. If the meat fell short, the hell with it. In the Bushmen idiom, I announced to all who would listen:

"I am a poor man and blind. If I have chosen one that is too old and too thin, we will eat it anyway and see if there is enough meat there to quiet the rumbling of our stomachs."

On hearing this speech, Ben!a offered me a rare word of comfort. "It's thin," she said philosophically, "but the bones will make a good soup."

At dawn Christmas morning, instinct told me to turn over the butchering and cooking to a friend and take off with Nancy to spend Christmas alone in the bush. But curiosity kept me from retreating. I wanted to see what such a scrawny ox looked like on butchering, and if there *was* going to be a fight, I wanted to catch every word of it. Anthropologists are incurable that way.

The great beast was driven up to our dancing ground, and a shot in the forehead dropped it in its tracks. Then, freshly cut branches were heaped around the fallen carcass to receive the meat. Ten men volunteered to help with the cutting. I asked /gaugo to make the breast bone cut. This cut, which begins the butchering process for most large game, offers easy access for removal of the viscera. But it also allows the hunter to spot-check the amount of fat on the animal. A fat game animal carries a white layer up to an inch thick on the chest, while in a thin one, the knife will quickly cut to bone. All eyes fixed on his hand as /gaugo, dwarfed by the great carcass, knelt to the breast. The first cut opened a pool of solid white in the black skin. The second and third cut widened and deepened the creamy white. Still no bone. It was pure fat; it must have been two inches thick.

"Hey /gau," I burst out, "that ox is loaded with fat. What's this about the ox being too thin to bother eating? Are you out of your mind?"

"Fat?" /gau shot back, "You call that fat? This wreck is thin, sick, dead!" And he broke out laughing. So did everyone else. They rolled on the ground, paralyzed with laughter. Everybody laughed except me; I was thinking.

I ran back to the tent and burst in just as Nancy was getting up. "Hey, the black ox. It's fat as hell! They were kidding about it being too thin to eat. It was a joke or something. A put-on. Everyone is really delighted with it!"

"Some joke," my wife replied. "It was so funny that you were ready to pack up and leave /ai/ai."

If it had indeed been a joke, it had been an extraordinarily convincing one, and tinged, I thought, with more than a touch of malice as many jokes are. Nevertheless, that it was a joke lifted my spirits considerably, and I returned to the butchering site where the shape of the ox was rapidly disappearing under the axes and knives of the butchers. The atmosphere had become festive. Grinning broadly, their arms covered with blood well past the elbow, men packed chunks of meat into the big cast-iron cooking pots, fifty pounds to the load, and muttered and chuckled all the while about the thinness and worthlessness of the animal and /ontah's poor judgment.

We danced and ate that ox two days and two nights; we cooked and distributed fourteen potfuls of meat and no one went home hungry and no fights broke out.

But the "joke" stayed in my mind. I had a growing feeling that something important had happened in my relationship with the Bushmen and that the clue lay in the meaning of the joke. Several days later, when most of the people had dispersed back to the bush camps, I raised the question with Hakekgose, a Tswana man who had grown up among the !Kung, married a !Kung girl, and who probably knew their culture better than any other non-Bushman.

"With us whites," I began, "Christmas is supposed to be the day of friendship and brotherly love. What I can't figure out is why the Bushmen went to such lengths to criticize and belittle the ox I had bought for the feast. The animal was perfectly good and their jokes and wisecracks practically ruined the holiday for me."

"So it really did bother you," said Hakekgose. "Well, that's the way they always talk. When I take my rifle and go hunting with them, if I miss, they laugh at me for the rest of the day. But even if I hit and bring one down, it's no better. To them, the kill is always too small or too old or too thin; and as we sit down on the kill site to cook and eat the liver, they keep grumbling, even with their mouths full of meat. They say things like, 'Oh this is awful! What a worthless animal! Whatever made me think that this Tswana rascal could hunt!' "

"Is this the way outsiders are treated?" I asked.

"No, it is their custom; they talk that way to each other too. Go and ask them."

/gaugo had been one of the most enthusiastic in making me feel bad about the merit of the Christmas ox. I sought him out first.

"Why did you tell me the black ox was worthless, when you could see that it was loaded with fat and meat?"

"It is our way," he said smiling. "We always like to fool people about that. Say there is a Bushman who has been hunting. He must not come home and announce like a braggard, 'I have killed a big one in the bush!' He must first sit down in silence until I or someone else comes up to his fire and asks, 'What did you see today?' He replies quietly, 'Ah, I'm no good for hunting. I saw nothing at all [pause] just a little tiny one.' Then I smile to myself," /gaugo continued, "because I know he has killed something big.

"In the morning we make up a party of four or five people to cut up and carry the meat back to the camp. When we arrive at the kill we examine it and cry out, "You mean to say you have dragged us all the way out here in order to make us cart home your pile of bones? Oh, if I had known it was this thin I wouldn't have come.' Another one pipes up, 'People, to think I gave up a nice day in the shade for this. At home we may be hungry but at least we have nice cool water to drink.'

If the horns are big, someone says, 'Did you think that somehow you were going to boil down the horns for soup?'

"To all this you must respond in kind. 'I agree,' you say, 'this one is not worth the effort; let's just cook the liver for strength and leave the rest for the hyenas. It is not too late to hunt today and even a duiker or a steenbok would be better than this mess.'

"Then you set to work neverthless; butcher the animal, carry the meat back to the camp and everyone eats," /gaugo concluded.

Things were beginning to make sense. Next, I went to Tomazo. He corroborated /gaugo's story of the obligatory insults over a kill and added a few details of his own.

"But," I asked, "why insult a man after he has gone to all that trouble to track and kill an animal and when he is going to share the meat with you so that your children will have something to eat?"

"Arrogance," was his cryptic answer.

"Arrogance?"

"Yes, when a young man kills much meat he comes to think of himself as a chief or a big man, and he thinks of the rest of us as his servants or inferiors. We can't accept this. We refuse one who boasts, for someday his pride will make him kill somebody. So we always speak of his meat as worthless. This way we cool his heart and make him gentle."

"But why didn't you tell me this before?" I asked Tomazo with some heat.

"Because you never asked me," said Tomazo, echoing the refrain that has come to haunt every field ethnographer.

The pieces now fell into place. I had known for a long time that in situations of social conflict with Bushmen I held all the cards. I was the only source of tobacco in a thousand square miles, and I was not incapable of cutting an individual off for noncooperation. Though my boycott never lasted longer than a few days, it was an indication of my strength. People resented my presence at the water hole, yet simultaneously dreaded my leaving. In short I was a perfect target for the charge of arrogance and for the Bushmen tactic of enforcing humility.

I had been taught an object lesson by the Bushmen; it had come from an unexpected corner and had hurt me in a vulnerable area. For the big black ox was to be the one totally generous, unstinting act of my year at /ai/ai, and I was quite unprepared for the reaction I received.

As I read it, their message was this: There are no totally generous acts. All "acts" have an element of calculation. One black ox slaughtered at Christmas does not wipe out a year of careful manipulation of gifts given to serve your own ends. After all, to kill an animal and share the meat with people is really no more than Bushmen do for each other every day and with far less fanfare.

In the end, I had to admire how the Bushmen had played out the farce—collectively straight-faced to the end. Curiously, the episode reminded me of the *Good Soldier Schweik* and his marvelous encounters with authority. Like Schweik the Bushmen had retained a thoroughgoing skepticism of good intentions. Was it this independence of spirit, I wondered, that had kept them culturally viable in the face of generations of contact with more powerful societies, both black and white? The thought that the Bushmen were alive and well in the Kalahari was strangely comforting. Perhaps, armed with that independence and with their superb knowledge of their environment, they might yet survive the future.

■ BAH, HUMBUG!

Marvin Harris

The distinguished anthropologist S. K. Lauss of the University of Thule was in town recently, doing some Christmas shopping. I invited him to the Faculty Club to see what I could learn about his latest Arctic research.

"Apropos of Christmas shopping," he said, "have you ever heard the Eskimo expression: 'Gifts make slaves, just as whips make dogs'?"

"Interesting," I said. "But that can't be an aboriginal proverb. How could they have known about Christmas and Macy's?"

"They didn't," he replied, adding, "they never had to worry about getting whipped by salespeople."

"Or getting crushed by shoppers," I said.

"Right," he declared. "Or the wage slavery of consumerism."

"Or debt slavery to a bank or loan company," I added.

"Precisely, and for the same reason. They had never even heard of Master Charge. Don't forget, people were exchanging gifts thousands of years before Christ, before there was money or prices or interest."

"So they must have been down on gifts for some reason intrinsic to the gift-giving process itself."

"You're beginning to see the light," he said.

Recalling the French anthropologist Marcel Mauss's turn-of-the-century book, *The Gift,* I said, "According to Mauss, there's an inborn human compulsion to reciprocate gifts."

Lauss picked up the thread: "And Levi-Strauss, who was Mauss's star pupil, has been trying to explain everything in terms of what he calls the 'most valuable gift of all—woman.' "

"A stroke of genius," I said. "What Frenchman could resist such a theory. No wonder he's the reigning French intellectual."

"Well, both Mauss and Strauss were wrong," said Lauss. "Gift giving and reciprocity are not the same thing. Gift giving is a form of reciprocity. But there are other ways to reciprocate."

"What do you mean by reciprocity?" I challenged.

"Reciprocity is the most important method of exchanging goods and services in small egalitarian communities, such as those in which the Eskimo live," he began. "Reciprocal exchanges are those in which the parties to the exchange never specify precisely what return is expected or when the return is to take place. When Eskimo reciprocity is at full strength, it looks to the observer as if valuables are merely being shared or taken without any obligation to provide equity or restoration."

Fearing that I was about to be swamped by Lauss's inexhaustible knowledge of Arctic cultures, I interrupted, "Give me an example from some other region."

"Robert Dentan makes the point beautifully for the Semai of Malaya. The Semai give and take portions of slain animals without any overt display of largesse on the part of the giver or of gratitude on the part of the taker. Even to say 'thank you' is a faux pas among the Semai, for it indicates that you are making mental calculations about how much you are getting. This implies that you are the kind of person who thinks it is unusual to be generous. Of course, each hunter eventually reciprocates to the best of his ability. That's reciprocity, but it's not gift giving."

"Thank you," I said.

"Never mind," he retorted. "Take my generosity for granted."

"Okay, how about another example?"

"Richard Lee's description of Bushmen. They're always belittling their own success as hunters. Anyone who starts to call attention to how good he is gets the cold shoulder. When a man brings down an enormous kudu that he can't carry back to camp, he goes home and smokes his pipe for a while. Sooner or later, someone asks him if he had any luck. The hunter then replies that he has caught a small, worthless kudu. So small and worthless that if he were not such a weakling, he would have carried it back to camp. When they hear this, the whole camp goes out to help him because the hunter is asking them to do him the favor of accepting his food. That's reciprocity, not gift giving."

"I can see that," I said." But now, I don't see why you persist in calling it an exchange. It seems all giving away, with nothing coming back."

"On the contrary, there is a definite underlying expectation of some sort of return. One party can continue to take from the other for months or years without embarrassing the taker or annoying the giver. Nevertheless, there are unstated limits beyond which the relationship begins to deteriorate. If the balance gets too far out of line, the freeloader will eventually acquire a reputation as an antisocial deviant. If misfortune strikes the community, he is likely to be the first one accused of practicing witchcraft. No girl will marry him, and the other hunters shun his companionship.

"But there may never be a direct tie-up between this punishment and the unbalanced reciprocity. People prefer to think of such deviants as bewitched, rather than as ungrateful. Under no circumstances will they admit that they owe each other anything simply because one has given something of value to the other."

"Well," I admitted, "you've explained the difference between reciprocity and gift giving. Now tell me why the Eskimo are down on gift giving."

"Get me another frozen daiquiri," said Lauss, "and I'll tell you."

When I returned, Lauss resumed: "Gift giving is a degenerate and historically self-destructive form of reciprocity. On the one hand, in the true spirit of reciprocity, gift giving is not supposed to establish any obligations for exchange. But at the same time, gift giving happens to violate the basic etiquette of reciprocal exchange by calling attention to one's generosity. So, despite assurances that gifts are not meant to be reciprocated, the pressure to reciprocate is much greater than in normal forms of reciprocal exchange. If the gift receiver wants to avoid feeling inferior and protect his reputation in the community, he must exert himself to provide a return gift. So egalitarian peoples are afraid of gifts. Gift giving tends to subvert the relationships based on purer forms of reciprocity. Gifts are like whips because failure to provide a return gift may result in permanently asymmetrical relationships."

Looking at me sharply, Lauss continued, Didn't you yourself recently suggest that social classes evolved out of the increasing centralization of asymmetrical redistributive networks?"

I was about to thank him for reading my latest article when he cut me off with a scowl. "Would you like to hear how my analysis applies to Christmas?" he asked.

"Sure," I said.

"You won't be offended?" he insisted.

"Of course not. I'm not ethnocentric."

"The contradictions of gift giving are nowhere more evident than in your culture at Christmas time. Aside from all the other hazards and penalties of your national lust for consumer goods, gift giving at this time of the year is a terrible threat to one's sanity. Everybody has to pretend that he wants to give away valuable items without expectation of equivalent items or anything at all in return.

"So the first rule of Christmas gift giving is that all price tags and sales slips must be removed from the gifts. This proves that the giver doesn't want the receiver even to think about the possibility of a return gift of equal value. But everybody knows that Christmas shoppers are experts at judging prices. So removal of price tags and sales slips never prevents anybody from accurately guessing the price of the items.

"The next routine requirement of the Christmas shopper," he went on, "is to clearly identify the item as a gift. It must not be confused with ordinary items in reciprocal exchange. This is done in two steps: the item is gift wrapped and the giver puts his name on a card that is tied or glued to the package. Gift wrapping by means of special brightly colored or shiny paper, ribbons and plastic baubles draws attention to the gift, and identifies it as a significant act of generosity. The name card suggests to whom one should be grateful until the act is reciprocated. Remember that when a Semai or a Bushman wants to provide valuables for his campmates, he doesn't begin by making a big fuss over it."

"Yes. Go on," I said, beginning to feel uncomfortable.

"As in true reciprocity, failure to match the value of a Christmas gift for a short time need cause no embarrassment. But a persistent imbalance, either above or below the actual price, will eventually lead to corrective action. Either the party on the high side lowers his desire to give, or the party on the low side raises his. Some of my informants have told me that close relatives and friends attempt to avoid this sort of unpleasantness by calling each other and agreeing beforehand on what kind of present each will give the other. Apparently, they may even indicate brand preferences. These items, however, can scarcely be called gifts, since the mode of exchange is closer to barter than to reciprocity.

"With certain revealing exceptions, persistent failure to reciprocate a Christmas gift will sooner or later result in getting oneself scratched off the gift giver's list. The exceptions are garbage men, janitors, secretaries, and children, all of whom your countrymen would like to treat as slaves, which is precisely what the Eskimo were afraid of."

"Wait a minute, Professor Lauss." I found myself quite agitated. "If you're so down on Christmas gift giving, how come you're in New York to do your Christmas shopping?"

Laying his finger to one side of his nose and winking as he quickly rose from the table, he answered, "I consider all forms of exchange, including reciprocity, inappropriate to the true spirit of Christmas.

"I'm never bothered with the foolishness of exchange because no one can ever find me to give me anything in return. You see, I just like to give things away."

And before I could say what I was going to give him for Christmas, he sprang out the door and into a taxi.

■ HOW TO BUY A HOUSE

Lawrence Durrell

"Last of all came the Greeks and inquired of the Lord for their gift.

" 'What gift would you like?' said the Lord.

" 'We would like the gift of Power,' said the Greeks.

"The Lord replied: 'Ah, my poor Greeks, you have come too late. All the gifts have been distributed. There is practically nothing left. The gift of Power has been given to the Turks, the Bulgarians the gift of Labour; the Jews of Calculation, the French of Trickery and the English of Foolishness.'

"The Greeks waxed very angry at this and shouted 'By what intrigue have we been overlooked?'

" 'Very well,' said the Lord. 'Since you insist, you too shall have a present and not remain empty-handed—may Intrigue be your lot,' said the Lord."

(Bulgarian Folk-tale)

The month or so of spring weather with its promise of summer to follow proved fraudulent. One day we woke to a sky covered in ugly festoons of black cloud and saw drift upon drift of silver needles like arrows falling upon the ramparts of Kyrenia castle. Thunder clamoured and rolled, and the grape-blue semi-darkness of the sea was bitten out in magnesium flashes as the lightning clawed at us from Turkey like a family of dragons. The stone floors turned damp and cold, the gutters brimmed and mumbled all day as they poured a cascade of rain into the street. Below us the sea dashed huge waves across the front where not a week ago we had been sitting in shorts and sandals, drinking coffee and *ouzo,* and making plans for the summer. It was a thrilling change, for one could feel the luxuriant grass fattening under the olives, and the spring flowers unwrapping their delicate petals on the anemone-starred slopes below Clepini.

It was hardly a propitious moment for Sabri to arrive, but arrive he did one black afternoon, wearing as his only protection a spotted handkerchief over his head against the elements. He burst through Panos' front door between thunder-flashes like an apparition from the underworld, gasping: "My dear." His suit was liberally streaked with rain. "I have something for you to see—but *please*" (in anguish almost) "don't blame me if it is not suitable. I haven't seen it myself yet. But it *may* be . . ." He accepted a glass of wine in chilled fingers. "It is in the village of Bellapaix, but too far from the road. Anyway, will you come? I have a taxi. The owner is a rogue of course. I can guarantee *nothing."*

I could see that he was most anxious that I should not judge his professional skill by what might turn out to be a mistake. Together we galloped across the rain-echoing courtyard and down the long flight of stairs by the church to where Jamal and his ancient taxi waited. The handles were off all the doors and there ensued a brief knockabout scene from a Turkish shadow-play among the three of us which finally resulted in our breaking into the vehicle at a weak point in its defences. (Jamal had to crawl through the boot, and half-way through the back seat, in order to unlatch for us.) Then we were off through a landscape blurred with rain and the total absence of windscreen wipers. Jamal drove with his head out of the window for the sake of safety. Outside, the rain-blackened span of mountains glittered fitfully in the lightning-flashes.

Just outside Kyrenia a road turned to the right and led away across a verdant strip of olive and carob land towards the foothills where Bellapaix stood in rain and mist. "Nevertheless," said Sabri thoughtfully, "it is a good day, for nobody will be out of doors. The café will be empty. We won't cause the gossips, my dear." He meant, I suppose, that in any argument over prices the influence of the village wiseacres would seriously affect the owner's views. A sale needed privacy; if the village coffee shop undertook a general debate on a transaction there was no knowing what might happen.

I was prepared for something beautiful, and I already knew that the ruined monastery of Bellapaix was one of the loveliest Gothic survivals in the Levant, but I was not prepared for the breath-taking congruence of the little village which surrounded and cradled it against the side of the mountain. Fronting the last rise, the road begins to wind through a landscape dense with orange and lemon trees, and noisy with running water. Almond and peach-blosom graze the road, as improbably precise as the décor to a Japanese play. The village comes down to the road for the last hundred yards or so with its grey old-fashioned houses with arched vaults and carved doors set in old-fashioned mouldings. Then abruptly one turns through an arc of 150 degrees under the Tree of Idleness and comes to a stop in the main square under the shadow of the Abbey itself. Young cypresses bent back against the sky as they took the wind; the broad flower beds were full of magnificent roses among the almond trees. Yet it all lay deserted in the rain.

The owner of the house was waiting for us in a doorway with a sack over his head. He was a rather dejected-looking man whom I had already noticed maundering about the streets of Kyrenia. He was a cobbler by trade. He did not seem very exuberant—perhaps it was the weather—but almost without a word spoken led us up the boulder-strewn main street, slipping and stumbling amongst the wet stones. Irrigation channels everywhere had burst their banks and Sabri, still clad in his handker-chief, gazed gloomily about him as he picked his way among the compost heaps where the chickens browsed. "It's no good, my dear," he said after we had covered about a hundred yards without arriving at the house. "You could never get up here." But still the guide led on, and curiosity made us follow him. The road had now become very steep indeed and resembled the bed of a torrent; down the centre poured a cascade of water. "My God," groaned Sabri, "it is a trout-stream, my dear." It certainly seemed like one. The three of us crept upwards, walking wherever possible on the facing-stones of the irrigation channel. "I am terribly sorry," said Sabri. "You will have a cold and blame me."

The atmosphere of the village was quite enthralling; its architecture was in the purest peasant tradition—domed Turkish privies in court-yards fanning out from great arched doors with peasant mouldings still bearing the faint traces of a Venetian influence; old Turkish screen-windows for ventilation. It had the purity and authenticity of a Cretan hamlet. And everywhere grew roses, and the pale clouds of almond and peach blossom; on the balconies grew herbs in window-boxes made from old petrol tins; and crowning every courtyard like a messenger from my Indian childhood spread the luxuriant fan of banana-leaves, rattling like parchment in the wind. From behind the closed door of the tavern came the mournful whining of a mandolin.

At the top of the slope where the village vanished and gave place to the scrubby outworks of the mountain behind, stood an old irrigation tank, and here our guide disappeared round a corner, drawing from his breast an iron key the size of a man's forearm. We scrambled after him and came upon the house, a large box-like house in the Turkish-Cypriot mode, with huge carved doors made for some forgotten race of giants and their oxen. "Very arty, my dear," said Sabri, noting the fine old windows with their carved screens, "but what a place"; and then he kicked the wall in an expert way so that the plaster fell off and revealed the mysteries of its construction to his practised eye. "Mud brick with straw." It was obviously most unsatisfactory. "Never mind," I said, stirred by a vague interior premonition which I could not put exactly into words. "Never mind. Let's look now we're here."

The owner swung himself almost off the ground in an effort to turn the great key in the lock which was one of the old pistol-spring type such as one sees sometimes in medieval English houses. We hung on to his shoulders and added our strength to his until it turned screeching in the lock and the great door fell open. We entered, while the owner shot the great bolts which held the other half of the door in position and propped both open with a faggot. Here his interest died, for he stayed religiously by the door, still shrouded in his sack, showing no apparent interest in our reactions. The hall was gloomy and silent—but remarkably dry considering the day. I stood for a while listening to my own heart beating and gazing about me. The four tall double doors were splendid with their old-fashioned panels and the two windows which gave internally on to the hall were fretted with wooden slats of a faintly Turkish design. The whole proportion and disposition of things here was of a thrilling promise; even Sabri glowed at the woodwork which was indeed of splendid make and in good condition.

The floor, which was of earth, was as dry as if tiled. Obviously the walls of the house offered good insulation—but then earth brick usually does if it is laid thickly enough. The wind moaned in the clump of banana trees, and at intervals I could still hear the whimper of the mandolin.

Sabri, who had by now recovered his breath, began to take a more detailed view of things, while I, still obscured by premonitions of a familiarity which I could not articulate, walked to the end of the hall to watch the rain rattling among the pomegranates. The garden was hardly larger than twenty square yards, but crammed with trees standing shoulder to shoulder at such close quarters that their greenery formed an almost unbroken roof. There were too many—some would have to go: I caught myself up with a start. It was early for me to begin behaving like the house's owner. Abstractedly I counted them again: six tangerines, four bitter lemons, two pomegranates, two mulberry trees and a tall leaning walnut. Though there were houses on both sides they were completely hidden by greenery. This part of the village with its steep slope was built up in tiers, balcony upon balcony, with the trees climbing up between. Here and there through the green one caught a glint of the sea, or a corner of the Abbey silhouetted against it.

My reverie was interrupted by a moan and I feared for a moment that Sabri had immolated himself in one of the rooms upon the discovery of some dreadful fact about the woodwork. But no. A heifer was the cause of the noise. It stood, plaintively chewing something in the front room, tethered to a ring in the wall. Sabri clicked his tongue disapprovingly and shut the door. "A bloody cow, my dear," he smiled with all the townsman's indulgence towards the peasant's quirks. "Inside of the house." There were two other rather fine rooms with a connecting door of old workmanship, and a couple of carved cupboards. Then came a landslide. "Don't open it!" shouted the owner and flew to the help of the gallant Sabri who was wrestling with a door behind which apparently struggled some huge animal—a camel perhaps or an elephant? "I forgot to tell you," panted the owner as we all three set our shoulders to the panels. The room was stacked breast-high with grain which had poured out upon Sabri as he opened the door. Together we got it shut but not before the observant Sabri had noticed how dry the grain was in its store. "This place is dry," he panted grudgingly. "So much I can say."

But this was not all; we were about to leave when the owner suddenly recollected that there was more to see and pointed a quavering finger at the ceiling in the manner of Saint John in the icons. "One more room," he said, and we now took a narrow outside staircase where the rain still drizzled, and climbed out upon a balcony where we both stood speechless. The view was indescribable. Below us, the village curved away in diminishing perspective to the green headland upon which the Abbey stood, its fretted head silhouetted against the Taurus range. Through the great arches gleamed the grey-gold fields of cherries and oranges and the delicate spine of Kasaphani's mosque. From this high point we were actually looking down upon Bellapaix, and beyond it, five miles away, upon Kyrenia whose castle looked absurdly like a toy. Even Sabri was somewhat awed by the view. Immediately behind, the mountain climbed into blue space, topped by the ragged outcrop and mouldering turrets of Buffavento. "My God," I said feebly. "What a position."

The balcony itself was simply a flat platform of earth with no balustrade. Up here in one corner of it was a rather lofty and elegant room, built on a bias, and empty of everything save a pair of shoes and a pile of tangerines. We returned to the balcony with its terrific panorama. The storm had begun to lift now and sun was struggling feebly to get out; the whole eastern prospect was suffused with the light which hovers over El Greco's Toledo.

"But the balcony itself," said Sabri with genuine regret, "my dear, it will need concrete." "Why?" He smiled at me. "I must tell you how the peasant house is built—the roof. Come down." We descended the narrow outside stair together, while he produced a notebook and pencil. "First the beams are laid," he said indicating the long series of magnificent beams, and at the same time scribbling in his book. "Then some reed mats. Then packets of osiers to fill the airspace, or perhaps dried seaweed. Then Carmi earth, then gravel. Finally it all leaks and you spend the whole winter trying to stop the leaks."

"But this house doesn't," I said.

"Some do sooner than others."

I pointed to the mason's signature upon the graven iron plaque which adorned the main door. It bore the conventional Orthodox cross embossed on it with the letters IE XR N (Jesus Christ Conquers) and the date 1897. Underneath, on the lower half of the plate, in the space reserved to record subsequent building or alteration was written only one date (9th September 1940), when presumably some restoration work had been undertaken. "Yes, I know, my dear," said Sabri patiently. "But if you buy this house you will have to rebuild the balcony. You are my friend, and so I shall insist for your own good."

We debated this in low tones on the way down the hill. Though the rain had slackened the village street was empty save for the little corner shop, a grocery store, where a thickset young man sat alone, amid sacks of potatoes and dry packets of spaghetti, playing patience on a table. He shouted good afternoon.

In the main square Jamal sat uneasily under the Tree of Idleness beneath an open umbrella, drinking coffee. I was about to engage the owner of the house in discussion as to the sort of price he had in mind for such a fine old relic when Sabri motioned me to silence. The coffee-house was gradually filling up with people and faces were turning curiously towards us. "You will need time to think," he said. "And I have told him you don't want to buy it at all, at any price. This will make the necessary despondence, my dear."

"But I'd like to have an idea of the price."

"My dear, he has no idea *himself*. Perhaps five hundred pounds, perhaps twenty pounds, perhaps ten shillings. He is completely vacant of ideas. In the bargaining everything will get cleared. But we must take time. In Cyprus time is everything."

I rode regretfully down the green winding ways to Kyrenia thinking deeply about the house which seemed more desirable in retrospect than it had in actual fact. Meanwhile Sabri talked to me in knowledgeable fashion about the drawbacks to buying out there. "You simply have not considered such problems," he said, "as water, for example. Have you?"

I had not, and I felt deeply ashamed of the fact. "Give me two days," said Sabri, "and I will find out about the land and water-rights of the property. Then we will ask the man and his wife for the big price-conversation at my office. By God, you will see how tricky we are in Cyprus. And if you buy the house I will send you to a friend of mine to do the rebuilding. He is a rogue, of course, but just the man. I only ask, give me time."

That night when I told Panos that I had seen what might prove to be a suitable house for me at Bellapaix he was delighted, for he had lived there for several years, teaching at the local school. "They are the laziest people in the world," he said, "and the best-natured in Cyprus. And you have honey, and also in the valley behind the house nightingales, my friend."

He did not mention silk, almonds and apricots: oranges, pomegranates, quince . . . . Perhaps he did not wish to influence me too deeply.

Sabri meanwhile retired into silence and contemplation for nearly a week after this; I imagined him sharpening himself for the coming contest of wills by long silent fasts—broken perhaps by a glass of sherbet—or perhaps even prayer for long stretches. The skies turned blue and hard again, and the orange-trees in the Bishopric put out their gleaming suns. The season was lengthening once more into summer, one felt; was stretching itself, the days beginning to unfold more slowly, the twilights to linger. Once more the little harbour filled up with its crowds of chaffering fishermen darning their nets, and of yachtsmen dawdling over caulked seams and a final coat of paint.

Then at last the summons came; I was to present myself at Sabri's office the next morning at eight. Panos brought me the message, smiling at my obvious anxiety, and telling me that Sabri was rather despondent because it now appeared that the house was owned not by the cobbler but by his wife. It had been her dowry, and she herself was going to conduct the sale. "With women," said my friend, "it is always a Calvary to argue. A Golgotha." Nevertheless Sabri had decided to go forward with the business. The intervening space of time had been valuable, however, because he had come into possession of a piece of vital information about the water supply. Water is so scarce in Cyprus that it is sold in parcels. You buy an hour here and an hour there from the owner of a spring—needless to say no quantity measure exists. The trouble lies here: that water-rights form part of property-titles of citizens and are divided up on the death of the owner among his dependants. This is true also of land and indeed of trees. Families being what they are, it is common for a single spring to be owned by upwards of thirty people, or a single tree to be shared out among a dozen members of a family. The whole problem, then, is one of obtaining common consent—usually one has to pay for the signatures of thirty people in order to achieve any agreement which is binding. Otherwise one dissident nephew and niece can veto the whole transaction. In the case of some trees, for example, one man may own the produce of the tree, another the ground on which it stands, a third the actual timber. As may be imagined the most elementary litigation assumes gigantic proportions—which explains why there are so many lawyers in Cyprus.

Now Sabri had got wind of the fact that the Government was planning to install the piped water supply to the village which had been promised for so long; moreover that the plans were already being drawn up. The architect of the Public Works happened to be a friend of his so he casually dropped into his office and asked to see where the various water-points were to be placed. It was a stroke of genius, for he saw with delight that there was to be a public water-point outside the very front door of the old house. This more than offset the gloomy intelligence that the only water the cobbler owned was about an hour a month from the main spring—perhaps sixty gallons: whereas the average water consumption of an ordinary family is about forty gallons a *day*. This was a trump card, for the cobbler's water belonged in equal part to the rest of his wife's family—all eighteen of them, including the idiot boy Pipi whose signature was always difficult to obtain on a legal document . . . .

I found my friend, freshly shaven and spruce, seated in the gloom of his office, surrounded by prams, and absolutely motionless. Before him on the blotter lay the great key of the house, which he poked from time to time in a reproachful way. He put his finger to his lips with a conspiratorial air and motioned me to a chair. "They are all here, my dear," he hissed, "getting ready." He pointed to the café across the road where the cobbler had gathered his family. They looked more like seconds. They sat on a semicircle of chairs, sipping coffee and arguing in low voices; a number of beards waggled, a number of heads nodded. They looked like a rugger scrum in an American film receiving last-minute instructions from their captain. Soon they would fall upon us like a ton of bricks and gouge us. I began to feel rather alarmed. "Now, whatever happens," said Sabri in a low voice, tremulous with emotion, "do not surprise. You must never surprise. And you don't want the house at all, see?"

I repeated the words like a catechism. "I don't want the house. I absolutely don't want the house." Yet in my mind's eye I could see those great doors ("God," Sabri had said, "this is fine wood. From Anatolia. In the old days they floated the great timbers over the water behind boats. This is Anatolian timber, it will last for ever"). Yes, I could see those doors under a glossy coat of blue paint . . . . "I don't want the house," I repeated under my breath, feverishly trying to put myself into the appropriate frame of mind.

"Tell them we are ready," said Sabri to the shadows and a barefooted youth flitted across the road to where our adversaries had gathered. They hummed like bees, and the cobbler's wife detached herself from the circle—or tried to, for many a hand clutched at her frock, detaining her for a last-minute consideration which was hissed at her secretively by the family elders. At last she wrenched herself free and walked boldly across the road, entering Sabri's shrine with a loud "Good morning" spoken very confidently.

She was a formidable old faggot, with a handsome self-indulgent face, and a big erratic body. She wore the white headdress and dark skirt of the village woman, and her breasts were gathered into the traditional baggy bodice with a drawstring at the waist, which made it look like a loosely furled sail. She stood before us looking very composed as she gave us good morning. Sabri cleared his throat, and picking up the great key very delicately between finger and thumb—as if it were of the utmost fragility—put it down again on the edge of the desk nearest her with the air of a conjurer making his opening dispositions. "We are speaking about your house," he said softly, in a voice ever so faintly curdled with menace. "Do you know that all the wood is . . ." he suddenly shouted the last word with such force that I nearly fell off my chair, "rotten!" And picking up the key he banged it down to emphasize the point.

The woman threw up her head with contempt and taking up the key also banged it down in her turn exclaiming: "It is not."

"It *is*." Sabri banged the key.

"It is *not*." She banged it back.

"It *is*." A bang.

"It is *not*." A counter-bang.

All this was not on a very high intellectual level, and made me rather ill at ease. I also feared that the key itself would be banged out of shape so that finally none of us would be able to get into the house. But these were the opening chords, so to speak, the preliminary statement of theme.

The woman now took the key and held it up as if she were swearing by it. "The house is a good house," she cried. Then she put it back on the desk. Sabri took it up thoughtfully, blew into the end of it as if it were a six-shooter, aimed it and peered along it as if along a barrel. Then he put it down and fell into an abstraction. "And suppose we wanted the house," he said, "which we don't, what would you ask for it?"

"Eight hundred pounds."

Sabri gave a long and stagy laugh, wiping away imaginary tears and repeating "Eight hundred pounds" as if it were the best joke in the world. He laughed at me and I laughed at him, a dreadful false laugh. He slapped his knee. I rolled about in my chair as if on the verge of acute gastritis. We laughed until we were exhausted. Then we grew serious again. Sabri was still fresh as a daisy, I could see that. He had put himself into the patient contemplative state of mind of a chess player.

"Take the key and go," he snapped suddenly, and handing it to her, swirled round in his swivel chair to present her with his back; then as suddenly he completed the circuit and swivelled round again. "What!" he said with surprise. "You haven't gone." In truth there had hardly been time for the woman to go. But she was somewhat slow-witted, though obstinate as a mule: that was clear. "Right," she now said in a ringing tone, and picking up the key put it into her bosom and turned about. She walked off stage in a somewhat lingering fashion. "Take no notice," whispered Sabri and busied himself with his papers.

The woman stopped irresolutely outside the shop, and was here joined by her husband who began to talk to her in a low cringing voice, pleading with her. He took her by the sleeve and led her unwillingly back into the shop where we sat pointedly reading letters. "Ah! It's you," said Sabri with well-simulated surprise. "She wishes to discuss some more," explained the cobbler in a weak conciliatory voice. Sabri sighed.

"What is there to speak of? She takes me for a fool." Then he suddenly turned to her and bellowed, "Two hundred pounds and not a piastre more."

It was her turn to have a paroxysm of false laughter, but this was rather spoiled by her husband who started plucking at her sleeve as if he were persuading her to be sensible. Sabri was not slow to notice this. "You tell her," he said to the man. "You are a man and these things are clear to you. She is only a woman and does not see the truth. Tell her what it is worth."

The cobbler, who quite clearly lacked spirit, turned once more to his wife and was about to say something to her, but in a sudden swoop she produced the key and raised it above her head as if she intended to bring it down on his hairless dome. He backed away rapidly. "Fool," she growled. "Can't you see they are making a fool of you? Let me handle this." She made another pass at him with the key and he tiptoed off to join the rest of her relations in the coffee-shop opposite, completely crushed. She now turned to me and extended a wheedling hand, saying in Greek, "Ah come along there, you an Englishman, striking a hard bargain with a woman. . . ." But I had given no indication of speaking Greek so that it was easy to pretend not to understand her. She turned back to Sabri, staring balefully, and banging the key down once more shouted "Six hundred," while Sabri in the same breath bellowed "Two hundred." The noise was deafening.

They panted and glared at each other for a long moment of silence like boxers in a clinch waiting for the referee to part them. It was the perfect moment for Sabri to get in a quick one below the belt. "Anyway, your house is mortgaged," he hissed, and she reeled under the punch. "Sixty pounds and three piastres," he added, screwing the glove a little to try to draw blood. She held her groin as if in very truth he had landed her a blow in it. Sabri followed up swiftly: "I offer you two hundred pounds plus the mortgage."

She let out a yell. "No. Never," and banged the key. "Yes, I say," bellowed Sabri giving a counter-bang. She grabbed the key (by now it had become, as it were, the very symbol of our contention. The house was forgotten. We were trying to buy this old rusty key which looked like something fitter for Saint Peter's key-ring than my own). She grabbed the key, I say, and put it to her breast like a child as she said: "Never in this life." She rocked it back and forth, suckled it, and put it down again.

Sabri now became masterful and put it in his pocket. At this she let out a yell and advanced on him shouting: "You give me back my key and I shall leave you with the curses of all the saints upon you." Sabri stood up like a showman and held the key high above his head, out of her reach, repeating inexorably: "Two hundred. Two hundred. Two hundred." She snapped and strained like a hooked fish, exclaiming all the time: "Saint Catherine defend me. No. No." Then quite suddenly they both stopped, he replaced the key on the desk and sat down, while she subsided like a pan of boiling milk when it is lifted off the fire. "I shall consult," she said briefly in another voice and leaving the key where it was she took herself off across the road to where her seconds waited with towels and sponges. The first round was a draw, though Sabri had made one or two good points.

"What happens now?" I said, and he chuckled. "Just time for a coffee. I think, you know, my dear," he added, "that we will have to pay another hundred. I feel it." He was like a countryman who can tell what the weather will be like from small signs invisible to the ordinary townsman. It was an enthralling spectacle, this long-drawn-out pantomine, and I was now prepared for the negotiations to go on for a week. "They don't know about the water," said Sabri. "They will let us have the house cheap and then try and sting us for the water-rights. We must pretend to forget about the water and buy the house cheaper. Do you see?" I saw the full splendour of his plan as it unfolded before us. "But," he said, "everything must be done today, now, for if she goes back to the village and makes the gossips nothing will be consummated." It seemed to me that she was already making the gossips in the café opposite, for a furious altercation had broken out. She was accusing her husband of something and he was replying waspishly and waving his arms.

After a while Sabri whispered: "Here she comes again," and here she came, rolling along with sails spread and full of the cargo of her misfortunes. She had changed her course. She now gave us a long list of her family troubles, hoping to soften us up; but by now I felt as if my teeth had been sharpened into points. It was clear that she was weakening. It was a matter of time before we could start winding her in. It was, in fact, the psychological moment to let out the line, and this Sabri Tahir now did by offering her another hundred ("a whole hundred," he repeated juicily in a honeyed voice) if she would clinch the deal there and then. "Your husband is a fool," he added, "and your family ignorant. You will never find a buyer if you do not take this gentleman. Look at him. Already he is weakening. He will go elsewhere. Just look at his face." I tried to compose my face in a suitable manner to play my full part in the pantomine. She stared at me in the manner of a hungry peasant assessing a turnip and suddenly sat herself down for the first time, bursting as she did so into heartrending sobs. Sabri was delighted and gave me a wink.

She drew her wimple round her face and went into convulsions, repeating audibly: "O Jesus, what are they doing to me? Destruction has overtaken my house and my line. My issue has been murdered, my good name dragged in the dust." Sabri was in a high good humour by this time. He leaned forward and began to talk to her in the voice of Mephistopheles himself, filling the interstices between her sentences with his insinuations. I could hear him droning on "Mortgage . . . two hundred . . . husband a fool . . . never get such an opportunity." Meanwhile she rocked and moaned like an Arab, thoroughly enjoying herself. From time to time she cast a furtive glance at our faces to see how we were taking it; she could not have drawn much consolation from Sabri's for he was full of a triumphant concentration now; in the looming shadows he reminded me of some great killer shark—the flash of a white belly as it turned over on its back to take her. "We have not spoken of the water as yet," he said, and among her diminishing sobs she was still able to gasp out, "That will be another hundred."

"We are speaking only of the house," insisted Sabri, and at this a look of cunning came over her face. "Afterwards we will speak of the water." The tone in which he said this indicated subtly that he had now moved over on to her side. The foreigner, who spoke no Greek, could not possibly understand that without water-rights the house itself was useless. She shot a glance at me and then looked back at him, the look of cunning being replaced by a look almost of triumph. Had Sabri, in fact changed sides? Was he perhaps also planning to make a killing, and once the house was bought . . . . She smiled now and stopped sobbing.

"All this can only be done immediately," said Sabri quietly. "Look. We will go to the widow and get the mortgage paper. We will pay her mortgage before you at the Land Registry. Then we will pay you before witnesses for the house." Then he added in a low voice: "After that the gentleman will discuss the water. Have you the papers?"

We were moving rather too swiftly for her. Conflicting feelings beset her; ignorance and doubt flitted across her face. An occasional involuntary sob shook her—like pre-ignition in an overheated engine which has already been switched off. "My grandfather has the title-deeds."

"Get them," said Sabri curtly.

She rose, still deeply preoccupied, and went back across the street where a furious argument broke out among her seconds. The white-bearded old man waved a stick and perorated. Her husband spread his hands and waggled them. Sabri watched all this with a critical eye. "There is only one danger—she must not get back to the village." How right he was; for if her relations could make all this noise about the deed of sale, what could the village coffee-shop not do? Such little concentration as she could muster would be totally scattered by conflicting counsels. The whole thing would probably end in a riot followed by an island-wide strike . . . .

I gazed admiringly at my friend. What a diplomat he would make! "Here she comes again," he said in a low voice, and here she came to place the roll of title-deeds on the table beside the key. Sabri did not look at them. "Have you discussed?" he said sternly. She groaned. "My grandfather will not let me do it. He says you are making a fool of me." Sabri snorted wildly.

"Is the house yours?"

"Yes, sir."

"Do you want the money?"

"Yes."

"Do you want it today?"

"Yes."

My friend leaned back in his chair and gazed up at the cobwebs in the roof. "Think of it," he said, his voice full of the poetry of commerce. "This gentleman will cut you a chekky. You will go to the Bank. There open the safe. . . ." His voice trembled and she gazed thirstily at him, entranced by the story-book voice he had put on. "They will take from it notes, thick notes, as thick as a honeycomb, as thick as salami" (here they both involuntarily licked their lips and I myself began to feel hungry at the thought of so much edible money). "One . . . two . . . three," counted Sabri in his mesmeric voice full of animal magnetism. "Twenty . . . sixty . . . a hundred" gradually getting louder and louder until he ended at "three hundred." Throughout this recital she behaved like a chicken with her beak upon a chalk line. As he ended she gave a sigh of rapture and shook herself, as if to throw off the spell. "The mortgage will have been paid. The widow Anthi will be full of joy and respect for you. You and your husband will have *three hundred pounds.*" He blew out his breath and mopped his head with a red handkerchief. "All you have to do is to agree. Or take your key."

He handed her the key and once more swivelled round, to remain facing the wall for a full ten seconds before completing the circle.

"Well?" he said. She was hovering on the edge of tears again. "And my grandfather?" she asked tremulously. Sabri spread his hands. "What can I do about your grandfather? Bury him?" he asked indignantly. "But act quickly, for the gentleman is going." At a signal from him I rose and stretched and said, "Well I think I . . ." like the curate in the Leacock story.

"Quick. Quick. Speak or he will be gone," said Sabri. A look of intense agony came over her face. "O Saint Matthew and Saint Luke," she exclaimed aloud, tortured beyond endurance by her doubts. It seemed a queer moment to take refuge in her religion, but obviously the decision weighed heavily upon her. "O Luke, O Mark," she rasped, with one hand extended towards me to prevent me from leaving.

Sabri was now like a great psychologist who divines that a difficult transference is at hand. "She will come," he whispered to me, and putting his fingers to his mouth blew a shrill blast which alerted everybody. At once with a rumble Jamal, who had apparently been lurking down a side street in his car, grated to the door in a cloud of dust. "Lay hold of her," Sabri said and grabbed the woman by the left elbow. Following instructions I grabbed the other arm. She did not actually resist but she definitely rested on her oars and it was something of an effort to roll her across the floor to the taxi. Apparently speed was necessary in this *coup de main* for he shouted: "Get her inside" and put his shoulder to her back as we propelled her into the back of the car and climbed in on top of her.

She now began to moan and scream as if she were being abducted—doubtless for the benefit of the grandfather—and to make dumb appeals for help through the windows. Her supporters poured out into the road, headed by a nonagenarian waving a plate and her husband who also seemed in tears. "Stop." "You can't do that," they cried, alerting the whole street. Two children screamed: "They are taking Mummy away," and burst into tears.

"Don't pay any attention," said Sabri now, looking like Napoleon on the eve of Wagram, "Drive, Jamal, drive." We set off with a roar, scattering pedestrians who were making their way to the scene of the drama, convinced perhaps that a shot-gun wedding was in progress. "Where are we going?" I said.

"Lapithos—the widow Anthi," said Sabri curtly. "Drive, Jamal, drive."

As we turned the corner I noticed with horror that the cobbler and his family had stopped another taxi and were piling into it with every intention of following us. The whole thing was turning into a film sequence. "Don't worry," said Sabri, "the second taxi is Jamal's brother and he will have a puncture. I have thought of everything."

In the brilliant sunshine we rumbled down the Lapithos road. The woman looked about her with interest, pointing out familiar landmarks with great good-humour. She had completely recovered her composure now and smiled upon us both. It was obviously some time since she had had a car-ride and she enjoyed every moment of it.

We burst into the house of the widow Anthi like a bomb and demanded the mortgage papers; but the widow herself was out and they were locked in a cupboard. More drama. Finally Sabri and the cobbler's wife forced the door of the cupboard with a flat-iron and we straggled back into the sunshine and climbed aboard again. There was no sign of the second taxi as we set off among the fragrant lemon-groves towards Kyrenia, but we soon came upon them all clustered about a derelict taxi with a puncture. A huge shout went up as they saw us, and some attempt was made to block the road but Jamal, who had entered into the spirit of the thing, now increased speed and we bore down upon them. I was alarmed about the safety of the grandfather, for he stood in the middle of the road waving his stick until the very last moment, and I feared he would not jump out of the way in time. I closed my eyes and breathed deeply through my nose: so did Sabri, for Jamal had only one eye and was unused to speeds greater than twenty miles an hour. But all was well. The old man must have been fairly spry for when I turned round to look out of the back window of the car I saw him spread-eagled in the ditch, but quite all right if one could judge by the language he was using.

The clerks in the Registry Office were a bit shaken by our appearance for by this time the cobbler's wife had decided to start crying again. I cannot for the life of me imagine why—there was nobody left to impress; perhaps she wanted to extract every ounce of drama from the situation. Then we found she could not write—Grandfather was the only one who could write, and she must wait for him. "My God, if he comes, all is lost again, my dear," said Sabri. We had to forcibly secure her thumbprint to the article of sale, which sounds easy, but in fact ended by us all being liberally coated with fingerprint ink.

She only subsided into normality when the ratified papers were handed to Sabri; and when I made out her cheque she positively beamed and somewhat to my surprise insisted on shaking hands with me, saying as she did so, "You are a good man, may you be blessed in the house."

It was in the most amiable manner that the three of us now sauntered out into the sunlight under the pepper trees. On the main road a dusty taxi had drawn up and was steadily disgorging the disgruntled remains of the defeated army. Catching sight of her they shouted vociferously and advanced in open order, waving sticks and gesticulating. The cobbler's wife gave a shriek and fell into her grandfather's arms, sobbing as if overtaken by irremediable tragedy. The old man, somewhat tousled by his expedition, and with grass in his eyebrows, growled protectively at her and thundered: "Have you done it?" She sobbed louder and nodded, as if overcome. The air was rent with execrations, but Sabri was quite unmoved. All this was purely gratuitous drama and could be taken lightly. With an expressive gesture he ordered Coca-Cola all round which a small boy brought from a barrow. This had the double effect of soothing them and at the same time standing as a symbolic drink upon the closing of a bargain—shrewdly calculated as were all his strokes. They cursed us weakly as they seized the bottles but they drank thirstily. Indeed the drive to Lapithos is a somewhat dusty one.

"Anyway," said the cobbler at last when they had all simmered down a bit, "we still have the water-rights. We have not yet discussed those with the gentleman." But the gentleman was feeling somewhat exhausted by now, and replete with all the new sensations of ownership. I possessed a house! Sabri nodded quietly. "Later on," he said, waving an expressive hand to Jamal, who was also drinking a well-earned Coca-Cola under a pepper tree. "Now we will rest." The family now saw us off with the greatest good humour, as if I were a bridegroom, leaning into the taxi to shake my hand and mutter blessings. "It was a canonical price," said the old greybeard, as a parting blessing. One could not say fairer than that.

■ HOW WOULD YOU LIKE TO BE A PEASANT?

Joseph Lopreato

By 1957, when migration from the south had already become quite voluminous, per capita yearly income in south Italy as a whole was about $200, compared to around $500 in the north.[1] It is easy to guess, furthermore, that the income of the southern peasants themselves was considerably lower than the southern average.

The general life conditions of the southern peasant are truly penurious. After a decade of miraculous economic boom in his nation, many a peasant's home is still a one-or-two-room hovel which he shares with his wife and three or four children, and very often with a donkey, a goat, or a pig. But the whims of history and terrain have also decreed that his hovel be often located in a village built high upon a hill. Not infrequently, therefore, the peasant spends several hours a day walking to and from his place of work loaded with his ancient hoe, a water receptacle, and a lunch bag consisting at best of bread, a piece of cheese, an onion, some olives, and dried fuit. When he arrives on the land, his body, already weakened by burden, disease, and starvation, is gravely fatigued by the interminable march in the mud or the dust. If by a supreme act of will and pride he succeeds in accomplishing a little work, too often it comes to nought.

After paying an exorbitant share to his landlord and losing much of

[1] Franco Angeli (ed.), *La Calabria*, Centro di Analisi di Opinione Pubblica e Mercato, Milano, 1958, p. 15.

his produce to thieves, birds, diseases, landslides, or drought, the peasant usually manages to store enough grain, fruit, or beans to keep him and his family barely alive until early spring, months before the new harvest. At such time, then, he is very frequently compelled to incur debts which keep him in continuous bondage. Writing about Butera, a Sicilian community of about 10,000 population, Sciortino Gugino has fittingly said:

> Woe to those who find it necessary to be in debt, be it with private persons or with banks. From then on the family has lost its peace. With banks, when all is counted, the interest rate amounts to 13 percent; very rarely, however, is a peasant judged a good risk by the director of the local bank. With usurers, interest rates are always higher than 20 percent and often reach 50 percent for a six-month loan or even for a two-month period in the spring.[2]

This state of chronic insolvency often induces the peasant to purchase a donkey, a goat, a pig, or sometimes even one or two calves. In his desperate estimate, the profit on the future sale of any of these may, and indeed sometimes does, permit him to make ends meet at the end of the year. But all too often the ends do not meet. Here is an actual case, admittedly extreme but in its basic elements not at all rare. In December 1962, a Calabrian sharecropper convinces his landlord to buy a calf at the cost of about $116. Four months later, in April 1963, the calf is sold for about $158. Total gross profit: $42. Sharecropper's share: $21. Daily gross profit: $116. Major expenses: hay and straw for a total market value of $10. The labor factor: inestimable. Suffice it to say that in order to be kept fed and safe from thieves, the calf required constant attention, whether it was on a Sunday, on Christmas, or Easter. Total net profit? In the colorful words of the peasant himself: "the hen's udders." And this was that peasant's way of accepting a familiar economic loss.

But things are not always so bad. There are times when, after a few months' assiduous care, a peasant clears a net profit of $60–80, and there are years when nature is generous, and he brings in a fair harvest. Assuming now that he has no rapidly multiplying debts to be paid, there is always a daughter to marry off, a lawyer to counsel with, an illness to be cured, or a funeral to pay. It is no accident that the peasant is an inveterate pessimist. Ask him, in a good year, "how is the harvest?" And the answer is likely to be: "poor." Ask the healthiest one about his health, and the answer is almost surely, "not very good." To answer otherwise would amount to disturbing that precarious and mysterious equilibrium that sometimes yields a moment of peace, or even to inviting the *iettatura* (evil eye.)

Rare is the peasant family in which there is not at least one member who does not suffer from illness. If it is not heart disease, it is a liver condition; if not anemia, it is kidney trouble; if not the eyes, then the

2 Carola Sciortino Gugino in U. Manfredi Editore, *Coscienza Collettiva e Giudizio Individuale nella Cultura Contadina,* Palermo, 1960, p. 44.

teeth; if it is not arthritis, it is hernia. Despite a relative abundance of medical doctors in south Italy, these disorders have a peculiar way of being persistent.

> Our ills are ours for the tomb

said an Abruzzese peasant recently.

The peasant's sickness is understandably a source of constant worry for him—and for more reasons than one. Given as he is to occasional arduous labor, not infrequently he breaks a bone or suffers a heart attack. At such times as these he has urgent need of medical care. Each town has a medical doctor appointed by the High Commissioner for Health, but all too often the doctor is nowhere to be found. His residence may be in another town, several miles away, where he may also have a private practice. Or he may travel daily to his native town many miles away to visit his parents or to eat his mother's food. Thus it is that when he finally returns to his official place of work, sometimes late at night, he often finds someone who asks him to write a death certificate, and a large number of suffering patients who have been waiting many hours for him. As a Roman doctor who knows this situation said recently in a personal conversation,

> then prescriptions for patent medicines start flying.

By then it may happen, however, that the pharmacies nearby are closed —legally or otherwise—and there is nothing that the peasant can do short of cursing under his breath against his God, his ill fate, his fellow-men, and his *Miseria*. Or in the hours of resigned and meditative protest, he may merely create a stanza such as the following:

> L'inferno è pieno
> di notari e giudici,
> uomini approbi (sic),
> speziali e medici.

> (Hell is full
> of notaries and judges,
> upright men,
> druggists, and doctors.)

A 1952 DOXA survey of Italian *braccianti* (farm hands) found that 68 percent of these workers were unhappy (*malcontenti*) of "their actual life conditions." No doubt, the percentage of unhappy southern *braccianti* was a great deal higher. The reasons given for their dissatisfaction were:

> little work, irregular work, little money, high prices, hunger, and other economic reasons and various difficulties.[3]

[3] Luzzato-Fegiz, *op. cit.*, p. 1018, Table 2.

These are largely economic expressions, and they are crucial. Nevertheless, depth interviewing by this writer and other students of south
Italian peasantry reveals additional important factors of another kind.[4]

INTERPERSONAL RELATIONS

The precariousness of the peasant's economy give rise to certain other
conditions that keep him in a constant state of insecurity, fear, distrust,
animosity, and conflict with his fellowmen. His life is in continual
anguish. A Calabrian peasant, who returned from Canada to visit his
parents and to satisfy his nostalgia for his birthplace, explained a few
years ago:

> The village is too small a world to live in. It is impossible to breathe freely
> in it. It is dirty; you must always hide something or from some one; every
> one lies about everything: wealth, eating, friendship, love, God. You are
> always under the eyes of someone who scrutinizes you, judges you, envies you,
> spies on you, throws curses against you, but smiles his ugly, toothless mouth
> out whenever he see you.

Suspicion of one's fellowmen is rampant in south Italian peasantry.
In its purest state it reveals in the peasant an individual engaged in a
one-man's war against all others. The nuclear family itself is not free
from intense internal conflict.[5] Basically this arises because an economy
of dire scarcity encourages instrumental relations based on domination-
submission terms within the family nucleus, and as a consequence, re-
sentment and hostility. Children are needed to "pitch in." Each of them
is an instrument of production and subsistence, and his energies are often
utilized to the maximum. The suffering child is quick in attributing
fault to his elders, and the positively affective aspect of family relations
is weakened. Thus it is that by the age of ten, many a south Italian child
has learned to bear a constant grudge against his father and his older
brothers who command him and reflect their animus for their father on
him. Communication is minimal, and then it is usually initiated by the
older person in the form of a dry, abrupt command to do something. On

[4] See for instance, Joseph Lopreato, "Social Stratification and Mobility in a South Italian
Town," *American Sociological Review*, XXVI (August, 1961), 585–596; "Interpersonal
Relations in Peasant Society: The Peasant's View," *Human Organization*, XXI (Spring,
1962), 21–24; "Alienazione nella Società e nella Comunità" (forthcoming), Istituto di
Statistica, Università di Roma. See also, Edward C. Banfield, *The Moral Basis of a Backward Society*, The Free Press, New York, 1958; Johan Galtung, "Componenti Psico-Sociali
nella Decisione di Emigrare" in Autori Vari (ed.), *op. cit.*, pp. 429–435; Carola Sciortino
Gugino, *op. cit.;* Guido Vincelli, *Una Comunità Meridionale*, Casa Editrice Taylor,
Torino, 1958.
[5] In his study of Montegrano, Banfield, *op. cit.*, has vividly discussed conflict in interpersonal relations, but he has failed to observe such conflict within the context of the
nuclear family itself.

those rare occasions in which the son addresses his father, he frequently does so in timid and formal language. When they return home from the fields, they often walk several yards apart. Their eyes hardly ever meet. They consume their evening meal in silence.

At home the father is considered a tyrant, frightful and ready to explode at the least provocation. It must be difficult to love such a person, to admire him, to feel friendly toward him. It is even difficult to talk with him. Is it then a surprise when we hear the lady of the home, who has just finished preparing the supper, call out curtly to her husband who has been waiting for it:

Don't you come to eat? What are you waiting for?

This statement comes at the end of an imagined but failed altercation in which she has vindicated her right to annul his arbitrary and afflicting authority. In her spiteful conclusion she seems to be saying:

It is ready, Mr. Belly. Come and choke on it!

On this topic of interpersonal hostility, an elderly and wise peasant recently explained to me:

Where there are hunger, grief, and uncertainty you can be sure that there is also carnage (*carneficina*) and not just among strangers, but also among friends and relatives. And mind you: things are getting worse. The young people are getting proud, demanding, and impatient. They get angry quickly and fall out with any one. In my youth I never heard of any one who killed his own father or brother with an axe. You would club a neighbor, alright. Today such cases happen frequently. We hear about them every day. . . . Nowadays everyone is every one else's enemy. In this village I could count on the fingers of one hand the young people who have not had a serious quarrel with their brothers or parents. It's frightful!

Whether in the family or in the community, interpersonal relations in peasant south Italy are stressful. It is not difficult to imagine why. In the last analysis stress and conflict in peasant society are rooted in the constant precariousness of its traditional economy.[6] In such economy, while the past evokes memories of painful hardships and the present is a tense and uncertain struggle for survival, the future constitutes a threat of hunger, sickness, humiliations, and futile toil. Under these circumstances, the peasant, like any other man, is *homo homini lupus*. He is constantly on guard against possible impingements on his meager share of the local "economic pie" and at the same time maneuvering against all but his own dependents to enlarge his own share so as to achieve a higher

[6] George M. Foster, "Interpersonal Relations in Peasant Society," *Human Organization*, XIX (Winter, 1960–1961), 174–178.

degree of comfort and security. It is such facts as these which explain such widely diffused maxims as:

> Do not trust even your brother, Friends with all, loyal with no one, Even your best friend is a traitor.

It may be objected that stress and conflict do not arise only in economically insecure societies, and they do not always arise here. What distinguishes the peasant economy from other types of economy at the present time is its rapidly changing nature. Whether it be in south Italy or in South America, in Africa or in Asia, strong winds of transformation are blowing. But the ensuing economic improvement is not equally distributed. It follows that the traditional power and prestige structures are disturbed, resulting in an intensification of the pre-existing, economically-derived and possibly latent, conflict.[7]

Indeed, the peasant is so insecure about his economy, and so accustomed to the idea of an inalterable partition of the economic pie, that he may negate even personal improvement in absolute terms. And it is understandable. From the perspective of the observer, it is not difficult to envision a future state of affairs in peasant society in which the traditional pie has been vastly enlarged to provide for each person a much larger share than he ever had in the past. But the traditional peasant himself can see the future only from the perspective of the past, and from here, any changes, any differential improvements are likely to suggest to him a diminution of his own share of the pie, unless they be clearly advantageous to him. The struggle for survival is accentuated, and with it, of course, stress, animosity, conflict.

The peasant's life, already burdened by hunger, ill health, hard labor, and insecurity becomes unbearably tiring and equally menacing. It is like living at the foot of a volcano that has been threatening to erupt. At his first chance, the peasant packs up his rags and leaves—he emigrates.

THE PRESTIGE STRUCTURE

Still another powerful set of circumstances, closely related to the above, induces the peasant to abandon his land.

> *Chi non ha non é* (He who has not is not)

states a Calabrian proverb. The peasant's economic poverty is translated into social insignificance, subordination, contemptibility. As sharecropper or farm hand, he is completely dependent on the capital of others for his minimal livelihood. Even as petty owner he disposes of little capital with which to exercise influence over any beyond his own family de-

[7] Joseph Lopreato, "Interpersonal Relations in Peasant Society: The Peasant's View," *op. cit.*, 24.

pendents. Lacking the support and the leadership to organize a protest, the traditional peasant seeks to insure his continued subsistence by practicing an abject servility. But such social response becomes the focus of general derision at his expense.

Again, his work conditions and habits are such that he is hardly ever present in the village, which is the center of social life and political affairs. It ironically happens, then, that in a village where peasants constitute as much as 90 percent of the total population, they are in fact a vast minority excluded from public participation. Furthermore, the peasant has little or no schooling; consequently, in "a country of the thousand foreign languages," he lacks the speech refinements of the most foreign, but most prestigeful, of them all: the mother language. Finally, in a society which has recently raised fashion to a national institution he lacks the most manifest of all symbols of social importance, correct dress. All this and the cruel fate of centuries of suffering stamped clearly on his face and on his back, render him clearly identifiable from a distance, and reduce him nearly to the level of an untouchable. And so it may happen that a young high-school student, proud of his talcum powder and hair tonic, prefers to walk two or three miles to a nearby town rather than taking a bus

crowded with fetid *contadini*.

In her study of the prestige structure of Butera, Sciortino Gugino observes that peasants

continue to make up the lowest stratum.

Nonfarming workers treat them with contempt; *pedi 'ncritati* (muddy feet) is their nickname. The peasant is credited with feeding everybody, and yet he is everybody's laughing-stock.

Viddanu si e di viddanu ti trattu. (You are a rustic, and as such I treat you.)[8]

It is no surprise that already in 1948, according to a DOXA national survey, only 14 percent of Italian parents wished their male children to become agricultural workers; yet the actual percentage of such workers was no less than 48.[9] And when in another such survey carried out in 1950 the respondents were divided by the four regional categories of North, Center, South, and Islands (Sardinia and Sicily), the percentages were respectively 25, 12, 8, and 19.[10] The people of the industrial north were more favorably disposed toward the agricultural way of life than the people of the agricultural south!

[8] *Ibid.,* 51.
[9] Luzzato Fegiz, *op. cit.,* p. 1037.
[10] *Ibid.,* p. 1050, Table 1.6.

In a nation where it is generally recognized that

ci vuole la raccomandazione per poter vivere (you need pull to be able to live),

the poor and unpolished peasant's life chances are very low indeed. In the shops, at the market place, in the hospital, in the army, in court, in church, in the post office, everywhere but in his own smoky and malodorous hut, the peasant is either neglected or altogether ridiculed and humiliated.

In the spring of 1963, for instance, I was at the post office of a southern market town to buy some stamps. Among the thick crowd of waiting clients there was a visibly exhausted peasant woman who had most likely left her little village at sunrise that morning to come to sell her score of eggs at the market. One by one, many fellow customers passed her by, oftentimes by their own initiative, sometimes because invited to do so by the postal clerk. When she could tolerate it no longer, she whispered to the clerk in a meek tone that could have aroused general shame and compassion:

Be charitable. I have been waiting an hour.

She must have wished she had never spoken! The clerk's immediate, violent reaction was to order her to hold her tongue until he would be ready to listen to her. Then he had a clever afterthought.

But what do you wish? [he jested] An express stamp [she begged]. But why, my good woman? Can you write?

That question was indeed clever. It had the effect of a clown act in a children's circus; the spectators exploded in laughter. One of them, who until then had been merrily conversing with the clerk at the nearby window about the exploits of an Italian soccer team, appeared to be one of the local police authority. He could not help but volunteer a bit of his own wisdom for the occasion:

And what do *you* know about the difficulty of dealing with these blessed peasants?

The tired and outraged lady retreated without the stamp and with the only form of protest open to her. In picking up her wicker basket from the floor, she exclaimed:

May you die with rabies, arrogant cowards!

Given her lowly social position, the whole thing ended there, for all but herself. When she returned home that day and heard her young son mention the possibility of going to seek work in Milan or Toronto, it is very likely that she did not discourage him.

■ THE CULTURE OF POVERTY

Oscar Lewis

Poverty and the so-called war against it provide a principal theme for the domestic program of the present Administration. In the midst of a population that enjoys unexampled material well-being—with the average annual family income exceeding $7000—it is officially acknowledged that some 18 million families, numbering more than 50 million individuals, live below the $3,000 "poverty line." Toward the improvement of the lot of these people some $1,600 million of Federal funds are directly allocated through the Office of Economic Opportunity, and many hundreds of millions of additional dollars flow indirectly through expanded Federal expenditures in the fields of health, education, welfare and urban affairs.

Along with the increase in activity on behalf of the poor indicated by these figures there has come a parallel expansion of publication in the social sciences on the subject of poverty. The new writings advance the same two opposed evaluations of the poor that are to be found in literature, in proverbs and in popular sayings throughout recorded history. Just as the poor have been pronounced blessed, virtuous, upright, serene, independent, honest, kind and happy, so contemporary students stress their great and neglected capacity for self-help, leadership and community organization. Conversely, as the poor have been characterized as shiftless, mean, sordid, violent, evil and criminal, so other students point to the irreversibly destructive effects of poverty on individual character and emphasize the corresponding need to keep guidance and control of poverty projects in the hands of duly constituted authorities. This clash of viewpoints reflects in part the infighting for political control of the program between Federal and local officials. The confusion results also from the tendency to focus study and attention on the personality of the individual victim of poverty rather than on the slum community and family and from the consequent failure to distinguish between poverty and what I have called the culture of poverty.

The phrase is a catchy one and is used and misused with some frequency in the current literature. In my writings it is the label for a specific conceptual model that describes in positive terms a subculture of Western society with its own structure and rationale, a way of life handed on from generation to generation along family lines. The culture of poverty is not just a matter of deprivation or disorganization, a term signifying the absence of something. It is a culture in the traditional anthropological sense in that it provides human beings with a design for living, with a ready-made set of solutions for human problems, and so serves a significant adaptive function. This style of life transcends national boundaries and regional and rural-urban differences within nations. Wherever it occurs, its practitioners exhibit remarkable similarity in the structure of their families, in interpersonal relations, in spending habits, in their value systems and in their orientation in time.

Not nearly enough is known about this important complex of human behavior. My own concept of it has evolved as my work has progressed and remains subject to amendment by my own further work and that of others. The scarcity of literature on the culture of poverty is a measure of the gap in communication that exists between the very poor and the middle-class personnel—social scientists, social workers, teachers, physicians, priests and others—who bear the major responsibility for carrying out the antipoverty programs. Much of the behavior accepted in the culture of poverty goes counter to cherished ideals of the larger society. In writing about "multiproblem" families social scientists thus often stress their instability, their lack of order, direction and organization. Yet, as I have observed them, their behavior seems clearly patterned and reasonably predictable. I am more often struck by the inexorable repetitiousness and the iron entrenchment of their lifeways.

The concept of the culture of poverty may help to correct misapprehensions that have ascribed some behavior patterns of ethnic, national or regional groups as distinctive characteristics. For example, a high incidence of commonlaw marriage and of households headed by women has been thought to be distinctive of Negro family life in this country and has been attributed to the Negro's historical experience of slavery. In actuality it turns out that such households express essential traits of the culture of poverty and are found among diverse peoples in many parts of the world and among peoples that have had no history of slavery. Although it is now possible to assert such generalizations, there is still much to be learned about this difficult and affecting subject. The absence of intensive anthropological studies of poor families in a wide variety of national contexts—particularly the lack of such studies in socialist countries—remains a serious handicap to the formulation of dependable cross-cultural constants of the culture of poverty.

My studies of poverty and family life have centered largely in Mexico. On occasion some of my Mexican friends have suggested delicately that I turn to a study of poverty in my own country. As a first step in this direction I am currently engaged in a study of Puerto Rican families. Over the past three years my staff and I have been assembling data on 100 representative families in four slums of Greater San Juan and some 50 families of their relatives in New York City.

Our methods combine the traditional techniques of sociology, anthropology and psychology. This includes a battery of 19 questionnaires, the administration of which requires 12 hours per informant. They cover the residence and employment history of each adult; family relations; income and expenditure; complete inventory of household and personal possessions; friendship patterns, particularly the *compadrazgo*, or god-parent, relationship that serves as a kind of informal social security for the children of these families and establishes special obligations among the adults; recreational patterns; health and medical history; politics; religion; world view and "cosmopolitanism." Open-end interviews and psychological tests (such as the thematic apperception test, the Rorschach test and the sentence-completion test) are administered to a sampling of this population.

All this work serves to establish the context for close-range study of a selected few families. Because the family is a small social system, it lends itself to the holistic approach of anthropology. Whole-family studies bridge the gap between the conceptual extremes of the culture at one pole and of the individual at the other, making possible observation of both culture and personality as they are interrelated in real life. In a large metropolis such as San Juan or New York the family is the natural unit of study.

Ideally our objective is the naturalistic observation of the life of "our" families, with a minimum of intervention. Such intensive study, however, necessarily involves the establishment of deep personal ties. My assistants include two Mexicans whose families I had studied; their "Mexican's-eye view" of the Puerto Rican slum has helped to point up the similarities and differences between the Mexican and Puerto Rican subcultures. We have spent many hours attending family parties, wakes and baptisms, responding to emergency calls, taking people to the hospital, getting them out of jail, filling out applications for them, hunting apartments with them, helping them to get jobs or to get on relief. With each member of these families we conduct tape-recorded interviews, taking down their life stories and their answers to questions on a wide variety of topics. For the ordering of our material we undertake to reconstruct, by close interrogation, the history of a week or more of consecutive days in the lives of each family, and we observe and record complete days as they unfold. The first volume to issue from this study is to be published next month under the title of *La Vida, A Puerto Rican Family in the Culture of Poverty—San Juan and New York* (Random House).

There are many poor people in the world. Indeed, the poverty of the two-thirds of the world's population who live in the underdeveloped countries has been rightly called "the problem of problems." But not all of them by any means live in the culture of poverty. For this way of life to come into being and flourish it seems clear that certain preconditions must be met.

The setting is a cash economy, with wage labor and production for profit and with a persistently high rate of unemployment and underemployment, at low wages, for unskilled labor. The society fails to provide social, political and economic organization, on either a voluntary basis or by government imposition, for the low-income population. There is a bilateral kinship system centered on the nuclear progenitive family, as distinguished from the unilateral extended kinship system of lineage and clan. The dominant class asserts a set of values that prizes thrift and the accumulation of wealth and property, stresses the possibility of upward mobility and explains low economic status as the result of individual personal inadequacy and inferiority.

Where these conditions prevail the way of life that develops among some of the poor is the culture of poverty. That is why I have described it as a subculture of the Western social order. It is both an adaptation and a reaction of the poor to their marginal position in a class-stratified, highly individuated, capitalistic society. It represents an effort to cope with feelings of hopelessness and despair that arise from the realization by the members of the marginal communities in these societies of the improbability of their achieving success in terms of the prevailing values and goals. Many of the traits of the culture of poverty can be viewed as local spontaneous attempts to meet needs not served in the case of the poor by the institutions and agencies of the larger society because the poor are not eligible for such service, cannot afford it or are ignorant and suspicious.

Once the culture of poverty has come into existence it tends to perpetuate itself. By the time slum children are six or seven they have usually absorbed the basic attitudes and values of their subculture. Thereafter they are psychologically unready to take full advantage of changing conditions or improving opportunities that may develop in their lifetime.

My studies have identified some 70 traits that characterize the culture of poverty. The principal ones may be described in four dimensions of the system: the relationship between the subculture and the larger society; the nature of the slum community; the nature of the family, and the attitudes, values and character structure of the individual.

The disengagement, the nonintegration, of the poor with respect to the major institutions of society is a crucial element in the culture of poverty. It reflects the combined effect of a variety of factors including poverty, to begin with, but also segregation and discrimination, fear, suspicion and apathy and the development of alternative institutions and procedures in the slum community. The people do not belong to labor unions or political parties and make little use of banks, hospitals, department stores or museums. Such involvement as there is in the institutions of the larger society—in the jails, the army and the public welfare system—does little to suppress the traits of the culture of poverty. A relief system that barely keeps people alive perpetuates rather than eliminates poverty and the pervading sense of hopelessness.

People in a culture of poverty produce little wealth and receive little in return. Chronic unemployment and underemployment, low wages, lack of property, lack of savings, absence of food reserves in the home and chronic shortage of cash imprison the family and the individual in a vicious circle. Thus for lack of cash the slum householder makes frequent purchases of small quantities of food at higher prices. The slum economy turns inward; it shows a high incidence of pawning of personal goods, borrowing at usurious rates of interest, informal credit arrangements among neighbors, use of secondhand clothing and furniture.

There is awareness of middle-class values. People talk about them and even claim some of them as their own. On the whole, however, they do not live by them. They will declare that marriage by law, by the church or by both is the ideal form of marriage, but few will marry. For men who have no steady jobs, no property and no prospect of wealth to pass on to their children, who live in the present without expectations of the future, who want to avoid the expense and legal difficulties involved in marriage and divorce, a free union or consensual marriage makes good sense. The, women, for their part, will turn down offers of marriage from men who are likely to be immature, punishing and generally unreliable. They feel that a consensual union gives them some of the freedom and flexibility men have. By not giving the fathers of their children legal status as husbands, the women have a stronger claim on the children. They also maintain exclusive rights to their own property.

Along with disengagement from the larger society, there is a hostility to the basic institutions of what are regarded as the dominant classes. There is hatred of the police, mistrust of government and of those in high positions and a cynicism that extends to the church. The culture of poverty thus holds a certain potential for protest and for entrainment in political movements aimed against the existing order.

With its poor housing and overcrowding, the community of the culture of poverty is high in gregariousness, but it has a minimum of organization beyond the nuclear and extended family. Occasionally slum dwellers come together in temporary informal groupings; neighborhood gangs that cut across slum settlements represent a considerable advance beyond the zero point of the continuum I have in mind. It is the low level of organization that gives the culture of poverty its marginal and anomalous quality in our highly organized society. Most primitive peoples have achieved a higher degree of sociocultural organization than contemporary urban slum dwellers. This is not to say that there may not be a sense of community and *esprit de corps* in a slum neighborhood. In fact, where slums are isolated from their surroundings by enclosing walls or other physical barriers, where rents are low and residence is stable and where the population constitutes a distinct ethnic, racial or language group, the sense of community may approach that of a village. In Mexico City and San Juan such territoriality is engendered by the scarcity of low-cost housing outside of established slum areas. In South Africa it is actively enforced by the *apartheid* that confines rural migrants to prescribed locations.

The family in the culture of poverty does not cherish childhood as a specially prolonged and protected stage in the life cycle. Initiation into sex comes early. With the instability of consensual marriage the family tends to be mother-centered and tied more closely to the mother's extended family. The female head of the house is given to authoritarian rule. In spite of much verbal emphasis on family solidarity, sibling rivalry for the limited supply of goods and maternal affection is intense. There is little privacy.

The individual who grows up in this culture has a strong feeling of fatalism, helplessness, dependence and inferiority. These traits, so often remarked in the current literature as characteristic of the American Negro, I found equally strong in slum dwellers of Mexico City and San Juan, who are not segregated or discriminated against as a distinct ethnic or racial group. Other traits include a high incidence of weak ego structure, orality and confusion of sexual identification, all reflecting maternal deprivation; a strong present-time orientation with relatively little disposition to defer gratification and plan for the future, and a high tolerance for psychological pathology of all kinds. There is widespread belief in male superiority and among the men a strong preoccupation with *machismo,* their masculinity.

Provincial and local in outlook, with little sense of history, these people know only their own neighborhood and their own way of life. Usually they do not have the knowledge, the vision or the ideology to see the similarities between their troubles and those of their counterparts elsewhere in the world. They are not class-conscious, although they are sensitive indeed to symbols of status.

The distinction between poverty and the culture of poverty is basic to the model described here. There are numerous examples of poor people whose way of life I would not characterize as belonging to this subculture. Many primitive and preliterate peoples that have been studied by anthropologists suffer dire poverty attributable to low technology or thin resources or both. Yet even the simplest of these peoples have a high degree of social organization and a relatively integrated, satisfying and self-sufficient culture.

In India the destitute lower-caste peoples—such as the Chamars, the leatherworkers, and the Bhangis, the sweepers—remain integrated in the larger society and have their own panchayat institutions of self-government. Their panchayats and their extended unilateral kinship systems, or clans, cut across village lines, giving them a strong sense of identity and continuity. In my studies of these peoples I found no culture of poverty to go with their poverty.

The Jews of eastern Europe were a poor urban people, often confined to ghettos. Yet they did not have many traits of the culture of poverty. They had a tradition of literacy that placed great value on learning; they formed many voluntary associations and adhered with devotion to the central community organization around the rabbi, and they had a religion that taught them they were the chosen people.

I would cite also a fourth, somewhat speculative example of poverty dissociated from the culture of poverty. On the basis of limited direct observation in one country—Cuba—and from indirect evidence, I am inclined to believe the culture of poverty does not exist in socialist countries. In 1947 I undertook a study of a slum in Havana. Recently I had an opportunity to revisit the same slum and some of the same families. The physical aspect of the place had changed little, except for a beautiful new nursery school. The people were as poor as before, but I was impressed to find much less of the feelings of despair and apathy, so symptomatic of the culture of poverty in the urban slums of the U.S. The slum was now highly organized, with block committees, educational committees, party committees. The people had found a new sense of power and importance in a doctrine that glorified the lower class as the hope of humanity, and they were armed. I was told by one Cuban official that the Castro government had practically eliminated delinquency by giving arms to the delinquents!

Evidently the Castro regime—revising Marx and Engels—did not write off the so-called *lumpenproletariat* as an inherently reactionary and anti-revolutionary force but rather found in them a revolutionary potential and utilized it. Frantz Fanon, in his book *The Wretched of the Earth,* makes a similar evaluation of their role in the Algerian revolution: "It is within this mass of humanity, this people of the shantytowns, at the core of the *lumpenproletariat,* that the rebellion will find its urban spearhead. For the *lumpenproletariat,* that horde of starving men, uprooted from their tribe and from their clan, constitutes one of the most spontaneous and most radically revolutionary forces of a colonized people."

It is true that I have found little revolutionary spirit or radical ideology among low-income Puerto Ricans. Most of the families I studied were politically conservative, about half of them favoring the Statehood Republican Party, which provides opposition on the right to the Popular Democratic Party that dominates the politics of the commonwealth. It seems to me, therefore, that disposition for protest among people living in the culture of poverty will vary considerably according to the national context and historical circumstances. In contrast to Algeria, the independence movement in Puerto Rico has found little popular support. In Mexico, where the cause of independence carried long ago, there is no longer any such movement to stir the dwellers in the new and old slums of the capital city.

Yet it would seem that any movement—be it religious, pacifist or revolutionary—that organizes and gives hope to the poor and effectively promotes a sense of solidarity with larger groups must effectively destroy the psychological and social core of the culture of poverty. In this connection, I suspect that the civil rights movement among American Negroes has of itself done more to improve their self-image and self-respect than such economic gains as it has won although, without doubt, the two kinds of progress are mutually reinforcing. In the culture of poverty of the American Negro the additional disadvantage of racial discrimination has generated a potential for revolutionary protest and organization that is absent in the slums of San Juan and Mexico City and, for that matter, among the poor whites in the South.

If it is true, as I suspect, that the culture of poverty flourishes and is endemic to the free-enterprise, pre-welfare-state stage of capitalism, then it is also endemic in colonial societies. The most likely candidates for the culture of poverty would be the people who come from the lower strata of a rapidly changing society and who are already partially alienated from it. Accordingly the subculture is likely to be found where imperial conquest has smashed the native social and economic structure and held the natives, perhaps for generations, in servile status, or where feudalism is yielding to capitalism in the later evolution of a colonial economy. Landless rural workers who migrate to the cities, as in Latin America, can be expected to fall into this way of life more readily than migrants from stable peasant villages with a well-organized traditional culture, as in India. It remains to be seen, however, whether the culture of poverty has not already begun to develop in the slums of Bombay and Calcutta. Compared with Latin America also, the strong corporate nature of many African tribal societies may tend to inhibit or delay the formation of a full-blown culture of poverty in the new towns and cities of that continent. In South Africa the institutionalization of repression and discrimination under *apartheid* may also have begun to promote an immunizing sense of identity and group consciousness among the African Negroes.

One must therefore keep the dynamic aspects of human institutions forward in observing and assessing the evidence for the presence, the waxing or the waning of this subculture. Measured on the dimension of relationship to the larger society, some slum dwellers may have a warmer identification with their national tradition even though they suffer deeper poverty than members of a similar community in another country. In Mexico City a high percentage of our respondents, including those with little or no formal schooling, knew of Cuauhtémoc, Hidalgo, Father Morelos, Juárez, Díaz, Zapata, Carranza and Cárdenas. In San Juan the names of Rámon Power, José de Diego, Baldorioty de Castro, Rámon Betances, Nemesio Canales, Lloréns Torres rang no bell; a few could tell about the late Albizu Campos. For the lower-income Puerto Rican, however, history begins with Muñoz Rivera and ends with his son Muñoz Marín.

The national context can make a big difference in the play of the crucial traits of fatalism and hopelessness. Given the advanced technology, the high level of literacy, the all-pervasive reach of the media of mass communications and the relatively high aspirations of all sectors of the population, even the poorest and most marginal communities of the U.S. must aspire to a larger future than the slum dwellers of Ecuador and Peru, where the actual possibilities are more limited and where an authoritarian social order persists in city and country. Among the 50 million U.S. citizens now more or less officially certified as poor, I would guess that about 20 percent live in a culture of poverty. The largest numbers in this group are made up of Negroes, Puerto Ricans, Mexicans, American Indians and Southern poor whites. In these figures there is some reassurance for those concerned, because it is much more difficult to undo the culture of poverty than to cure poverty itself.

Middle-class people—this would certainly include most social scientists

—tend to concentrate on the negative aspects of the culture of poverty. They attach a minus sign to such traits as present-time orientation and readiness to indulge impulses. I do not intend to idealize or romanticize the culture of poverty—"it is easier to praise poverty than to live in it." Yet the positive aspects of these traits must not be overlooked. Living in the present may develop a capacity for spontaneity, for the enjoyment of the sensual, which is often blunted in the middle-class, future-oriented man. Indeed, I am often struck by the analogies that can be drawn between the mores of the very rich—of the "jet set" and "café society"—and the culture of the very poor. Yet it is, on the whole, a comparatively superficial culture. There is in it much pathos, suffering and emptiness. It does not provide much support or satisfaction; its pervading mistrust magnifies individual helplessness and isolation. Indeed, poverty of culture is one of the crucial traits of the culture of poverty.

The concept of the culture of poverty provides a generalization that may help to unify and explain a number of phenomena hitherto viewed as peculiar to certain racial, national or regional groups. Problems we think of as being distinctively our own or distinctively Negro (or as typifying any other ethnic group) prove to be endemic in countries where there are no segregated ethnic minority groups. If it follows that the elimination of physical poverty may not by itself eliminate the culture of poverty, then an understanding of the subculture may contribute to the design of measures specific to that purpose.

What is the future of the culture of poverty? In considering this question one must distinguish between those countries in which it represents a relatively small segment of the population and those in which it constitutes a large one. In the U.S. the major solution proposed by social workers dealing with the "hard core" poor has been slowly to raise their level of living and incorporate them in the middle class. Wherever possible psychiatric treatment is prescribed.

In underdeveloped countries where great masses of people live in the culture of poverty, such a social-work solution does not seem feasible. The local psychiatrists have all they can do to care for their own growing middle class. In those countries the people with a culture of poverty may seek a more revolutionary solution. By creating basic structural changes in society, by redistributing wealth, by organizing the poor and giving them a sense of belonging, of power and of leadership, revolutions frequently succeed in abolishing some of the basic characteristics of the culture of poverty even when they do not succeed in curing poverty itself.

5 POLITICS AND LAW

People in groups get into at least two kinds of conflict: 1) conflict between the freedom of individuals and the welfare of the society in general; 2) conflict between people over allocation of scarce resources. The resolution of conflict in an orderly fashion is the business of politics and law.

Because these kinds of conflict are found in all human groups, it follows that all groups have legal and political systems. One of the primary functions of any political system is to give the members of a conflict an opportunity to work out their differences through compromise. When compromise won't work, political-legal systems channel the use of violence to settle disputes. Most compromises are worked out through customary (non-written) law. In many societies customary law is the *only* law. Even in our own culture, it is fair to say that most conflict never gets into court and is resolved without reference to any written law.

Among preliterate peoples, law is the *sentiment* of the group. Because most preliterate social groups are fewer than about 150–200 persons, this system works quite well. If a person does something wrong, it is fairly easy for leaders to assess how strongly the group feels and what everyone thinks should be done to the offender. Under these conditions ridicule and ostracism are the ultimate weapons to keep people in line. The first selection, by Colin Turnbull, shows how the Pygmies use these weapons to maintain law and order in their society.

When preliterate groups come into contact with complex, modern nation-states, legal action becomes more complex. Certain crimes may be adjudicated on the local level, whereas very serious ones may be sent to national courts. In Otomi Indian communities in Mexico, for example, each village has an elected judge who "represents" the national law in his village. He may be illiterate and have no knowledge whatever of Mexican national law, but this is unimportant. Most disputes within the community are settled by the judge according to traditional law and local sentiment. In one case a man stole another man's goat. The case came before the judge and the guilty party pleaded that his family was desperately hungry, so he stole a nanny-goat for milk. The judge ordered the goat returned and further ordered the owner to give the thief a weekly portion of milk. It turned out that the aggrieved party was the thief's brother-in-law. The thief had asked for food assistance but had been turned down, in spite of the fact that the goat produced more milk than the owner required. By customary law the man who stole the goat was entitled to make legitimate demands for assistance on his brother-in-law. It was declared that the goat had been borrowed and no crime committed except that of refusing to assist a relative. The second selection, by Hortense Powdermaker, is a recorded, word-for-word account of a local court in action.

Ostracism, ridicule, and local court action are not the only means by which people maintain order and resolve conflict. The ultimate sanction is violence.

All societies prohibit the unrestrained use of personal violence. They also regulate the use of collective violence, or war. Two widely different societies have been chosen here to demonstrate the systematic, controlled use of violence as a mechanism of social order and unity. The Dani of New Guinea wage a constant war with nearby groups. The wars are limited, however, to restoring the balance of life that is put out of kilter by ambush attacks on one another. Both sides are on constant alert, but inevitably an ambush is successful and a life is taken.

The warring parties may meet on an open field of battle, and as soon as anyone is killed or seriously injured the two sides retreat to assess the current balance. In the selection here we see how the death of Weake, a young boy, is avenged, and how the use of controlled violence functions in the Dani society.

The Albanian hill tribes were a peasant people living in the mountains, isolated from the Turkish and other national governmental structures that ruled the country. Like the people of northern Crete, the Mani of the Peloponnese in Greece, the Corsicans, and the Sicilians, the people of rural Albania had a highly formalized system of vendetta violence. Like the Dani, the balance was always off; but instead of whole societies going to war, the battles were fought between families.

Looking around the world we see numerous systems of formalized, channeled violence. There can be little doubt that constant vendetta warfare has dramatic effects on demographic patterns. The number of young men in the population is reduced; fewer women get married; population slumps occur, and so on. On the other hand, one can point to World War I, the Civil War, and possible nuclear war for more serious demographic consequences.

In light of this, it is tempting to say that formalized violence, such as is practiced by the Dani and the Albanians, is more rational. Some people are also prompted to conclude that such systems are evidence of people's cultural ways for keeping their "killer instinct" in check.

Do people have a killer instinct? Are human beings essentially violent beasts whose culture keeps the violence from going too far? Or are they peaceful creatures whose culture teaches them to kill and maim? Two famous writers, Konrad Lorenz and Robert Ardrey, have advocated the former view. Many physical anthropologists, however, hold the latter view; the argument that humans learn through their culture to be violent is given in the fifth selection here.

If we learn to kill, why don't we unlearn it? We may fool ourselves into believing that primitive peoples don't know any better. The selection on the Dani, however, shows how much compassion and pathos people everywhere have for those killed in violent acts. In any case, why do so-called civilized people continue to use war as a political instrument for conflict resolution? In the final selection, Charles Moskos shows that a battle soldier's first concern is for his personal safety. It is painfully obvious that if it were left to the soldiers (Dani, Albanian, American, or Viet Cong), war would not be a likely occurrence. We may be stuck with war because it's too hard to unlearn. But the evidence is mounting that collective social violence is a product of culture and of people rather than the other way around.

■ THE GIVER OF THE LAW

Colin M. Turnbull

Cephu had committed what is probably one of the most heinous crimes in Pygmy eyes, and one that rarely occurs. Yet the case was settled simply and effectively, without any evident legal system being brought into force. It cannot be said that Cephu went unpunished, because for those few hours when nobody would speak to him he must have suffered the equivalent of as many days solitary confinement for anyone else. To have been refused a chair by a mere youth, not even one of the great hunters; to have been laughed at by women and children; to have been ignored by men—none of these things would be quickly forgotten. Without any formal process of law Cephu had been firmly put in his place, and it was unlikely he would do the same thing again in a hurry.

This was typical of all Pygmy life, on the surface at least. There was a confusing, seductive informality about everything they did. Whether it was a birth, a wedding, or a funeral, in a Pygmy hunting camp or in a Negro village, there was always an unexpected casual, almost carefree attitude. There was, for instance, little apparent specialization; everyone took part in everything. Children had little or no voice in adult affairs, but the only adult activities from which they seemed to be rigidly excluded were certain songs, and of course the molimo. Between men and women there was also a certain degree of specialization, but little that could be called exclusive.

There were no chiefs, no formal councils. In each aspect of Pygmy life there might be one or two men or women who were more prominent that others, but usually for good practical reasons. This showed up most clearly of all in the settling of disputes. There was no judge, no jury, no court. The Negro tribes all around had their tribunals, but not the Pygmies. Each dispute was settled as it arose, according to its nature.

Roughly, there were four ways of punishing offenses, each operating as an efficient deterrent but without necessitating any system of outright punishment. In a small and co-operative group no individual would want the job either of passing judgment or of administering punishment, so like everything else in Pygmy life the maintenance of law was a co-operative affair. Certain offenses, rarely committed, were considered so terrible that they would of themselves bring some form of supernatural retribution. Others became the affair of the molimo, which in its morning rampages showed public disapproval by attacking the hut of the culprit, possibly the culprit himself. Both these types of crime were extremely rare. The more serious of the other crimes, such as theft, were dealt with by a sound thrashing which was administered co-operatively by all who felt inclined to participate, but only after the entire camp had been involved in discussing the case. Less serious offenses were settled in the simplest way, by the litigants themselves either arguing out the case, or engaging in a mild fight.

I came across only one instance of the first type of crime. We had all eaten in the evening and were sitting around our fires. It was with Kenge and a group of the bachelors, talking about something quite trivial, when all of a sudden there was a tremendous wailing and crying from Cephu's camp. A few seconds later there was shouting from the path connecting the two camps and young Kelemoke came rushing through our camp, hotly pursued by other youths who were armed with spears and knives. Everyone ran into the huts and closed the little doorways. The bachelors, however, instead of going in with their families, ran to the nearest trees and climbed up into the lower branches. I followed Kenge up one of the smaller trees and sat among the ants, whose persistent biting I hardly noticed. What was going on below took all my attention.

Kelemoke tried to take refuge in a hut, but he was turned away with angry remarks, and a burning log was thrown after him. Masisi yelled at him to run to the forest. His pursuers were nearly on top of him when they all disappeared at the far end of the camp.

At this point three girls came running out of Cephu's camp, right into the middle of our clearing. They also carried knives—the little paring knives they used for cutting vines and for peeling and shredding roots. They were not only shouting curses against Kelemoke and his immediate family, but they were weeping, with tears streaming down their faces. When they did not find Kelemoke, one of them threw her knife into the ground and started beating herself with her fists, shouting over and over again, "He has killed me, he has killed me!" After a pause for breath she added, "I shall never be able to live again!" Kenge made a caustic comment on the logic of the statement, from the safety of his branch, and immediately the girls turned their attention to our tree and began to threaten us. They called us all manner of names, and then they fell on the ground and rolled over and over, beating themselves, tearing their hair, and wailing loudly.

Just then there came more shouts from two directions. One set was from the youth who had evidently found Kelemoke hiding just outside the camp. At this the girls leaped up and, brandishing their knives, set off to join the pursuit. The other shouts, for the first time from adult men and women, came from the camp of Cephu. I could not make out what they were about, but I could see the glow of flames.

I asked Kenge what had happened. He looked very grave now and said that it was the greatest shame that could befall a Pygmy— Kelemoke had committed incest. In some African tribes it is actually preferred that cousins should marry each other, but among the Ba-Mbuti this was considered almost as incestuous as sleeping with a brother or sister. I asked Kenge if they would kill Kelemoke if they found him, but Kenge said they would not find him.

"He has been driven to the forest," he said, "and he will have to live there alone. Nobody will accept him into their group after what he has done. And he will die, because one cannot live alone in the forest. The forest will kill him. And if it does not kill him he will die of leprosy," Then, in typical Pygmy fashion, he burst into smothered laughter, clapped his hands and said, "He has been doing it for months; he must have been very stupid to let himself be caught. No wonder they chased him into the forest." To Kenge, evidently, the greater crime was Kelemoke's stupidity in being found out.

All the doors to the huts still remained tight shut. Njobo and Moke had both been called on by the youths to show themselves and settle the matter, but they had both refused to leave their huts, leaving Kelemoke to his fate. Now there was an even greater uproar over in Cephu's camp, and Kenge and I decided to climb down from the tree and see what was going on.

One of the huts was in flames, and people were standing all around, either crying or shouting. There was a lot of struggling going on among a small group of men, and women were brandishing fists in each other's faces. We decided to go back to the main camp, which by then was filled with clusters of men and women standing about discussing the affair. Not long afterward a contingent from Cephu's group came over. They swore at the children, who, delighted by the whole thing, were imitating the epic flight and pursuit of Kelemoke. The adults, in no joking frame of mind, sat down to have a discussion. But the talking did not center around Kelemoke's act so much as around the burning of the hut. Almost everyone seemed to dismiss the act of incest. One of Kelemoke's uncles, Masalito, with whom he had been staying since his father died, had great tears rolling down his cheeks. He said, "Kelemoke only did what any youth would do, and he has been caught and driven to the forest. The forest will kill him. That is finished. But my own brother has burned down my hut and I have nowhere to sleep. I shall be cold. And what if it rains? I shall die of cold and rain at the hands of my brother."

The brother, Aberi, instead of taking up the point that Kelemoke had dishonored his daughter, made a feeble protestation that he had been insulted. Kelemoke should have taken more care. And Masalito should have taught him better. This started the argument off on different lines, and both families quarreled bitterly, accusing each other for more than an hour. Then the elders began to yawn and say they were tired; they wanted to go to sleep; we would settle it the next day.

For a long time that night the camp was alive with whispered remarks, and not a few rude jokes were thrown about from one hut to another. The next day I went over to Cephu's camp and found the girl's mother busy helping to rebuild Masalito's hut; the two men were sitting down and talking as though nothing much had happened. All the youths told me not to worry about Kelemoke, that they were secretly bringing him food in the forest, he was not far away.

Three days later, when the hunt returned in the late afternoon, Kelemoke came wandering idly into the camp behind them, as though he too had been hunting. He looked around cautiously, but nobody said a word or even looked at him. If they ignored him, at least they did not curse him. He came over to the bachelor's fire and sat down. For several minutes the conversation continued as though he were not there. I saw his face twitching, but he was too proud to speak first. Then a small child was sent over by her mother with a bowl of food, which she put in Kelemoke's hands and gave him a shy, friendly smile.

Kelemoke never flirted with his cousin again, and now, five years later, he is happily married and has two fine children. He does not have leprosy, and he is one of the best liked and most respected of the hunters.

I have never heard of anyone being completely ostracized, but the threat is always there, and is usually sufficient to insure good behavior. The two attitudes which disturb the Pygmy most are contempt and ridicule. Contempt is most effectively shown by ignoring someone, even if he comes and sits at the same fire. But it is difficult to maintain for long because hunters cannot afford to ignore a fellow hunter. So ostracism of this kind is infrequent and does not last. Almost as effective, and of much longer duration, is ridicule. The BaMbuti are good-natured people with an irresistible sense of humor; they are always making jokes about one another, even about themselves, but their humor can be turned into an instrument of punishment when they choose.

Such a case was a great fight between the same two brothers who had fallen out over Kelemoke's misdemeanors, Aberi and Masalito. This incident shows as well as any how a tiny, and often imagined, insult can be magnified out of all proportion until it becomes a serious issue, threatening the peace of the camp. In any small, closed community, there are hidden tensions everlastingly at play. They are capricious, they are fluctuating and vapid, but every one of them is potentially explosive.

Of the two brothers Aberi was the elder. He was aggressive and ugly, and he considered himself the head of the family. The oldest brother, Kelemoke's father, had died. But Kelemoke had been brought up by Masalito rather than Aberi because everyone agreed that Masalito, if younger, had much more sense. He was also a better hunter, a better singer, a better dancer, and considerably better-looking. He had a prettier wife too; Aberi's wife had lost half her face, which had been eaten away by yaws. So between these two brothers there were always strained feelings. Open conflict was avoided because Masalito usually lived with the main group, of which his wife was a member, while Aberi always hunted with Cephu, his cousin.

But Masalito was kindly and liked peace and quiet, so when Cephu joined the main group at Apa Lelo he often used to visit his brother in Cephu's camp. Aberi's wife was a hard-working woman, and although it was difficult to look at her without flinching, she was loved by everyone. One afternoon, on a rainy day, Masalito wandered over to visit his brother. Rainy days are not happy days in a hunting camp; they are often oppressive, and of course hunting is impossible. People are couped up in their tiny leaf huts, thinking of all the game that is going uncaught. Aberi was sleeping, so Masalito sat down beside his sister-in-law, Tamasa, and asked her for a smoke. She passed him the clay pipe bowl and a little tobacco, and a long stem cut freshly from the center of a plantain leaf. She had recently come back from a visit to a Negro village and had brought several of these stems with her, as they give by far the best smoke.

Masalito smoked a few puffs, then passed the pipe to Tamasa. But instead of accepting it she abruptly turned it upside down and knocked the remaining tobacco out into the dirt. This was not only wasteful, but a deliberate insult. Masalito did not want to take offense, so he gave Tamasa the chance to re-establish good relations. He asked her to give him one of the new pipestems to take back to his hut for himself and his wife to enjoy. To refuse her husband's brother would be an open act of aggression quite uncalled for, and if she made the gift she would automatically cancel the previous insult. Masalito thought that he had not only maneuvered the political situation to his advantage but also won for himself and his wife a new pipestem. Unfortunately he had chosen a bad day.

Tamasa felt that Masalito was trying to get the better of her, and to get her to give away her husband's property while he was asleep, without asking him. She said, "Certainly I will give you a pipestem." Then she went behind the hut, where all the rubbish was thrown, and came back with a withered and smelly stump of a pipe. It had been pared away so often between smokes, to keep the mouthpiece fresh, that it was now only two feet long instead of six or seven. And instead of being fresh and green and juicy it was stale and brown and dry, reeking of old tobacco and spittle. This she presented to Masalito, who was so upset that he cried with rage, and asked why she and Aberi always treated him so badly. Tamasa promptly retorted that it was not bad treatment to feed him and give him tobacco every time he came over from his camp. Didn't his wife look after him, that he had to come and scrounge from his brother?

This was too much for Masalito, who had wanted only to be on good terms with everyone. He called Tamasa a name that one should never use to one's brother's wife, and Tamasa started crying. This awakened Aberi, who came out of his hut sleepily, looking uglier than ever. Without trying to explain, Masalito, still sobbing tearlessly with rage, hit his brother over the head with the withered pipestem Tamasa had given him. Brandishing the offending article above his head he stalked back to the main camp shouting at the top of his voice what miserable wretches his brother and his sister-in-law were. The dirty old pipe was damning evidence, and all sympathy was with Masalito. Njobo's wife took her husband's pipestem and gave it to Masalito, who quickly regained his good humor. But by now Aberi was aroused, and came storming into the camp, saying that his brother had insulted Tamasa. He declared that is was a matter for serious action; Masalito should be thrashed.

Everybody thought this was a great joke, and burst into laughter. Only children and youths got thrashed, and Masalito was a father. Aberi did not like being laughed at and he went over to where Masalito was sitting down on a log, smoking his new pipe. He demanded an apology. Masalito, now completely composed, simply picked up the old pipestem and threw it at his brother's feet, saying, "There! That is for her!" By now a crowd had gathered around, and the hotter Aberi became the more relaxed Masalito seemed to be.

Aberi shook his fists and said that if nobody else was going to thrash Masalito he was. This brought more laughs as Aberi was positively puny beside Masalito, who himself was little more than four feet tall. Masalito invited his brother to come and try. Aberi then pretended that he was holding a spear, and in a high-pitched voice, squeaking with anger, he cried out, "I am going to get my spear and I am going to kill you completely!" Whereupon he imitated a spear thrust in Masalito's direction. There was a gasp of horror, as this is something one does not say to one's brother even in jest. But Masalito replied calmly, "Go and get your spear, then, and come back and kill me. I'll still be here. You don't have the courage to kill your brother." He said a lot of other things, goading Aberi on to an even higher pitch of fury. Aberi tried to make himself more impressive by a graphic dance, which was meant to show exactly how he was going to leap in the air and twist around and drive the spear home. But he was not a good dancer, and when he tried to illustrate the leap he fell flat on his face.

That was the end of the matter for Aberi. For weeks he was ridiculed, everyone asking him if he had lost his spear, or telling him to be careful not to trip and fall. But it was not quite the end of the matter for Masalito. He felt more angry than ever at his brother, because Aberi had made himself, and so the whole family, an object of ridicule. Masalito felt this an added insult to himself. Even Kelemoke was furious. So relations between the two brothers got worse and worse, and every time there was a silence in the camp Masalito would complain in a loud voice about his brother and his brother's wife.

At first this was tolerated, but finally it threatened to split the camp in two. Masalito began naming all his friends and relatives to support him in ignoring Aberi; he refused to say a word to his brother. Of course his brother could claim support from the same relatives and friends, and tension was spreading throughout both camps. That was when the molimo stepped in and showed public disapproval of Masalito. The original source of the dispute, and Alberi's undoubted wrongdoing, were forgotten. Masalito was guilty of the much more serious crime of splitting the hunting band into opposing factions. He himself was then ridiculed and shamed into silence. After that is was only one or two days before the two brothers became good friends and hunting companions once again.

Disputes were generally settled with little reference to the alleged rights and wrongs of the case, but chiefly with the intention of restoring peace to the community. One night Kenge slipped out of our hut on an amorous expedition to the hut of Manyalibo, who had an attractive daughter, one of Kenge's many admirers. Shortly afterward there was a howl of rage and Kenge came flying back across the clearing with a furious Manyalibo hurling sticks and stones after him. Manyalibo then took up a position in the middle of the clearing and woke the whole camp up, calling out in a loud voice and denouncing Kenge as an incestuous good-for-nothing. Actually Kenge was only very distantly related to the girl, and the flirtation was not at all out of order, though marriage might have been. Several people tried to point this out to Manyalibo, but he became increasingly vociferous. He said that it wasn't so much that Kenge had tried to sleep with his daughter, but that he had been brazen enough to crawl right over her sleeping father to get at her, waking him up in the process. This was a considered insult, for any decent youth would have made a prior arrangement to meet the girl elsewhere. He called on Kenge to justify himself. But Kenge was too busy laughing and only managed to call out "You are making too much noise!" This seemed a poor defense, but in fact it was not. Manyalibo set up another hue and cry about Kenge's general immorality and disrespect for his elders, and strode up and down the camp rattling on the roofs of huts to call everyone to his defense.

Moke took the place in the center of the camp where Manyalibo had stood, and where everyone stands who wants to address the whole camp formally. He gave a low whistle, like the whistle given on the hunt to call for silence. When everyone was quiet he told Manyalibo that the noise was giving him a headache, and he wanted to sleep. Manyalibo retorted that this matter was more serious than Moke's sleep. Moke replied in a very deliberate, quiet voice, "You are making too much noise—you are killing the forest, you are killing the hunt. It is for us older men to sleep at night and not to worry about the youngsters. They know what to do and what not to do." Manyalibo growled with dissatisfaction, but he went back to his hut, taunted by well-directed remarks from Kenge and his friends.

Whether Kenge had done something wrong or not was relatively immaterial. Manyalibo had done the greater wrong by waking the whole camp and by making so much noise that all the animals would be frightened away, spoiling the next day's hunting. The Pygmies have a saying that a noisy camp is a hungry camp.

Some misdemeanors are very simply dealt with. A Pygmy thinks nothing of stealing from Negroes; they are, after all, only animals, as seen by Pygmy eyes. But among themselves theft is virtually non-existent. For one thing, they have few possessions, and for another there is no necessity for theft except through laziness.

Pepei was such a lazy Pygmy, and he was always stealing from the Negroes. But out in the forest he was forced to work for his food, to build his own hut if he wanted one (he was a bachelor but liked having his own hut, sharing it with his younger brother), and he had to make his own bows and arrows and hunting net, and to cook his own food. This was hard on Pepei, and although he meant no harm he could not resist slipping around the camp at night, taking a leaf from this hut and a leaf from that, until he had enough to thatch his own hut— which he made by acquiring saplings in a similar manner. Food used to disappear mysteriously, and Pepei had always seen a dog stealing it. But finally he was caught in the act by old Sau, Amabosu's mother, who was a very strange and frightening old lady. Pepei crept into her hut one night and was lifting the lid of a pot when she smacked him hard on the wrist with a wooden pestle. She then grabbed him by the arm, twisting it behind his back, and forced him out into the open.

Nobody really minded Pepei's stealing, because he was a born comic and a great storyteller. But he had gone too far in stealing from old Sau, who had lost her husband and was supported by her son Amabosu and his wife. So the men ran out of their huts angrily and held Pepei, while the youths broke off thorny branches and whipped him until he managed to break away. He went running as fast as he could into the forest; he cried bitterly and wrapped his arms around himself for comfort. He stayed in the forest for nearly twenty-four hours, and when he came back the next night he went straight to his hut, unseen, and lay down to sleep. His hut was between mine and Sau's, and I heard him come in, and I heard him crying softly because even his brother wouldn't speak to him.

The next day Pepei was his old self, and everyone was glad to see him laughing; they were happy to be able to listen to his jokes, and they all gave him food so that he wouldn't have to steal again.

But sometimes a dispute cannot be settled in any of these ways. It blows up too quickly to be ended by ridicule; the participants are too old to be thrashed; yet it is not serious enough to merit ostracism. Such disputes are usually trivial in origin, and often arise from the confined and close conditions of living. Personal relations become very involved in a hunting group, particularly when both members of a sister-exchange marriage are living in the same group.

Under this system, when a boy chooses a wife he becomes obliged to find a "sister"—actually any girl relative—to offer in exchange to his bride's family for one of their bachelor sons. This can be quite a chore, as it may be difficult to find a "sister" who is willing to marry the youth his in-laws have in mind as a groom, and whom the groom himself will also like.

Amabosu had married Ekianga's sister, and Ekianga had married, as his third wife, Amabosu's sister, the beautiful Kamaikan. He had just had a child by her, while Amabosu was still childless. Since Kamaikan was nursing a child, Ekianga was under an obligation not to sleep with her, and his two other wives were happy that at last they could expect him to pay them some attention. But to everyone's dismay he continued to sleep with Kamaikan. And one day Amabosu started making loud remarks across the camp about his sister's health.

This was not at Apa Lelo, but at a later camp. Apa Kadiketu, Amabosu's hut was to my right, and it faced directly across toward the first of Ekianga's huts, the largest and the best, built by himself and Kamaikan. Amabosu was sitting down at his fire at the time, and his wife was sitting near him, peeling mushrooms for the evening meal. Ekianga was inside the hut with Kamaikan, who had given the baby to her old mother, Sau, to look after for a few hours. At first Amabosu's remarks brought no response from the closed hut. But he became more and more explicit, denouncing Ekianga's shame in considerable and intimate detail, hinting that what was going on inside the hut at that moment was precisely what every new mother should avoid if she was to be able to look after the baby properly and give it lots of milk.

At last Ekianga retorted angrily from inside the hut. Amabosu continued to sit quietly, staring into the fire, with his wide, strange eyes. He answered in as caustic tones as he could find. In the end, Ekianga's door burst open and Ekianga appeared, spear in hand. He looked wild with fury and shame, and he flexed his muscles and hurled the spear at Amabosu with all his might. Amabosu looked up from the fire for the first time, but sat perfectly still with not a flicker of emotion on his face, his eyes still wide and cold and staring. The spear struck the ground within twelve inches of his feet, which was probably exactly where it had been intended to land. Amabosu calmly rose, pulled the spear free, and tossed it behind his hut into the rubbish dump. This was just about as insulting a gesture as he could have made at that moment, and it started one of the most dramatic fights I have seen in a Pygmy camp, and one of the most complicated.

As long as it was between the two men all was well, but the wives were torn between their loyalties as wives and as sisters. Amabosu's wife entered the fray by swearing at her husband for throwing her brother's spear into the rubbish dump. Amabosu countered by smacking her firmly across the face. Normally Ekianga would have approved of such manly assertion of authority over a disloyal wife, but as the wife was his sister he retaliated by going into his hut and dragging out Kamaikan, whom he in turn publicly smacked across *her* face. Kamaikan was made of tough stock. She picked up a log from the fire and beat her husband over the back with it. It is difficult to remember just exactly what the sequence of events was after that.

The two wives began fighting tooth and nail, quite literally. The men battled with burning logs, three or four feet long, swinging them from the cool end, but always just missing each other. Every now and again one of the girls would break free and go to the assistance of her brother, and the other would run and pull her away.

As always, a large crowd gathered—men, women and children. But nobody volunteered to stop the fight or to adjudicate in any way. They took one side or the other, either according to the rights and wrongs of the issue, or merely on the grounds that one or the other was the better fighter and more likely to win. The general opinion was that Ekianga should certainly not be sleeping with Kamaikan while she was nursing a baby, but since Kamaikan was equally at fault, Amabosu was wrong in defending her. By and large, however, the onlookers were more interested in the fight than the issue at stake.

As the fight grew more serious, and some visible damage was being done to all four parties, first relatives and then friends began to take sides more vigorously, and it looked as though fighting were going to break out all over the camp. At that moment Arobanai, Ekianga's senior wife, came striding out of her hut and announced in her deep contralto voice that she couldn't rest with all this noise going on, so it would have to stop. To make her impartiality quite plain she added that her animal of a husband could sleep with anyone he wanted to as far as she was concerned. She then went to where the two girls were locked together, both looking very much the worse for wear. She pulled them apart, and having given Amabosu's wife a hefty kick she took Kamaikan tenderly and led her back to her own hut.

At this, old Sau, who had been sitting on the ground throughout, with Kamaikan's baby on her lap, handed the baby to her weeping daughter-in-law and slowly got to her feet. Her son and Ekianga were now both armed with stout sticks, about four inches thick and three feet long, and they were lashing out with no reservations. Sau hobbled up to them and calmly pushed her way between; then she turned and put her head against Ekianga's stomach and her backside against her son's legs, and forced them apart. They continued trying to fight each other around the old lady, reaching out far so as not to hit her, but it was just too difficult. Ekianga was the first to throw away his weapon, which he did over Sau's head, with all his might. But Amabosu ducked and it missed him. Amabosu then threw his club on the ground and led his mother back to his hut. His wife meanwhile had been joined by Kamaikan, and they both were playing happily with the baby.

This incident illustrates one of the most remarkable features of Pygmy life—the way everything settles itself with apparent lack of organization. Co-operation is the key to Pygmy society; you can expect it and you can demand it, and you have to give it. If your wife nags you at night so that you cannot sleep, you merely have to raise your voice and call on your friends and relatives to help you. Your wife will do the same, so whether you like it or not the whole camp becomes involved. At this point some-one—very often an older person with too many relatives and friends to be accused of being partisan—steps in with the familiar remark that everyone is making too much noise, or else diverts the issue onto a totally different track so that people forget the origin of the argument and give it up.

Issues other than disputes are settled the same way, without leadership appearing from any particular individual. If it is a matter involving the hunt, every adult male discusses it until there is agreement. The women can throw in their opinions, particularly if they know that the area the men have selected is barren of vegetable foods. But the men usually know this anyway.

If the question is one of marriage, and a father announces that he does not like the girl his son has chosen, his son can call on all his friends to help him. If he is strong and holds out, the whole group will be assembled to discuss the case. If they agree with the father, then either the boy has to give up his talk of matrimony or else make up his mind to marry the girl anyway. In the latter case he would probably go and live with her hunting group. But it is seldom that things come to such a pass.

In fact, Pygmies dislike and avoid personal authority, though they are by no means devoid of a sense of responsibility. It is rather that they think of responsibility as communal. If you ask a father, or a husband, why he allows his son to flirt with a married girl, or his wife to flirt with other men, he will answer, "It is not my affair," and he is right. It is *their* affair, and the affair of the other men and women, and of their brothers and sisters. He will try to settle it himself, either by argument or by a good beating, but if this fails he brings everyone else into the dispute so that he is absolved of personal responsibility.

If you ask a Pygmy why his people have no chiefs, no lawgivers, no councils, or no leaders, he will answer with misleading simplicity, "Because we are the people of the forest." The forest, the great provider, is the one standard by which all deeds and thoughts are judged; it is the chief, the lawgiver, the leader, and the final arbitrator.

■ THE MAN WHO KNOCKED AT THE WRONG WOMAN'S DOOR

Hortense Powdermaker

INTRODUCTION

Unlike the fight between the women, some cases were not considered important enough to take to court. These were settled immediately by the parties concerned, following the same principles and similar procedures of the more formal courts. Friends and neighbors acted as witnesses and judges. Such a case was that of Mr. Harry Chomba (Bemba tribe), a miner without any European education, who when drunk had come knocking on Mrs. Mwenda's door while her husband was working on a night shift. The immediate suspicion was that Mr. Chomba had adulterous intentions; the face-to-face personal relations of the people concerned and of their neighbors demanded that his and Mrs. Mwenda's guilt or innocence be established immediately.

Africans have long had a well-defined system of customary law, and in this area native courts were continued under British administration. The functional principle underlying the law was, and still is, the establishment of a peaceful equilibrium through compensation for wrongs. Litigants acted as their own lawyers, and tribal authorities attempted to reconcile the conflicting interests and assess the amount of compensation.

Fundamental to African law was the concept of "the reasonable man," nicely illustrated in this case and, also, in much of the African's everyday thinking.

Mr. Chomba's case was heard in front of Mrs. Mwenda's house on the day following his midnight knock at her door. Mr. Mwenda, who was a brother of Mrs. Mwenda and who slept in her house, was a witness, as were also the neighbors, Mr. and Mrs. Kabeyo, Mr. Mwape, and Mr. Chomba's wife. Mr. Mhango and Mr. Chomba were the main parties in the case. Three men served as judges: one was a friend of Mr. Mhango; another, a friend of Mr. Chomba; and the third was not a friend of either.

HARRY CHOMBA: Yesterday, I drank a lot of beer at Section One and came home late. I started quarreling with my wife. But I did not want to quarrel, and so I told my wife that I was going to sleep in the kitchen because I was drunk and wanted to keep from quarreling. I left my clothes in the house and went out to the kitchen in my underwear. But I did not stay there. I came out in my underwear and tried to go to Section One for more beer, but I found myself at Section Two. Then I tried to go home, and I thought I had arrived at my house, but instead I was here. I started knocking hard at the door. This boy who sleeps here is the one who answered and told his sister that someone was knocking at the door. But even when he was saying that, I did not know I was lost; I thought it was my wife who was asking who I was. Then Mrs. Mwenda opened the door, and I realized I was lost. She asked my name, and I only answered, "I am." She went to get the light and looked at my face and she said, "Are you the father of Samuel?" I agreed. She asked me where I came from, and I explained how I came here and that I was lost. Then she went to tell Mr. Mwape and Mr. and Mrs. Kabeyo, so that they could be witnesses in the morning, in case either her husband or my wife or other people would be suspicious. Then Mr. Kabeyo and Mr. Mwape and Mrs. Mwenda took me to my wife, and she also explained to them how I left the house to go and sleep in the kitchen and that she thought I was there.

FIRST JUDGE: We have heard what Mr. Chomba has told us. He says he got
(*friend of Mr.* lost because he was drunk.
Mhango):

SECOND JUDGE: Is it usual for you, Mr. Chomba, to leave your house after a
(*friend of Mr.* quarrel and go to sleep in the kitchen?
Chomba):

HARRY CHOMBA: No, it only happened yesterday.

THIRD JUDGE: We do not act in the same way always. You cannot say, "I do not do this always, so I cannot do it now!" when people are drunk they do not reason much. Please, Mrs. Chomba, tell us how your husband left the house.

ALICE CHOMBA: My husband came very late after he had been drinking beer. I was annoyed at him because he was so late and was drunk, and he said, "I am going to sleep in the kitchen because you are talking too much." He left all his clothes in the house and went out in his underwear. I slept, thinking he was in the kitchen. The next time I saw him was when he was brought home by Mr. Mwape and Mr. Kabeyo and the owner of this house, Mrs. Mwenda. She explained how he came to her house and how she called Mr. Mwape and Mr. Kabeyo to be witnesses.

THIRD JUDGE: We have heard from his wife. We can now hear from the owner of this house, who knows how the man came.

MARY MWENDA: It was very late at night when he came to knock at the door. I did not hear the knocking, but my brother who sleeps in this front room did. Then my brother shouted, "Someone is knocking at the door." That was after he had asked him who he was, and the reply had been, "I am." I went to open the door and found a man only in his underwear. I asked who he was, and the answer was, "I am." I then went to collect the lamp and looked at his face and found that he was Mr. Chomba. I said, "Are you Mr. Chomba:" and he answered, "Yes." Then I asked why he was naked. He told me he had lost his house. He said, "After I left my house, I went to sleep in the kitchen; then after that I decided to go for beer to Section One, and when I was coming back, I knocked at this door, thinking I had arrived home." So I decided to call Mr. Mwape and Mr. and Mrs. Kabeyo to come and witness. I explained the matter to them, and then we took him to his house. This morning he came and found me at the washing stand and told me that he was very sorry and would come after work to apologize to my husband with the witnesses present.

FIRST JUDGE: We have now heard the case from the owner of the house.

SECOND JUDGE: The matter is quite all right. It was only a mistake, as we have heard from the main evidence of the owner of the house.

THIRD JUDGE: It is also important to get evidence from witnesses who were there. What do you say, Mr. Mwape?

RICHARD MWAPE: I cannot say more than what you have already heard from the three people. Moreover, the main thing you should all know is how Mr. Chomba came to the house and what he said. If you also find those two things to be important, then let us ask the biggest witness, her brother, to tell us, since he was the first person to hear him.

PETER MWENDA:	When I first heard him knocking I was half dreaming. I woke up and then heard him knocking very hard.
FIRST JUDGE:	He was sure he had come to his own house.
SECOND JUDGE:	Yes, otherwise he should have been knocking very softly, or not at all.
PETER MWENDA:	Then I asked who it was. He answered, "I am," with a very strong voice.
SECOND JUDGE:	He did not doubt that it was his house where he was knocking.
PETER MWENDA:	Then I called my sister, and she came to see who it was and recognized him. My sister asked him why he had come to her house at that time. He explained in the same way my sister has done. All his words he spoke showed me that he was really lost. There was no word out of his mouth that would make me suspicious of his coming to this house at that time.
SECOND JUDGE:	We have heard now the evidence from all of them, and the matter is straightforward. He was only drunk.
FIRST JUDGE:	It usually happens that when one is drunk he becomes totally useless. This beer we drink is no good.
SECOND JUDGE:	It is what I have already seen. One man at home [in the village] drank a lot of beer. He went to his house and found another woman sleeping on his bed and thought she was his wife. His wife, who was drunk, too, slept outside on the veranda, and he thought she was another woman. When his friends came, he told them that there was a woman on the veranda and they could get her. One of his friends went to the veranda, and since the woman too had drunk too much she thought he was her husband. So they slept. Later on, the husband realized that he was sleeping with another woman and that the woman on the veranda was his wife. So he realized he had given his own wife to his friends. That is the trouble with drinking too much beer.
HARRY CHOMBA:	I was very sorry when I realized I was lost.
SECOND JUDGE:	Oh yes, one can be worried because other people will be talking about it in many different ways, such as saying they found you committing adultery, or you wanted someone's wife, and many other bad things.
JAMES MHANGO:	I heard about this thing at my friend's house Mr. Nyawale when I was coming from work. I was told Mr. Chomba went to my house at night for my wife. I was very sorry because I have been with this man for very many years now and we have never quarreled. When I came here I was told about it and that is why I came to call you all. Now we have all heard the evidence you have given and there is, as I have found out, nothing that can make me suspicious. I know that it is the work of beer to confuse people. I was also lost last

week. I could not find my house at all. I came from Section
Nine through here to the Welfare Center. Fortunately, I met
a kind person who led me home. So I ask you, Mr. Chomba,
not to feel unhappy about this. Nearly everyone makes such
mistakes.

■ UNDER THE MOUNTAIN WALL

Peter Matthiessen

For several days the Wittaia, unable to effect a death in battle or in their
field raids from the Tokolik, had attempted a raid near the river, coming across early in the morning from the Turaba. The akuni were aware
of this, and Weaklekek's kaio had been strengthened by Aloro, Husuk,
and other warriors, who attempted to ambush the raiders; despite several
alarms, no real battle had occurred.

This morning the men did not go to the kaio, for the feast of the
Wilil was taking place. Aloro was an important Wilil, Weaklekek an important guest, and Husuk went off to war on the north frontier. No
women were permitted in Weaklekek's fields, and the kaio was abandoned
for the day. The Aike frontier, with the looming Turaba, had always
been a dangerous place, and as Weaklekek's absence, like all other important matters, was common knowledge, no trouble was expected.

But the day was hot, and in the afternoon the solitary Woluklek went
to the river to drink water. The people tire of the stale, silted waters of
the ditches—they have no drink but water—and in dry weather will
often go a long way to the river, where they squat on the bank and
drink slowly and steadily for minutes. Woluklek took with him three
little boys who were playing near Mapiatma.

One of the boys was Weake, whose father had been killed the year
before on the Waraba. His mother had since run off to the Wittaia, and
Weake was now the ward of his uncle, the warrior Huonke. He was a
small yegerek, a friend of Tukum, with the large eyes and thick eyebrows which make many of the children beautiful. His name meant
"Bad Path," and recently he had hurt his leg. For this reason, on this
day, he was slower than his friends.

Near the Aike, on a little rise just short of the side path to Weakle-
kek's kaio, Woluklek and the three boys were ambushed by a party of
Wittaia; the raiders sprang from the low reeds and bushes. Afterward
Woluklek was not sure about their numbers, but a raiding party is
usually comprised of about thirty men. There was nothing to be done.
He dropped his spear and fled, the boys behind him.

All his life Weake had been taught to hate and fear the enemy, and when he saw the strange men with their spears he turned with the rest and ran. But he was not fast enough and was almost immediately run down. He screamed for help, but the others were running for their lives and did not turn. The face of a man, of several men, loomed above him on the bright blue sky, with harsh, loud breathing. The men rammed their spears through him over and over, pinning him to the ground, and then they were gone, and Weake was carried home.

The cry of *Kaio, kaio* carried swiftly past Homuak and to the pig feast: the hot stone fragment that had burned Huonke must have struck him close to the same instant that his nephew had been pierced by the long spears. While the rock fire was still steaming, word came from Abulopak about the boy. The two villages almost adjoin, and the pilai where Weake lived was scarcely a hundred yards across the fences from the Wilil fire. Huonke and Tamugi, his brother-in-law, ran toward Abulopak, where the women's wailing had already started.

In the long yard of the sili two women were kneeling, facing the mute pilai. The sili lies under the mountain, at the north end of the great grove of araucaria, and the pilai at its southern end is shaded by the tall pines against the hill. Inside the pilai were a few old men, and then Asikanalek arrived, and Tamugi and Huonke, and Siloba.

Weake lay on a banana frond beside the fire. He was still alive, and his clear childish voice seemed out of place in the brown solemnity of the men's round house: it cut through the decrepit snuffling of the old men as the shaft of daylight in the doorway cut through the motes of dust. Weake spoke of his own etai-eken, his seed-of-singing, the life he clung to with all his strength, as if the mourning he could hear must be some dark mistake. *An etai-eken werek!* But I'm alive! Though he not once screamed or whined, his voice was broken as he spoke by little calls of pain, and the blood flowed steadily onto the frond beneath him.

Huonke tried to quiet him, repeating the same terse phrase over and over, like a chant: *Hat nahalok loguluk! Hat nahalok loguluk!*—But you're not going to die! Huonke's voice was the only firm one in the pilai. Tamugi, a large-muscled man whose ready smile is bolder than his nature, sobbed as loudly as he could, while Asikanalek cried silently. The boy's voice answered Huonke obediently—*Oh, oh,* he repeated gently. Yes, yes. But now and then pain or terror overcame him, and he cried out and fought to escape the death that he felt in their hands. Huonke held his left arm and Siloba his right, while Tamugi and Asikanalek held down his legs, Siloba neither talked nor cried, but breathed earnestly and ceaselessly into the boy's ear, oo-Phuh, oo-Phuh: this ritual breathing, which brought health, would be used in the next hour on the wisa pig meat in the pilai of the Wilil.

Weake twisted in their grasp, his back arching; his legs were released and he drew his knees up to his chin, covering the gleam of the neat spear holes at his navel and lower belly. The old cut on the boy's leg still had its green patch of leaf dressing, but the spear holes, like small mouths in his chest and sides, his arm and leg and stomach, had not been tended. Some fresh leaf was brought at last, and the two stomach wounds were bound up hastily, almost carelessly, as if the true purpose of the leaf was to protect the pilai floor from blood; in their distress the men handled him ineptly, and he cried out. The figures hunched over him in the near-darkness, with the old men's snuffling and the steady oo-Phuh, oo-Phuh, and the harsh tearing of the leaf.

Behind Huonke, in the shadows, a woman sat as rigid as a stone. The custom excluding women from the pilai had been waived while the child lived, but nevertheless she maintained silence: when she spoke, but once, out of the darkness, her voice came clear and tragic, like a song. The woman was Huonke's sister, married to Tamugi; she has a wild sad quality in her face and is one of the handsomest women in the Kurelu. She counseled the men to take the boy down to the stream.

Weake clung to life and would not die. His writhings had covered him with blood, and he lay in a pool of darkness. When the woman finished speaking, the men agreed to take him to the water, which, entering his wounds, would leach out the dark blood of illness. He was picked up and carried outside, Siloba holding his head up by the hair. The women in the yard began an outcry, but the men did not pass through the yard. They took Weake through a hole in the back fencing, across a pig pasture, over a stile, down through a small garden to a ditch. There they laid him in the muddy water, so that it lapped up to his chest.

Tamugi did not come. After leaving the pilai with the other men, he kept on going, for the Wilil fire was now open, and he wished some pig. The others accompanied Huonke to the ditch. Soon they too left, for there was nothing to be done. Only Siloba remained, and his friend Yonokma. Yonokma sat in water up to his waist, holding the legs, while Huonke and Siloba, their own lower legs submerged, held the child's arms: Weake's head rested on Huonke's right thigh.

Fitfully Weake talked and now and then cried out: the voice rang through the silent garden, against the soft background of lament and the low hum of the men's voices at the pig feast. Once he cried, *Tege! Tege!* in terror of the spears, and Huonke shouted him down: *Hat ninom werek! Hat ninom werek!*—over and over and over: You are here with us, you are here with us! He said this dully every time Weake called out. You are here with us. Then Weake would resume his own meek, rhythmic *Oh, oh, oh,* of assent. *Hat ninom werek—oh. Hat ninom werek —oh.* His eyes closed, opened wide, and closed again; he seemed to doze. In the muddy ditch, with its water spiders, round black beetles, and detritus of old leaves, his blood drifted peacefully away. Against the firmament above soared the great arches of the banana trees, and the hill crest in a softening light, and the blue sky. Taro and hiperi grew about him, and the blue-flowered spiderwort lined the steep banks. Swiftlets coursed the garden, hunting insects, and the mosquitoes came; the men slapped one another.

Huonke sighed and leaned his head against the bank. In grief Huonke's face had lost its hard, furtive quality and become handsome. Yonokma, sitting in the water, yawned with cold. Okal, who had gone with Weake to the river, came and stared down at his friend; he looked restless and unhappy and soon went away again.

In his last sleep Weake cried, a small, pure sound which came with every breath. When pain awakened him, he tried to talk, but his voice was faint and drowsy. Siloba breathed fitfully into his ear, but his efforts were disheartened: he only did it, guiltily, when the little boy called out. The small slim body had more than twenty wounds, and the wonder was that the boy had lived so long. But Weake would live until the twilight, asleep in the healing water, while the men attending him grew tired and cold. They coughed and slapped themselves and stared into the water, and the little boy's chest twitched up and down, up and down. Sometimes Siloba poured water on the wounds above the surface, and more blood was drawn forth, flowing down his side. Huonke said, You will stay with us, You will stay with us, and the child said Yes, yes, yes, and did not speak again.

Siba came and stared at the little boy. He broke off the stem of a taro leaf and with it probed the wound on the left side. The belly leaf was floating, and the small horim: Siba attempted to push back a trace of white intestine which protruded near the navel as if, by concealing the evidence of hurt, he might somehow be of help. Weake was failing rapidly and did not cry out; his mouth was open, and his lips had puffed and dried. In the attack he had received a heavy blow, for the side of his face had grown swollen and distorted.

Yonokma leaned forward and removed a bit of straw from the dry lips.

Siba ran across the garden and sprang onto the roof of the pig shed by the fence. There, with a great cracking sound like anger, he broke off a banana frond and hurled it down into the sili yard: this leaf would be the little boy's last bed. Returning, he picked Weake up out of the water and carried him homeward through the garden. Huonke and the two elege trailed Siba through the dusk, shaking with cold.

The small body was limp, with one foot lying on the other, and arms hanging: the blood dripped very slowly on the weeds. His breathing had silenced, and his eyes, half closed, had glazed, like those of a fresh-killed animal. Nilik, Werelowe, and Polik had come to look at him in his pilai, but it was evening now and he was dead.

The next morning, in the middle of the yard, Huonke and Tamugi built the chair. Four women emerged from the cooking shed and kneeled before it, and more women were already climbing the stile which separated the small sili from the main yard of Wereklowe. The wailing had commenced, and the Alua clan was coming through the fields from all across the southern Kurelu.

In the pilai crouched Asikanalek, twisted by grief. Against the wall, where sunlight filtered through the chinks, sat Weake's small silhouette, already arranged in the position he would be given in the chair. Asikanalek went to him and carried him outside into the day. Still holding the boy, he kneeled in the bright sun before the pilai and, staring upward at the sky, lamented. The men about him looked disheveled and distraught, and Asikanalek's shoulders were smeared with yellow clay. Weake's appearance in the yard had caused a stir among the women; the long day of fierce wailing had begun.

Weake was draped with two large shell bibs, which covered not only his mutilated chest but his torn stomach; the wife of Tamugi kneeled before him, binding up his legs. A man adjusted a new funeral horim to replace the one which had floated off in the brown ditch. Beside the chair Huonke and Tamugi cried out and rubbed their legs. Now and then Huonke would rub his hands together in a strange, stiff-fingered way, and glance about him, as if uneasy in the light of day.

Weake was carried to his chair. His bound legs were hung over the cross piece, and his head was held up by a strip of leaf passed by Tamugi beneath his chin. At the foot of the chair, wailing, Tamugi's wife crouched upon the ground and mopped at it with torn-up grass; she made a circular motion with her hand, scarring the earth. Other women, with girls and small children, filed steadily into the yard and arranged themselves upon the ground before lending their voices to the waves of sound.

A lizard darted from the fence to seize an insect. It gulped busily, its small head switching back and forth, and moved in quick fits and starts back to the shadows. Above, a honey eater bounded to the limb of an albizzia. It too cocked its head, unsettled by the wailing, but calmed before it fled, and sat there preening. In the blue sky over the hill the kites harassed one another, screeching.

The men draped shell belts on Weake, binding his brow with the bright colors and building the belts into a kind of crown. But his head was small, and most of the belts were laid along his sides and down the chair arms. While his attendants scratched and shuffled and thought thoughts, in the warm doldrums of their existence, the child sat alone in cold serenity. He seemed to grieve, nevertheless, as if oppressed by all his trappings; when the women came and draped their nets, they almost hid him in the shadows. Huonke came and smeared him with fresh pig grease, and his shins, still in the sun, took on a gleam: Tukum, himself gleaming from the pig grease of the day before, perched by the fence on a small stone and watched Weake. Tukum was one of the few children who seemed upset, though, like all his companions, he had seen many funerals and would see many more.

A group led by Polik sang wheezily and long the ancient chants of mourning, working the ground with gnarled old toes and rubbing spavined thighs. One of them, his wrinkled skin reptilian, felt peevishly for the tobacco roll buried in the pouch strung on his back. At the same time he contributed his mourning, a frail *woo, woo, woo,* and his long nose ran tumultuously with all the rest: the hole for boars' tusks in his septum had stretched wide with old age, so that the light shone through it.

Some of the men brought belts, and Huonke called out to them in greeting, a loud *wah-h, wah-h,* somehow impertinent, and at the same time self-ingratiating. He and his brother-in-law stood at the chair and haggled covertly about the placement of the belts. While haggling, Tamugi contrived to sob, rolling his eyes in the frank, open face of cant.

Four pigs came forth, and the pilai's owner destroyed them with a kind of sad authority. All four died speedily, snouting the ground, legs kicking, as if they were trying to bore into the earth. They were dressed swiftly, and the yegerek brought logs. Weake's friend Okal was among them: he wore the yellow clay of mourning and a pad of leaves to protect his shoulder from the wood. Like all the other boys, he played a large part in the funeral of his friend.

Nilik, with his affinity for pig, had come in time to finger the bloody pieces, which were hung on a rack behind the chair. Before the chair an old woman beat her breast with stumpy hands: *Aulk, aulk, aulk, aulk,* she cried—*Loo, loo, loo, loo.* The yellow clay was crusted in the skin folds of old breasts, of fallen hips. On the far side of the yard a giant butterfly, dead white and black, danced out of the shadows of the woods and, passing through the akuni, danced back again.

Huonke and Tamugi cried loud and long, mouths trembling and eyes alert. They watched the entrance of Weaklekek, his people behind him carrying three large flat *ye* stones decorated around the middle with fur and cowries. The ye stones are valuable but not sacred, though they may later become so; they are used, like cowrie belts, as a medium of exchange. *Wah! Wah!* cried Huonke. *Wah! Wah!* cried Tamugi. The party stopped before the chair to grieve, and then the men went onward toward the pilai, while the women and small children remained in the upper yard.

Weaklekek sat down quietly and stared into the earth. He was one of Weake's namis, and plainly he blamed himself for the boy's death, since it was his kaio that had been abandoned. But the raid and death were part of akuni existence, and neither Weaklekek nor Woluklek was blamed by any of the others. Even so, Woluklek, who had been unwise enough to lead the three boys to the river, did not come to the funeral at all.

U-mue's wives had come, and with them the children of his sili. Aku and Holake joined the little girls of the village, who were going about on small self-conscious errands; the girls smiled modestly at everyone, in the pretty illusion that all eyes were upon them. Nylare, who is very young, had a poor grasp of the situation, but she took up the wail of mourning, humming it contentedly to her own rhythms. Natorek, escaping his mother repeatedly, played in the narrow path through the massed women; like most akuni children, he accepted his mother's cuffs and cries in great good spirits and smiled expansively at all and everything even when late-comers stepped upon him. He was finally placed under the care of his brother Uwar, who took him to a corner of the yard and picked his lice.

While the food cooked, more men arrived; they overflowed into the woods behind the fencing. The mourning faltered in the midday pall, and nothing stirred. Only the stinging bees, black and yellow, toiled remorselessly on a small open hive, hanging upside down from a pandanus leaf beyond the fence; they hung in the air below the hive, their hair legs dangling, or clasped one another in dry, delicate embrace.

Near the main entrance of Abulopak the tips of the long grasses had been tied together in three places in the weeds: the tied grass forbids trespassing. The signs were a warning to the women, who were nearly two hundred strong, and whose use of the near weeds to urinate had become an offense to Wereklowe.

The rock fire was dismantled, and pig distributed among the men: a few bits were borne to certain women. Asikanalek's daughter Namilike walked around with her small net stuffed with hiperi, passing it out; Weake's little sister Iki Abusake was also there, as pretty in a baby way as Namilike herself. Iki Abusake's curious name means "Hand That Could Not Help Itself," the expression used by the akuni to account for the phenomenon of pig-stealing.

During the eating, soft waves of mourning rose and fell. The sun, sliding down into the west, burned hotly on Weake, and women tried to shield him with their nets. But now the men came forward and stripped him of his belts: the meal was over, and the day's business must begin. The belts were stretched on a frond before the pilai, with the kains seated in a line along each side. When the belts had been admired for a time, and their destiny decided, Wereklowe stood up to dispense them.

Until this time Wereklowe had remained out of the way, ceding the administration of the funeral to Asikanalek: Asikanalek was not only a sub-kain of the Alua but a fine warrior who had killed two, and a close relative of the dead boy. But the exchange of goods was an end purpose of the funeral, and the greatest leader of the clan usually directs it. With a weighty pause between the names, Wereklowe gave out the belts; he was attended by respectful silence. One belt was awarded to Weaklekek, but Weaklekek was still morose and waved it off; in his despair, and despite all his rich gifts, he felt he did not deserve it. Lakaloklek, more practical, came forth and took it in her husband's name.

Despite the great amount of grieving there seemed small hint of outrage. Huonke complained that the *pavi* should not have done it, but then, Huonke has killed once himself, a harmless woman found near the frontier who had run away from the Siep-Elortak. Revenge there would be, inevitably, but without moral judgments. Nevertheless, for the funeral of a small boy, well over two hundred people had pushed into the small sili: more presents were brought, and more pigs killed, than for the funeral of Ekitamalek, a kain's son and a warrior. Only a few could have come there in real sorrow, and only a few for the exchange of goods. The rest had come because the killing of a child, despite its ancient sanctions, had made them unhappy and uneasy.

His back to Wereklowe, the child sat naked in the chair. The women came to remove the nets, and Weake stirred; his head dropped slowly to his breast, for his chin strap had been loosened from behind. Then suddenly a man began to shout, and a complete silence fell. The speaker was Polik, and he was warning the people that they might be in danger.

In the fortnight previous Amoli, the violent kain of the Haiman, had killed the young brother of a man with whom he was having a dispute: taking the life of a relative of one's antagonist, or even that of his small child, is not unusual, being not only a more subtle punishment but a less dangerous one. The man had fled to the Siep-Kosi but had sworn revenge, and Polik, on behalf of Amoli, warned any of the latter's friends or kinsmen to be on guard. The fugitive's wife was ordered to come to him the next morning in Abulopak, so that he and Wereklowe might have a full explanation of the affair: it is one of the duties of the great kains to settle feuds within the tribe, not infrequently at the expense of their own pigs. When Polik had finished speaking, the guests fidgeted uneasily, but after a while the voices mounted once again, and the women returned to remove Weake's nets.

People were already departing from the sili. The thongs were loosened, and Weake was carried back to the banana leaves where the shell belts had lain. The yegerek, grim, brought timber for the pyre: Tukum looked frightened and was openly upset. The mourning quickened. Huonke greased the body a last time and, when he was finished, took up the bow and arrow. Another man held up the great thatch bundle. The arrow was shot into it, releasing the spirit from the body, and the man ran with the bundle up the yard; he laid the bundle on the sili fence.

The fire had been assembled quickly, and a loud outcry erupted with the flames: the body was hurried to its pyre. Weake was laid upon his side, in the way that small boys sleep, with a rough timber pillowing his head. The flames came up beside him, and more wood was laid on top of him, and he disappeared.

The mourning died after a time, and the sili emptied quickly. Huonke brought out a red parrot feather and performed the purification ceremony on the men who had handled the boy's body. The men, seated in a circle, held out both their hands, and Huonke passed the parrot feather through the air above the outstretched fingers. Afterward, as much was done for him.

The last of Weake was a sweet choking smell, carried upward by an acrid smoke from the crackling pyre, and diffusing itself at last against the pine trees, the high crest of the mountain wall, the sky . . . .

One afternoon in this period four strangers came on a visit to Abulopak. Though the men were of the Asuk-Palek people, a group allied ordinarily with the Wittaia, they considered themselves safe because two of them had close relatives in the sili of Wereklowe.

But, despite the new turn in their fortunes, the Kurelu considered the revenge of Weake and Yonokma incomplete; in addition, a man arrowed in the inner thigh on the afternoon that the Kurelu were routed from the Waraba had since died of this wound in the mountain villages. It was therefore decided to attack the two strangers who had no clansmen, with the excuse that the two had doubtless come to kill somebody.

A fierce howling burst the twilight air. One man fled the sili and, as dark was near, escaped entirely in the heavy brush which lies just opposite Abulopak. The second took refuge in the loft of the pilai; he was dragged out to the yard and speared to death. As most of the men involved were Wilil, U-mue took loud credit for his clan, a credit which, in high excitement, he shortly transferred to himself.

The body was taken by the heels and dragged out along the muddy paths, all the way from Abulopak to the Liberek. Tegearek led in the hauling, beside himself with the joy of violence.

Some boys had been playing in the fields as twilight came, and these now danced along beside the body. Okal and Tukum among them, and jabbed at it with their cane spears. Though Tukum took part, he seemed frightened by what he was doing, and the next day broke the toy spear he had used over his own head.

The Asuk-Palek was of middle age and strongly made, with a large forehead. He had been breathing when the spearing stopped, a short, ragged sound, but he was dead long before he reached the Liberek. He lay on his back beneath a high, hard moon, his eyes wide open, an eager smile upon his face. The face looked oddly trusting and untroubled.

The people were gathering; they danced beneath the stars.

Husuk came from the Kosi-Alua, an ax gripped in his hand. Taking the body by the hair, he wrenched it into a seated position and inspected the spear holes in the back. The man's mouth fell slack and the eyes stared; for a moment it seemed that Husuk would sever the head.

He let the body fall.

Tegearek, excited still, dragged the body to the field edge. Behind a low fence there lay a slough from which yellow clay is taken in time of war or funeral or etai. The body was dumped over the fence, then thrown face down into the ditch. The men prodded it with spears until it slid beneath the surface, and black bubbles rose. Grass was thrown on top of it.

Later in the evening the body was taken from the ditch, and the two Asuk-Paleks who had not been attacked carried it off beyond the Elokera. The following day a large etai was held, for the score had been settled at long last, and the faltering etai-eken of the people had been restored.

■ COURSE OF THE BLOOD FEUD

Margaret Hasluck

The fatal shot fired, a murderer's life was in such instant danger from the avenger that it behoved him to fly with all speed. But often his "blood seized him" so that "his legs gave way under him" and he was rooted to the spot from shock. Custom therefore prescribed in Shkodër,

Lumë and Godolesh that he must drop on the ground a cartridge or an article of clothing such as his fez, sash, or handkerchief; in Elbasan, Shpat and Çermenikë that he must lick the muzzle of his rifle or pistol; alternatively, in Elbasan that he must inhale the smoke of the gunpowder or let his comrades slap his face; in Labinot that he must hold the cartridge case in his mouth and bite his little finger and suck the blood, and in Mat that he must eat a little gunpowder. That done successfully, "his blood was set free," "the seizure passed," and he was able to run away.

When an article of clothing was left behind, it served to identify the murderer; where none was left, word had to be sent to the victim's family. It was everywhere "held dishonourable" to kill and not to tell. It was also thought unfair for reasons that varied with the locality. In Mirditë the victim's relatives might go mad if they did not know the identity of the murderer; in north Albania the murderer's kinsmen would not know to hide while the avenger's blood was boiling; in south Albania the crime might be laid at the wrong door. Besides, the normal murder was matter for boasting; committed only to avenge some wrong or insult, it showed that the murderer was spirited enough to resent ill-treatment.

Latterly, when the government was attempting to repress murder, the murderer, certain of arrest, left no token and did not inform the relatives. The community, however, was always on the watch and from its members' observation of those who came from the direction of the shots and from their knowledge of the whereabouts of the victim's enemies at the time, the murderer's identity was established—at all events to the satisfaction of the community.

In the early days of a feud the father or brother of the victim might in his furious rage kill the murderer and shoot a second time at the lifeless corpse. When the feud was older, it was not permitted to kill and shoot again. A murderer seldom looked at the corpse, a fact which gave men quick-witted enough to feign death a chance to escape. In some places, such as Mirditë, the murderer was expected to turn the dead man in the right direction for one of his religion—with his head towards the east if Christian, whether Catholic or Orthodox, towards Mecca if Mohammedan, and to rest his rifle against his head; if unable to touch him, he had to tell the first man he met to attend to those matters. In Shpat the murderer left the cartridge-case by his victim, allegedly not to "set his own blood free," as in Lumë, but to avoid carrying away a thing that was unlucky because stained with blood and sin. In Mat and the Malësi e Madhe, the murderer's own life being in grave danger from the avenger, it was thought "brave" to tread in the victim's blood as a last insult.

A murderer must not rob his victim; he had killed him only to defend his honour and not to enrich himself. As was popularly said, "low-class fellows" take a man's rifle, watch, money or clothes; "good-class men" take only vengeance. In some places sanctions reinforced public dis-approval of the robber-murderer. In Lumë he saddled himself with one and a half feuds, i.e. the need to pay for the murder with blood money as well as a life; in Mirditë, where he was expected to lay the dead man's rifle against his head, he incurred two feuds. Certain exceptions to the rule were admitted. A murderer could everywhere, except in Mirditë, take his victim's rifle to prove that he "had really trodden in his blood," but he must afterwards send the weapon to the family. On similar terms he might take the dead man's watch also. When the murderer was a hired assassin, he commonly took a token from his victim, usually his cap, to prove to his paymaster that he had earned his money. When a man's enemy lived at a distance, he might again take his cap to prove to his own friends and neighbours that he had killed him. Robbery of the corpse by a third person was not to be feared; since everybody within range, the dead man's relatives included, rushed up at the sound of the shot, there was publicity enough to prevent such an outrage. As for the supernatural dangers thought to beset the bodies of persons dead in ordinary circumstances, it was well known that Satan feared a rifle too much to approach the body of the murdered man.

When describing how Albanian men used to shave their heads except for a tuft on the crown, as a few old men and young boys still do, the Highlanders of north Albania asserted that a murderer had licence to cut off his victim's head. The tuft, they said, was left so that an enemy might conveniently carry the head when he cut it off; failing such a handle, he would thrust his finger into the dead man's mouth, an intolerable insult. The veracity of this story appears doubtful, since although the Highlanders, Slavs, and Turks all cut off heads, Albanians as far inland as Elbasan shaved their head save for the tuft on the crown, and it is unlikely that all anticipated murder by Slavs or Turks. Whatever the purpose, the tuft was not confined to Albanians, but was seen in 1926 worn by small boys in the Turkish villages in south Serbia where the population was of mixed Turkish and Bulgarian stock.

A murderer usually announced his crime to the victim's family by a crude message to fetch him from such-and-such a place and bury him. He was always expected to surrender the body, but if a feud was unusually bitter, the murderer might forbid the body to be buried in the cemetery in the ordinary way. If he was backed by enough men to make his ban effective, the body was buried in the secrecy of night. Sometimes he forbade it to be taken even at night to the cemetery; in that event it had to be buried elsewhere. A story comes from Sopot in Dibër. About 1893 Abas Kamber's enemy killed one of his men and forbade him to carry the body to the cemetery. Abas, strong though he was, could do nothing but bury it in the courtyard of his house. Just before it was lowered into the grave, the enemy repented and sent him leave to bury it in the cemetery. To show that he was not always prepared to do the enemy's bidding, Abas sent back the message that he would not dig up the body again and concluded that burial as it had begun.

Hiding the body was universally deprecated. When men stole a grazing cow, it was said they killed it, roasted and ate what they could of the meat and hid the remainder. But it was not to eat a man's flesh that they killed him and they must not conceal his body like the cow's. If they did, the feud was doubly embittered.

By rights a man was never buried where he was killed. Even if the spot were two days distant, or if, like Kol Mali's victim, he had lain three weeks undiscovered, he was carried home for burial. "He had been theirs," his relatives said, and neither distance nor a natural repugnance could prevent them from doing their duty by him. In the northern mountains, in Mirditë and in Kurbin, a heap of stones was made where he was killed; on this every passer-by was expected to throw a green leaf, a blade of grass or a pebble while expressing a wish for the repose of his soul. In Shkrel, according to one informant, a stone was stuck at the head and another at the foot, as though the place was a real grave, but a *muranë* was not made. Any relatives who wished to mourn him went to his grave, not to the place where he had been killed. Exceptionally, what seem real graves may be seen near the meadows of Tërnovë above Zerqan; ten or twelve in number, each roughly outlined with stones, they are known as "the murdered graves" and are said to contain the bodies of men who fell there in a long-past battle between the villages of Tërnovë and Sopot. Again exceptionally, when Muharrem Bajraktar of Lumë fled in 1934 to Yugoslavia, the Spahi family, his hereditary enemies, killed one of his servants. Muharrem said this man was not to be buried in Bicaj, his native village, but by the wayside where he fell, so that when he himself returned from exile he should see the grave and be reminded to take vengeance.

The ideal was to take vengeance as soon as possible. In Kurbin the piled stones served to make the dead man's kinsmen hasten to take vengeance, reminding them of his death and so "heating their blood." For the same purpose the Catholics of the north frequently buried the man in his blood-stained clothes; the Mohammedans, however, obedient to the dictum that all who profess their faith must go to the grave in a clean winding sheet, discarded this custom. A still stranger reminder of the need to take vengeance, a little bottle filled with the dead man's blood, was used all over north Albania and in Kosovë. This bottle the relatives looked at day and night. As soon as the blood "boiled," i.e. fermented, they seized their rifles, cocked their skull-caps over one ear to show their determination, and rushed forth to kill the murderer. If the blood did not "boil," they might accept a money indemnity instead of taking a life. In western Mat they dipped a rag in the dead man's blood; when it looked stained and brown, they knew the hour to avenge him had struck. None of these reminders was found as far south as Çermenikë and Shpat.

Public opinion also spurred the avenger on. A man slow to kill his enemy was thought "disgraced" and was described as "low-class" and "bad." Among the Highlanders he risked finding that other men had contemptuously come to sleep with his wife, his daughter could not marry into a "good" family and his son must marry a "bad" girl. As far south as Godolesh on the outskirts of Elbasan, he paid visits at his peril; his coffee cup was only half-filled, and before being handed to him it was passed under the host's left arm, or even his left leg, to remind him of his disgrace. He was often mocked openly.

All over north Albania it was permissible for the victim's kin to burn down the murderer's house. The veteran Mirash Nue of Vuksan in Shalë boasted that once he saved his house from this fate by sending a message to the avenger which ran: "Spare the ashes on my hearth for the sake of the open house I've kept." The avenger, touched by the reminder of Mirash's noted hospitality, yielded to the plea. In 1935 a Dibran took to the mountains after wounding a fellow-villager with whom he was at feud; on recovering, his victim did not dare to sleep at home in case he returned under cover of darkness to repair his bad marksmanship by setting fire to the house and burning him to death. In hot blood an avenger might in some places do as much material damage as possible to the murderer, burning his hay as well as his house, scything his ripening grain and harrowing over his growing maize. For fear of reprisals in kind he could nowhere harm his children or animals.

Burning down a murderer's house is said in Martanesh to have been a recent innovation, and in Dibër and Lumë to have been formerly much more common than in recent times. Various considerations suggest that the latter view is correct. The reason given in Lumë for the waning of the custom is that it grew progressively more serious as people abandoned the straw huts in which they once lived and built themselves stone houses; the huts were cheap and easy to rebuild, but the houses were not so easily replaced. With poverty as general and murder as frequent as they used to be, it is obvious that if burning the murderer's stone house and destroying his crops had been freely permitted, the life of the tribe could not have gone on. To restrict the attacks on property, sanctions were introduced. In Dibër an avenger guilty of incendiarism was banished in perpetuity by the community. In Krujë the crime was deprecated as doubly unwise; it might cause further deaths, so involving the avenger in further feuds, and women and children might be among the victims, in which case the avenger would be covered with disgrace. In Shpat an avenger who burned his enemy's house found the whole community against him as a man willing to burn women and children to death and to harm property; in Shpat property was so sacrosanct that one must not touch even "the leaf of the leek" belonging to one's enemy.

When the community decided to burn out a man whom they had sentenced to banishment for committing a heinous murder, their numbers and their power to exclude him completely from the tribal life made it impossible for him to resist. It was otherwise with the victim's kin. For want of power to exclude the murderer from more than their own section of tribal life they could not make him submit tamely, and in their attempts to use force they were often baffled by the fire-resisting principles on which most mountain houses were built. With the walls of stone, only the roof and the outer door were inflammable, and with no matches available these could only be set alight by blazing brands, probably of pitch pine, brought from another house. If the murderer was a rich man, he lived in a house surrounded by a courtyard wide enough to keep incendiaries at a safe distance from both roof and doorway; one or two towers in the walls of the courtyard sufficiently protected its gateway. If the murderer was poor, his house had no courtyard. But like the rich man's, it consisted of two or more storeys, the stable on the ground floor and the living-rooms above. The roof was, therefore, too high for the avenger to throw firebrands among the rafters. The door was surmounted by machicoulis through which the defenders could shoot or pour boiling water, and loopholes at the corners of the living-rooms commanded the approaches; in cases of bitter feud the door was sometimes covered outside with tin plates. Windows in a stable being thought unnecessary, the door was the only break in the solid walls of the ground floor. Sometimes avengers who were weak in guns hired men to fire the murderer's house. These hirelings came especially from Mirditë, for Mirdites were notoriously brave enough to face the risk entailed and poor enough to think only of the money offered; this amounted to some thirty napoleons (£40 in the 1930's) per man.

When an avenger burned down the murderer's house in hot blood, his motive was to do the murderer as much damage as possible. When he burned it down in cold blood, his motive was to drive the murderer into the open to be shot at. A murderer not infrequently shut himself up in his house during the daytime and stirred outside only at night, so remaining beyond the avenger's reach. When his house was set on fire, he knew that if he remained inside the blazing building, his death was certain, and that if he came out, he had a sporting chance of escaping the avenger's bullets. He had, therefore, no choice but to leave the burning house. In the same way when gendarmes surrounded a house in which a desperate criminal was hidden, he preferred to run the gauntlet of their fire rather than wait tamely to be seized and led off perhaps to death as a menace to society. This was particularly true of Turkish times, when dangerous criminals were generally shot out of hand when arrested.

■ WHY MEN FIGHT

Charles C. Moskos, Jr.

Few stories to come out of the Vietnam War are so poignant as the story of Company A of the 196th Light Infantry Brigade, Third Battalion. As told by Associated Press reporters Horst Fass and Peter Arnett in a cable dated August 26, 1969, Company A had been pushing for five days through enemy-held territory in an effort to recover the bodies of eight Americans killed in a helicopter crash 31 miles south of Da Nang. Now, its strength halved to 60 men, its platoon leaders dead or wounded, Company A was ordered to move down a jungled rocky slope of Nuilon Mountain. They refused. Most of the men were 19 to 20 years old, draftees, and many of them had only a short time to go before being rotated back to the States. They were ordered to move out and they refused.

The rest of the story is unimportant; as far as the military command is concerned the whole story is unimportant. But for many Americans, Company A's refusal to fight that day must have raised terrible questions—perhaps above all questions about one's own personal courage, but questions too about how and why American soldiers continue to expose themselves to death and pain in a war that few civilians any longer believe in.

The most popular notion of how men are brought to kill and be killed in combat has to do with the presumed national character of the soldiers. Different national armies perform better or worse according to the putative martial spirit of their respective citizenries. Italians make "poor" soldiers, Germans "good" ones. Another view has it that combat performance is basically a consequence of the operation of the formal military organization—the strict discipline, military training, unit esprit de corps and so forth. This viewpoint is, naturally enough, found in traditional military thought; but the importance of military socialization is similarly emphasized—albeit from different premises—by antimilitarists concerned with the perversions that military life allegedly inflicts on men's minds. Another interpretation—often the hallmark of political rhetoric—holds that combat performance depends on the soldier's conscious allegiance to the stated purposes of the war. Whether motivated by patriotism or a belief that he is fighting for a just cause, the effective soldier is ultimately an ideologically inspired soldier.

Yet another explanation of combat motivation developed out of the social science studies of World War II. This interpretation deemphasizes cultural, formal socialization and ideological factors and focuses attention instead on the crucial role of face-to-face or "primary" groups. The motivation of the individual combat soldier rests on his solidarity and social intimacy with fellow soldiers at small-group levels. This viewpoint was characteristic of the studies that Samuel Stouffer and his associates reported in *The American Soldier,* as well as of the analysis of the *Wehrmacht* by Edward Shils and Morris Janowitz. The rediscovery of the importance of primary groups by social scientists was paralleled in the accounts given by novelists and other writers about combat behavior such as Norman Mailer, James Jones, J. Glenn Gray and S. L. A. Marshall. In a few of the more extreme elaborations of this theory, primary relations among men in combat were viewed as so intense that they overrode not only preexisting civilian values and formal military goals, but even the individual's own sense of self-preservation.

My own research among American soldiers in Vietnam has led me to question the dominant influence of the primary group in combat motivation on at least two counts. First, the self-serving aspects of primary relations in combat units must be more fully appreciated. War is a Hobbesian world and, in combat, life is truly short, nasty and brutish. But, to carry Hobbes a step farther, primary group processes in combat are a kind of rudimentary social contract, a contract that is entered into because of its advantages to oneself. Second, although the American soldier has a deep aversion to overt political symbols and patriotic appeals, this fact should not obscure his even deeper commitments to other values that serve to maintain the soldier under dangerous conditions. These values—misguided or not—must be taken into account in explaining the generally creditable combat performance American soldiers have given. Put most formally, I would argue that combat motivation arises out of the linkages between individual self-concern and the shared beliefs of soldiers as these are shaped by the immediate combat situation.

THE COMBAT SITUATION

To convey the immediacy of the combat situation is hard enough for the novelist, not to say the sociologist. But to understand the fighting soldier's attitudes and behavior, it is vital to comprehend the extreme physical conditions under which he must try to live. It is only in the immediate context of battle that one can grasp the nature of the group processes developed in combat squads. For within the network of his relations with fellow squad members, the combat soldier is also fighting a very private war, a war he desperately hopes to leave alive and unscathed.

The concept of relative deprivation—interpreting an individual's evaluation of his situation by knowing the group he compares himself with—has been one of the most fruitful in social inquiry. We should not, however, forget that there are some conditions of life in which deprivation is absolute. In combat, a man's social horizon is narrowly determined by his immediate life chances in the most literal sense. The fighting soldier, as an absolutely deprived person, responds pragmatically to maximize any and all short-run opportunities to improve his chances of survival. For the soldier the decisions of state that brought him into combat are irrelevant, meaningless.

Under fire, the soldier not only faces an imminent danger of his own death and wounding; he also witnesses the killing and suffering of his buddies. And always there are the routine physical stresses of combat life —the weight of the pack, tasteless food, diarrhea, lack of water, leeches, mosquitos, rain, torrid heat, mud and loss of sleep. In an actual firefight with the enemy, the scene is generally one of terrible chaos and confusion. Deadening fear intermingles with acts of bravery and, strangely enough, even moments of exhilaration and comedy. If prisoners are taken, they may be subjected to atrocities in the rage of battle or its immediate aftermath. The soldier's distaste for endangering civilians is overcome by his fear that any Vietnamese, of any age or sex, could very well want him dead. Where the opportunity arises, he will often loot. War souvenirs are frequently collected, either to be kept or later sold to rear-echelon servicemen.

As Stendahl and Tolstoy noted long ago, once the fight is over, the soldier still has little idea of what has been accomplished in a strategic sense. His view of the war is limited to his own observations and subsequent talks with others in the same platoon or company. The often-noted reluctance of soldiers to discuss their war experiences when back home doesn't hold true in the field. They talk constantly, repetitiously, of the battles and skirmishes they have been through. They talk about them not just to talk, but more importantly to nail down tactics that may save their lives in future encounters with the enemy.

DEROS AND AGAPE

For the individual soldier, the paramount factor affecting combat motivation is the operation of the rotation system. Under current assignment policies Army personnel serve a 12-month tour of duty in Vietnam. Barring his being killed or severely wounded, then, every soldier knows exactly when he will leave Vietnam. His whole being centers on reaching his personal "DEROS" (Date Expected Return Overseas). It is impossible to overstate the soldier's constant concern with how much more time—down to the day—he must remain in Vietnam.

Within the combat unit, the rotation system has many consequences for social cohesion and individual motivation. The rapid turnover of personnel hinders the development of primary group ties, even as it rotates out of the unit men who have attained fighting experience. It also, however, mitigates those strains (noted in World War II in *The American Soldier*) that occur when new replacements are confronted by seasoned combat veterans. Yet because of the tactical nature of patrols and the somewhat random likelihood of encountering the enemy, a new arrival may soon experience more actual combat than some of the men in the same company who are nearing the end of their tour in Vietnam. Whatever its effects on the long-term combat effectiveness of the American forces as a whole however, the rotation system does largely account for the generally high morale of the combat soldier.

During his one-year stint in Vietnam, the fighting soldier finds his attitude undergoing definite changes. Although attitudes depend a good deal on individual personality and combat exposure, they usually follow a set course. Upon arrival at his unit and for several weeks thereafter, the soldier is excited to be in the war zone and looks forward to engaging the enemy. After the first serious encounter, however, he loses his enthusiasm for combat. He becomes highly respectful of the enemy's fighting abilities and begins to fear and scorn the South Vietnamese. He grows skeptical of victory statements from headquarters and of the official reports of enemy casualties. From about the third to the eighth month of his tour, the soldier operates on a kind of plateau of moderate commitment to his combat role.

Toward the ninth and tenth months, the soldier begins to regard himself as an "old soldier," and it is usually at this point that he is generally most effective in combat. As he approaches the end of his tour in Vietnam, however, he begins noticeably to withdraw his efficiency. He now becomes reluctant to engage in offensive combat operations; and increasingly, he hears and repeats stories of men killed the day they were to rotate back home.

It is significant, though, that "short-timer's fever" is implicitly recognized by the others, and demands on short-timers are informally reduced. The final disengagement period of the combat soldier is considered a kind of earned prerogative which those earlier in the rotation cycle hope eventually to enjoy.

Overall, the rotation system reinforces a perspective which is essentially private and self-concerned. Somewhat remarkably, for example, I found little difference in the attitudes of combat soldiers in Vietnam over a two-year interval. The consistency was largely due, I believe, to the fact that each soldier goes through a similar rotation experience. The end of the war is marked by the date a man leaves Vietnam, and not by its eventual outcome—whether victory, defeat or stalemate. Even discussion of broader military strategy and the progress of the war—except when directly impinging on one's unit—appears irrelevant to the combat soldier: "*My* war is over when I go home."

When the soldier feels concern over the fate of others, it is for those he personally knows in his own outfit. His concern does not extend to those who have preceded him or will eventually replace him. Rather, the attitude is typically, "I've done my time; let the others do theirs." Or, as put in the soldier's vernacular, he is waiting to make the final entry on his "FIGMO" chart—"Fuck it, got my order [to return to the United States]." Whatever incipient identification there might be with abstract comrades-in-arms is flooded out by the private view of the war fostered by the rotation system.

Conventionally, the primary group is described as a network of interpersonal relationships in which the group's maintenance is valued for its own sake rather than as a mechanism that serves one's own interests. And, as has been noted, social science descriptions of combat motivation in World War II placed particular emphasis on the importance of groupings governed by intimate face-to-face relations. Roger Little's observations of a rifle company during the Korean War differed somewhat by pointing to the two-man or "buddy system" as the basic unit of cohesion rather than the squad or platoon.

My observations in Vietnam, however, indicate that the concept of primary groups has limitations in explaining combat motivation even beyond that suggested by Little. The fact is that if the individual soldier is realistically to improve his survival chances, he must *necessarily* develop and take part in primary relationships. Under the grim conditions of ground warfare, an individual's survival is directly dependent upon the support—moral, physical and technical—he can expect from his fellow soldiers. He gets such support to the degree that he reciprocates to the others in his unit. In other words, primary relations are at their core mutually pragmatic efforts to minimize personal risk.

Interpreting the solidarity of combat squads as an outcome of individual self-interest can be corroborated by two illustrations. The first deals with the behavior of the man on "point" in a patrolling operation. The point man is usually placed well in front of the main body, in the most exposed position. Soldiers naturally dread this dangerous assignment, but a good point man is a safeguard for the entire patrol. What happens, as often as not, is that men on point behave in a noticeably careless manner in order to avoid being regularly assigned to the job. At the same time, of course, the point man tries not to be so incautious as to put himself completely at the mercy of an encountered enemy force. In plain language, soldiers do not typically perform at their best when on point; personal safety overrides group interest.

The paramountcy of individual self-interest in combat units is also indicated by the letters soldiers write. Squad members who have returned to the United States seldom write to those remaining behind. In most cases, nothing more is heard from a soldier after he leaves the unit. Perhaps even more revealing, those still in the combat area seldom write their former buddies. Despite protestations of life-long friendship during the shared combat period, the rupture of communication is entirely mutual, once a soldier is out of danger. The soldier writes almost exclusively to those he expects to see when he leaves the service: his family and relatives, girl friends, and civilian male friends.

Do these contrasting interpretations of the network of social relations in combat units—the primary groups of World War II, the two-man relationships of the Korean War, and the essentially individualistic soldier in Vietnam described here—result from conceptual differences on the part of the commentators, or do they reflect substantive differences in the social cohesion of the American soldiers being described? If substantive differences do obtain, particularly between World War II and the wars in Korea and Vietnam, much of this variation could be accounted for by the disruptive effects on unit solidarity caused by the introduction of the rotation system in the latter two wars.

LATENT IDEOLOGY

Even if we could decide whether combat primary groups are essentially entities *sui generis* or outcomes of pragmatic self-interest, there remain other difficulties in understanding the part they play in maintaining organizational effectiveness. For it has been amply demonstrated in many contexts that primary groups can hinder as well as serve to attain the formal goals of the larger organization. Thus, to describe effective combat motivation principally in terms of primary group ties leaves unanswered the question of why various armies—independent of training and equipment—perform differently in times of war. Indeed, because of the very ubiquity of primary groups in military organizations, we must look for supplementary factors to explain variations in combat motivation.

I propose that primary groups maintain the soldier in his combat role only when he has an underlying commitment to the worth of the larger social system for which he is fighting. This commitment need not be formally articulated, nor even perhaps consciously recognized. But the soldier must at some level accept, if not the specific purposes of the war, then at least the broader rectitude of the society of which he is a member. Although American combat soldiers do not espouse overtly ideological sentiments and are extremely reluctant to voice patriotic rhetoric, this should not obscure the existence of more latent beliefs in the legitimacy, and even superiority of the American way of life. I have used the term "latent ideology" to describe the social and cultural sources of those beliefs about the war held by American soldiers. Latent ideology, in this context, refers to those widely shared sentiments of soldiers which, though not overtly political, nor even necessarily substantively political, nevertheless have concrete consequences for combat motivation.

Students of political behavior have too often been uninterested in answers that do not measure up to their own standards of expressiveness. When a person responds in a way that seems either ideologically confused or apathetic, he is considered to have no political ideology. But since any individual's involvement in any polity is usually peripheral, it is quite likely that his political attitudes will be organized quite differently from those of ideologists or political theorists. Yet when one focuses on underlying value orientations, we find a set of attitudes having a definite coherence—especially within the context of that individual's life situation.

Quite consistently, the American combat soldier displays a profound skepticism of political and ideological appeals. Somewhat paradoxically, then, anti-ideology itself is a recurrent and integral part of the soldier's belief system. They dismiss patriotic slogans or exhortations to defend democracy with "What a crock," "Be serious, man," or "Who's kidding who?" In particular, they have little belief that they are protecting an outpost of democracy in South Vietnam. United States Command Information pronouncements stressing defense of South Vietnam as an outpost of the "Free World" are almost as dubiously received as those of Radio Hanoi which accuse Americans of imperialist aggression. As one soldier put it, "Maybe we're supposed to be here and maybe not. But you don't have time to think about things like that. You worry about getting zapped and dry socks tomorrow. The other stuff is a joke."

In this same vein, when the soldier responds to the question of why he is in Vietnam, his answers are couched in a quite individualistic frame of reference. He sees little connection between his presence in Vietnam and the national policies that brought him there. Twenty-seven of the 34 combat soldiers I interviewed defined their presence in the war in terms of personal misfortune. Typical responses were: "My outfit was sent over here and me with it," "My tough luck in getting drafted," "I happened to be at the wrong place at the wrong time," "I was fool enough to join this man's army," and "My own stupidity for listening to the recruiting sergeant." Only five soldiers mentioned broader implications—to stop Communist aggression. Two soldiers stated they requested assignment to Vietnam because they wanted to be "where the action is."

Because of the combat soldier's overwhelming propensity to see the war in private and personal terms, I had to ask them specifically what they thought the United States was doing in Vietnam. When the question was phrased in this manner, the soldiers most often said they were in Vietnam "to stop Communism." This was about the only ideological slogan these American combat soldiers could be brought to utter; 19 of the 34 interviewed soldiers saw stopping Communism as the purpose of the war. But when they expressed this view it was almost always in terms of defending the United States, not the "Free World" in general and certainly not South Vietnam. They said: "The only way we'll keep them out of the States is to kill them here," "Let's get it over now, before they're too strong to stop," "They have to be stopped somewhere," "Better to zap this country than let them do the same to us."

Fifteen of the soldiers gave responses other than stopping Communism. Three gave frankly cynical explanations of the war by stating that domestic prosperity in the United States depended on a war economy. Two soldiers held that the American intervention was a serious mistake initially; but that it was now too late to back out because of America's reputation. One man even gave a Malthusian interpretation, arguing that war was needed to limit population growth. Nine of the soldiers could give no reason for the war even after extensive discussion. Within this group, one heard responses such as: "I only wish I knew" "Maybe Johnson knows, but I sure don't" and "I've been wondering about that ever since I got here."

I asked each of the 19 soldiers who mentioned stopping Communism as the purpose of the war what was so bad about Communism that it must be stopped at the risk of his own life. The first reaction to such a question was usually perplexity or rueful shrugging. After thinking about it, and with some prodding, 12 of the men expressed their distaste for communism by stressing its authoritarian aspects in social relations. They saw Communism as a system of excessive social regimentation which allows the individual no autonomy in the pursuit of his own happiness. Typical descriptions of Communism were: "That's when you can't do what you want to do," "Somebody's always telling you what to do," or "You're told where you work, what you eat, and when you shit." As one man wryly put it, "Communism is something like the army."

While the most frequently mentioned features of Communism concerned individual liberty, other descriptions were also given. Three soldiers mentioned the atheistic and antichurch aspects of Communism; two specifically talked of the absence of political parties and democratic political institutions; and one man said Communism was good in theory, but could never work in practice because human beings were "too selfish." Only one soldier mentioned the issues of public versus private property ownership.

I should stress once again that the soldiers managed to offer reasons for the war or descriptions of communism only after extended discussion and questioning. When left to themselves, they rarely discussed the goals of America's military intervention in Vietnam, the nature of Communist systems, or other political issues.

AMERICANISM

To say that the American soldier is not overtly ideological is not to deny the existence of salient values that do contribute to his motivation in combat. Despite the soldier's lack of ideological concern and his pronounced embarrassment in the face of patriotic rhetoric, he nevertheless displays an elemental American nationalism in the belief that the United States is the best country in the world. Even though he hates being in the war, the combat soldier typically believes—with a kind of joyless patriotism—that he is fighting for his American homeland. When the soldier does articulate the purposes of the war, the view is expressed that if Communist aggression is not stopped in Southeast Asia, it will be only a matter of time before the United States itself is in jeopardy. The so-called domino theory is just as persuasive among combat soldiers as it is among the general public back home.

The soldier definitely does *not* see himself fighting for South Vietnam. Quite the contrary, he thinks South Vietnam is a worthless country, and its people contemptible. The low regard in which the Vietnamese— "slopes" or "gooks"—are held is constantly present in the derogatory comments on the avarice of those who pander to G.I.s, the treachery of all Vietnamese, and the numbers of Vietnamese young men in the cities who are not in the armed forces. Anti-Vietnamese sentiment is most glaringly apparent in the hostility toward the ARVN (Army of the Republic of Vietnam, pronounced "Arvin") who are their supposed military allies. Disparaging remarks about "Arvin's" fighting qualities are endemic.

A variety of factors underlie the soldier's fundamental pro-Americanism, not the least of them being his immediate reliance on fellow Americans for mutual support in a country where virtually all indigenous people are seen as actual or potential threats to his physical safety. He also has deep concern for his family and loved ones back home. These considerations, however, are true of any army fighting in a foreign land. It is on another level, then, that I tried to uncover those aspects of American society that were most relevant and important to the combat soldier.

To obtain such a general picture of the soldier's conception of his homeland, I asked the following question, "Tell me in your own words, what makes America different from other countries?" The overriding feature in the soldier's perception of America is the creature comforts that American life can offer. Twenty-two of the soldiers described the United States by its high-paying jobs, automobiles, consumer goods and leisure activities. No other description of America came close to being mentioned as often as the high—and apparently uniquely American—

material standard of living. Thus, only four of the soldiers emphasized America's democratic political institutions; three mentioned religious and spiritual values; two spoke of the general characteristics of the American people; and one said America was where the individual advanced on his own worth; another talked of America's natural and physical beauties; and one black soldier described America as racist. Put in another way, it is the materialistic—and I do not use the word pejoratively—aspects of life in America that are most salient to combat soldiers.

THE BIG PX

The soldier's belief in the superiority of the American way of life is further reinforced by the contrast with the Vietnamese standard of living. The combat soldier cannot help making invidious comparisions between the life he led in the United States—even if he is working class —and what he sees in Vietnam. Although it is more pronounced in the Orient, it must be remembered that Americans abroad—whether military or civilian—usually find themselves in locales that compare unfavorably with the material affluence of the United States. Indeed, should American soldiers ever be stationed in a country with a markedly higher standard of living than that of the United States, I believe they would be severely shaken in their belief in the merits of American society.

Moreover, the fighting soldier, by the very fact of being in combat, leads an existence that is not only more dangerous than civilian life, but more primitive and physically harsh. The soldier's somewhat romanticized view of life back home is buttressed by his direct observation of the Vietnamese scene, but also by his own immediate lower standard of living. It has often been noted that front-line soldiers bitterly contrast their plight with the physical amenities enjoyed by their fellow countrymen, both rear-echelon soldiers as well as civilians back home. While this is superficially true, the attitudes of American combat soldiers toward their compatriots are actually somewhat more ambivalent. For at the same time the soldier is begrudging the civilian his physical comforts, it is these very comforts for which he fights. Similarly, they envy rather than disapprove of those rear-echelon personnel who engage in sub rosa profiteering.

The materialistic ethic is reflected in another characteristic of American servicemen. Even among front-line combat soldiers, one sees an extraordinary amount of valuable paraphernalia. Transistor radios are practically de rigueur. Cameras and other photographic accessories are widely evident and used. Even the traditional letter-writing home is becoming displaced by tape recordings. It seems more than coincidental that American soldiers commonly refer to the United States as "The Land of the Big PX."

Another factor that plays a part in combat motivation is the notion of masculinity and physical toughness that pervades the soldier's outlook toward warfare. Being a combat soldier is a man's job. Front-line soldiers often cast aspersions on the virility of rear-echelon personnel ("titless WAC's"). A soldier who has not experienced combat is called a "cherry" (i.e. virgin). Likewise, paratroopers express disdain for "legs," as nonairborne soldiers are called. This he-man attitude is also found in the countless joking references to the movie roles of John Wayne and Lee Marvin. These definitions of masculinity are, of course, general in America and the military organization seeks to capitalize on them with such perennial recruiting slogans as "The Marine Corps Builds Men" and "Join the Army and Be a Man."

Needless to say, however, the exaggerated masculine ethic is much less evident among soldiers after their units have been bloodied. As the realities of combat are faced, more prosaic definitions of manly honor emerge. (Also, there is more frequent expression of the male role in manifestly sexual rather than combative terms, for example, the repeatedly heard "I'm a lover not a fighter.") That is, notions of masculinity serve to create initial motivation to enter combat, but recede once the life-and-death facts of warfare are confronted. Moreover, once the unit is tempered by combat, definitions of manly honor are not seen to encompass individual heroics. Quite the opposite, the very word "hero" is used to describe negatively any soldier who recklessly jeopardizes the unit's welfare. Men try to avoid going out on patrols with individuals who are overly anxious to make contact with the enemy. Much like the slacker at the other end of the spectrum, the "hero" is also seen as one who endangers the safety of others. As is the case with virtually all combat behavior, the ultimate standard rests on keeping alive.

THE FIGHTING MAN'S PEACE DEMONSTRATION

On both of my trips to Vietnam I repeatedly heard combat soldiers —almost to a man—vehemently denounce peace demonstrators back in the United States. At first glance such an attitude might be surprising. After all, peaceniks and soldiers both fervently want troops brought home. In fact, however, the troops I interviewed expressed overt political sentiments only when the antiwar demonstrations came up in the talk. Significantly, the soldier perceived the peace demonstrations as being directed against himself personally and not against the war. "Did I vote to come here? Why blame the G.I.?" There was also a widespread feeling that if peace demonstrators were in Vietnam they could change their minds. As one man stated: "How can they know what's happening if they're sitting on their asses in the States. Bring them here and we'd shape them up quick enough." Or as one of the more philosophically inclined put it, "I'd feel the same way if I were back home. But once you're here and your buddies are getting zapped, you have to see things different."

Much of the soldier's dislike of peace demonstrators is an outcome of class hostility. To many combat soldiers—themselves largely working class—peace demonstrators are socially privileged college students. I heard many remarks such as the following: "I'm fighting for those candy-asses just because I don't have an old man to support me." "I'm stuck here and those rich draft dodgers are having a ball raising hell." "You'd think they'd have more sense with all that smart education."

The peace demonstrators, moreover, were seen as undercutting and demeaning the losses and hardships already suffered by American soldiers. Something of this sort undoubtedly contributed to the noticeable hawk-like sentiments of combat soldiers. "If we get out now, then every G.I. died for nothing. Is this why I've been putting my ass on the line?" Here we seem to have an illustration of a more general social phenomenon: the tendency in human beings to justify to themselves sacrifices they have already made. Sacrifice itself can create legitimacy for an organization over a short period of time. It is only after some point when sacrifices suddenly seem too much, that the whole enterprise comes under critical reevaluation. But sharp questioning of past and future sacrifices does not generally occur among combat soldiers in Vietnam. I believe this is because the 12-month rotation system removes the soldier from the combat theater while his personal stake remains high and before he might begin to question the whole operation. The rotation system, in other words, not only maintains individual morale but also fosters a collective commitment to justify American sacrifices.

The soldier's hostility toward peace demonstrators is reinforced by his negative reactions to the substance of certain antiwar arguments. For while the combat soldier is constantly concerned with his own and his fellow American's safety, as well as being a fundamental believer in the American way of life and profoundly apolitical to boot, the radical element of the peace movement mourns the suffering of the Vietnamese, is vehement in its anti-Americanism, and is self-consciously ideological. At almost every point, the militant peace movement articulates sentiments in direct opposition to the basic values of the American soldier. Statements bemoaning civilian Vietnamese casualties are interpreted as wishes for greater American losses. Assertions of the United States' immorality for its interventionism run contrary to the soldier's elemental belief in the rectitude of the American nation. Arguments demonstrating that the Viet Cong are legitimate revolutionaries have no credence both because of the soldier's ignorance of Vietnamese history and —more importantly—because the Viet Cong are out to kill him. As one man summed it up: "I don't know who are the good guys or the bad guys, us or the V.C. But anybody who shoots at me ain't my friend. Those college punks are going to answer to a lot of us when we get back."

It must be stressed, however, that the soldier's dislike of peace demonstrators is reactive and does not imply any preexisting support for the war. Paradoxically, then, the more militant peace demonstrations have probably created a level of support for the war among combat soldiers that would otherwise be absent. This is not to say that the soldier is immune to antiwar arguments. But the kind of arguments that would be persuasive among soldiers (e.g. Vietnam is not worth American blood, South Vietnam is manipulating the United States, the corruptness of the Saigon regime and ineptitude of the ARVN make for needless U.S. casualties) are not the ones usualy voiced by radical peace groups. *The combat soldier is against peace-demonstrators rather than for the war.* For it should also be known that he has scant affection for "support-the-boys" campaigns in the United States. Again, the attitude that "they don't know what it's all about" applies. As one soldier succinctly put it—and his words spoke for most: "The only support I want is out."

RESEARCH IN THE COMBAT ZONE

The information for this article is based on my observations of American soldiers in combat made during two separate stays in South Vietnam. During the first field trip in 1965, I spent two weeks with a weapons squad in a rifle platoon of a paratrooper unit. The second field trip in 1967 included a six-day stay with an infantry rifle squad, and shorter periods with several other combat squads. Although identified as a university professor and sociologist, I had little difficulty gaining access to the troops because of my official status as an accredited correspondent. I entered combat units by simply requesting permission from the local headquarters to move into a squad. Once there, I experienced the same living conditions as the squad members. The novelty of my presence soon dissipated as I became a regular participant in the day-to-day activities of the squad.

The soldiers with whom I was staying were performing combat missions of a patrolling nature, the most typical type of combat operation in Vietnam. Patrols are normally small-unit operations involving squads (9–12 men) or platoons (30–40 men). Such small units made up patrols whose usual mission was to locate enemy forces which could then be subjected to ground, artillery or air attack. Patrols normally last one or several days and are manned by lower-ranking enlisted men, noncommissioned officers leading squads and lieutenants heading platoons.

In the vast majority of instances these patrols turn out to be a "walk in the sun," meeting only sporadic or no enemy resistance. Even when enemy contact is not made, however, patrols suffer casualties from land mines and booby traps. But it is primarily on those occasions when enemy forces are encountered that casualty rates are extremely high. Upon return to the permanent base camp, members of the patrol are able to enjoy a modicum of physical comfort. They live in large tents, eat hot food, get their mail more or less regularly, see movies, and can purchase beer, cigarettes and toilet articles at field Post Exchanges. They spend the bulk of their time in camp on guard duty and maintaining equipment.

In both the 1965 and 1967 field trips, I collected data through informal observations and personal interviewing of combat soldiers. During the second field trip I also conducted 34 standardized interviews with the men of the particular squads with whom I was staying. Some of the information contained in these 34 interviews is amenable to tabular ordering. Yet even when given in tabular form the data are not to be conceived as self-contained, but rather as supportive of more broadly based observations. The attitudes expressed by the formally interviewed soldiers constantly reappeared in conversations I had with numerous other combat soldiers in both 1965 and 1967. Again and again, I was struck by the common reactions of soldiers to the combat experience and their participation in the war. By myself being in the combat situation, I could conduct lengthy interviews on an intimate basis. I assert with some confidence that the findings reflect a set of beliefs widely shared by American combat soldiers throughout Vietnam during the period of the field work.

A prefatory comment is needed on the social origins of the men I interviewed. The 34 soldiers had the following civilian backgrounds prior to entering the service: ten were high-school dropouts, only two of whom were ever regularly employed; 21 were high-school graduates, six directly entering the service after finishing school; and three were college dropouts. None were college graduates. Eighteen of the 34 men had full-time employment before entering the service, 12 in blue-collar jobs and six in white-collar employment. About two-thirds of the soldiers were from working-class backgrounds with the remainder being from the lower-middle class.

As for other social background characteristics: eight were black; one was a Navajo; another was from Guam; the other 20 men were white including three Mexican-Americans and one Puerto Rican. Only seven of the squad members were married (three after entering the service). All the men, except two sergeants, were in their late teens and early twenties, the average age being 20 years. Again excepting the sergeants, all were on their initial enlistments. Twenty of the men were draftees and 14 were Regular Army volunteers. Importantly, except for occasional sardonic comments directed toward the regulars by the draftees, the behavior and attitudes of the soldiers toward the war were very similar regardless of how they entered the service.

■ THE FASHIONABLE VIEW OF MAN AS A NAKED APE IS:
1) **An Insult to Apes**
2) **Simplistic**
3) **Male-Oriented**
4) **Rubbish**

David Pilbeam

As we turn to man, let's consider for a while human groups as they were before the switch to a settled way of life began. For at least 2½ million to 3 million years, man and his ancestors lived as hunters and gatherers. The change from hunting to agriculturally based economics began a mere 10,000 years ago, a fractional moment on the geological time scale. Hunting has been a highly significant event in human history; indeed, it is believed by most of us interested in human evolution to have been an absolutely vital determinant, molding many aspects of human behavior.

There are a number of societies today that still live as hunters. Congo Pygmies, Kalahari Bushmen, and Australian aborigines, are three well-known examples. When comparisons are made among these hunting societies we can see that certain features are typical of most or all of them, and these features are likely to have been typical of earlier hunters.

In hunting societies, families—frequently monogamous nuclear families are often grouped together in bands of 20 to 40 individuals; members of these hunting bands are kinsmen, either by blood or marriage. The band hunts and gathers over wide areas, and its foraging range often overlaps that of adjacent groups. Bands are flexible and variable in composition—splitting and re-forming with changes in the seasons, game and water availability, and whim.

Far from life being "short, brutish and nasty" for these peoples, recent studies show that hunters work on the average only 3 or 4 days each week; the rest of their time is leisure. Further, at least 10 per cent of Bushman, for example, are past 60 years of age, valued and nurtured by their children. Although they lack large numbers of material possessions, one can never describe such peoples as savages, degenerates or failures.

The men in these societies hunt animals while the women gather plant food. However, women often scout for game, and in some groups may also hunt smaller animals, while a man returning empty-handed from a day's hunting will almost always gather vegetable food on his way. Thus the division of labor between sexes is not distinct and immutable; it seems to be functional, related to mobility. The women with infants to protect and carry simply cannot move far and fast enough to hunt efficiently.

Relations between bands are amicable; that makes economic sense as the most efficient way of utilizing potentially scarce resources, and also makes sense because in the practice of exogamy—marrying out—adjacent groups will contain kinsmen, and kinsmen will not fight. Within the group, individual relations between adults are cooperative and based upon reciprocity; status disputes are avoided. These relations are a formalized part of cultural behavior, since such actions are positively valued and rewarded. Aggression between individuals is generally maintained at the level of bickering, in cases where violence flares, hunters generally solve the problem by fission: the band divides.

Data on the child-rearing practices of hunters are well-known only about Bushmen, and we don't yet know to what extent Bushmen are typical of hunters. According to Patricia Draper, a Harvard anthropologist, Bushman children are almost always in the company of adults; because of the small size of Bushman societies, children rarely play in large groups with others of their own age. Aggression is minimal in the growing child for two principal reasons. First, arguments between youngsters almost inevitably take place in the presence of adults, and adults break these up before fights erupt; the socialization process gives children little opportunity for practicing aggressive behavior. Second, because of the reciprocity and cooperativeness of adults, children have few adult models on which to base the learning of aggressiveness.

Thus, the closest we can come to a concept of "natural man" would indicate that our ancestors were, like other primates, capable of being aggressive, but they would have been socialized culturally in such a way as to reduce as far as possible the manifestation of aggression. This control through learning is much more efficient in man than in other primates, because we are culture creatures. The term "culture," a special one for the anthropologist, describes the specifically human type of learned behavior in which arbitrary rules and norms are so important. The appropriate or correct behavior varies from culture to culture; exactly which one is appropriate is arbitrary. This sort of behavior is known as "context-dependent behavior" and is, in its learned form, pervasively and almost uniquely human. So pervasive is it, indeed, that most of the time we are unaware of the effects of context dependence on our behavior. It is important to realize that although a great deal of ape and monkey behavior is learned, little of it is context-dependent in a cultural, human sense.

As such a cultural creature, man has the ability to attach positive value to aggression-controlling behavior. Thus, Bushmen value and thereby encourage peaceful cooperation. Their culture provides the young with nonviolent models. Other cultures promote the very opposite. Take, for example, the Yanomamö Indians of Venezuela and Brazil; their culture completely reverses our ideals of "good" and "desirable." To quote a student of Yanomamö society: "A high capacity for rage, a quick flash point, and a willingness to use violence to obtain one's ends are considered desirable traits." To produce the appropriate adult behavior, the Yanomamö encourage their children, especially young boys, to argue, fight and be generally belligerent. Such behavior, I should emphasize, is learned, and depends for its encouragement upon specific cultural values. Our own culture certainly provides the young with violent, though perhaps less obtrusive, models. These, I should emphasize again, are learned and arbitrary, and we *could* change them should we choose to do so.

So far we have seen that fierce aggression and status-seeking are no more "natural" attributes of man than they are of most monkey and ape societies. The degree to which such behavior is developed depends very considerably indeed upon cultural values and learning. Territoriality, likewise, is not a "natural" feature of human group living; nor is it among most other primates.

As a parting shot, let me mention one more topic that is of great interest to everyone at the moment—sex roles. Too many of us have in the past treated the male and female stereotypes of our particular culture as fixed and "natural"; in our genes, so to speak. It may well be true that human male infants play a little more vigorously than females, or that they learn aggressive behavior somewhat more easily, because of hormonal differences. But simply look around the world at other cultures. In some, "masculinity" and "femininity" are much more marked than they are in our own culture; in others the roles are blurred. As I said earlier, among Bushmen who are still hunters, sex roles are far from rigid, and in childhood the two sexes have a very similar upbringing. However, among those Bushmen who have adopted a sedentary life devoted to herding or agriculture, sex roles are much more rigid. Men devote their energies to one set of tasks and women to another, mutually exclusive set. Little boys learn only "male" tasks, little girls exclusively "female" ones. Maybe the switch to the sedentary life started man on the road toward marked sex-role differences. These differences, though, are almost entirely learned, and are heavily affected by economic factors.

So, what conclusions can be drawn from all this? It is overly simplistic in the extreme to believe that man behaves in strongly genetically deterministic ways, when we know that apes and monkeys do not. Careful ethological work shows us that the primates closely related to us—chimps and baboons are the best known—get on quite amicably together under natural and undisturbed conditions. Learning plays a very significant part in the acquisition of their behavior. They are not highly aggressive, obsessively dominance-oriented, territorial creatures.

There is no evidence to support the view that early man was a violent status-seeking creature; ethological and anthropological evidence indicates rather that preurban men would have used their evolving cultural capacities to channel and control aggression. To be sure, we are not born empty slates upon which anything can be written; but to believe in the "inevitability of beastliness" is to deny our humanity as well as our primate heritage—and, incidentally, does a grave injustice to the "beasts."

6

RELIGION

Philosophers, theologians, and anthropologists can all agree on at least one characteristic of people. Humans are the only creatures who know they are going to die. This may be the root cause of religion; we do not know. We do know, however, that every human society on earth deals with this annoying knowledge in a systematic way.

Many peoples postulate the existence of supernatural forces or beings as one way of relating to death. In addition, the supernatural is often given credit for all sorts of other things over which people do have effective control. Religion is minimally the belief that there are supernatural beings and/or forces that have to be dealt with in order to ensure a good life.

How we deal with the supernatural depends on how we view our gods and ghosts in the first place. Some gods require that we plead with them for favors. Others won't listen to prayers and so they have to be bullied, harassed, threatened, and manipulated to get them to do our wishes. A reverent, supplicative approach to the supernatural is usually termed *religious* behavior. Attempting to overcome the supernatural and force it to do what you want is *magic*. Sometimes coercive magic is used only after religious methods fail. In Mexico, many researchers have noticed this among various Indian groups during droughts. The images and statues of the saints to whom people pray for rain may be taken out to the fields and left to bake in the sun. The idea is that when the gods get thirsty and uncomfortable enough they will bring rain.

Of course, we engage in magic all the time; our soaps have mysterious "cleaning power"; our tooth pastes and deodorants have mysterious sexual powers or "sex appeal"; we imagine our physicians to have healing powers rather than healing skills.

It should be clear from all this that religion is a complicated thing. In this section I have chosen a few readings that give some of the breadth of this topic. In the first article, Howells considers the basics: What is religion? How can anthropologists study it most effectively? The second article, by LaBarre, shows how much any definition of religious behavior depends on who is defining and who is behaving. LaBarre imagines what an anthropologist from a black African civilization might make of our ritualized behavior at cocktail parties. What the African anthropologist finds, of course, is that Americans engage in strange, ritualistic behavior at these affairs. This approach has been used by several anthropologists and the results are usually sobering as well as hilarious. The classic in this genre is Horace Miner's analysis of the Nacirema (not reprinted here) who spend long hours of prayer in a shrine called the *toilet*. Miner wrote the Nacirema article in 1959, long before television was saturated with advertisements for underarm sprays, vaginal sprays, mouth sprays, and a dozen other products to help us worship in the toilet.

The personnel of religion are as important as the beliefs. Religion in primitive societies is handled within the family. Everyone knows the rituals and the beliefs, and each person is responsible for carrying them out at the proper time. In complex societies we find full-time practitioners of religion who belong to formally organized ecclesiastical groups. In many ways these full-time religious personnel (priests) take the burden off the rest of us for participation in the religion itself. But they are more than this in any community, especially in the closed agricultural communities of peasant society. In the third selection, by Irwin Sanders, we see how the priest functions in the Greek community—how he fits in to the total framework of the village society.

Although the priest represents the benevolent practitioner, many religions also include evil doers such as witches. The fourth selection, from Kluckholn and Leighton's famous study of the Navaho, describes the ghosts and witches in the Navaho religion.

Finally, we must consider the nature of the religious experience and the role of ritual and ceremonial in creating that experience. In a ceremony, a group of people come together on a regular basis to perform a series of ritual acts. One of the key functions of such acts is the strengthening of emotional bonds in the community that celebrates the ceremony. In the final article, Jeff Greenfield shows how a secular ceremony—one that does not convene for the purpose of relating to the supernatural—can perform the same social functions as a religious cermony. Reading the description of Americans' behavior at the Indy 500 forces us to consider again the definition of religion in the first place.

■ THE NATURE OF RELIGION

William Howells

Whatever religion may be, the human material for it is probably similar in all men and all tribes of men. There may be differences in its expression. One group may appear more religious, another less. Or one tribe may go in for the appeasement of local ghosts, another for the worship of remote high gods, and a third for magic to open the rain clouds and lure the game. But all give signs of satisfaction with their own observances, and primitive societies without religion have never been found.

As to the people themselves, there are those who are pious and those who are not. And there are those who may have doubts about what they are told, and those who may be extra gullible about witches and demons. But such individual notions matter little; most people get their beliefs straight out of the public pool and accept them implicitly. These are the ideas that have social force and do the work; they are the ones that people talk about and act upon together. They are the things I shall deal with, and what I say hereafter is meant to apply to public religion rather than private.

This does not let the individual out entirely, of course, because we have to look at society through him—it is the individual, not society, who acts religiously, though society tells him how to do it. When we consider religions we must first consider man, because religion is rooted in man and would of course not exist without him. It is a human manifestation. It is made by man. This is something different from the old epigram: "Man made God in his own image." It is not a question of the existence or non-existence of supernatural beings, for there could be no religion connected with them if man himself did not exist and feel the need of it.

It is, instead, a question of what there is in man, or about him, which makes him religious. I do not mean a quality of religion, like a phrenologist's head bump, something which might almost be dressed up and put in an allegory. There has in the past been brisk discussion of a religious emotion, or "instinct," as the one responsible factor, and such a thing has been accepted and sought for in other supposed emotions, or derivations or combinations of them: awe, love, fear, shame, conscience, as well as diverted sexual or social longings, and so forth and so on. Now of course the things signified by such terms may have strong connections with religious behavior, in different individuals and to different degrees, but this is a far cry from supposing that there may be found a particular, recognizable instinct, drive, or type of reaction which might be isolated like a bacillus and accepted as the one thing explaining why societies inevitably turn to religion like a flower to the sun. The quest for some factor has not succeeded. In any event it is a subject for the psychologists, if they care to have it. What I am leading up to is different; it is a matter of certain palpable facts about man and his past which tend to show that it is not one lone element within him, but rather his whole organism and life which predispose him to "religious" behavior—which cause him to produce religious ideas and then to respond so readily to them.

First of all there are some important characteristics of man himself. We are fearfully and wonderfully made, and we can get a better idea of how fearfully and wonderfully by comparing ourselves with some of Noah's other passengers. Among all animals, the warm-blooded mammals are the most active, with the most intricate organization and the best-developed nervous systems. Among these, in turn, it is the Primates (especially the monkeys, the anthropoid apes, and men) which have, on the whole, the largest brains and the most refined and acute set of senses, so that their awareness of the world around them is increased beyond that of all living things. The highest of these animals not only possess good hearing, sensitive hands, and excellent muscular control, but have undoubtedly the best eyes in all of nature; they see stereoscopically (focusing on the same object from different points), so that they judge size and distance most accurately. Only men, apes, and monkeys completely enjoy this ability, and only these same animals are able to see so full a range of colors. With this fullness of vision we (and our low-brow relatives) absorb more of our surroundings than all other creatures —without realizing quite how well endowed we are, we nevertheless experience great pleasure in gazing at landscapes and living things. Lacking his range of senses and muscular refinement, think how handicapped an animal man would be. Compare yourself with a dog. He sees a grayish world tinged only with blue and brown, and he can feel and understand very little through the use of his paws, let alone accomplish anything with them, like playing billiards. There is only one thing he can do better than you: starting from scratch, he can smell you before you can smell him.

So man, approached only by his zoological next of kin, is constructed in such a way as to feel the impact of the physical world much more forcibly than any of the beasts. Thus far we have considered only the nature of what his senses receive, and how they receive it, like currency coming into a cash register. How is the money used? This, of course, is a question of brain, and here again man has no peers, for in relative size and complexity his brain outclasses all others. This is so obvious that I need not go on about it, except to remark that the only animals who can be induced to proceed any distance in reasoning along human patterns are the apes and monkeys. Accordingly, although they fall woefully short, they resemble us in this as in other things, and represent a stage from which we ourselves must have arisen.

For a purely animal existence, our large brains are a luxury rather than a necessity. While other creatures can retain sensory and motor nervous patterns—i.e., do a certain amount of remembering—the plenteousness of our own brains not only makes them act as much vaster storehouses but also allows us to think about things we have never actually experienced—to imagine. Therefore, if what our senses receive is a multiplication of what most mammals can take in, and if what our brain can then make of it is also a great multiplication of what a simpler brain can do, then it is easy to see that the final effect of beholding a lake, a bolt of lightning, or a dead man can be infinitely greater on us than on any of our four-footed friends.

Even so, the effect would be naught if we were stolid creatures, unroused by such a wealth of sensation. But we are not. Our nervous organization is matched by, and related to, a highly excitable temperament or emotional nature. You might say that any species of mammal which had evolved into a man, and had come to experience so much, had every right to an excitable disposition and a parlous insanity rate. Probably there is justice in this; however, by referring to some of the other Primates again I think it is possible to see that this keyed-up temperament is, partly at least, an organic inheritance, belonging to the monkeys and apes generally. While temperament is something which cannot be measured properly, it can be said that all the apes appear to be subject to temper tantrums like a child's. Chimpanzees seem to have a normal excitability much like ours, though somewhat higher, while gorillas, outwardly more placid and contented, may really be inhibiting their natural emotionalism more than chimps, being actually capable of marked emotional disturbances. To make an analogy, it is rather as though among the higher Primates and ourselves the emotional motors idled at a high rate, capable of quick acceleration.

There are other important qualities in which our relatives resemble us, indicating that they are old traits and that we did not acquire them only on becoming human beings. One such quality is gregariousness. All men live in societies, or at least families, a hermit being very much of an exception. Of the higher Primates, the orangutan apparently often lives in solitude, but the others are typically extremely clannish; they either live in close family groups, like gibbons, or go about in sizable bands, which are not chance groupings but solidly knit affairs which will admit an occasional stranger only after he has hung around at a respectful distance long enough to become familiar. This cohesiveness is based on the fact that the individuals of a group are all socially or psychologically adjusted to one another, and it may show itself in a number of ways. One way is the above hostility to strangers, or meanness to a new colleague in the zoo. Another is the misery some animals will show if they are separated from their accustomed fellows, and the sympathy and affection of which they are capable toward one another, much more marked than, for example, among dogs. Yet others are the sensitivity they have for the moods of their companions, and the susceptibility to suggestions from one another or from human overlords, and the adaptability to the general mood of the group, or to demands made upon them by students putting them through tests. All this responsiveness and malleability is a sign of a rich and flexible nervous organization, capable of a great range of adjustment and not, as in lower animals, limited and hampered by a lot of ready-formed patterns, popularly known as instinctive behavior.

What I have said about human and Primate nature is based on serious investigation of matters of fact, and not on my own assumptions. I have been trying to hold up man's own physique and psyche as things legitimately founded in his evolutionary past; in other words, to show man not as an inexplicable what-is-it in the scheme of things but rather as the culmination of a trend producing creatures capable in the highest degree of receiving, and reflecting on, stimuli from their surroundings, and of great sensitiveness in reacting personally and adjusting themselves thereto. I do not think, however, that I need appeal to fact in order to state that this trend has not yet produced a sublimely happy animal, but only one capable of variable internal weather and of uncomfortable awareness of his difficulties. Nonetheless, in order to preserve the scientific tone of this dissertation, I will introduce one exhibit.

The Grant Study of Harvard University, in an attempt to reverse the field of medicine, has been studying the characteristics of "normal" young men[1] by selecting suitable Harvard sophomores over a period of four years up to a total of 259 students. These men were not meant to be unusual; on the contrary, they were meant to be as usual as possible, with the following qualifications. They were Harvard boys, of course, and Harvard is not the easiest college to enter. They were passed by the Hygiene Department as having no marked physical disabilities such as diabetes, infantile paralysis, deformities, and so on, and no psychological abnormalities; and all were doing satisfactorily in college, none having fallen afoul of the dean by day or by night. "Actually, some attempt was made to enlist those whose adjustments were superior. That the group was superior, in various categorizations, to the population at large and to the average college undergraduate, should be obvious."[2] Nevertheless, of these 259 normal or better-than-average students, 232 had at least one personal problem that either bothered them sufficiently to make them ask advice of the Grant Study staff, or made itself obvious to the staff members themselves. Only a small proportion of problems was acute (17 per

[1] See Clark W. Heath, *What People Are: A Study of Normal Young Men* (1945); Earnest Hooton, *Young Man, You Are Normal* (1945); C. W. Heath and Lewise W. Gregory, "Problems of Normal College Students and Their Families," *School and Society*, Vol. 63 (1946).
[2] Heath, *What People Are . . .*, p. 12.

cent of cases), but none of them was frivolous and all were disquieting, and most of the boys had more than one problem apiece. Remark now that 232 out of 259 is, to the nearest figure, 90 per cent. Who, then, is "normal"? If you were one of the 10 per cent, out of a generally superior physical and intellectual group, to whom life is all serene, you could count yourself lucky, since it seems more "normal" to have at least one fly in your ointment. It is true, of course, that these boys had not reached the Age of Discretion, and were still floundering in the adolescent Age of Worry; but this does not change the fact of man's great capacity for apprehensiveness. What does it batten on? This brings us from human nature to human history.

Man's life is hard, very hard. And he knows it, poor soul; that is the vital thing. He knows that he is forever confronted with the Four Horsemen—death, famine, disease, and the malice of other men. And because he can speak and so frame ideas for himself and his mercurial imagination, he is nature's great and only worrier; he can worry alone and he can worry in unison, always with justice. It is among people living a primitive existence, however, that this should be particularly true.

Man is distinguished from all other animals by culture. Culture, which largely is made possible by language, comprises everything which one generation can tell or teach the next; in other words, its non-physical inheritance. The complexity of our own culture shows what man is capable of, but the most primitive of surviving tribes, small bands of wandering hunters, show the kind of culture in which man has lived for perhaps a million years, including, for many thousands of years, some of our own ancestors in Europe, who must have had brains as good as our own. This was a bitterly harsh existence made harsher because, as I have said, he knew the worst; unlike animals, he was aware of the precariousness of his life and of the fact of death.

We today have some recompenses: our expectancy of life is long and we can make false teeth. Truly primitive people may keep only one jump ahead of nature, instead of our two or three. We can fetch our food from far away; they must depend on the weather and the game in one small region. We can cure disease or prevent it; they can only palliate it. We may still have nightmares of being chased by bears or lions; they may encounter the real thing, armed only with a stone-headed spear or ax. For primitive or ancient men, therefore, culture has been a thin shield indeed, so that they have been forced to use their resources to the utmost. And religion is related to all this because religion is one of their resources.

Taking two of the Four Freedoms will make this a little clearer. Freedom of speech and freedom of religion are of no concern to the compact society of a savage people. They are solely preoccupied with freedom from want and freedom from fear, and I will seize on this to make a somewhat exaggerated distinction. Freedom from want they achieve by their own practical efforts, while freedom from fear they achieve by religion. That is to say, they feed and clothe themselves, and also protect their goods, by everyday material tools and techniques which they have invented and which they understand perfectly: they will use a bow made partly of bone to strengthen it, to shoot an arrow expertly tipped and feathered, and perhaps poisoned, and will accompany this with delicate tricks to quiet the quarry's fears, or call it to the hunter; and they make their clothes and houses in perfectly practical ways, according to climate and material. It is all hard work but it is satisfying because it is direct and dependable. Freedom from fear (including, note well, the fear of want) is something else, however, because it can seldom be attained directly. Want is a physical hazard; fear is a mental hazard.

Now by "fear," I should like to say clearly, I do not mean simply fright: that funk induced by something in the dark, or by the threat of pain, or by a terrible mistake. I use "fear" because I need a short Anglo-Saxon word to stand for a number of longer Latin words like anxiety, insecurity, frustration, maladjustment, apprehensiveness, inadequacy, dissatisfaction, disappointment, vulnerability, and so on—all those lesser cares which rot the apple of content and keep life from its fullness. Such corrosive feelings may exist for some clear reason which cannot be removed. Or they may come from a dimmer consciousness of accumulating wrongs and ills. Or they may arise in small common neuroses, with no direct cause at all. But, though it may seem so unnecessary, this kind of heckling is constant, and a natural part of existence, the debit side of the ledger.

We have managed to compress our fears into a much smaller compass, because we have spread such a wide scientific control over many of the things, such as pestilence, which might threaten our security, but a backward society has so little that can be called science at its disposal that it is left with no certain answer to a great many of its urgent necessities, let alone its minor complaints. And an answer it must have, to forestall fear, or even panic. (This is true even of ourselves.) The principal answer is religion, which is thus used to piece out the ground between what man can attend to himself and what his imagination tells him must be attended to. It is the extension of his wishes and beliefs beyond the edges of what his senses grant him; it is what lies outside the light of the campfire. It is the notions he feels he must accept if life is to be satisfactory, or even safe. In other words, religion is composed of all the serious things man feels obliged to take for granted.

Religion therefore may be said to complement science. The latter has been defined best, I think, as a system of knowledge which admits of no internal contradictions. It is a body of facts which continually grows but does so only by adding new facts which are acceptable in the light of those already known. If two apparent facts are in conflict, then one of them is wrong or else the principle used in relating them is in error. For anthropological purposes, however, I should define science simply as the understanding of the correct explanation or principle for anything at all. If this is so, then the simplest technical exercise, like baiting a hook so that a fish will want to bite it, is scientific, while putting a spell on the same hook and bait to make the fish bite, regardless of his appetite, is religious. Thus people solve their problems either by science or by religion, since, if science hasn't an answer, religion has.

This is only a preliminary characterization of religion, and is not meant to be a full-fledged definition. It introduces the anthropological view; it attempts to say what religion does, without necessarily saying what it is. The fact is that no satisfactory definition of religion has ever been made. One good reason for this is that each definition has depended on the approach of the person making it, which takes us back to the six blind men and the elephant. A philosopher says, "Religion is x." But then a psychologist says: "What about y?" And an anthropologist says, "Yes, and what about z?" If you then lamely concede that "Religion is $x + y + z$," you are surrounding it, not defining it. I say this in the hope that I may sound less awkward when I shortly begin to talk in a circle myself.

E. B. Tylor[3] defined religion simply as the belief in spiritual beings, of any kind, and called this belief "animism." Marrett[4] simplified it further, to a feeling compounded of awe, fear, and wonder, aroused by the supernatural, and called this "pre-animism." But in these there appears no idea of action on this belief or feeling; this was inserted by Sir James Frazer and William James. Said the latter: ". . . the religious life consists of the belief that there is an unseen order and that our supreme good lies in harmoniously adjusting ourselves thereto."[5] This, however, is callous; respectful as it sounds, it is much like H. L. Mencken's disparaging dictum: "Its single function is to give man access to the powers which seem to control his destiny, and its single purpose is to induce those powers to be friendly to him. . . . Nothing else is essential."[6] Frazer,[7] however, insisted not only on the necessity of both belief and practice, but also that of religious feeling, or humility; but Frazer, in so doing, chose to exclude magic (sorcery, the use of spells, etc.) from religion.

These men put forward the original anthropological idea, but, as Marrett pointed out, they were concerned with religion in the individual, and neglected the social nature of religion, which was stressed by the French sociologist Durkheim.[8] The latter was also led by his argument to exclude magic from religion, like Frazer. According to his definition, a sense of the sacredness of certain things gives rise to beliefs and practices which become a communal affair, i.e., a church, and he considered this last element indispensable.

Other definitions have been coined in plenty. The first recent philos-

---

[3] *Primitive Culture* (1871).

[4] R. R. Marrett, *The Threshold of Religion* (1909).

[5] William James, *The Varieties of Religious Experience* (1902).

[6] *Treatise on the Gods* (1930).

[7] J. G. Frazer, *The Golden Bough* (1890; abridged edition, 1922).

[8] E. Durkheim, *The Elementary Forms of the Religious Life, a Study in Religious Psychology* (1915).

ophers who had the nerve to define religion at all spoke of it as man perceiving the infinite, or something of the sort; Kant called it the recognition of our duties as divine commands. The opposite extreme, the most detached view, is that of Reinach, who termed religion "a sum of scruples which impede the free exercise of our faculties."[9] To paraphrase him, religion is inhibitions. This sounds cynical, but it has the sense of the compulsive nature of religion in it; it is better as an epigram, however, than as a definition. On the whole, the anthropological efforts remain much the best, and modern students take the same line, usually rewording the older definitions so carefully and fulsomely that they sound as though they had been written by a lawyer. They do not satisfy, however, because religion needs a description rather than a definition. It has too rounded a nature to be expressed as a single idea or to be delimited by means of a single characteristic.

For example, the best attempted definitions have included as necessary elements belief, practice, emotional attitude, and the social nature of religion. But these things themselves need further qualification. Belief, in religion, is typically not simply the acceptance of an idea, like the moon being made of green cheese; it is more intense, it is an attitude, and need not even be formulated very clearly. It is the strong sense that there is more power in the universe than is present on the surface, and that such power may have a personal interest in you; and this strong sense acts as a compulsion, not simply as an argument. It is a matter beyond experience and does not require to be known by any of the ordinary means of perception. Practice or ritual also has a strong feeling of compulsion in it; it often contains the force of a wish, and it is accompanied by the conviction that there is more in your action than is put there by your mind and your arm. Furthermore, whether it is prayer, spell, or any other form, ritual is something established and accepted, so that in this sense it is always ceremonial. And the social aspect of religion means more than popular enthusiasm for the cult; it means that it serves some positive function for society itself, usually highly beneficent. Note, however, that none of this includes ethical ideas, or a belief in gods, or even a clear notion of what the power in the background may be.

If I were to try a definition here, I should say that a religion is a set of earnest policies which a group of people adopts under an unconscious compulsion in order to tidy up their distraught relationships with each other and with the universe as they perceive it, without the aid of science. In man's own eyes, perhaps, religion is a diplomatic conspiracy against the invisible, and since he keeps the score himself he usually manages to be satisfied with the results. But I would go completely around him and define it still again, as the normal psychological adjustment by which human societies build a barrier of fantasy against fear. And since, like any psychological adjustment, it is born in stress, it is therefore a source of emotion.

9 S. Reinach, *Orpheus,* English translation (1909).

■ PROFESSOR WIDJOJO GOES TO A KOKTEL PARTI

Weston La Barre

"Of course," mused Professor Widjojo, the eminent anthropologist of the University of Nyabonga, "the natives of the U.S.A. have many strange and outlandish customs; but I must say the drinking rituals of the Usans impressed me the most. These rituals occur yearly during an extended period in the calendrical round, beginning at the time of the harvest rites of Thanks-for-Blessings and ending largely at the drinking bouts at the New Year. This is called The Season, after which those who can afford it usually leave their homes entirely and flee southward into retirement for recuperation."

"Rather like our Nyabongan puberty ordeals?" asked a brilliantly dark matron dressed in a handsome apron of tiki feathers and little else.

"Well, no, not exactly," said Professor Widjojo, fingering his nose-stick politely before replying. "Perhaps I could describe it best by telling you of the Usan *koktel parti,* as they call it. You know, of course, that the Usan women, despite their rigid tribal clothing taboos, in general take off more clothes at their gatherings, depending upon the time of day. The neckline drops more and more, both in front and in back, as the *parti* is held later and later in the evening. They are entirely covered in the daytime, but this night-time disrobing is considered to be more formal. At the same time the length of the skirt increases, until it reaches the ground or even drags on it.

On the other hand, men put on more and more clothes as the formality of the occasion increases. The interesting point, however, is that the men, at *koktel partis,* do not ordinarily wear the beetle coats and white cloth neck-chokers of their most formal rituals, but dress rather more moderately as for church; furthermore, the women keep their hats on at *koktel partis,* thus clearly establishing the ritual significance of these *koktel partis.*

"Social status is indicated by the number of *partis* that a couple is invited to attend—and, of course, wealth, since a woman cannot wear the same dress and hat to more than one *parti.* People complain bitterly at the number they have to go to—sometimes even during the *parti* they are attending—but it is nevertheless plain that they are proud of their ability to sustain many ordeals, and this is a form of polite boasting. This point comes out most clearly in the *aignawg partis* when they are heard to boast, after they have stayed long enough at one to save face, that they must 'get on' to a number of other New Year *partis* before midnight. They always say they 'hate to go' though it is plain that they would really hate to stay.

"Not that these other rituals are any different, or that they provide escape from the ordeal," continued Professor Widjojo, "for at all of them the natives receive the same ritualized drink called *aignawg*. Everybody hates it, and freely says so in private, but they must drink some of it so as not to offend their hostess. Despite the superficial phonetic resemblance, *aignawg* has no connection whatever with eggs. It is really skimmed milk, made commercially and thickened with seaweed jelly; and the cream, if any, is whipped and placed on top of the handled cup they must drink it in.

"The ordeal aspect of the ritual is indicated in the fact that the hostess presses more and more cups upon her guests, who must pretend to praise the virtues of the drink—but even more so in the fact that they sprinkle *nutmaig* powder on top which, in larger quantities, of course is a violent poison inducing fainting, convulsions and death. But this *aignawg* has only enough *nutmaig* on it to make the people ill for several days. The Usan natives pride themselves on 'holding their liquor' so that this ceremony is plainly a contest between a hostess and her guests.

"But I am getting ahead of my chronology. Really, the drinking season of the Usans begins in the fall of the year, after a wholesome summer vacation, at the time of the *futbol* games. The purpose of the Usan colleges is to collect young men by competitive subsidies to engage in these mock battles, during which they rush ferociously at one another wearing padded armor and ritually kill one another. It seems to be some sort of contest over a sacred pigskin, and everyone gets up alive after each act in the ceremony. Rarely is a young man killed. However, the warriors are often 'punch-drunk' (an odd phrase because they are not allowed to drink, in contrast with spectators) and they may suffer broken legs, or faces mutilated by the nailed shoes of their opponents.

"Colleges seem once to have been trade schools where tribal lore was taught, but this was long ago and is now hardly remembered. The importance of a college nowadays is rated by the number of *futbol* games its team wins, and this in turn attracts further desirable young warriors to that college. The watchers urge on the warriors with blood-curdling chants, and between acts there are military maneuvers of a more rigorous form than in the battle itself. Afterward, they either celebrate their victory or 'drown their sorrows' in mourning if the warriors have sustained too many broken bones to win.

"These *futbol* ceremonies seem to be totemistic celebrations mainly, for each side has an animal totem—such as a bulldog, a tiger or a goat—which symbolizes the mystical unity of each side in their oddly named *alma mater,* or 'protective mother,' probably so called because she is the patron mother goddess of the young warriors frequently invoked in the battle hymns at these war games. Strangely, however, these totems do not govern marriage rules either inside or outside the *alma mater* group. I collected figures on this critical matter and found it is about as common to marry outside one's totem as within. In fact, *futbol* games are a recognized way to meet young people belonging to another totem."

"Are there totems governing marriage in the *koktel* gatherings you mentioned earlier?" asked a young girl just past her puberty ceremonial.

"No, I would think not," replied Professor Widjojo, thoughtfully. "On the contrary, the *koktel parti* more resembles a primitive orgy, with no reference to marriage bonds whatever. You see, as a point of etiquette husbands and wives do not remain near one another at *koktel partis*, but circulate around making conquests. After a few drinks, the males display their 'lines,' which are ritualized ways of approaching the brightly decorated and painted females—a strange custom, incidentally, since it is the males naturally who ought to be painted, as among us Nyabongans.

"The sexual nature of these ceremonies is shown in the magic plants called *mislto* which they hang up at these winter rituals in particular. These are parasitic plants with white berries that grow on oak trees—both of which have symbolical significance—but they are by no means necessary as a sanction or encouragement for pawing and kissing, especially at a New Year's *koktel parti* in full swing. The idea seems to be to crowd as many people together as possible, to increase inescapable physical contacts. Many times people moving restlessly about in search of new partners spill drinks on one another's fine clothes, and then the person who does this is allowed to rub the other ritually with a pocket-cloth, pretending to be much distressed at the accident."

"Are these *koktel partis* always orgies?" inquired a plump, middle-aged Nyabongan man.

"Not entirely, perhaps," replied Professor Widjojo. "There is one which is called a *literari koktel*, the ostensible reason for which is to celebrate the birth of a new book. Naturally, no one ever discusses the book being celebrated, since no one has read it, although everybody expresses a readiness to analyze it critically. Mostly, the people talk about their own books, past, projected or purely conjectural. They allude meaningfully to the amount of their royalties, complain about editors and publishers, mention their translation into Japanese and other languages including the Scandinavian, and make the most they can of some tenuous dickering for movie rights or 'coming out in paperbacks.' *Literari koktel partis* are mainly an opportunity to advertise books other than the one by the publisher giving the *parti*. At these there is much *karakter-as-asination,* or verbal witchcraft, designed to decrease the sales of rival authors and to increase one's own reputation for cleverness of expression and literary insight."

"Do the same people always go to one another's *partis?*" asked the tiki-attired matron.

"Well, this is largely the case," said the distinguished Nyabongan anthropologist. "However, hostesses complain proudly of the number of 'people we hardly know' whom they invite to their *partis*. The reason for this is probably owing to the fact that both host and hostess are too busy seeing that drinks are replenished to have more than a few words with any one person. But it is a matter of prestige, as guests, to meet the same people briefly at two successive rituals on one evening, and in this manner they can gather more people they hardly know for their own next gathering.

"Hostesses also compete with one another in exotic foodstuffs. Smoked oysters, fish pastes, rare fish eggs, sea-spider and shrimp purées are commonplaces, as are foreign cheeses; the successful hostess is one who uses something like *kashu-nut* butter on new and unfamiliar wafers before these in turn become commonplace. Some like to present new drink mixtures with names like Rag-Pickers' Toddy or Purple Nose or Longshoreman Slugger, but mostly *koktels* are of the same few types, like Manhattans (named after an island off the Usan mainland to the east), poured into an inverted conical or hemispherical stemmed glass—quite unlike the *aignawg* cup—with an onion or a stuffed olive or a cherry, which of course no one is required to eat, this being a sign of naïveté. Sometimes there are 'tall ones,' so called because of the long glass cylinders they are served in. But all these drinks contain some sort of drug that makes the people fatuous, foolish, talkative, tearful or amorous."

"Where does this word *koktel* come from?" another interested Nyabongan listener inquired.

"Well, literally, the word means the hind feathers of a male chicken or cock," replied the professor. "But, though Usan natives readily admit this derivation upon questioning, no one seems to know why they are called this. They claim that *koktels* began only as late as the Nineteen Twenties when they were forbidden and had to be obtained in secret ritual underground chambers called *speekeezies* or from *butlaigers*."

"But don't the Usans get exhausted running from one *koktel parti* to another, especially in this restricted season?"

"Oh, yes, and they frequently say as much," answered the Nyabongan savant. "There is another institution, though, that is protectively exploited in these circumstances. This is the *baybisitter*. The Usans do not have the extended family that we Nyabongans do, but live in one-family units called houses or apartments. For this reason they have to hire a *baybisitter* to take care of the children in their absence; of course, they couldn't bring the children to these ceremonies, because they would be trampled underfoot in their crowded ritual chambers.

"The word does not mean, despite its form, that they hire a *baybi* or infant to sit, for these persons are often someone else's grandmother. It seems, rather, that they hire someone to sit on the *baybi*, to prevent its destroying the furniture while they are gone. *Koktel*-goers are able to invent the most fantastic and transparent excuses involving these *baybisitters* which require the imminent presence of the parents back home. Other parents at the *parti* commiserate, thcugh disbelieving these excuses, and the couple is allowed to leave without losing face."

"Strange people, these Usan natives," said the fat, middle-aged Nyabongan.

"That they are, that they are!" echoed Professor Widjojo, touching his nosestick thoughtfully.

■ RELIGION AND THE GREEK PEASANTS

Irwin Sanders

ORTHODOXY AND GREEKNESS

To start any discussion of religion and the Greek peasant, it is necessary to state clearly and unequivocally that adherence to the official religion of Greece, the Greek Orthodox Church, is tantamount to being Greek. Only 2 to 3 percent of the population of the country are not members of the Orthodox Church. Though those comprising this small fraction may have political citizenship, may speak the Greek tongue, and may take pride in the legacy of ancient Greece, they are at best suspect Greeks if they do not nominally at least belong to the Orthodox Church.

But what is the syncretism that is called Orthodoxy? This question can be answered on at least two levels: first, that of the peasant and, second, that of the educated Greek. To the peasant, the coming of Christianity did not mean an important break with many of his previous practices, beliefs, and even deities. What were formerly deities became saints, with some of the more powerful deities becoming identified with the most powerful saints, such as the Holy Virgin. It seemed perfectly fitting and not at all surprising to find an old, old church dedicated to St. Theodore in the southern Peloponnesos, two of whose columns were from an ancient pre-Christian temple standing on their original pediments. Many scholars have described in considerable detail various aspects of this easy transition from pagan to Christian worship.[1] William Miller, a keen student of Greek life, has pointed out that the saints play a very important part in Greek life: their functions and names often prove that they are the legitimate descendants of the old Greek gods, the new religion having been grafted on to the old. He indicates that Helios, the sun god, has been succeeded by the Prophet Elias (Elijah), whose chapels crown almost every eminence in Greece; the Virgin has replaced Athena Parthenos, and the Parthenon in the Middle Ages was the Church of St. Mary, whether as a Greek Cathedral or as a Latin minister; St. Dionysios has dethroned Dionysis; St. George and the Dragon are the Christian version of Theseus and the Minotaur, so that the Theseum naturally became in Christian times the Church of St. George.[2]

Marcu Beza, who describes many pagan survivals with Christian names which are found throughout the Balkans, speaks of the rich texture of

[1] See a classic work on the subject by John C. Lawson, *Modern Greek Folklore and Ancient Greek Religion: A Study in Survivals* (Cambridge, Eng., 1910).
[2] William Miller, *Greek Life in Town and Country* (London, 1905), p. 73.

Christianity there, which came to the Balkan nations in the shape of Byzantine Orthodoxy and which meant a particular culture, comprising art, literature, and theology, in the service of the Church.[3]

One has only to review the brief description of the peasant and nature of the peasant approach to sickness and child care in earlier chapters to see how lively is the environment for any peasant who believes in the Evil Eye or the omens of spiders, birds in flight, or the hooting of an owl.[4] The peasant, instead of being made over into some sort of revolutionary Christian image, was able to take early Christianity and make it over into the even earlier Greek image. That is what survives in rural Greece today.

The educated Greek went through almost the same process, but on a much more sophisticated level. Instead of equating the sun god with St. Elijah, he equated Platonic teachings with the doctrines of St. Paul. Thanassis Aghnides sets forth this theme:

> As regards religious life, let us not forget that the New Testament was written in Greek, and most of the principles of Christianity are loans from Greek moral philosophy. Plato's ideas could find no better means of diffusion in the world than the New Testament.
>
> Thus a Greek never feels that the Christian religion is a Jewish gift to the world. When he reads the New Testament he is reminded of the highest precepts of the Greek classical period. Here again the modern Greek is not very conscious of the lines of demarcation between the high precepts of Christianity, and, let us say, those of Socrates. The latter's principles and those of the Galilean are derived from the same source. The modern Greek is confusedly aware of this. He may not say it in as many words but he feels the modern ethical standards of the Christian world as being part and parcel of his own heritage from his classical ancestors.[5]

In support of this point of view among the peasants, I can mention the consternation shown by some Greek village women when, for the first time, they learned that Christ was a Jew. They had always assumed that he was Greek and would not believe otherwise until they had gone to check with the priest.

Orthodoxy and Greekness are tied in together not only because of the continuity between ancient traditions and Christian doctrine; the Orthodox Church was also the vehicle through which Greekness was preserved under alien conquerors. Church and politics went hand in hand. The Greek Orthodox Church, which was the basic institution of the Byzantine Empire, continues as such within the modern Greek nation, and contemporary Greeks, like the Byzantines, find it hard to accept political

[3] Marcu Beza, *Heritage of Byzantium* (London, 1947), p. 89.
[4] See also B. P. D'Estournelles, "The Superstitions of Modern Greece," *The Nineteenth Century*, no. 62 (April 1882).
[5] Thanassis Aghnides, "What Ancient Greece Means to the Modern Greek," *John Rylands Library Bulletin*, XXVII (1943), 263–64.

ideas which do not assume the complete unification of church and state. Today the church is still an integral part of the Greek government, its affairs administered within the Ministry of Education and Religion, the salaries of the clergy paid by the state as civil servants, and religious belief a part of national patriotism. Nothing really fundamental can be done in the nation down to the smallest commune without clerical interest and participation. This is not written law, but deep-seated custom.[6]

Greeks view contemporary events in terms of their own adaptation of New Testament teachings and claim that the Greek nation, though it has suffered many "Golgothas," has recovered from these disasters to experience a "resurrection" each time.[7] Such comparisons with the life and sufferings of Christ are also intelligible to the Greek peasant, who has little difficulty in identifying them with the sufferings of Greece through which the rest of the world will be saved. Greeks give episodes in Greek history, such as their defeat of the Italians in World War II and their fighting back the spread of Communism in postwar years, a political-religious interpretation highly charged with emotion because these touch upon what is sacred in the Greek national tradition—the unique contribution Greece has over and over again made to the preservation of Western civilization through the frequent ordeals she has endured.

THE VILLAGE PRIEST AND HIS PARISH

An American walking down the street with a Greek friend is usually surprised when the Greek hits him on the shoulder and says, "I give you the priest." This act supposedly transfers to someone else the misfortune that might follow from meeting the *papas*, or priest, who passes dressed in his flowing black robes and his tall stovepipe brimless hat, and wearing a handsome black beard and his long hair neatly done up into a bun. Should he be accompanied by a woman, she is probably his wife, for in the Greek Orthodox Church there are both married and unmarried priests. The married priests can take the ordination vows after marriage, but no priest can marry after ordination. The married priests are usually the parish priests, and it is rare to find the village priest unmarried. On the other hand, the unmarried priest, recruited among the monks, can alone rise to high administrative positions in the church. He may, for instance, be a bishop over one of the sixty-seven dioceses or, if properly qualified, eventually be one of the twelve bishops comprising the Holy Synod which guides the church under the presidency of the Metropolitan of Athens, the actual head of the church. The Patriarch of Constantinople at Istanbul is the titular head, but this is more of a

[6] Harold F. Alderfer, "Greece and the West Today," ECA Memorandum, Athens, April 13, 1951, p. 8. Also see Alderfer's *I Like Greece* (State College, Pa., 1956), chap. 10, "The Church Is the Foundation."

[7] Floyd A. Spencer, *War and Postwar Greece: An Analysis Based in Greek Writings* (Washington, D.C., 1952), p. 153.

traditional and honorary office, since the Metropolitan is looked upon as the chief functionary. In Greece the king has no authority over the church.

In the village the parish priest, married as he is, settles down, digs his roots in deeply, so to speak. He knows that he has no opportunity for advancement in the church hierarchy; so there is no need for him to spend his time "politicking" for appointment to some choice position in the church courts. The village priest, therefore, acquires land and farms, in many cases just as diligently as the other villagers; he may even embark upon a few small-scale business enterprises on the side. His regular salary from the state gives him a steady income which the rest of the local people usually lack. This, combined with thrift and diligence, helps him acquire a little more property than the average farmer and enjoy a slightly higher standard of living. This is not guaranteed, of course, and one can call to mind many village priests who obviously were living on the barest minimum. At the same time, the priest is able to maintain what has been called a "comradely equality" with his people.[8]

The priest, however, is not necessarily a permanent fixture. The bishop appoints him to a post and the local congregation can refuse him, or it can raise objections to a bishop about a priest who conducts himself in ways the local people do not like. In most cases, the bishop tries to find the kind of priest that the local parishioners prefer. Since the priest often acquires land, as has been pointed out, he wants to pass that on to his children. He may try to persuade one son at least to follow him in the service of the church. In one Peloponnesian village I found that a priest's son now off at the seminary was coming back to succeed his father, thus making a fourth generation of priests from the same family serving that parish. When I mentioned this to bishops and others familiar with church matters, they pointed out that this was a common phenomenon, and even gave the names of villages where a fifth-generation member from the same family was ministering to the same parish.

Should a parish vacancy occur, the bishop, who is informed about it as a matter of course, announces in the local papers as well as in the church papers that there is a vacancy in such and such a village and that all qualified people may apply. He goes through the applications, selects the eligible candidates, and posts their names on the door of the cathedral, with the notice that anyone who knows any reason why these people should not serve as priests should inform the bishop. After due time has elapsed, he makes the choice, giving heavy weight, according to one bishop who discussed this, to educational qualifications and moral considerations.

In pursuing in greater detail the relationship between the parish priest and the state, I learned that it was under the leadership of Archbishop (Metropolitan) Damaskinos, who played such an important part in helping his country through the politically troubled waters from

8 Alderfer, "Greece and the West Today," p. 8.

German occupation back to self-government, that the priests were put on a salary paid by the state. Before that, they had been paid from fees and also by products from the parishioners. *Kondota,* or the subscription by families of so much wheat, eggs, olive oil, and such, to the priest if he would serve them was widely practiced before the present salary arrangement was made. In round figures, the parishes now contribute about one fourth of the amount needed to pay the priests' salaries, with the difference coming from state revenue. Also, the local parishes have to pay an amount equal to 6 percent of their priest's salary to the bishop toward the retirement fund for the local priest.

For salary purposes, the priests are divided into four classes: those who have gone through the theological faculty of the university; those who have attended the seminary, perhaps one or two years beyond gymnasium; those who have no seminary but who have finished gymnasium; and those put in a miscellaneous category. There are apparently sufficient candidates for the priesthood now, and some effort is being made to fashion their curriculum to prepare them to serve village needs more effectively; even the older priests are encouraged to come back for periods of study. One member of the Holy Synod thought that the priests ought to know more about agriculture, economics, and first aid, so that they might play a more vital part in community life. His view of the priest's role was that "he is to help people with their problems of all kinds and settle any disputes among the villagers."

But what part does the village priest really play? As has already been indicated, the Greeks are ambivalent toward the priest.[9] "As an individual, he commands respect, and gives advice to those who seek it. However, he is also a figure of ridicule and of ill omen."[10] A great deal depends upon the personality of the priest himself. One informant told me that when he was a boy their village had had a wonderful priest who was very important. Today, even though the people are probably just as much attached to their religion, the present priest is not popular. In the course of an extended conversation with the people in a village near Volos, we asked what kind of priest they had. "Oh, our priest is from around Karpenesi. He has five children and is a good family man." He was not singled out for praise because of any priestly performance, but because of his conformity to basic village values. But children in that same village must have heard many, many times the local account of what happened to some monks who lived in a monastery not far from the village. This had been built in 1714 as an annex of a Mount Athos establishment, but in due course of time the monks became "naughty" in that they called to and teased the women who were on their way to work

---

[9] For observations on the village clergy, see Sir Charles Eliot, *Turkey in Europe* (London, 1908), and H. D. F. Kitto, *In the Mountains of Greece* (London, 1933), p. 16.

[10] See Dorothy D. Lee, "Greek Tales of Priest and Priestwife," *Journal of American Folklore,* April–June 1947, p. 163. This article contains nine stories about the priest and his wife, some of them Chaucerian in tone. He is either interested in an attractive parishioner whose husband eventually deals drastically with him, or his wife is involved with a lover whom the priest may or may not outwit.

in the fields. Finally the villagers could stand this no longer, so the men took the monks to a rock overlooking the sea and told them to jump. The monks jumped and were never heard of again. The present priest, unlike the monks, is "a good family man."

Very persistent and widespread is the belief, already mentioned, that an encounter with the priest brings bad luck. If peasants starting on some new venture meet a priest, they will turn back home and not begin it on that day for fear of failure. Anyone who meets a priest, in addition to "giving" the bad luck to a companion by hitting him on the shoulder, can tie a knot in a handkerchief, thereby putting the priest under his control so he will do no harm. But, bad luck or not, the priest is indispensable. At numerous repasts celebrating a christening, a nameday, or some other important event, we had to wait what seemed an interminable length of time because the priest could not arrive any earlier. Without him, nothing could get under way. One serious student of Greek rural life said: "In Greece when a priest is missing, it is a great calamity, for the Greek is not used to praying by himself without a priest."[11] In earlier days when the belief in vampires was much more widespread than today, it was the priest, the minister of God, who alone had any power over them. He could calm the fears of the people.

The responsibility for the local parish does not fall entirely upon the priest, although the chief responsibility is his. There is a church board, consisting of three to five members, with the priest as president. The nominations for this board are submitted to the bishop by the priest, and the bishop designates them as official members of the board. One member of the board is the treasurer. When these local officials are asked just what their duties are, they usually include in their replies: to help the priest, to look after the finances, and to care for the church building. This board has as one of its chief duties the sale of the candles in the church vestibule and can use the proceeds of the sale for local church needs. In most communities it is considered a great honor to serve as a member of this board, although this position requires much work and frequently has more responsibility than the presidency of the local cooperative.

A recent development is the growth of the Sunday school, held after the regular morning service. Young boys, girls, and a few women are usually found in attendance, although young people up to the age of twenty are urged to attend. Throughout much of Greece the priest gives the instruction, although in Northern Greece we found many villages where the teacher had taken over this extra duty. Usually the same lesson is given to all age groups at the same time. It is customary in some places, such as the Attic villages we visited, for the school to be held on a weekday by the teacher, in which case it was not called Sunday school but "the preaching school."

The heart, however, of the Greek Orthodox Church—as of many other Christian bodies—is the Sunday-morning Mass. Anyone attending cannot

11 Angelike Chatzemichale made this observation.

help but notice the building itself, usually in the shape of a Greek cross, with the ends terminating in apses. Over the center there is a dome representing heaven. In front, the altar screen (*eikonostasion*), on which one finds the icons or pictures of various saints, separates the altar (*vema*), which no woman can enter, from the nave, where the worshippers congregate.[12] The priest moves back and forth between altar and nave in what seems a random manner to the uninitiated. As he turns to face the altar, the icon of Christ is on his right and that of St. John the Baptist next to it. To his left one sees on the altar the icon of the Virgin, and farther to the left the icon of the saint for whom the church was named.

The congregation stands during the service, except for a few infirm who can lean against supports along the wall; there is no instrumental music, as the priest and the chanter carry the service themselves in a language that much of the time is unintelligible to the worshippers. The gospels are read in Koine, or New Testament Greek, and the liturgy, written by St. John Chrysostom toward the end of the fourth century, is in the Greek of that period. When the priest delivers a sermon, he uses his version of katharevousa, if he is sufficiently schooled; otherwise, he speaks in demotike. Apparently the worshippers are moved by the ceremony, the procession, the swinging censers, and the chanting even more than by the actual meaning of the words to which they listen. Now and then in the liturgy, however, come familiar passages which most can understand because of having learned their meaning in school or from some relative.

The worshippers, among whom small children may be running or tugging, include very few men. They come out for special festival services but show no interest in the regular Sunday-morning service, which is viewed as the woman's social hour. Even during the service women catch up on the latest happenings throughout the village.

The priest, however, is busy at other times, too. Dorothy Lee describes it this way:

Religion permeates Greek life, punctuating it with ritual. No Greek, urban or rural, would think of initiating anything important without a religious inauguration. Schools open with the inaugurative *agiasmos*, "making holy"; the foundation stone of every house is laid with *agiasmos;* merchants begin new undertakings with the proper religious inauguration. On Epiphany, the sea is made holy for those who journey on it. In the country, blessed water is carried from the Epiphany Mass to sprinkle on the fields. The Virgin and the Saints are invoked, but not mainly as correctives; their main function is to endow an undertaking with good and success, it is not primarily to prevent or correct . . . . Priests are called in, and Saints and the Virgin invoked, also, when difficulties arise. Vows are made for the recovery of a loved one; the priest is called when

<hr />

[12] The material for this whole paragraph is adapted from Anne Anthony, *Meet the Greeks* (Athens, 1950), pp. 37–41.

the family has had a run of misfortune, to "make holy" and exorcise the evil. Priests conduct a rain litany to break a drought.[13]

The parish as such consists of no such array of organized groups as comprise an American congregation; the priest is not trying to convert the unbeliever or change the daily life of his people. He is there to help them meet life's emergencies, to instill a love for their religion and their country, and to act as peacemaker when disputes threaten the harmony of the community.[14]

■ GHOSTS AND WITCHES

Clyde Kluckhohn and Dorothea Leighton

GHOSTS

Not all the powerful beings who are always present as potential threats to the well-being of the Navaho are Holy People. Perhaps the most fearful of all to them are the ghosts of Earth Surface People.

The Navahos seem to have no belief in a glorious immortality. Existence in the hereafter appears to be only a shadowy and uninviting thing. The afterworld is a place like this earth, located to the north and below the earth's surface. It is approached by a trail down a hill or cliff, and there is a sandpile at the bottom. Deceased kinfolk, who look as they did when last seen alive, come to guide the dying to the afterworld during a journey that takes four days. At the entrance to the afterworld, old guardians apply tests to see if death has really occurred.

Death and everything connected with it are horrible to The People. Even to look upon the bodies of dead animals, except those killed for food, is a peril. Dead humans are buried as soon as possible, and with such elaborate precautions that one of the greatest favors which a white person can do for Navahos is to undertake this abhorrent responsibility.

This intense and morbid avoidance of the dead and of everything connected with them rests upon the fear of ghosts. The other Earth Surface People who have fearful powers—witches—are also very terrible, but they are, after all, living beings who can be controlled in some measure and, if necessary, killed. Ghosts are, as it were, the witches of the

13 D. Lee, "Greece," *Cultural Patterns and Technical Change*, p. 84.
14 One of the most vivid accounts in English of the prominent role of the priest is found in Nikos Kazantzakis, *The Greek Passion* (New York, 1954), a fictionalized account of what happened in an Asia Minor Greek community when some of its characters in a passion play began to play their roles seriously in real life.

world of the dead, a shadowy impalpable world altogether beyond the control of the living.

Most of the dead may return as ghosts to plague the living. Only those who die of old age, the stillborn, and infants who do not live long enough to utter a cry or sound do not produce ghosts, and for them the four days of mourning after burial need not be observed, since they will not be injurious to the living. Otherwise, any dead person, no matter how friendly or affectionate his attitude while he was living, is a potential danger.

A ghost is the malignant part of a dead person. It returns to avenge some neglect or offense. If a corpse has not been buried properly, if some of his belongings which he wished interred with him have been held out, if not enough animals have been killed at his grave, or if the grave has been disturbed in any way, the ghost will return to the burial place or to the former dwelling.

Ghosts appear after dark or just before the death of some family member, in human form or as coyotes, owls, mice, whirlwinds, spots of fire, or indefinite dark objects. They are usually dark or black. They may change form or size before one's eyes or make recognizable sounds (as of familiar birds or animals) and noises of movement. Whistling in the dark is always evidence that a ghost is near. Since ghosts appear only at night, adult Navahos are afraid to go about in the dark alone, and all sorts of night shapes and sounds are fearful.

Ghosts may chase people, jump upon them, tug their clothes, or throw dirt upon them. Not only are their actions frightening in themselves but they are omens of disaster to come. When a Navaho thinks he has seen a ghost or one appears in his dreams, he is sure that he or a relative will die unless the proper ceremonial treatment is successfully applied.

Both the type of experience with ghosts which is commonly related among Navahos and the way in which children at boarding school interpret events there in terms of the old beliefs are illustrated in this passage from an autobiography.

One time I was sure scared. I was at school in California and two men were doing the shot put. And one man got hit behind the ear and they took him to the hospital. I sprained my ankle and every day I went to the hospital and the next day I asked for him and they said he is dead. And I said I want to see him so they took me up. And I was surprised—he was lying there with his eyes open and he didn't look dead. Everyone was sorry he was dead. He was our best football player. He played quarter back. So we dressed him in his football clothes and took his picture and then we put him in his citizen clothes and took his picture. We had a funeral and we all marched and the band played slow music. His bed was next to mine. We slept on a porch. And I went to bed and pretty soon I heard someone coming and then he opened the screen door. I didn't see his face. He came in and sat on the foot of that boy's bed. I reached for a flashlight under my pillow and I turned it on and he had disappeared. Boy, I sure was scared. I didn't believe in those things before that but I got out of bed and ran into the house where the other boys were. And I told them.

And then we heard somebody coming another night. I was scared all right. So they gave me a bed upstairs and I was looking out the window and I saw somebody coming a long ways off. It was like something black and it came nearer. And I turned my flashlight on him and there was nobody there. The disciplinarian didn't believe it and I said well you go and sleep down there on the porch, so he did. And that night he heard somebody coming and he sure ran.

When I came home from school my father rode toward Perea one night and I was with my sister in the hogan. Pretty soon we heard my father galloping toward us and when he got to the door he fell off his horse onto the ground and he lay there and didn't know anything. So I got on the horse and I rode as fast as I could to a medicine man over there [pointing] by the mesa. And he didn't stop to get a horse. He just took his bundle and got on my horse and I rode behind him. He had a hard time with my father. He sang most of the night before he got him conscious. The next day my father said he was riding home and two black things came after him. They were on each side of him. And they rode down on him and one of them tried to get his reins. He rode around dodging them and finally he got away from them.

WITCHES

The Navahos believe that by witchcraft evil men and women, acting separately or in a group, can obtain property and produce the illness or death of those whom they hate. Like ghosts, these malevolent people are active mainly at night. They often wear the hide of a coyote, a wolf, or some other animal. English-speaking Navahos talk about them as "human wolves" or "Navaho wolves." They are ghouls, and they practice incest.

A witch may use four principal techniques against his victims. He may feed them "corpse poison," a preparation made of powdered human flesh, or blow it in their faces. He may utter spells, particularly over something closely associated with the victims—nail parings or hair or a fragment of clothing—which the witch secretes in a grave. Or he may magically shoot into the victims small objects, especially something connected with corpses, like a bone or a bit of ash from a hogan in which someone has died. (This is commonly "diagnosed" by the presence of a small bump on the head.) The fourth technique involves the use of a narcotic plant and is said to be employed primarily in seducing women, in gambling, and in trading. The principal symptoms manifested by the supposed victims are fainting, "epileptic" seizures, sudden onset of pain, emaciation, or a sharp pain in a localized area with a lump or other evidence of a foreign object there.

Witchcraft is a subject which most Navahos are unwilling to discuss, sometimes even to mention, before whites. This is in part because they anticipate ridicule or violent disapproval if they confess such a belief, in part because of their own intrinsic fear and dislike of talking about such an unpleasant subject. Consequently, some whites live for years in the Navaho country with only a vague awareness that Navahos suspect others as witches, gossip about them, hold trials, and occasionally carry out "executions." Occasionally accounts of witch killings get into the papers, like that near Fruitland, New Mexico, in 1942 when a man who thought witchcraft had caused the death of his children killed four "witches" and then committed suicide. Witchcraft belief is extraordinarily persistent. Navahos who seem to be completely "emancipated" from other aspects of their religion will still show tremendous fear of witches, once a situation takes on a certain coloring.

Various plants and other substances are believed to afford protection against witches. Still stronger protection is held to be afforded by possessing ceremonial knowledge and power and by having frequent ceremonies held over one. Curing is possible through certain ceremonials, when the witchcraft has not gone too far. Special features may also be added to help out victims of witchcraft. For example, if a person is convinced that he knows who the witch-aggressor is, he may have performed over him the Enemy Way ceremonial popularly called the "squaw dance." After the first night of chanting over the patient in the ceremonial hogan, a group of mounted Navahos ride off to another hogan some miles distant. The Indian mounted on the fastest horse carries a small bundle tied to a pole. If the patient thinks he has been bewitched, this bundle contains something belonging to the supposed witch (one of his hairs or a piece of his hat which has absorbed his sweat, for example). Upon reaching the second hogan this party is met by other mounted Indians, and a mock battle takes place. The net result of all this procedure is thought to be that the evil will be turned away from the patient and back upon the witch. The Navaho theory under all circumstances is that if the intended victim is too strong or too well protected the witch's evil backfires upon himself.

All ceremonial cures, if successful, are believed to cause the death of the witch before long, and various deaths are accounted for in this way. Some Navahos also believe that witches are commonly struck down by lightning. When public feeling is sufficiently aroused, the supposed witch is made to confess, which ensures his "magical" death within a year, or he is actually put to death, sometimes by bloody and brutal means.

The following stories, told (in 1944) by a fifteen-year-old school boy to the boys' adviser in his school, are typical of the tales about witches which are constantly circulating around the Navaho country.

There is one of them down there towards those hills. They cover themselves with a skin of a dog, or a bear. They dig up the dead men, then they make them small so that they can fit in the hand and take it home. Then they sing and make the small dead man get big again. Then they put something on that dries them up, and they grind it up. Then they put the powder in a deerskin bag and carry it with them even if they don't have their skin on. When they put this powder on you, you die.

Last summer when I was herding sheep, I was by myself and it was midnight. I saw a big dog standing in the middle of the sheep so I took out the 440 [410 gauge shotgun, no doubt] and shot at him. I missed him and hit a sheep on the other side. Then my sister came and I went to the other side. I shot at him and hit him this time right here [indicating his upper arm]. I saw him on top of one of the sheep, but when I hit him he jumped up and ran away . . . . When I saw the sheep, he had a cut on his neck this long [two inches], but the sheep was still alive when I saw it in the morning. Then the next morning, one man told me that he was going to the sing and wanted me to go with him. I didn't go with him, but after he was gone I went to the place he said the sing was. When I got there, it was dark. I went into the hogan and sat in a corner that was dark. I saw a man with some bandages on his arm right here [indicating his upper arm]. I asked his sister what was wrong with the man and she said that he got his arm in the wheel of the wagon and got it hurt. I knew that that was the man that I shot.

Another man told me last summer that he watched where the Navaho Wolfs hold their meetings. They dig a big hole, about this size [3 feet diameter] and dig it for a long ways, almost over to that building there [30 yards] on the side of the mountain. He went inside and found a curtain; when he crawled about five feet more, there was another curtain. He went farther and passed about five more curtains. Then the last curtain, he could see through because it was thin. He saw about fourteen men sitting in a circle, and five women, with no clothes on. They were all singing, and there was a feather standing up and moving like this [indicating an up and down motion]. When the feather stands up like that, the Navaho Wolf who is out is all right but when the feather falls down, then it means that the Navaho Wolf is dead. When this man saw that, he went out and went about one hundred feet and climbed a tree and waited for the Wolf to come back. About five o'clock he came back, and this man went back and told all of the Navahos about it. They came back on horses, and made a big circle. They waited for a long time, and when these Navaho Wolfs came out, they got them and took them to Shiprock and got $1,000 for them. They took them with their skins.

Jack told us about a Navaho Wolf that he chased when he was looking for his horse. He chased him down about five miles, and then this wolf ran under a bridge. When Jack saw him he took his skin down to his pants, and there was lines on the man. He told Jack to look that way, but Jack did not look that way because when a man looks that way, the Navaho Wolf takes out a gun and shoots him. Then the Navaho Wolf told Jack to come down to near Tohatchi where he lived, and he would give him two hundred dollars, if he did not tell anybody. Jack said that he wouldn't tell nobody, but he didn't go. When you go far away, you get tired and hungry, this Navaho Wolf will give you something to eat; but you will die if you eat that because he puts some powder on it. At the squaw dances you see some Navahos with long hair in a knot in the back. These are the ones that you have to be scared of.

The other night, like I told you, William see a man come to the dormitory. He was about this small [4 feet], and then he gets real big, then he gets small again. He couldn't hear his tracks. Then two nights passed and another man came in, but he could hear his tracks. He could hear when he shut the door.

If the Navaho Wolf catches you at the meeting, they bring you inside and ask you if you want to learn or die. If you want to learn, they bring you inside and say, "Who do you want, your sister or brudder?" If you say "brudder," two days after that he will die. Then they will send you after him, like they show you, and you bring him back. It is like paying to learn, only you don't pay in money. You have to pay with your brudder or sister.

The Navaho Wolf travels fast. Fast like the automobile or horse. They live over near Chinle, but they can come to Shiprock and go back in one night. Last year there was a boy here at school whose name was Albert. He died just about this time. His father was caught, and he named Albert too. They took him to Shiprock and he died there. [This boy died at the Shiprock Hospital on January 17, 1943, from complications of a mastoid operation.] They brought him over here and let everybody see him, but his brudders and sister and father didn't cry. Now the father is a Navaho Wolf.

The Navaho Wolfs are rich. The other day a teacher asked how a man can get rich, and William or James wrote on the blackboard, "Be a Navaho Wolf." When a Navaho Wolf unburies a dead man, he takes away his silver belt and sells it at Farmington, or away over at Phoenix. They don't sell it to the traders near where they dig up the man because the people know about it. They sell it far away.

■ MIDDLE AMERICA HAS ITS WOODSTOCK, TOO

Jeff Greenfield

It is a warm night, and the sky overhead is lit up by searchlights. Cars, campers, trucks, buses, station wagons—thousands of vehicles with thousands of people in and milling around them—are parked in ragged rows that stretch back and forth across the huge field at 30th Street off Georgetown Road in the All-American city of Indianapolis, Indiana.

A cacophany of jazz, pop, rock and roll blasts into the night from speakers hooked to radios, tape decks, and stereos. Hundreds of barbecue grills broil steaks, hamburgers, hot dogs. Oceans of beer, surely more than 100,000 bottles and cans of it, are popped and twist-snapped open. The whine of motorcycles, their single lights cutting through the dark, speed up and down the fire lanes between the rows of cars. Grown men with wives and children shout their *macho* yearnings at young women.

"Hey, sister, I'd sure like to get my dipstick into you!"

"Hey! Any of you girls wanna be liberated, you just come on over to this here camper, you hear? Sleeps six and lays twelve! Ha-ha-ha."

Almost as often, the men invoke another common denominator as well:

"Hey! Whattya drinkin'?"

"Coors! Great beer!"

"Aw, that's crap!"

"Goddamn, you don't know your beer!"

At the edge of the field, on a flat-bed truck, a pleasant, balding man in his sixties, who could be the principal of a small-town junior high school, is trying to spread the good word of the Gospel.

"You boys and girls, you've got to please God by faith. How about you, young lady? Would you like to be called a child of God tonight? How 'bout you, young fella? Will you overcome the world?"

"Somebody get the preacher a beer!" shouts a crew-cut boy of fifteen, who well might be singing in the preacher's choir on another weekend. But not this weekend. This is the Friday midnight of Memorial Day weekend, and for these thousands, it is a time for furious revelry, release, and a strange blend of fellowship and indulgence, all part of one of the most extraordinary conglomerations I have ever attended anywhere: The Indianapolis 500 Mile International Sweepstakes.

Every year more than 300,000 people pack the fields and stands around the track of the Indianapolis Speedway, ostensibly to witness the running of the 500 Mile Race, with its million dollars in prize money, record-breaking speeds, and a constant promise of fiery death. It is the single biggest event held in America; on any given year more Americans meet in one place at one time here at the speedway than anywhere else in the country.

From May 1, when the speedway opens for practice runs, through the time trials to determine who qualifies for entry into the race, up through the neosacred Race Day, a fever begins to build all through Indianapolis. Indiana newspapers fill page upon page with history, legend, predictions, and interviews with everyone from the hot-dog concessionaires to John MacKenzie, the man who carries into Victory Lane the ponderous Borg-Warner trophy with which to honor the winner. More than 100,000 people attend the time trials on the weekends before Memorial Day. By the Friday night before the race, fans who drive here from as far away as California and Oregon are settled in their beer-swilling camping areas, ready for the gates to swing open at 5:00 a.m. on Race Day, so they can guide their cars into the enormous infield area of the track. From this vantage point, where not more than a tenth of the track can be seen, the fans set up platforms and chairs on the tops of vehicles. The resulting cluster of humanity is something like a tract of suburbia writ small, each family or group carving out a few square feet of land. And there, under an increasingly hot sky, inhaling the stench of gasoline, burning rubber and charcoal, the fans eat and drink away the dawn and the morning and finally the climactic afternoon during which thirty-three drivers in exotic-looking automobiles flash by them.

Why do the people come? Certainly, the city of Indianapolis is no part of the attraction. This is perhaps the worst metropolis in the entire United States—a city with endless miles of indifferent gray structures, Burger Chefs, and Kentucky Fried Chicken stands and a political climate that welcomed such spasms of paranoia as the Klan during the Twenties and the Birchers in the Sixties. Even if the Indy fans were drawn to such a city, none of them would leave their valued places at the speedway to journey downtown.

Still, it is not simply, or even primarily, the race that attracts the fans. It is the awesome, terrifying, hilarious spectacle surrounding the race, a spectacle that holds within itself a welter of contradictory yearnings tearing at what is left of our national spirit: glory, speed, wealth, fellowship, and death. After witnessing the Indy for a weekend, I came away with an overriding sense of sorrow at what we have done to each other and to ourselves.

The 500 itself is, in part, a celebration of technology, the continuation of an old American tradition, rooted in another age, when people traveled great distances from their isolated communities to hear Chautauqua speakers or witness the new marvels of the machine age: horseless carriages, dirigibles, airplanes, and the wonders of science that promised, at the turn of the twentieth century, to turn the United States into a streamlined technological paradise.

The first 500 Mile Race at Indianapolis was run in 1911. It was dreamed up by Carl Fisher, a local promoter-businessman and speed demon, who had originally built the track on which the races were run in order to test improvements for automobiles. Within a few years the race was attracting thousands of spectators from around the country, and it proved a powerful magnet as well for manufacturers, who saw a chance for free publicity by underwriting the cost of machines built with their parts. During the gasoline-scarce days of World War II, the speedway was abandoned. After the war it was brought back to life by Tony Hulman, its present owner and president, and since then the ties between the race and big business have become thoroughly entwined. Piston-ring makers, tire manufacturers, sparkplug producers, and the like help finance the machines, which cost up to $200,000, counting the maintenance costs. And the businessmen of Indianapolis have for fifteen years or so whipped up a promotional effort of Babbitt-sized proportions. Checkered flags, like those used to wave autos across the finish line, decorate the city. Throughout the month of May a series of events progressively builds up excitement: Festival queens are chosen, there are gin rummy and golf tournaments, a mayor's breakfast, and finally an eve-of-race parade down streets painted with the checkered flag pattern. So ingrained is the race that even the soul-saving evangelists working the camping area pass out tracts bearing the checkered-flag emblem and titled, "Souvenir Victory Edition."

Boosterism, however, cannot by itself attract tens of thousands of people to Indianapolis for a week of sleeping in open fields or in the back of campers. The race itself, of course, is a powerful magnet. Each year the cars are lower, sleeker, and more ingeniously designed. This year, for example, their surprisingly fragile fiber-glass bodies are equipped with a small wing in front and a wider wing in the rear; the air pressure against these wings pushes the car down, holding it to the road at speeds that, on the straightaways, approach 200 miles per hour.

The sheer power of thirty-three cars roaring around the speedway is unbelievable. From the turn, you hear a high-pitched, angry whine, like a brigade of enraged, giant hornets. Suddenly, the cars appear, hurtling around the banked track and seeming to fly straight at you. Then in a flash of energy, light, sound, dirt, and with an assault of rubber and gasoline smells, they zoom by. It seems odd, given supersonic airplanes and rockets to the moon, that automobiles can be so awesome in their speed. The reason they are, of course, is that the high-speed auto fits into a fantasy that is grafted onto everyday experience. Watching the race at Indy is like attending a Walter Mitty Memorial Convention. Every fan imagines himself behind the wheel of an Olsonite-Eagle or a Ford-McLaren thundering and skidding around the track.

"Boy," says Jennings, head of a family of a half-dozen that journeys here every year from eastern Pennsylvania. "I'd love to get in my Chevy and drive around that track just once. They got a little bus that'll give you a tour of the track for fifty cents, but, aw, I'd love to drive around it, just once. Or even get in one of those cars. I don't see why they don't have an old car they'd let you sit in and take a picture. You'd think they'd set it up for the fans."

Along with the specter of glory, fame, and speed, of course, is the specter of death. Driving a car at three times the maximum speed permissible on a superhighway is, to say the least, unsafe; running over a piece of metal on the track, making a slight miscalculation in braking or steering in a turn, can send the car smashing into a wall. And while no visitor will admit openly that it is the prospect of witnessing death that draws him to the race, the anticipation of danger is clearly present in many minds.

"Yeah," says Paul, a shipping clerk from Iowa. "I was here in '39 when Floyd Roberts got it, and I remember '64 when Eddie Sachs and MacDonald were burned up. Jeez, that was something. And in '68 I was right there when a guy got killed. Got a great picture of that wreck."

For Mike, a state trooper from Ohio who is half-Indian, witnessing the race in person cannot be equaled by television because "the thing that's wrong with TV, they try not to show the grisly part of it when it happens. Now you take this Jim Malloy, who got wrecked in the trials this year. Well, when it first happened, they didn't show the grisly stuff—you know, when he actually hit the wall, how bad it really was."

"You'd be surprised," says Cleek, a sun-reddened harvest hand in his sixties who drove in by himself from Oregon in a pickup. "Ninety-nine-and-nine-tenths of 'em come to see wrecks. You hear 'em say, 'Wasn't no good race, no wrecks.' Just like people watching a man on a ledge, most of 'em want him to jump. That's what a lot of people come here for, I believe. I dunno, I see it the other way. That just about ruins it for me. People gettin' pretty damned hard-hearted now. They don't give a damn about their fellow man."

The strange mixture of honor and bloodshed, sudden wealth and sudden death, courage and the mechanical skill involved in building a championship car and keeping it moving (a task assigned the "pit" crews who service the cars with the frantic speed and competence of a team of open-heart surgeons) can get a hold on a fan that lasts for a life-time. It happened to Clyde de Botkin, who was stationed near the speedway during World War II, when it lay idle. "I said to myself, 'If they ever have a race here again, I want to see it.' I came back in '47, and that was it," he recalls.

Now in his late forties, Clyde is a round-faced, pleasant man who works as a handy man in Kaycee, Wyoming. For the last twenty-seven years the only vacation Clyde has taken has come between April and early June. Every year, he has driven—most years by himself—to Indian-apolis, taken a room in a boardinghouse, and stayed at the track from April 28 to June 5. He usually hangs out in Gasoline Alley, where the cars are stored and worked on; he has come to know the mechanics and pit crews by sight. The pride of his life is Special Pit Pass Number 777, which a speedway official gave Clyde a decade ago after he had noticed him at the 500 year after year; the pass permits him to watch the mechanics and drivers at work. The Indy is the only event outside of his daily routine that Clyde de Botkin has experienced in his adult life. He has never even seen another part of America.

"Why should I want to?" Clyde says. "This is the most exciting place in the world." Too exciting, in fact. Clyde has an enlarged heart, and he must lie down several times a day in the air-conditioned press room to safeguard his health. "I know it's dangerous," he says; "but if I couldn't be here on Race Day, I just wouldn't . . . ." He shrugs.

Unlike Clyde de Botkin, who is caught up in the drama of the long, grueling challenge, a remarkable number of Indy fans are almost totally uninterested in the race. "I'd guess about one hundred thousand people here never see the cars in action, don't know who won, and couldn't care less," says a race reporter. For the fans who pack the infield, in fact, the race is almost impossible to watch. Even the more affluent spectators in the upper grandstand can see barely a fourth of the track —it's just too big to see in its entirety.

"We'll be watching the backstretch," says Sam, a shipping clerk. "We'll only see a tenth of the race. But when they go by, we'll see this one's first, this one's second, and so on. So if their positions change, we'll know somebody passed."

For a sports junkie like me, this was odd to contemplate; it was as if I could watch a hockey game only from a ten-foot-wide stretch of ice, or a baseball game from an obstructed view that revealed only a six-foot chunk of base path. What kind of sports fan would watch an event where he could not see who scored, how, and what outstanding achievements won or lost the game?

"See, that's the thing," explains Bill, who has been here since Monday to be first on line to drive through the gate to the infield. "You could just not run the race, and most people here wouldn't give a damn. The main thing is that people get together, and there's no fighting or anything . . . . I know these guys—they been coming here for years. They all park in the same spot at the gate, they mess around for three or four days with each other before the race starts, buying each other beer . . . they take care of each other. When we get inside the track, there'll be friends on both sides of us where we park, everybody sharing everything, and they all have a ball. No, we don't see each other the rest of the year. Just here. And we talk about the times we had and party it up."

What Bill says is echoed by many of the hard-core Indy spectators. They come because it is a "good time" and "the world's biggest party." For three or four days they live away from the home, the factory, or office. ("Why do I come here?" asks a Bendix-Westinghouse worker from Elyria, Ohio. "Four days away from the kids, with my buddies.") They move outside their existence. They see friends who are friends for a weekend each year. They drink endless cases of beer, grill their steaks together, and yell at the young girls in hot pants and T-shirts with no bras underneath.

"You know what this is like?" asks a dark-haired, muscular auto worker. "This is just like that Woodstock. Only those hippies had their music and their dope; we got beer and racing."

"Yeah," a buddy interrupts. "Only nobody around here is taking off their clothes and running around bare-ass. Goddamnit." He laughs.

There *is* a sense of Woodstock here, a sense of camaraderie. That sense is kindled by staying up all night together on Friday, waiting for the aerial bombs to explode at 5:00 a.m. Saturday signaling the opening of the track, and then the furious, Oklahoma-land-rush sprint to the best positions in the track ("The real race is at 5:00 a.m.," says a security guard. "The car race, that's just an anticlimax.") But there is also a fierce sense of personal, material pride: in the outfitting of the campers ("We got four bunk beds here, paneling, a can, running water, air conditioning") and the food ("Now, most folks have cold fried chicken. Hell, we got eggs any style, bacon, ham, home fries, and then steak, baked potato and sour cream, salad with blue cheese dressing"). The dull glow of television sets flickers in the late night air, that umbilical link with reality that cannot be turned off and left home.

I could not help thinking that we have at Indianapolis a metaphor for the way we live: Here before me are decent, hard-working people, seeking a sense of community and excitement beyond their individual lives, waiting patiently to be packed together with their small luxuries and large discontents, being told what is happening by electronic tote boards and a loudspeaker system, seeking what fun they can find from a spectacle whose drama they cannot very clearly see. Much of the pomp and majesty of the race—the start, the solemn intonation, "Gentlemen, start your engines," the pit stops, the salute to the victor— all of these important events go unwitnessed by those who have come the farthest and endured the most to be "where the action is."

An hour before the race ends, hundreds of spectators' cars are already streaming out of the speedway, under a cloud of gasoline fumes, dust, and heat, heading for home. They will not see the climax of the race, the victorious driver receiving his kiss on the cheek from the queen, the victor's slow, triumphal circuit of the track, nor the winning driver acknowledging the cheers from the grandstand. They have gotten what they came for in the revelry and release and camaraderie; and most of them will be back again next year.

"I been goin' to my sister's place for Memorial Day since 1938," says Cookie, a factory hand in his fifties who made his first visit to the Indianapolis 500 this year. "This is the first time I missed going to my sister's. And I think she's never going to see me no more."

"One thing about this," observed Cookie, speaking as one of the latest initiates to Middle America's perennial Woodstock. "I guess you either love it or you hate it. And I love it."

7

THE LIFE CYCLE

In this section we examine some of the important times and experiences in the human life cycle: infancy and childhood, adolescence, sex, marriage, and death. People everywhere confront these things, but the confrontations are different from culture to culture. All people deal with the birth of young; but in some societies the woman is pampered for months before and after delivery, whereas in others she is expected to resume her normal life rapidly. In some cultures men practice the *couvade;* they go through sympathetic labor and recovery pains after birth.

Some cultures provide a smooth transition from childhood to adulthood. Others make adolescence a trauma. When Margaret Mead went to study the Arapesh and other Pacific peoples in 1931, people in America assumed that adolescents were "naturally" rebellious and anxiety-ridden about sex. Of course, as it turned out, Professor Mead showed that anxiety in adolescence was a product of our culture. People learn to be what they are. Their culture teaches them how to occupy the status of child, the status of father, the status of sick person, and so on.

The process of learning how to behave correctly in one's own society is called socialization. The selections here explore some of the ways in which different cultures deal with the life-cycle and socialize humans to act in the "correct" way according to local tradition. In the first article, Martha Wolfenstein shows how differently American and French children are raised. American infants are encouraged to share and to be gregarious; French children are given to understand that their security lies in not being too friendly with others. American boys complain about their kid-brother tagging along. French boys learn to desire the company of younger siblings and to admire babies—a behavior that is peculiarly linked to girls in our culture. Wolfenstein's article shows clearly how early learning molds the attitudes and behavior of adults in different ways from society to society. Because adult per-

252

sonality is linked to early childhood experience, we can see how similar experience can lead to similar results.

In complex societies roles are taught more formally than in simpler societies. In America, for example, one of the best places to see role socialization in action is in the primary school. One of the first anthropologists to use ethnographic observation in schools was Jules Henry. Professor Henry's study of the formal socialization process was very revealing and disturbing. "[The student must] learn that the proper way to sing is tunelessly . . . and the proper way to paint is the way the teacher says, not the way he sees it." Henry found that American school children were alienated and that they came to accept alienation as the natural order of things. There is a price we pay for giving impersonal institutions like schools the essential job of socializing our young. According to Henry, "School is indeed a training for later life not because it teaches the three R's (more or less), but because it instills the essential cultural nightmare—fear of failure, envy of success, and absurdity."

The Siriono are a primitive people of Bolivia, who were described by Alan Holmberg. Childhood among the Siriono is a benign, gentle experience and very permissive. But this does not mean that the Siriono child is deprived of his basic education. To the contrary, as Holmberg shows, "although only three or four years of age [the child] has already experienced a major part of his natural environment and participated deeply into his culture." He has seen death and disease, and learned what plants to eat. Boys are given lessons in hunting with a miniature bow from the time they can walk, and girls are given miniature spindles. The lack of formal, institutionalized socialization does not diminish Siriono schooling at all.

Contrasting with the permissive, rather happy-appearing environment of the Siriono childhood is that of Pilaga Indians. Jules Henry described this group of people living in Argentina. Among the Pilaga, weaning is abrupt and difficult, and "deprived of warmth, the Pilaga child remains a poor hostile little flounderer for a number of years until he at last begins to take his place in the adult economic activity."

Adolescence is sampled here among modern Sioux Indians of South Dakota, middle-class white Americans, and the Alorese, a people who live an isolated island existence on the eastern end of the Java chain. Rosalie Wax was interested in why adolescent Sioux boys dropped out of school. She found that many of the boys were push-outs rather than drop-outs, because the school was crippling to

253

their needs as Sioux. The Sioux peer group had its own internal discipline, but the white-run school ignored it and stifled fulfillment for the boys.

The quintessence of youth in America is the glorification of pubescent womanhood in the Miss America pageant. A good irreverent look at the pageant by Judith Martin (a columnist for the *Washington Post*) tells a lot about middle-American values on adolescence in general and on beauty in particular. In contrast to these values are those of the Alorese, who are described by Cora Dubois. Tatooing and tooth filing are vital in the beautification of Alorese girls and boys; hardly the sort of thing for Miss America.

Marriage is described here for four societies: Sicilian, Taiwanese, American, and Gusii. The first two are peasant societies; the third is a complex society; the Gusii are a primitive Bantu-speaking people of Kenya. After reading the first two selections, many American students (especially women) agree with Cadwallader's article on marriage as a "wretched institution," because it pits people (men and women) against one another in an adversary relationship. To show that this is not particularly Western or even particularly common to complex industrial or agricultural societies, Robert Levine describes the often violent "sex battle" among the Gusii. We do not know the basic cause of sexual antagonism in human populations; but it seems to be evident in almost all societies. Among the Gusii, however, the antagonism is given institutionalized expression.

Finally, at the end of the life cycle, there is death. We have already contrasted Alorese and American values on beauty and adolescence. These same two societies are contrasted by Cora Dubois and Jessica Mitford. After studying many Alorese funerals, Dubois concluded that "the expediency and realism in human relationships is basically a shallowness of positive affect." Considering the commercialism of American funerals, as described by Mitford, and the way in which the grieving parties go along with it, Dubois could be correct. Further studies of emotion and emotional expression in many societies are needed before such a generalization can be supported. But the possibility that humans are essentially shallow pragmatists is intriguing and a little unsettling.

■ FRENCH PARENTS TAKE THEIR CHILDREN TO THE PARK

Martha Wolfenstein

THE "FOYER" IN THE PARK

For the French each family circle is peculiarly self-inclosed, with the family members closely bound to one another and a feeling of extreme wariness about intrusion from outside.[1] This feeling is carried over when parents take their children to play in the park. The children do not leave their parents to join other children in a communal play area. In fact, there are few communal play facilities—an occasional sand pile, some swings and carrousels, to which one must pay admission and to which the children are escorted by the parents. The usual procedure is for the mother (or other adult who brings the children to the park) to establish herself on a bench while the children squat directly at her feet and play there in the sand of the path. Where there is a sand pile, children frequently fill their buckets there and then carry the sand to where mother is sitting and deposit it at her feet. What one sees in the park, therefore, is not so much groups of children playing together while the adults who have brought them for this purpose sit on the side lines, but rather a series of little family enclaves. In a similar spirit the adults bring food from home for the children's mid-afternoon snack (*goûter*); it is rare for them to buy refreshments in the park (and, in keeping with the small demand, there are few facilities for this).

The adults do not seem interested in friendly overtures between children of different families, showing little of the usual eagerness of American parents that their children should make friends and be a success with their age mates. French adults seem to be much more on the alert for negative behavior of other children toward their charges.

These tendencies are illustrated in the behavior of a grandmother and her two-and-a-half-year-old grandson, Marcel. The grandmother seats herself on a bench facing the sand pile, to which Marcel goes, waving back at her across a few feet as if it were a long distance. He keeps looking at her while he plays, and she praises his sand pies. When a little girl steps on one of them, the grandmother scolds her roundly. Repeatedly the grandmother enters the sandbox and takes the little boy away from the others, telling him to stay in his own little corner. She makes frequent negative comments about the other children, remarking to me: "Have you ever noticed in children how some of them have the spirit of evil [*l'esprit du mal*]? Marcel, however, never destroys other children's things; he is very well brought up [*très bien*

---

[1] Cf. Métraux and Mead, 1954, Part I.

élevé]." The little boy, though on the whole he seems friendly toward other children, has the idea of demarcating his own little space and safeguarding it from intrusion. Thus, when another boy sits down on the cement edge of the sandbox where Marcel has a row of prized sand pies that grandmother has helped him make, he is anxious about the other boy getting too close and makes a barrier with his hand between the other boy and the sand pies; then, becoming increasingly uneasy about these fragile possessions, he starts gently pushing the other boy away (Sèvres-Babylone, July 23, 1953). In such little daily experiences the child learns from the attitude of the adult to carry over into the world outside the home the feeling of separateness and the need to guard one's own against possibly dangerous intruders.

There seems to be a continual mild anxiety that possessions will get mixed up in the park. Mothers are constantly checking on the whereabouts of their children's toys and returning toys to other mothers. One woman hands a toy shovel to another, saying: *C'est à vous, madame?* (Sèvres-Babylone, July 21, 1953). Toys seem to be regarded as the possessions of the parents, and mislaid ones are usually restored to them. While parents are concerned to keep track of their own child's toys, they seem particularly upset if their child has picked up something belonging to another and are apt to slap the child for it. This happens regardless of whether there has been any dispute and where the owner may be quite unaware that another child has picked up something of his.

The following incidents illustrate these attitudes. A girl of about two is holding a celluloid fish belonging to a boy of about the same age. Though the boy makes no protest, the attendant of the girl scoldingly tells her to give it to him, pushes her forward, and after the girl has handed the fish to the boy, hustles her back to her own bench (Parc Monceau, September 10, 1947).

A girl of about two has picked up a leather strap from a neighboring group. Her nurse reproves her, takes her by the hand, and returns the strap. A little later a boy of about the same age, belonging to this neighboring family, plays with the little girl, picks up her pail, and keeps it while the little girl is fed by her nurse. The boy's grandmother becomes aware that he has the pail, hits him on the buttocks, scolds, and, taking him by the hand, returns the pail to the girl's nurse. In front of the nurse she repeatedly hits the boy about the head and ears (Parc Monceau, September 10, 1947).

A three-year-old boy has been playing with a borrowed scooter, when his mother notices that the handlebar grip is torn. She takes hold of the scooter with one hand and the child with the other, goes over to the mother to whom the scooter belongs, apologizes, and scolds the boy in front of her (Luxembourg, September 11, 1947).

Among American children issues of ownership versus sharing tend to arise when two children dispute about the use of a toy. What is considered desirable is that the child should learn to share his playthings, which are his property, with others. French children seem to be taught something quite different. Toys are familial property, and those belonging to each family must be kept separate. Just as the children with their parents or other familial adults form a close little circle in the park, so their belongings should remain within this circle. The child who brings into this circle something from outside seems to be introducing an intrusive object, which arouses all the negative sentiments felt, but from politeness not directly expressed, toward outsiders. At the same time it is an offense to the outsiders, whose belongings are thus displaced, and restitution and apologies to them are required. Also, as French adults are much preoccupied with property and with increasing their own, they have to ward off the temptation to do so by illegitimate means. The child's easy way of picking up others' things may evoke in adults impulses to take which they strive to repress in themselves and which they therefore cannot tolerate in the child.

Friendly behavior between children of different families is not encouraged by the adults. A pretty nine-year-old girl is playing with a boy of the same age and his sister, about a year older. The boy clowns a great deal to impress the girl, who is rather severe and unamused. Having finally won a smile from her, he flirtatiously pinches her chin and asks her name. She does not answer. Her grandmother, watching this, remarks humorously to the boy: "She didn't tell you?" The grandmother seems quite content with the girl's aloofness and a bit mocking toward the frustrated little boy[2] (Luxembourg, July 21, 1953).

Adults also seemed apt to interpret children's approaches to one another as more negatively motivated than they were. The mother of a five-year-old boy who is approaching a three-year-old repeatedly calls to him: *Claude, laisse le petit garçon!* It is not clear at first whether Claude is more interested in the other boy or in a ball which he is holding. However, when the ball has been taken by the younger boy's mother, the two children sit in the sand and play together quite amicably. Claude makes the younger boy laugh. At no time had the little one shown any sign of not wanting Claude to play with him (Luxembourg, September 11, 1947). In thus underestimating the children's positive impulses toward one another, the adults may be projecting their own negative feelings toward strangers. It would be mistaken to infer, on the grounds of this adult discouragement, that the capacity for friendship fails to develop in children and adolescents. Other evidence suggests that just the opposite is true.[3] Parental approval or urging does not constitute the only auspices under which the child can find a friend. Sometimes the most intense friendships develop without the encouragement or against the discouragement of the older generation.[4]

[2] Cf. in *The Remembrance of Things Past,* Proust's account of Marcel's long-term childhood attachment to Gilberte, whom he used to see only in the park.

[3] Métraux and Mead, 1954, Part I.

[4] Roger Peyrefitte's *Amitiés particulières* (1945) recounts a special case of intense homosexual attachment in a strict Catholic school where any meeting of two boys alone together was taboo.

SECRET SOLIDARITY OF BROTHERS

In the following incident one can observe the friendly relation of two brothers which becomes more outspoken when they get by themselves, away from the adults.[5] The two boys, of about six and seven, very neat, dressed alike in blue jerseys and white shorts, are playing together in the sand of the path. Their father sits talking with two women, who appear to be friends of the family, and the boys' sister, about a year older, sits on a bench with her doll. As the younger boy moves into the father's field of vision, the father slaps his hands and face, presumably because he has got himself dirty. This puts an end to the sand play; the two boys sit down, subdued, on the bench, and as the father turns away, the older presents the younger with a cellophane bag—a gesture of sympathy and compensation. After a time the father suggests to the girl that the children take a walk around the park, and they immediately set out. On their walk the boys keep close together, leaving the girl to herself. As they get farther away from the father, the boys begin putting their arms around each other's shoulders. They become much more animated and point things out to each other as they go. As they get nearer to the father again on the return path, they drop their arms from each other's shoulders, drift apart, and again become more subdued. Having returned, they seat themselves quietly again on the bench (Parc Monceau, September 4, 1947).

ACCEPTANCE OF THE LITTLE ONES

French children show a great readiness to play with children younger than themselves, in a way which contrasts strikingly with the behavior of American children. It is typical of American boys particularly to be intolerant of the "kid brother" who wants to tag along and get into the big boys' game when he isn't good enough.[6] An American boy of seven will complain that he has no one of his own age to play with; the neighbors' little boy is six. In America there tends to be a strict age-grading, which the children themselves feel strongly about.

In contrast to this, French children appear interested in younger children and ready to accept them in their games. A boy of eight or nine will play ball with a smaller boy, a five-year-old or even a two-year-old, without showing any impatience at the ineptitude of the younger one. The two children may be brothers or may belong to families that know each other (Sèvres-Babylone, July 21 and 23, 1953). A slender blond boy of about seven seems completely absorbed in a little

5 The importance of dyadic relations in the family is indicated in Métraux and Mead (1954), Part I.
6 Margaret Mead has pointed out the position of the American "kid brother," whom the older boys regard as a nuisance because he tries to get into their games and he isn't good enough. The recent film, *The Little Fugitive,* gives a vivid instance of this.

girl of two or three whom he follows around, bending over to speak to her. The mothers of the two children are acquainted with each other, and the boy and his mother both shake hands with the little girl's mother when she leaves the park. The boy looks quite disconsolate without his little friend; eventually, at his mother's suggestion, he picks up his scooter and slowly pushes off on it (Parc Monceau, September 18, 1953).

Such interest, particularly on the part of boys, in younger children differs markedly from the American pattern, where interest in babies becomes strictly sex-typed for girls only and out of keeping with the boy's ideal of masculine toughness.

On another occasion I observed a group of seven children, ranging in age from about nine to under two, who had been brought to the park by two nurses. They played a number of group games in which the six- to nine-year-olds regularly included a three-year-old little girl, who was given her turn like the rest. In an interval of play, the children sat on a bench, and a couple of the older girls and a boy of about eight took turns in holding and cuddling the baby boy, who was less than two and who accepted their embraces quite complacently (Luxembourg, September 22, 1953).

This sort of grouping which includes a considerable age range may derive from the requirement of staying within the family circle or the circle of children whose parents know one another. Where the American child is expected from an early age to become a member of a peer group outside the family, for the French child the family and the contacts which the adults make with other families remain decisive. While, from the American point of view, this may appear restrictive, it also facilitates friendly relations between older and younger children, including notably affectionate quasi-paternal feelings of older boys toward small children.

It should perhaps be added that in school there seems to be a sharp awareness of small gradations of age. Thus a six-year-old little girl, the child of some friends of mine, informed me that in her class in school the children were seated according to age and that it was mainly the "babies" who were punished by the teacher (who put them in the wastebasket, according to my young informant, or consigned them to the place under her desk). The little girl telling this was evidently not one of the "babies." However, the order of precedence prevailing in the classroom does not seem to carry over outside it.

To the extent to which I was able to observe exclusive groupings, these seemed to be more in terms of sex than of age, though this also appeared much less sharp than among American children. The pair of brothers, of whom I spoke earlier, who were so closely allied but excluded their sister illustrate this. On another occasion I observed a group of girls of various ages (from about four to about seven) playing together at making a garden in the sand of the path (laying down rows of pebbles, etc.) and brusquely throwing out any little boy who intruded ("Boys aren't allowed in the garden. Only girls are allowed in, because we made it.") (Luxembourg, September 11, 1947). This, however, was not frequent; usually boys and girls played quite readily together.

GROWNUPS STOP CHILDREN'S AGGRESSION

French children are not taught to fight their own battles, to stick up for their rights, in the American sense of these terms. If one child attacks another, even very mildly, the grownups regularly intervene and scold the aggressor. The child who is attacked is likely to look aggrieved or to cry, to look toward his mother or go to her. He does not hit back, nor is he encouraged to do so. An attack is thus not a challenge which must be met by the attacked to save his self-esteem. It is a piece of naughty behavior to be dealt with by the adults.

In the following instances one can see how quickly adults intervene in even very slight manifestations of aggression. Among a group of small children playing on a sand pile, a girl of about two and a half takes a shovel from her four-year-old sister and walks away with it, looking back in a mildly provocative way. The older girl remains seated and simply looks dismayed. The younger one is already going back to return the shovel when the mother comes over and scolds her, calling her *vilaine*. The little one gives back the shovel, and the two resume their digging (Parc Monceau, September 4, 1947).

Two girls about three years old are seated on the sand pile. One takes hold of the other's pail, not removing it but only holding on to the rim. The owner of the pail cries but makes no other defense. An elderly woman, grandmother or nurse of the attacker, intervenes, reprimands, and the girl lets go. The woman reassures the victim, who stops crying. The woman continues to scold her charge, who moves away from the sand pile (Parc Monceau, September 4, 1947).

In an incident cited earlier, where a little girl stepped on a little boy's sand pie, the boy looked toward his grandmother with an expression of amazement and distress. The grandmother promptly launched into a biting verbal attack on the little girl: *Vilaine! Vilaine fille! Tu commences maintenant à faire des sottises!* A little later when another girl was throwing sand into the sand pile, the grandmother scolded her repeatedly, telling her it could get into children's eyes. The girl's mother, a little way off, then chimed in and told the girl to stop. Protective as she was of her little grandson, the grandmother was equally ready to interfere in an aggressive act of his. Thus, when he was pushing another boy, who did not even seem to notice the rather gentle pressure, the grandmother called to him to stop, that he would make the other boy get a *bo-bo*, and the grandson stopped (Sèvres-Babylone, July 23, 1953).

Thus what French children learn is not the prized Anglo-Saxon art of self-defense or the rules that determine what is a fair fight.[7] What they learn is that their own aggression is not permissible.

A consequence of the prohibition against physical aggression is that verbal disputes are substituted for it.[8] Also, in the case of any serious conflict there is a tendency for everything to come to a standstill, for all involved to become immobilized.[9] This was illustrated in a family of five children whom I observed, where a quarrel between two of them brought their play to a complete stop. The four older children (three boys of about twelve, nine, and eight and a girl of about seven) were playing hide-and-seek, while the youngest girl (about six) sat beside her mother, who was knitting. The goal was the chair on which the youngest child was sitting. It happened repeatedly that the second oldest boy, Philippe, a snub-nosed mischievous-looking fellow, did not come out of hiding when he was called. The eldest, a slender, quick, excitable boy, became quite desperate about this, shouting repeatedly: "Philippe! Philippe!" when his brother refused to appear, but not running to look for him. The mother chided him for his shouting, saying, *C'est suffisant.* (Shouting, incidentally, is very rare in Paris parks.) When Philippe finally showed up, in his own good time, smiling provocatively, his elder brother scolded him. Philippe disappeared behind a pedestal against which his mother was sitting; the older boy followed, and evidently hit him, because Philippe was crying when they emerged. The mother appeared to rebuke the older boy. There then followed a prolonged acrimonious dispute between the older brother and Philippe, the game giving way entirely to this dispute. The younger girl and boy, who had participated in the game in a gay and lively way, now became immobile, not joining in the argument or demanding that the game go on or instituting a game of their own, but just standing and gazing abstractedly into the distance. The mother continued to knit, and the father, who had joined them, read his newspaper.

I had the feeling that American children in similar circumstances would, out of a greater urgency for physical activity, have managed to get their game going again. The aggressive feelings would have become dissipated in strenuous action. For the French, the prohibition of fighting seems to extend itself to a general inhibition of motor activity where a conflict has arisen. Everyone becomes immobilized, while protracted and inconclusive verbal hostilities ensue. (This paralyzing effect of conflict is also exemplified in French politics, where *l'immobilisme* in the face of contradictory demands from opposing sides is acknowledged as a central reality.[10])

---

[7] Margaret Mead describes how, on an American playground, mothers keep admonishing their children to stick up for their rights, to fight for themselves, and to fight fair (Mead, 1942, pp. 141–42).

[8] A stock French parental injunction is: *Disputez, mais ne vous battez pas.*

[9] Abel, Belo, and Wolfenstein, 1954.

[10] Nathan Leites, unpublished research in French politics.

RESTRAINT IN MOTOR ACTIVITY

To an American visitor it is often amazing how long French children can stay still. They are able to sit for long periods on park benches beside their parents. A typical position of a child in the park is squatting at his mother's feet, playing in the sand. His hands are busy, but his total body position remains constant. Children are often brought to the park in quite elegant (and unwashable) clothes, and they do not get dirty. The squatting child keeps his bottom poised within an inch of the ground but never touching, only his hands getting dirty; activity and getting dirty are both restricted to the hands. While sand play is generally permissible and children are provided with equipment for it, they seem subject to intermittent uncertainty whether it is all right for their hands to be dirty. From time to time a child shows his dirty hands to his mother, and she wipes them off.

Among some children between two and three I noticed a particularly marked tendency to complete immobility, remaining in the same position with even their hands motionless, and staring blankly or watching other children. A French child analyst suggested that this is the age when children are being stuffed with food and are consequently somewhat stuporous. Occasionally one could see children of these ages moving more actively and running about. But the total effect contrasted with the usual more continuous motor activity which one sees in American children. Also, French children seemed more often to walk where American children would run.

The same French child analyst told me about a "hyperactive" six-year-old child who had been referred to her for treatment. The teacher had brought it to the mother's attention that he was never seated, but constantly moving around at school. I asked whether this was so unusual and was told that the teacher had never seen anything like it, so she knew the boy was ill. Ordinarily, children of this age sit quite motionless in school; as the analyst put it, it is so quiet you can hear a fly flying. As we spoke of the greater activity of American children, the analyst, who had lived for some time in America, remarked that she found many American children *insupportable* in their tendency to keep incessantly in motion.

Thus there appears to be considerable adult intolerance for children's motor activity, which is effectively communicated to the children. The requirement of keeping clean and the inhibition on physical aggression contribute to the restriction of motor activity, and so does the distrustful feeling about alien space, outside the family circle. The relation between restraint on aggression and on large-muscle activity was remarked upon by another French child analyst, who had treated both French and American children.[11] She observed that an American child in

11 Cf. Françoise Dolto, "French and American Children as Seen by a French Child Analyst," in Margaret Mead and Martha Wolfenstein (eds.), *Childhood in Contemporary Cultures* (Chicago: The University of Chicago Press, 1955), p. 408.

an aggressive mood would throw things up to the ceiling, while a French child would express similar angry impulses by making little cuts in a piece of clay.

Forceful activity on the part of children is apt to evoke warning words from the adults: "Gently, gently." Two brothers about nine and six were throwing a rubber ball back and forth. The younger had to make quite an effort to throw the ball the required distance; his throws were a bit badly aimed but did not come very close to any bystanders. His mother and grandmother, who were sitting near him, repeatedly cautioned him after every throw: *Doucement! Doucement!* I had the feeling that it was the strenuousness of his movements which made them uneasy, though they may also have exaggerated the danger of his hitting someone (Sèvres-Babylone, July 23, 1953). Similarly, when two little girls about four and five were twirling around, holding each other's hands, an elderly woman seated near by kept calling to the older girl: *Doucement, elle est plus petite que toi.* To which the child answered that they were not going very fast (Parc Monceau, September 18, 1953). The implication here seems to be that any rapid or forceful movement can easily pass into a damaging act.

The tendency to talk rather than act appears not only in substituting verbal disputes for fighting but also in prolonged talking, which postpones activity, where the activity is not of an aggressive nature. The preponderance of talk over action was striking in the following incident. The younger of two brothers, about six and eight, has a toy airplane of which he is winding up the propeller. The older boy reaches for the plane, but the younger one keeps it, and the older does not persist. Several slightly bigger boys gather around interestedly (this airplane was the only toy of its sort which I saw in the park). A prolonged discussion ensues about how to launch the plane, whether at this angle or at that. They talk and talk, and the boy with the plane continues to wind the propeller. Watching them, I began to feel rather acutely that there was no action: how about trying actually to fly the plane? Finally, it was set off and was a complete failure, nose-diving about four feet from the takeoff. The interest of the boys, however, did not diminish; they continued their discussion while the owner of the plane again began winding up the propeller. Though a subsequent flight was as bad as the first, no one seemed to draw the conclusion that the plane was incapable of flying. Interest continued, despite failure in action; none of the older boys took the plane out of the hands of the younger one; and the discussion did not lose its zest, despite its lack of practical results (Parc Monceau, September 18, 1953).

On the same occasion the play of another boy whom I observed, with a paper airplane, seemed to demonstrate very nicely the feeling about remaining within a small space. When American boys make planes out of folded paper, these planes are generally long and narrow, with a sharp point, with the aim of their being able to fly as fast and far as possible. In contrast to this prevailing American style, the French boy had folded his paper plane in a wide-winged, much less pointed shape. It moved more slowly through the air and did not go any great distance, but within a small space described many complicated and elegant loops.

Another time I observed a game where an active chase was led up to by elaborate preliminaries in which action was slight. This seemed comparable to the protracted talk postponing action. Five children (of about six to nine) were playing together with a young nursemaid. The nursemaid sat on a bench while the children performed charades in front of her, the performance being preceded by considerable consultation among themselves as to the subject they would enact. As the nursemaid ventured various guesses, the children interrupted their act several times to explain the exact rules of the game to her. When she finally uttered the right word, this was the signal for them to run and her to chase them. Any child she caught before they reached a certain tree then joined her on the bench and helped to guess and to chase the next time round. But before the next brief chase there were again the consultations and the pantomime. Other children's games in which an introductory ritual precedes a chase are common, but I am not familiar with any in which the less active preparatory phase is so elaborate, where talk and small movements occupy such a large part of the game and the chase comes only as a brief finale.

THE CHILD ALONE

French children manifest a greater tolerance for being alone than American children do. Just as they do not show the urge to be incessantly in motion, which one sees in American children, so also they do not show the need to be constantly with other children. When I speak of a child being alone, I mean alone with the adult who has brought him to the park. But this may mean in effect being very much alone, since, as a rule, the adult pays little attention to him. There is usually little interchange in the park between adults and children over one and a half. While mothers and nurses direct a good deal of affectionate talk to a baby in a carriage, they tend to ignore the three-year-old squatting at their feet or sitting on the bench beside them. The child who is able to walk around is, as it were, on his own, even if he is moving around very little. Most of the time the adults read, or knit, or just sit, or talk with other adults of their acquaintance. The child who does not have siblings to play with or other children of families with whom his parents are acquainted may play with a doll or play in the sand or sometimes just sit beside mother without a word being exchanged. There were instances where a mother or a father, a grandmother or nurse, kept up a more lively contact with a child, talking and even playing with him, but this seemed to be the exception rather than the rule.

Where children have others to play with and participate eagerly in common games, they still do not show the need for unbroken social contact. There are intermissions in their play when each may go off by himself. In the group of children of whom I spoke before, seven children of various ages, accompanied by two nurses, a series of organized games (such as charades) were played, which the children seemed to enjoy very much. They could also play in a less organized way, as when they took turns in cuddling the baby or carrying him around. But there came an interlude when they separated. One of the older girls had gone off to take the baby to the toilet, having been given five francs for this purpose by the nurse (this, incidentally, showed an exceptional scruple, as generally children up to six or seven were permitted to urinate in the open). The boy of eight then went a little apart and stood on a chair. He gazed around, looked toward the tennis courts, fingered his collar and his lips, and picked his nose. While in the games he had been lively, smiling, agreeable, and occasionally clowning, he now appeared immobile and abstracted. At a little distance his older sister leaned against a tree, watching one of the younger girls play with a toy that was thrown into the air and caught with a string. While these children came together again shortly afterward, they had chosen for a while to be detached and alone. The moments of detachment, particularly clearly in the case of the boy who was fingering his nose and lips, suggest that the child does not feel so uneasy about autoerotic activities or solitary fantasies that he must be constantly with others to guard against them (Luxembourg, September 22, 1953).

Where there is a choice of either playing alone or with others, playing alone may be preferred (which again I think would be very rare among American children). Three girls of about thirteen were playing near one another, each with the kind of toy which is whirled into the air from a string and caught again, a game requiring considerable skill. The three of them, all quite proficient, continued this play, each by herself, for at least an hour before they joined together and began passing the whirling object from one to another (Luxembourg, September 22, 1953).

For the French child, being alone is partly enforced by the closed family circle, where he is confined with adults, who are often aloof from him. There is some evidence that the child in the circle of adults, preoccupied with their own affairs, may feel painfully abandoned.[12] However, he also seems to achieve a certain tolerance for being by himself, so that, where various possibilities are open to him, he exhibits a range of activities, alternately social and solitary.

It may be added that for the French the mere presence of others, even if there is no overt interaction with them, appears to constitute a valued form of sociability. This would apply to the child who plays by himself alongside other children in the park as well as to the adult who sits alone with his drink and his newspaper at a café table.

LOOKING

Children frequently become absorbed in watching other children. A child walking past where others are playing will come to a standstill and

12 Cf. Prévert, 1951.

watch. Children sitting on a bench watch others playing ball. A child in the sand pile becomes immobile, forgets the shovel in his hand and his half-filled pail, as he watches other children. This absorption in looking seems in part related to the obstacles in the way of free contact with others. Sometimes the closest the child can get is to stand a little way off and look. Then, with the inhibition of motor activity, looking may become, in a compensatory way, intensified.[13] But also French children learn by looking more than by doing. They are taught to watch activities for which they are not yet ready but which they will be able to perform later on.[14] This was expressed, for instance, in the way in which parents held up small children to watch older ones on the swings. A mother with a one-year-old boy in her arms stops by the swings and says: *C'est la balançoire, mon petit chéri,* and holds him so that he can watch. A father with a baby of about six months holds the child up to watch, saying, *Regarde. C'est bon?* (Luxembourg, September 23, 1953).

ADULTS ARE ABOVE THE EMOTIONS OF CHILDREN

Adults seem to look down from a considerable height on both the griefs and the joys of children. Childhood and adulthood are two very distinct human conditions. From the vantage point of the adult, the emotions of the child do not seem serious: they are not, after all, about anything very important. The adult is likely to be detached in the face of the child's distress. Where the child is elated, the adult, though sympathetic, may regard the child humorously, perhaps a bit mockingly: how he overestimates these little childish things!

On an occasion when a mother punished a little boy, she appeared quite unconcerned about his rage and grief and was amused when he later came to fling his arms around her. I did not see what it was that provoked the mother's punishment. My attention was attracted when I saw the boy, of about six or seven, running, with his mother, a sturdy, athletic-looking woman, hard at his heels. When she overtook him, she gave him several hard whacks on the behind, and the boy burst into tears. The mother then sat down on the bench beside her husband, who was holding the baby; for her the episode seemed finished. The boy, however, continued crying, his posture very tense, with an expression of raging protest. He stalked off, still crying, looking helplessly angry and hurt, and walked around the playground, where several other children and mothers turned to look at him. His own mother was not looking but after a while glanced in his direction, smiling, seemingly not at him

---

[13] Abel, Belo, and Wolfenstein (1954) suggest that prohibitions against nocturnal looking intensify the wish to look.

[14] French girls, for instance, learn to cook by watching their mothers (cf. Métraux and Mead, 1954, Part I).

but about him. The boy returned to the parents' bench, stood first in front of his father, then threw his arms around his mother and put his head in her lap. The mother put her arms around him and turned to a woman on the other side of the bench and laughed. The other woman laughed back. The boy remained for some time with his head buried in his mother's lap. The mother had apparently been unperturbed by the boy's stormy tears and by his gesture of walking away, while his return to her, as his love and longing overpowered his angry feelings, seemed to her humorous. In laughing with another adult about it, she seemed to express: that's the way children are; that's all that comes of their little scenes (Sèvres-Babylone, July 24, 1953). Such discrepancies between the feelings of children and adults, where the adults remain detached while the child is undergoing violent emotions, may produce in the child a sense of painful abandonment.

Where the child is pleased with himself over some achievement, the adults may be more sympathetic, but with a nuance of gentle mockery, expressing a feeling of the smallness of these childish feats. This was the case with the grandmother of the little boy, Marcel, whom I mentioned before. The boy had been trying very hard to make sand molds with his pail. When, after numerous less successful attempts, he turned out a complete one, he threw back his head, beaming with elation. The grandmother was greatly amused by this, laughing and remarking to me: *Il est fier! Comme il est fier!* She was very sympathetic to the little boy, but at the same time found the child's great pride in having made such a thing as a sand pie humorous (Sèvres-Babylone, July 23, 1953). The nuance here is a delicate one. I would say it consists in the adult's never quite putting himself in the child's place but retaining a double position: in part empathizing with the child, but in part seeing the child's concerns as such a small matter that the child's strong feeling about them appears disproportionate and hence comic.

At other times, when children are having fun together, an adult who is with them may be simply unamused, not feeling at all impelled to participate in the children's mood or to smile at what makes them laugh. I observed such a discrepancy of mood where two boys were playing together very gaily while the mother of one of them sat on a bench beside them, reading, very unsmiling, addressing to her son from time to time a slight reprimand and then turning back to her book. Jean, her son, and Michel, his friend, both about seven, were chattering and laughing as they built a sand fort. Jean jumped up to show his mother his muddy hands (he remained otherwise immaculate), saying, *Regarde, maman!* His mother looked up briefly to say in a perfunctory tone, *Quelle horreur,* and continued reading. Jean returned to the fort, jumped up now and then to prance around in a clowning way, then seated himself on the shoulders of Michel, who was squatting over the fort, and playfully bounced up and down. Michel giggled. The mother repeatedly, unsmilingly, told Jean not to do this, without, however, interrupting the play or the good humor of the boys. When the mother announced it was time to leave, the boys began by slow stages to demolish their fort, the operation ending with Michel sitting down on it. The boys thought this very funny (probably the more so since throughout their play they had carefully squatted with their behinds poised an inch or so above the ground). At this final foolishness the mother smiled for the first time, saying: *Michel, tu es bête* (Parc Monceau, September 18, 1953). In such circumstances as these, the adult's detachment is mingled with disapproval. The children's way of having fun, which here included getting dirty and physical contacts which produced giggles, seems to the adult slightly naughty or at best silly.

I think this latter instance particularly contrasts with the way in which American adults are likely to respond to children's play. For Americans, there is not such a cleavage between childhood and adulthood, nor is adulthood so decidedly the advantageous position. To be able to play like children and with children is a highly valued capacity. The sour-faced adult who is a killjoy to the children's sport is likely to arouse negative reactions not only in children but in adults as well. Adults generally do not like to think of themselves in this role. They are eager to show children that they are good sports, that they have a sense of humor, and this involves falling in with children's playful moods.

CHILDREN MIMIC ADULTS

I observed very little of the sort of make-believe play in which children assume the roles of imaginary characters of drama or story, such as the frequent cowboy play of American little boys. Perhaps such dramatic play is carried on more at home than out in the open. I saw a few little boys with toy guns, but their play was far from aggressive by American standards, and if shooting noises were simulated, they were quite soft. A boy of about seven or eight, holding a gun, told a playmate, *Haut les mains,* in a tone of instructing him how to play the game rather than as a convincing dramatic threat. The second boy obligingly put up his hands and walked smilingly in front of his friend, who held the gun pointed at the other's back (Parc Monceau, September 18, 1953).

More often children mimic the familiar gestures and intonations of adults. Here they show excellent observation, combined with mockery. Their performance has much more zest and vividness than the mild *Haut les mains* of the friendly little gunman. The handshaking ritual of the adults is repeatedly imitated. For instance, as a group of boys pass a brother and sister, one of the boys calls: *Salut!* and the girl takes his hand and shakes it rather hard. Her brother starts shaking hands with the other boys with more show of politeness, saying, *Bonjour, Monsieur* (Parc Monceau, September 18, 1953).

A group of six- and seven-year-old girls who have been working at laying out a garden in the sand of the path take time out to sit on a bench and gossip. After a while, one of them interrupts their talk, exclaiming, like a busy woman who has let herself be distracted from her tasks: "But what are we doing chattering [*bavarder*] like this?" They laugh and return to their work. When smaller children unwittingly get in their way, the girls pick them up and put them to one side, with a *Qu'est-ce que tu fais, petite?* uttered in a tone of simulated amazement, combined with resignation, well imitated from the adults (Luxembourg, September 11, 1947).

At a band concert, a boy of nine, showing off to a pretty little girl, applauds exaggeratedly and cries, "Bravo! bravo!" after every piece. Later, when the concert is over, he mounts the bandstand and imitates the conductor, with autocratic gestures and a grandoise air, while a few other little boys sit in the places of the musicians and pretend to play different instruments (Luxembourg, July 21, 1953).

For the French, adulthood is decidedly the desirable time of life. Simply assuming the role of adults as he knows them is gratifying to a French child; no extraneous glamour need be added. At the same time, the adults in their role of authority rouse impulses of rebellious mockery in children, which they express in parodying the adults among themselves. This motive is liable to persist and to be permitted much stronger expression when the children grow up, in the mockery of authority figures, particularly in the political sphere, which is so prominent in French life.[15]

In contrast to this, for American children the adults they know are far from glamorous. Father is no superman.[16] Cowboys and spacemen provide models that better express the children's aspirations to strenuous and violent activity. The choice of models for children's make-believe play is perhaps reflected in the different styles of adult acting which we find in American and French films. There is little fine mimicry in facial expression, gestures, or tone of voice on the part of the American film hero. As the man on horseback, the man with the gun, fast-moving, triumphant in violent action, he fulfills the small boy's dream, at the same time exemplifying the heroic qualities which daddy lacks. In French films the actors show rather a mastery of small nuances of voice and manner, expressive of different characters that seem to have been unerringly observed. Such acting appears to be the highly elaborated sequel of the children's keen mimicry of adults. The contrast previously indicated between American and French children in respect to large and small movements is also relevant here.

CHILDHOOD IS NOT FOR FUN[17]

For the French, enjoyment of life is the prerogative of adults. Childhood is a preparation. Then everything must be useful, not just fun; it must have an educational purpose. The hard regime of French school

[15] Cf. the peculiarly irreverent political satire of *Le Canard enchaîné*.
[16] Mead, 1942, 1949.
[17] Cf. Françoise Dolto, "French and American Children as Seen by a French Child Analyst," in Meade and Wolfenstein, op. cit., p. 408.

children, with its tremendous burden of work, is well known. Probably nothing in later life is such a terrible ordeal as the dreaded *bachot* (the examination at the conclusion of secondary school). It is a real *rite de passage,* a painful test to which youths on the verge of maturity are subjected by their elders.

The attitude that everything for children, even the very young, must serve a useful purpose and not be just amusing is well exemplified around the carrousel in the Luxembourg Gardens. There are various rides for the children, among them rows of large rocking horses. A sign describes these as: *Chevaux hygiéniques. Jeu gymnastique pour les enfants développant la force et la souplesse.*

At the carrousel, as soon as the ride began, an old woman with spectacles and red hair done up in a bun on top of her head and wearing an old-fashioned gray coat (she seemed to me a benevolent witch), handed out to each child in the outer circle a stick (*baguette*). She then held out to them a contraption which dispensed rings and encouraged them to catch the rings on their sticks. Throughout the duration of the ride, the old woman directed to the children an incessant didactic discourse, urging them to pay attention and work very hard to catch the rings. *Attention! Regarde ton travail! Regarde bien, chouchou! Au milieu,* indicating with her finger the middle of the ring at which the child should aim. *Doucement!* When a child used his stick to beat time instead of to catch the rings, the old woman scolded him for this frivolity. At the end of the ride, she commended a boy who had caught many rings: *Tu as bien travaillé. Tu es gentil.* There was no other premium for catching the rings. On the next ride, a girl of about seven who failed to catch the rings where younger children were succeeding smiled with self-conscious chagrin. The elderly woman who had brought the girl there urged her to do better: *Attention! Regarde bien, Françoise* (Luxembourg, September 23, 1953). Thus, even on the carrousel, children have a task to perform. The elders direct, commend, and rebuke them. They are not there just for fun.

The paradox from the American point of view is that the French grow up with a great capacity for enjoyment of life. The adult enters fully into the pleasures which have not been permitted to the child. There seems to be a successful realization that pleasure is not taboo, but only postponed. The song of Charles Trenet, *Quand j'étais petit,* ends with the triumphant, *On n'est plus petit!*—everything is now permitted. It remains one of the puzzles of French culture how this effect is achieved: that the restraints to which children are subjected have only a temporary influence and do not encumber the adult with lasting inhibitions.

If we compare Americans and French, it seems as though the relation between childhood and adulthood is almost completely opposite in the two cultures. In America we regard childhood as a very nearly ideal time, a time for enjoyment, and end in itself. The American image of the child, whether envisaged in the classical figures of Tom Sawyer and Huckleberry Finn, or in the small hero of the recent film *The Little*

Fugitive, who achieves a self-sufficient existence at Coney Island, is of a young person with great resources for enjoyment, whose present life is an end in itself.[18] We do not picture children as longing for adult prerogatives from which they are excluded. Adults tend to feel nostalgic for the carefree times of childhood, or at any rate adolescence. Young adults in their middle twenties may feel old and wish they were back in college. It is in adulthood that the ceaseless round of activities which are means to further ends sets in: the job which is a steppingstone to a better job, the social entertainments which may lead to some advancement, etc. In this continual planning ahead which absorbs adults, the capacity for immediate sensuous enjoyment is often lacking. With the French, as I have said, it seems to be the other way around. Childhood is a period of probation, when everything is a means to an end; it is unenviable from the vantage point of adulthood. The image of the child is replete with frustration and longing for pleasures of the adults which are not for him.[19] It is in adulthood that the possibility of living in the moment is achieved. Not that this precludes much scheming and planing as far as careers or business advantage is concerned. But this is not allowed to interfere with sensuous pleasure, which are an end in themselves. The attainment of these end-pleasures, notably in eating and in lovemaking, is not a simple matter. Much care and preparation are required, and changing stimuli may be needed to keep pleasure intense. Concern with such pleasures and ingenuity in achieving them are persistent in adult life. It is with the prospect of these pleasures that the individual has served his hardworking childhood, and it is now, as an adult, that he can lose himself in the pleasures of the moment.

■ GOLDEN RULE DAYS: AMERICAN SCHOOLROOMS

Jules Henry

THE REALM OF SONG

It is March 17 and the children are singing songs from Ireland and her neighbors. The teacher plays on the piano, while the children sing. While some children sing, a number of them hunt in the index, find a song belonging to one of Ireland's neighbors, and raise their hands in order that

---

[18] Cf. Martha Wolfenstein, "The Image of the Child in Contemporary Films," in Mead and Wolfenstein, op. cit., p. 277.

[19] *Ibid.*

they may be called on to name the next song. The singing is of that pitchless quality always heard in elementary school classrooms. The teacher sometimes sings through a song first, in her off-key, weakishly husky voice.

The usual reason for having this kind of a song period is that the children are broadened, while they learn something about music and singing.

It is true that the children learn something about singing, but what they learn is to sing like everybody else, in the standard, elementary school pitchlessness of the English-speaking world—a phenomenon impressive enough for D. H. Lawrence to have mentioned it in *Lady Chatterly's Lover*. The difficulty in achieving true pitch is so pervasive among us that missionaries carry it with them to distant jungles, teaching the natives to sing hymns off key. Hence on Sundays we would hear our Pilagá Indian friends, all of them excellent musicians in the Pilagá scale, carefully copy the missionaries by singing Anglican hymns, translated into Pilagá, off key exactly as sharp or as flat as the missionaries sang. Thus one of the first things a child with a good ear learns in elementary school is to be musically stupid; he learns to doubt or to scorn his innate musical capacities.

But possibly more important than this is the use to which teacher and pupils put the lesson in ways not related at all to singing or to Ireland and her neighbors. To the teacher this was an opportunity to let the children somehow share the social aspects of the lesson with her, to democratically participate in the selection of the songs. The consequence was distraction from singing as the children hunted in the index and raised their hands to have their song chosen. The net result was to activate the competitive, achievement, and dominance drives of the children, as they strove with one another for the teacher's attention, and through her, to get the class to do what they wanted it to do. In this way the song period on Ireland and her neighbors was scarcely a lesson in singing but rather one in extorting the maximal benefit for the Self from *any* situation. The first lesson a child has to learn when he comes to school is that lessons are not what they seem. He must then forget this and act as if they were. This is the first step toward "school mental health"; it is also the first step in becoming absurd. In the first and second grades teachers constantly scold children because they do not raise their hands enough—the prime symbol of having learned what school is all about. After that, it is no longer necessary; the kids have "tumbled" to the idea.

The second lesson is to put the teachers' and students' criteria in place of his own. He must learn that the proper way to sing is tunelessly and not the way *he* hears the music; that the proper way to paint is the way the teacher says, not the way he sees it; that the proper attitude is not pleasure but competitive horror at the success of his classmates, and so on. And these lessons must be so internalized that he will fight his parents if they object. The early schooling process is not successful unless it has accomplished in the child an acquiescence in its criteria, unless the child *wants* to think the way school has taught him to think. He must have accepted alienation as a rule of life. What we see in the kindergarten and the early years of school is the pathetic surrender of babies. How could it be otherwise?

Now, if children are taught to adopt alienation as a way of life, it follows that they must have feelings of inadequacy, for nothing so saps self-confidence as alienation from the Self. It would follow that school, the chief agent in the process, must try to provide the children with "ego support," for culture tries to remedy the ills it creates.

Hence the effort to give recognition; and hence the conversion of the songfest into an exercise in Self-realization. That anything essential was nurtured in this way is an open question, for the kind of individuality that was recognized as the children picked titles out of the index was mechanical, without a creative dimension, and under the strict control of the teacher. Let us conclude this discussion by saying that *school metamorphoses the child, giving it the kind of Self the school can manage, and then proceeds to minister to the Self it has made.*

Perhaps I have put the matter grossly, appearing to credit the school with too much formative power. So let us say this: let us grant that American children, being American, come to school on the first day with certain potentialities for experiencing success and failure, for enjoying the success of their mates or taking pleasure in their failure, for competitiveness, for cooperation, for driving to achieve or for coasting along, et cetera. But school cannot handle variety, for as an institution dealing with masses of children it can manage only on the assumption of a homogeneous mass. Homogeneity is therefore accomplished by defining the children in a certain way and by handling all situations uniformly. In this way no child is directly coerced. It is simply that the child must react in terms of the institutional definitions or he fails. The first two years of school are spent not so much in learning the rudiments of the three Rs, as in learning definitions.

It would be foolish to imagine that school, as a chief molder of character, could do much more than homogenize the children, but it does do more—it sharpens to a cutting edge the drives the culture needs.

If you bind or prune an organism so it can move only in limited ways, it will move rather excessively in that way. If you lace a man into a strait jacket so he can only wiggle his toes, he will wiggle them *hard*. Since in school children are necessarily constrained to limited human expression, under the direction of the teacher, they will have a natural tendency to do with exaggerated enthusiasm what they are permitted to do. They are like the man in the strait jacket. In class children are usually not permitted to talk much, to walk around much, to put their arms around each other during lessons, to whistle or sing. But they are permitted to raise their hands and go to the pencil sharpener almost at will. Thus hand-raising, going to the pencil sharpener, or hunting in the back of a song book for a song for the class to sing are not so much activities stemming from the requirements of an immediate situation as expressions of the intensified need of the organism for relief from the five-hour-a-day pruning and confining process. This goes under the pedagogical title of "release of tension"; but in our view the issue is that what the children are at length permitted—and invited—to do, and what they therefore often throw themselves into with the enthusiasm of multiple pent-up feelings, are cultural drive-activities narrowly construed by the school. In that context the next example is not only an expression by the children of a wish to be polite, but an inflated outpouring of contained human capacities, released enthusiastically into an available—because approved—cultural channel.

ON HANGING UP A COAT

The observer is just entering her fifth-grade classroom for the observation period. The teacher says, "Which one of you nice, polite boys would like to take [the observer's] coat and hang it up?" From the waving hands, it would seem that all would like to claim the title. The teacher chooses one child, who takes the observer's coat. The teacher says, "Now, children, who will tell [the observer] what we have been doing:"

The usual forest of hands appears, and a girl is chosen to tell. . . . The teacher conducted the arithmetic lessons mostly by asking, "Who would like to tell the answer to the next problem?" This question was usually followed by the appearance of a large and agitated forest of hands, with apparently much competition to answer.

What strikes us here are the precision with which the teacher was able to mobilize the potentialities in the boys for proper social behavior, and the speed with which they responded. One is impressed also with the fact that although the teacher could have said, "Johnny, will you please hang up [the observer's] coat?" she chose rather to activate all the boys, and thus give *them* an opportunity to activate their Selves, in accordance with the alienated Selfhood objectives of the culture. The children were thus given an opportunity to exhibit a frantic willingness to perform an act of uninvolved solicitude for the visitor; in this way each was given also a chance to communicate to the teacher his eagerness to please her "in front of company."

The mere appearance of the observer in the doorway sets afoot a kind of classroom destiny of self-validation and actualization of pupil–teacher communion, and of activation of the cultural drives. In the observer's simple act of entrance the teacher perceives instantly the possibility of exhibiting her children and herself, and of proving to the visitor, and once again to herself, that the pupils are docile creatures, eager to hurl their "company" Selves into this suburban American tragicomedy of welcome. From behind this scenery of mechanical values, meanwhile, the most self-centered boy might emerge a *papier maché* Galahad, for what he does is not for the benefit of the visitor but for the gratification of the teacher and of his own culturally molded Self. The large number of waving hands proves that most of the boys have already become absurd; but they have no choice. Suppose they sat there frozen?

From this question we move to the inference that the skilled teacher sets up many situations in such a way that *a negative attitude can be construed only as treason.* The function of questions like, "Which one of you nice polite boys would like to take [the observer's] coat and hang it up?" is to bind the children into absurdity—to compel them to acknowledge that absurdity is existence, to acknowledge that it is better to exist absurd than not to exist at all.

It is only natural, then, that when the teacher next asks, "Now who will tell what we have been doing?" and "Who would like to tell the answer to the next problem?" there should appear "a large and agitated forest of hands," for failure to raise the hand could be interpreted only as an act of aggression. The "arithmetic" lesson, transformed by the teacher, had become an affirmation of her matriarchal charisma as symbol of the system.

The reader will have observed that the question is not put, "Who *has* the answer to the next problem?" but "Who *would like to tell* it?" Thus, what at one time in our culture was phrased as a challenge to skill in arithmetic, becomes here an invitation to group participation. What is sought is a sense of "groupiness" rather than a distinguishing of individuals. Thus, as in the singing lesson an attempt was made to deny that it was a group activity, in the arithmetic lesson the teacher attempts to deny that it is an individual one. The essential issue is that *nothing is but what it is made to be by the alchemy of the system.*

In a society where competition for the basic cultural goods is a pivot of action, people cannot be taught to love one another, for those who do cannot compete with one another, except in play. It thus becomes necessary for the school, without appearing to do so, to teach children how to hate, without appearing to do so, for our culture cannot tolerate the idea that babes should hate each other. How does the school accomplish this ambiguity? Obviously through competition itself, for what has greater potential for creating hostility than competition? One might say that this is one of the most "creative" features of school. Let us consider an incident from a fifth-grade arithmetic lesson.

AT THE BLACKBOARD

Boris had trouble reducing "12/16" to the lowest terms, and could only get as far as "6/8". The teacher asked him quietly if that was as far as he could reduce it. She suggested he "think." Much heaving up and down and waving of hands by the other children, all frantic to correct him. Boris pretty unhappy, probably mentally paralyzed. The teacher, quiet, patient, ignores the others and concentrates with look and voice on Boris. She says, "Is there a bigger number than two you can divide into the two parts of the fraction?" After a minute or two, she becomes more urgent, but there is no response from Boris. She then turns to the class and says, "Well, who can tell Boris what the number is?" A forest of hands appears, and the teacher calls Peggy. Peggy says that four may be divided into the numerator and the denominator.

Thus Boris' failure has made it possible for Peggy to succeed; his depression is the price of her exhilaration; his misery the occasion for her rejoicing. This is the standard condition of the American elementary school, and is why so many of us feel a contraction of the heart even if someone we never knew succeeds merely at garnering plankton in the Thames: because so often somebody's success has been bought at the cost of our failure. To a Zuñi, Hopi, or Dakota Indian, Peggy's performance would seem cruel beyond belief, for competition, the wringing of success from somebody's failure, is a form of torture foreign to those noncompetitive Indians. Yet Peggy's action seems natural to us; and so it is. How else would you run our world? And since all but the brightest children have the constant experience that others succeed at their expense they cannot but develop an inherent tendency to hate—to hate the success of others, to hate others who are successful, and to be determined to prevent it. Along with this, naturally, goes the hope that others will fail. This hatred masquerades under the euphemistic name of "envy."

Looked at from Boris' point of view, the nightmare at the blackboard was, perhaps, a lesson in controlling himself so that he would not fly shrieking from the room under the enormous public pressure. Such experiences imprint on the mind of every man in our culture the *Dream of Failure,* so that over and over again, night in, night out, even at the pinnacle of success, a man will dream not of success, but of failure. *The external nightmare is internalized for life.* It is this dream that, above all other things, provides the fierce human energy required by technological drivenness. It was not so much that Boris was learning arithmetic, but that he was learning the *essential nightmare. To be successful in our culture one must learn to dream of failure.*

From the point of view of the other children, of course, they were learning to yap at the heels of a failure. And why not? Have they not dreamed the dream of flight themselves? If the culture does not teach us to fly from failure or to rush in, hungry for success where others have failed, who will try again where others have gone broke? Nowadays, as misguided teachers try to soften the blow of classroom failure, they inadvertently sap the energies of success. The result will be a nation of chickens unwilling to take a chance.

When we say that "culture teaches drives and values" we do not state the case quite precisely. One should say, rather, that culture (and especially the school) provides the occasions in which drives and values are *experienced in events* that strike us with *overwhelming and constant force.* To say that culture "teaches" puts the matter too mildly. Actually culture invades and infests the mind as an obsession. If it does not, culture will not "work," for only an obsession has the power to withstand the impact of critical differences; to fly in the face of contradiction; to engulf the mind so that it will see the world only as the culture decrees that it shall be seen; to compel a person to be absurd. The central emotion in obsession is fear, and the central obsession in education is fear of failure. In order not to fail most students are willing to believe anything and to care not whether what they are told is true or false. Thus one becomes absurd through being afraid; but paradoxically, *only by remaining absurd can one feel free from fear.* Hence the immovableness of the absurd.

In examining education as a process of teaching the culture pattern, I have discussed a singing lesson, an arithmetic lesson, and the hanging up of a coat. Now let us consider a spelling lesson in a fourth-grade class.

"SPELLING BASEBALL"

The children form a line along the back of the room. They are to play "spelling baseball," and they have lined up to be chosen for the two teams. There is much noise, but the teacher quiets it. She has selected a boy and a girl and sent them to the front of the room as team captains to choose their teams. As the boy and girl pick the children to form their teams, each child chosen takes a seat in orderly succession around the room. Apparently they know the game well. Now Tom, who has not yet been chosen, tries to call attention to himself in order to be chosen. Dick shifts his position to be more in the direct line of vision of the choosers, so that he may not be overlooked. He seems quite anxious. Jane, Tom, Dick, and one girl whose name the observer does not know, are the last to be chosen. The teacher even has to remind the choosers that Dick and Jane have not been chosen. . . .

The teacher now gives out words for the children to spell, and they write them on the board. Each word is a pitched ball, and each correctly spelled word is a base hit. The children move around the room from base to base as their teammates spell the words correctly. With some of the words the teacher gives a little phrase: "Tongue, watch your tongue, don't let it say things that aren't kind; butcher, the butcher is a good friend to have; dozen, twelve of many things; knee, get down on your knee; pocket, keep your hand out of your pocket, and anybody else's. No talking! Three out!" The children say, "Oh, oh!"

The outs seem to increase in frequency as each side gets near the children chosen last. The children have great difficulty spelling "August." As they make mistakes, those in the seats say, "No!" The teacher says, "Man on third." As a child at the board stops and thinks, the teacher says, "There's a time limit; you can't take too long, honey." At last, after many children fail on "August" one child gets it right and returns, grinning with pleasure, to her seat. . . . The motivation level in this game seems terrific. All the children seem to watch the board, to know what's right and wrong, and seem quite keyed up. There is no lagging in moving from base to base. The child who is now writing "Thursday" stops to think after the first letter, and the children snicker. He stops after another letter. More snickers. He gets the word wrong. There are frequent signs of joy from the children when their side is right.

Since English is not pronounced as it is spelled, "language skills" are a disaster for educators as well as for students. We start the problem of "spelling baseball" with the fact that the spelling of English is so mixed up and contradictory and makes such enormous demands on the capacity for being absurd that nowadays most people cannot spell. "Spelling baseball" is an effort to take the "weariness, the fever, and the fret" out of spelling by absurdly transforming it into a competitive game. Over and over again it has seemed to our psychologist designers of curriculum scenery that the best way to relieve boredom is to transmute it into competition. Since children are usually good competitors, though they may never become good spellers, and although they may never learn to *spell* "success" (which really should be written *sukses*), they know what it *is,* how to go after it, and how it feels not to have it. A competitive game is indicated when children are failing, because the drive to succeed in the *game* may carry them to victory over the *subject matter.* At any rate it makes spelling less boring for the teacher and the students, for it provides the former with a drama of excited children, and the latter with a motivation that transports them out of the secular dreariness of classroom routine. "Spelling baseball" is thus a major effort in the direction of making things seem not as they are. But once a spelling lesson is cast in the form of a game of baseball a great variety of *noise* enters the system, because the sounds of *baseball* (the baseball "messages") cannot but be *noise* in a system intended to communicate *spelling.* Let us therefore analyze some of the baseball noise that has entered this spelling system from the sandlots and the bleachers.

We see first that a teacher has set up a choosing-rejecting system directly adopted from kid baseball. I played ball just that way in New York. The two best players took turns picking out teammates from the bunch, coldly selecting the best hitters and fielders first; as we went down the line it didn't make much difference who got the chronic muffers (the kids who couldn't catch a ball) and fanners (the kids who couldn't hit a ball). I recall that the kids who were not good players danced around and called out to the captains, "How about me, Slim? How about me?" Or they called attention to themselves with gestures and intense grimaces, as they pointed to their chests. It was pretty noisy. Of course, it didn't make any difference because the captains knew whom they were going to try to get, and there was not much of an issue after the best players had been sorted out to one or the other team. It was an honest jungle and there was nothing in it that didn't belong to the high tension of kid baseball. But nobody was ever left out; and even the worst were never permitted to sit on the sidelines.

"Spelling baseball" is thus sandlot baseball dragged into the schoolroom and bent to the uses of spelling. If we reflect that one could not settle a baseball game by converting it into a spelling lesson, we see that baseball is bizarrely *irrelevant* to spelling. If we reflect further that a kid who is a poor speller might yet be a magnificent ballplayer, we are even further impressed that learning spelling through baseball is learning by absurd association. In "spelling baseball" words become detached from their real significance and become assimilated to baseballs. Thus a spelling game that promotes absurd associations provides an indispensable bridge between the larger culture, where doubletalk is supreme, and the primordial meaningfulness of language. It provides also an introduction to those associations of mutually irrelevant ideas so well known to us from advertising—girls and vodka gimlets, people and billiard balls, lipstick and tree-houses, et cetera.

In making spelling into a baseball game one drags into the classroom whatever associations a child may have to the impersonal sorting process of kid baseball, and in this way some of the *noise* from the baseball system enters spelling. But there are differences between the baseball world and the "spelling baseball" world also. Having participated in competitive athletics all through my youth, I seem to remember that we sorted ourselves by skills, and we recognized that some of us were worse than others. In baseball I also seem to remember that if we struck out or muffed a ball we hated ourselves and turned flips of rage, while our teammates sympathized with our suffering. In "spelling baseball" one experiences the sickening sensation of being left out as others are picked —to such a degree that the teachers even have to remind team captains that some are unchosen. One's failure is paraded before the class minute upon minute, until, when the worst spellers are the only ones left, the conspicuousness of the failures has been enormously increased. Thus the *noise* from baseball is amplified by a *noise* factor specific to the classroom.

It should not be imagined that I "object" to all of this, for in the first place I am aware of the indispensable social functions of the spelling game, and in the second place, I can see that the rendering of failure conspicuous, the forcing of it on the mind of the unchosen child by a process of creeping extrusion from the group, cannot but intensify the quality of the essential nightmare, and thus render an important service to the culture. Without nightmares human culture has never been possible. Without hatred competition cannot take place.

One can see from the description of the game that drive is heightened in a complex competitive interlock: each child competes with every other to get the words right; each child competes with all for status and approval among his peers; each child competes with the other children for the approval of the teacher; and, finally, each competes as a member of a team. Here failure will be felt doubly because although in an ordinary spelling lesson one fails alone, in "spelling baseball" one lets down the children on one's team. Thus though in the game the motivation toward spelling is heightened so that success becomes triumph, so does failure become disaster. The greater the excitement the more intense the feeling of success and failure, and the importance of spelling or failing to spell "August" becomes exaggerated. But it is in the nature of an obsession to exaggerate the significance of events.

We come now to the *noise* introduced by the teacher. In order to make the words clear she puts each one in a sentence: "Tongue: watch your tongue; don't let it say things that aren't kind." "Butcher: the butcher is a good friend to have." "Dozen: twelve of many things." "Knee: get down on your knee." "Pocket: keep your hand out of your pocket, and anybody else's." More relevant associations to the words would be, "The leg bends at the knee." "A butcher cuts up meat." "I carry something in my pocket," etc. What the teacher's sentences do is introduce a number of her idiosyncratic cultural preoccupations, without clarifying anything; for there is no *necessary* relation between butcher and friend, between floor and knee, between pocket and improperly intrusive hands, and so on. In her way, therefore, the teacher establishes the same irrelevance between words and associations as the game does between spelling and baseball. She amplifies the *noise* by introducing ruminations from her own inner communication system.

CARPING CRITICISM

The unremitting effort by the system to bring the cultural drives to a fierce pitch must ultimately turn the children against one another; and though they cannot punch one another in the nose or pull each other's hair in class, they can vent some of their hostility in carping criticism of one another's work. Carping criticism is so destructive of the early tillerings of those creative impulses we cherish, that it will be good to give the matter further review.

Few teachers are like Miss Smith in this sixth-grade class:

The Parent-Teachers Association is sponsoring a school frolic, and the children have been asked to write jingles for publicity. For many of the children, the writing of a jingle seems painful. They are restless, bite their pencils, squirm in their seats, speak to their neighbors, and from time to time pop up with questions like, "Does it have to rhyme, Miss Smith?" At last she says, "Alright, let's read some of the jingles now." Child after child says he "couldn't get one," but some have succeeded. One girl has written a very long jingle, obviously the best in the class. However, instead of using "Friday" as the frolic day, she used "Tuesday," and several protests were heard from the children. Miss Smith defended her, saying, "Well, she made a mistake. But you are too prone to criticize. If *you* could only do so well!"

In our six years of work, in hundreds of hours of observation in elementary and high schools, Miss Smith is unique in that she scolded the children for tearing down the work of a classmate. Other teachers support such attacks, sometimes even somewhat against their will.

"For many of the children, the writing of a jingle seems painful" says the record. "They are restless, bite their pencils, squirm in their seats. . . ." What are they afraid of but failure? This is made clear by

Miss Smith's angry defense of the outstanding child as she says to her critics, "If only *you* could do so well!"

In a cooperative society carping is less likely to occur. Spiro says of the *kibbutz:*

> . . . The emphasis on group criticism can potentially engender competitive, if not hostile feelings among the children. Frequently, for example, the children read their essays aloud, and the others are then asked to comment. Only infrequently could we detect any hostility in the criticisms of the students, and often the evaluations were filled with praise.[1]

But in Miss Smith's class, because the children have failed while one of their number has succeeded, they carp. And why not? However we may admire Miss Smith's defense of the successful child, we must not let our own "inner Borises" befog our thinking. A competitive culture endures by tearing people down. Why blame the children for doing it?

Let us now consider two examples of carping criticism from a fifth-grade class as the children report on their projects and read original stories.

> Bill has given a report on tarantulas. As usual the teacher waits for volunteers to comment on the child's report.

> MIKE: The talk was well illustrated and well prepared.

> BOB: Bill had a *piece of paper* [for his notes] and teacher said he should have them on *cards.* . . .

Bill says he could not get any cards, and the teacher says he should tear the paper the next time he has no cards.

> BOB: He held the paper behind him. If he had had to look at it, it wouldn't have been very nice.

The children are taking turns reading to the class stories they have made up. Charlie's is called *The Unknown Guest.*

"One dark, dreary night, on a hill a house stood. This house was forbidden territory for Bill and Joe, but they were going in anyway. The door creaked, squealed, slammed. A voice warned them to go home. They went upstairs. A stair cracked. They entered a room. A voice said they might as well stay and find out now; and their father came out. He laughed and they laughed, but they never forgot their adventure together.

> TEACHER: Are there any words that give you the mood of the story?

> LUCY: He could have made the sentences a little better. . . .

[1] Melford Spiro, *Children of the Kibbutz.* Harvard University Press, 1958, p. 261.

TEACHER: Let's come back to Lucy's comment. What about his sentences?

GERT: They were too short.

Charlie and Jeanne have a discussion about the position of the word "stood" in the first sentence.

TEACHER: Wait a minute; some people are forgetting their manners . . . .

JEFF: About the room: the boys went up the stairs and one "cracked," then they were in the room. Did they fall through the stairs or what?

The teacher suggests Charlie make that a little clearer . . . .

TEACHER: We still haven't decided about the short sentences. Perhaps they make the story more spooky and mysterious.

GWYNNE: I wish he had read with more expression instead of all at one time.

RACHEL: Not enough expression.

TEACHER: Charlie, they want a little more expression from you. I guess we've given you enough suggestions for one time. [Charlie does not raise his head, which is bent over his desk as if studying a paper.] Charlie! I guess we've given you enough suggestions for one time, Charlie, haven't we? [Charlie half raises his head, seems to assent grudgingly.]

It stands to reason that a competitive system must do this; and adults, since they are always tearing each other to pieces, should understand that children will be no different. School is indeed a training for later life not because it teaches the 3 Rs (more or less), but because it instills the essential cultural nightmare fear of failure, envy of success, and absurdity.

■ THE SIRIONO CHILDREN

Allan Holmberg

INFANCY

When the period of couvade is over, the infant, who is then regarded as a definite member of the nuclear and extended family, stays almost constantly with his mother until he is about a year old. Most of the duties pertaining to his care fall to her. Whenever the mother is in the house, the infant lies across her lap; whenever she leaves the house, he is placed in the baby sling and carried astride her hip. He is freely offered the breast whenever he is awake, and if he cries, his mother tries her best to pacify him by this method. She grooms him frequently, watching for the appearance of wood ticks, lice, and skin worms; she carefully protects him from the bites of mosquitoes and other harassing insects which cause him no end of discomfort and distress.

During this early period, infants are carefully watched that they do not play with their feces. The Siriono appear to have made the connection between contact with feces and such ailments as hookworm and dysentery. Consequently, whenever the infant defecates, the excreta are immediately cleaned up by the mother (she generally uses a hard shell of motacú fruit for this purpose), wrapped in a leaf, and stored in a special depository basket. When this basket becomes full, the mother carries it some distance into the forest and empties the contents where the child can have no contact with them.

In spite of the care with which mothers watch their young babies, I frequently observed infants playing with their feces. On one occasion Acíba-eóko and his family were busily engaged consuming a batch of manioc. His first wife's baby, a boy about six months of age, was lying on the ground near the hammock. The baby defecated while the mother was eating, and she did not see him. After lying in the excreta for several minutes, he began to smear them over himself and shortly thereafter he put some of them into his mouth. At this moment the mother observed what he was doing. She grabbed the infant by the arm, put her finger into his mouth, and cleaned out the excreta, saying at the same time, "*abacikwaia ikwa nde*" ("You are an evil spirit"). Although the baby was badly soiled, he was not bathed, but was wiped with a large leaf. The mother continued to eat without washing her hands.

An infant receives no punishment if he urinates or defecates on his parents. Almost no effort is made by the mother to train an infant in the habits of cleanliness until he can walk, and then they are instilled very gradually. Of course, if a mother hears her infant fart or feels that he is about to defecate on her, she holds him away from her body so as not to be soiled, but about the only punishment that an infant is subjected to by defecating on her is that of being set aside for a while until she cleans up the mess. Children who are able to walk, however, soon learn by imitation, and with the assistance of their parents, not to defecate near the hammock. When they are old enough to indicate their needs, the mother gradually leads them further and further away from the hammock to urinate and defecate, so that by the time they have reached the age of three they have learned not to pollute the house. Until the age of four or five, however, children are still wiped by the mother, who also cleans up the excreta and throws them away. Not until a child has reached the age of six does he take care of his defecation needs alone.

Little training is given a child in the matter of urination. Contact with urine is not regarded as harmful, and I frequently observed mothers who did not even move when babies on their laps urinated. Since no clothes are worn by either the mother or the child, the urine soon dries or can readily be washed off. Grown children frequently urinate in the house without censure, and even adults seldom go more than ten feet from the house to urinate.

Infants are usually bathed at least once a day. If the band is on the march, infants often receive shower baths from the frequent rains that fall. If the band is settled, the mother usually repairs to the water hole or stream in the late afternoon to bathe both herself and the baby. If not, she usually bathes the baby in the house from a calabash of water. In washing the infant's hands, which she may do more frequently, the mother fills her mouth with water and squirts it on the baby's hands, rubbing them briskly at the same time.

Until a baby is about six months of age, he gets no other nourishment than mother's milk. Soon after, however, he may be given a bone to suck on, and his mother begins to supplement his diet with a certain amount of premasticated food. As the infant grows older, he is given more and more premasticated food, so that by the time he is one year of age, about 25 per cent of his diet consists of foods other than mother's milk. During this time, however, he is never denied the breast if he wants it. In fact, children are rarely, if ever, fully weaned until they are at least three years of age, and occasionally one sees a child of four or five sucking from his mother's breast.

Weaning, like toilet training, is a very gradual process. The rapidity with which it occurs depends largely on how soon another child is expected in the family. If the mother soon becomes pregnant, the infant is discouraged from sucking; if no child is expected, the process may be lengthened considerably. In weaning, the mother usually applies beeswax to her breasts, so that the child receives no reward for his sucking. This method is also employed when the mother is ill and does not want her child to suck. Foul-tasting substances, such as excrement, are never smeared on the breasts to discourage a child from nursing.

Because of the limited time which I spent with the Siriono, I am unable to supply accurate information concerning the age at which such habit patterns as creeping, standing, walking, and talking first appear in children. In all of these respects, however, Siriono infants seem to fall within the normal human range. Parents do little to hasten the maturation process. As habits begin to form, of course, an infant is encouraged to develop them for himself, but if it represents any strain for him to creep, to stand, or to walk, little attempt is made to force him. If, for instance, an infant is lying on the floor near his mother's hammock and wishes to come to her, he is encouraged to do so by creeping or, if old enough, by walking, but if he starts to cry, which is recognized as a sign that it is too difficult for him, the mother gets up from her hammock and picks him up.

One of the most painful and frustrating experiences that every infant must regularly undergo is that of having his eyebrows and the hair from his forehead depilated. A newborn baby receives his first haircut the day after birth and is subjected to periodic depilations about every two weeks thereafter. These are not endured without avoidance and pain. Mothers almost always have to hold infants very forcibly while giving them a haircut, and it is only after a child has reached the age of about three years that he resigns himself to this operation without whimpering. Whenever I heard infants howling terrifically, I could be sure they were receiving their semi-monthly grooming.

The Siriono are proud parents. They spend a great deal of time in fondling and playing with their children and are delighted to display them to anyone foreign to their camp. I found that one of the best ways to gain the confidence of the Indians was by taking an interest in their children: in bringing them presents, in playing with them, and in curing them of such ailments as hookworm. Their interest in children was also clearly reflected in their conversations with me, for I was bombarded with questions as to how many children I had, where they were living, etc. In order to avoid some explanation of my bachelorhood, which they would not have understood or which would have seemed ridiculous to them, I always told them that I had a wife and several children (I even supplied the names) waiting for me at home, and that as soon as I had obtained the information which my "father" had sent me to gather, I was going to return to my family.

Males are definitely preferred. If asked the sex of her infant, a mother proudly holds up a boy and demonstrates his penis; if her infant is a girl, she contents herself merely with replying *"eréN"* ("Vulva," i.e., female). A pregnant woman, too, always expresses a desire to give birth to a boy. The preference for males, however, is not much reflected in the amount of love or care given an infant. Parents spend as much time fondling a girl as a boy. Even clubfooted children and other deformed infants are shown no lack of partiality in this respect.

Babies are tickled a great deal in the neck region and on the genitals. When they are nursing, their mothers often excite them sexually. The pleasure derived from play and fondling is often noticably reciprocal. Nursing infants sometimes fondle their mothers' breasts and bring them into sharp erection. Not infrequently one observes a mother play with her young boy's penis until it becomes erect and then rub it over her vulva. I have also seen men get partial erections while playing with the genitals of their infants.

Parents are very proud of a display of sexual desire on the part of their infants. One afternoon, Eantándu was fingering the penis of his young son, who was sleeping. The boy got an erection. Eantándu called my attention to it and proudly said: *"eráNkwi eánta túti; čúki čúki etúhenia ekwásu mosé"* ("Very hard penis; when grown, he will have a lot of intercourse").

CHILDHOOD

The transition from infancy to childhood in Siriono society is a very gradual one. Not only are there no sharp breaks in the process of growing up, but from the time one is a child until one assumes the role of an adult, life is relatively carefree and undisciplined. In fact, this pattern of freedom so carries on throughout adult life that it can be truly said of the Siriono that they are a highly undisciplined people.

In contrast to many primitive societies, where a maternal or paternal relative often assumes the responsibility of formally educating the child, the system of education among the Siriono may best be characterized as informal, random, and haphazard. If there is a general theory of education, it can hardly be more than the necessary one of gradually teaching the child to be as independent as possible of his family, so that by the time he has reached the age of maturity he will be able to shift for himself. Since the amount of knowledge that a child has to absorb to survive in this culturally backward society is small in comparison with what he would have to learn in many other societies, the period of childhood offers more than ample time to instill the patterns of adult behavior without a great deal of formal education.

Until a child can walk or talk, at about the age of three, he is taught almost everything he knows by his parents and his older siblings, and during the early phases of the education of the child, of course, it is the mother who plays the predominant role. Not only does she feed and care for the child, but she is largely responsible, since the father is away a great deal on the hunt, for teaching him to walk, to talk, and to observe the rules of cleanliness. Young children are, therefore, usually "mothers' boys" or "mothers' girls."

In instilling the habits of prescribed behavior in a child, the principles of reward and punishment are clearly recognized. A mother who is teaching her child to walk, for instance, frequently rewards him, after he has reached his destination, with a bit of wild bee honey or some other tidbit. But if he is violating some taboo, such as eating dirt or a forbidden animal, not only are the rewards withdrawn, but the child may be roughly picked up and set aside to cry by himself for a while. A disobedient child may also be warned that if he repeats a forbidden act he will be bitten by a snake or carried off by an evil spirit. An unruly child is never beaten, however. At worst, his mother gives him a rough pull or throws some small object at him.

During all of my residence among the Siriono, I observed only one extreme outburst of aggression on the part of a mother against her child. This took place one evening about dusk. Erakúi, a nickname meaning "Pointed-one," had just begun to eat a chunk of broiled peccary meat which she had received from one of her relatives. Her young son, Erámi ("Oldbuck"—so called because he looked like an old man), although he had just eaten, began to complain that he had not had enough to eat. Erakúi paid little attention to him at first, but as he continued to complain, she made a few sharp remarks and finally said to him: "You have already had enough to eat." He replied: "You lie," and made a gesture of grabbing for the meat that she was eating. Suddenly she lost her temper, picked up a spindle lying nearby, and gave the boy a sharp rap on the shoulders. He began to howl and made a dash for the other end of the house to avoid more blows. She followed him a short distance, threw the spindle at him, and then returned to her hammock, where she, too, began to cry. (Mothers almost always cry after they have expressed aggression against their children.) The boy continued to wail at the other end of the house for about twenty minutes, after which, since it was getting very dark, he sneaked back and climbed in a hammock with his father. In the morning all had been forgotten.

Children are generally allowed great license in expressing aggression against their parents, who are both patient and long-suffering with them. A young child in a temper tantrum may ordinarily beat his father and his mother hard as he can, and they will just laugh. When children are neglected or teased by their parents, they often pick up a spindle or stick and strike them with considerable force without being punished. I have even heard fathers encouraging their young sons to strike their mothers. Eantándu told me that such expressions of anger in a child were a sign that he would grow up to be a valiant adult.

Food habits are among the first patterns of behavior that every young child must learn. After weaning, taboo foods are simply withheld from a child, but as he grows older and more omnivorous, he is threatened with disease and abandonment if he partakes of forbidden foods to which he may be exposed while his parents are not around. The list of foods taboo to him, however, is not long. Among the animals he must never eat is the harpy eagle. This taboo is easy to obey, since this bird is rarely bagged; only two were shot during my residence at Tibaera. The harpy eagle is regarded as the king of the birds by the Siriono, and the eating of its flesh is believed to cause illness (it is never stated what kind) to anyone but an old person. Likewise taboo until one is aged are the anteater, lest one sire or give birth to club-footed children, and the howler monkey, because it is an "old" animal with a beard and therefore dangerous to eat when one is young. Children are also forbidden the meat of the owl monkey, lest they spend sleepless nights and be restless, and the coati, lest they break out with sores on their bodies. Embryos and the young offspring of animals also cannot be eaten by children, lest they have miscarriages in adulthood.

There are few instances when the above-mentioned food taboos cause a child to suffer from lack of meat. Sometimes, however, hunters return with nothing but a howler monkey or an anteater, and the child is denied a share. On such occasions parents attempt by exchange to secure some edible meat for the child, but in some instances he may be forced to go meat-hungry for a day or two. As a last resort, parents sometimes neglect the food taboos in order to satisfy a hungry and whimpering child. I have observed a father offer his crying son anteater meat, for instance, even though it was strictly taboo for the child to eat it. Generally speaking, however, taboo foods are withheld from children, who themselves learn what foods not to eat by the time they have reached the age of six.

When a child is able to walk and talk, his relations outside the family begin to broaden. By this time, of course, his education is well under way. Having traveled extensively through jungle and swamp, he has already become acquainted with the plants and animals. He knows which ones are good to eat and which ones must be avoided. He has felt the prick of spines. He has experienced the sting of mosquitoes, of scorpions, and of ants. He has seen where animals live and how they are shot. He has watched them being cleaned, gutted, quartered, cooked, and eaten. He has gone hungry and eaten to excess. He has been sick with malaria, hookworm, and dysentery. He has watched children be born and die. He has seen the aged and sick abandoned. He has observed his parents get drunk, dance, and fight. He has heard of evil spirits, and has been admonished not to venture out of the house at night lest he be carried off by one. In short, although only three or four years of age, he has already experienced a major part of his natural environment and participated deeply into his culture.

At about the age of three, although still largely dependent upon his parents, the child begins to stray from family fire—to play with other children, and to learn those habit patterns which gradually increase his self-reliance and lessen his dependency on the family. His first contacts with people of his own age are generally those with his half brothers, half sisters, and his cousins, who are not only closely related to him genealogically but spatially as well, since the extended family tends to cluster together in the house. A child's first play group, in fact, seldom contains members outside his extended family. As he grows older, children of the same sex and age from other extended families join the play group, so that at puberty there is usually not more than one play group for each sex in the entire band. Since the local group is small, play groups seldom contain over five or six members.

Since the aim to which Siriono male aspires is to be an excellent hunter, young boys get an early education, through play, in the art of the chase. Before a boy is three months of age his father has made him a miniature bow and arrows which, although he will not be able to use them for several years, are symbolic of his adult role as a hunter. By the time a boy is three years of age he is already pulling on some kind of bow, and with his companions he spends many pleasant hours shooting his weapons at any non-living target that strikes his fancy. As he grows older and more skillful with his bow, he begins to select living targets, such as butterflies and insects, and when his marksmanship is perfected he is encouraged to stalk woodpeckers and other birds that light on branches near the house. Consequently, by the time a boy is eight he has usually bagged some game animal, albeit only a small bird.

Like young boys, girls too, through play, get an early exposure to some of the household tasks which they have to perform when they are adults. As the bow symbolizes the hunting role of the boy, so the spindle symbolizes the spinning role of the girl. Before a girl is three years of age her father has made her a miniature spindle with which she practices the art of spinning as she matures.

Strikingly enough, miniature bows and arrows for boys and spindles for girls are the only toys which the Siriono make for their children. There is a conspicuous lack of dolls, animal figures, puzzles, cradles, stilts, balls, string figures, etc., so commonly found in other primitive societies. Occassionally a baby tortoise or the young of some animal is brought in from the forest for a child to play with, but such pets are usually treated so roughly that they die within a few days' time. Moreover, such common amusements for children as games of tag, hide-and-seek, and racing are unknown in Siriono society. Organized games and contests for children (except wrestling for boys) seem to be entirely lacking.

Besides playing with their bows and arrows, boys amuse themselves in other ways: climbing trees, playing in the water, fishing, learning to swim, chasing one another around camp, and wrestling. They also spend a great deal of time lying in their hammocks, a custom they seem readily to learn from their parents.

Girls play especially at house: making baskets and pots, spinning cotton thread, and twining bark-fiber string. They also frequently assist their mothers in performing such simple household tasks as shelling maize, roasting wild fruits, and carrying water. Young girls also spend a great deal of time grooming each other, depilating the hair from their foreheads and picking out and eating the lice from their heads. In general, by the time they have reached the age of eight girls have learned to weave baskets, to twine bark-fiber string, to spin cotton thread, and to perform most of the tasks which the society assigns to the adult female.

Within play groups aggression is freely expressed. When boys are playing with their bows and arrows (boys' arrows always have blunt ends, and their bows shoot with little force), accidents sometimes occur, and occasionally one child shoots another intentionally, even though boys are admonished not to point their weapons at any human target. When such accidents or shootings occur (children are seldom wounded as a result of them), a fight usually breaks out, and the child who has been hit often strikes back at the boy who shot him. Adults generally take no part in these fights (they usually laugh at them), but the loser almost always runs crying to his parents for protection.

Considerable teasing and torturing—such things as pinching of the genitals, poking fingers in the eyes, and scratching—of young children by older children takes place. A young child most often protects himself from such attacks with a brand of fire or a digging stick, and if he catches off guard the older child who molested him, he may burn him rather severely or give him a sharp rap on the head. Older girls, too, sometimes tease young children by pretending to suck from their mothers' breasts, and this invariably arouses anger in the latter, who sometimes strike their tormentors with considerable force. Under such circumstances, older children are not allowed to express counteraggression.

Sibling rivalry does not seem to be intense. If a quarrel breaks out between siblings, parents almost always take the part of the younger child. There seems, in fact, to be a clear recognition by the Siriono that the younger a child the less responsible he is for his acts. As between sisters and brothers, there seems to be a slight preference in the treatment of boys, though this is scarcely noticeable until puberty. Generally speaking, however, boys receive more food and less discipline than girls.

At about the age of eight, a boy begins to accompany his father on the hunt. This is really the beginning of his serious education as a hunter. Until this time most of his hunting has been confined to the immediate environs of the hut. When a boy first starts to accompany his father, he makes only about one excursion per week, but as he gradually becomes hardened to the jungle, his trips away from camp become more frequent and of longer duration. On these expeditions the boy gradually learns when, where, and how to track and stalk game. His father allows him to take easy shots, so as to reinforce his interest in hunting. The boy is given light loads of game to carry in from the jungle, and if he kills an animal of any importance, such as a peccary or coati, he is decorated like a mature hunter. During all this time, of course, he is also learning to make bows and arrows and to repair those which have been broken on the hunt. Hence, by the time a boy has reached the age of twelve, he is already a full-fledged hunter and is able to supply a household of his own with game. At this age girls, too, are ready for the responsibilities of adulthood.

■ THE DEVELOPMENT OF THE CHILD'S PERSONALITY

Jules Henry

When the baby is very young it is the object of constant attention. At the first wimper it is nursed by its mother, or in her absence, sometimes by its grandmother. It is bathed and kept free of lice, and its mother carefully plucks out its eyelashes to make it beautiful. She kisses it over and over again, rubbing her mouth violently on the baby's in an ecstasy of pleasure. The baby is passed around from hand to hand and people in the house and visitors take turns mouthing it. But as time passes, as the baby's personality begins to develop, and as the baby becomes more and more interested in the things around it, it gets less and less attention from everyone, for the adults regard the child's expanding interests as a rejection.

The withdrawal of attention takes place by almost imperceptible degrees, and is evident at first only in the mother's increased slowness in stopping her work to nurse her weeping baby, and in a diminishing of the mouth rubbing.

At about the eighth month of the infant's life two important factors operate with particular vigor to undermine the child's security. These factors are his mother's work and the absence of solidarity within the household. In order to gather in the crops of wild fruits the child's mother must spend hours away from home. She often cannot take the child with her, for the distance she has to go is too great and the baby too heavy to carry in addition to her burden of wild fruit. In some primitive communities where similar conditions exist the mother can leave her child with some other woman who will suckle it if it grows hungry or weeps. Among the Pilaga, however, this does not occur because there is so little solidarity within the household and because the reluctance to take food from others forces all of the able-bodied women and many of the weak and the aged out to look for food. Often, therefore, the baby is left with an old and feeble (sometimes blind) grandparent who can do little for it.

The period of greatest suffering for the baby begins, however, when it can walk a little. This is the time when it begins to explore the world outside the house.[1] Now, alone, outside the familiar circle of its housemates, the child is afraid. Little children tear past at breakneck speed, screaming, or tumble about on the ground in violent play. Strangers walk by. The baby bursts into tears, but its elders are slow to reassure it.

During the period when the baby is investigating the outer world it is almost continously in tears. Not only is it frightened by contact with strangers, but its mother leaves it more and more alone as she goes about her work. Formerly she had left the baby alone for hours; now she leaves it alone for a whole day. It eats a little pounded corn or drinks a little honey water, but the baby is hungry, and by evening it is so wrought up that when its tired mother comes home it cannot wait to be picked up but has a tantrum at her feet.

Although as the Pilaga child grows older he receives the breast less often, partly because he eats other things, partly because he is busy playing, and often because his mother is away working, he can still have access to her breast frequently. He is still very much the object of his mother's attention, and he spends many hours sitting on her thighs as she parts his hair looking for lice. Once a new sibling appears, however, this is radically changed. Though his mother may nurse him even while she is in labor, when the new child is born the older sibling is absolutely denied the breast. Not only this, but the attention his mother and father once gave him is now directed to the new baby. Formerly when he wept he was given the breast and comforted by his mother. Now he is told to "Be quiet" and sent to play outdoors or to a relative, who may afford him some casual comfort in the form of a morsel of food.

---

[1] The babies are often encouraged by their mothers to go outside.

This situation leaves the older sibling stunned. He wanders disconsolately about near the house and whimpers continually, apparently without cause. When he comes home it is not infrequently to try out little schemes for doing away with the new baby, and his mother must be very watchful lest he injure the new sibling. Naturally this only intensifies the situation, for the mother's redoubled attention serves to isolate the older sibling even more.

In some cultures the shock of rejection may be somewhat lessened through a marked change in the status of the older sibling, or through some device whereby he is given considerable prestige or made to feel important. In other cultures again, the older sibling becomes the care of some special relative who takes the child everywhere and is a constant companion. Among the Pilaga, however, these things do not occur. The Pilaga have no device for giving status or prestige to anyone below the rank of chief, and one of the outstanding facts of Pilaga life is that no one troubles himself much about a child with a younger sibling. In view of the foregoing discussion of Pilaga social structure we can readily understand why no one other than the parents should bother much about the child, but why fathers should show such indifference is another matter. It is not that all Pilaga fathers are completely indifferent to the child who has just been weaned. Indeed, some fathers take them visiting, buy them gifts, and even delouse them. But their interest in the child never extends to the play and fondling that is typical for the responsive father in our society. Over and over again among the Pilaga the picture is of the apathetic father who suffers his little child to squat between his knees. There is good reason, in the social arrangements in this tribe, as we have seen for the jealousy of their infants which Pilaga fathers explicitly remark upon, and warmth does not develop between fathers and children.

Thus, without status and deprived of warmth, the Pilaga child remains a poor hostile little flounderer for a number of years until at last begins to take his place in the adult economic activity.

Dr. David M. Levy has described earlier the doll experiments performed by Mrs. Henry and me. They amplify and confirm in a clear-cut way the results of our long day-by-day observation of the Pilaga children, viz., that feelings of hostility towards parents and siblings are intense enough to show themselves in the patterns Dr. Levy has already demonstrated as typical for similar situations in our own culture. That is to say, the day-by-day and experimental play behavior of the children is characterized by destructive attempts against the parents and siblings, by attempts at restitution, and by regression.[2]

---

[2] It is not yet clear, however, that there is evidence of self-punishment in day-by-day behavior.

■ THE WARRIOR DROPOUTS

Rosalie Wax

Scattered over the prairie on the Pine Ridge reservation of South Dakota, loosely grouped into bands along the creeks and roads, live thousands of Sioux Indians. Most live in cabins, some in tents, a few in houses; most lack the conventional utilities—running water, electricity, telephone, and gas. None has a street address. They are called "country Indians" and most speak the Lakota language. They are very poor, the most impoverished people on the reservation.

For four years I have been studying the problems of the high school dropouts among these Oglala Sioux. In many ways these Indian youths are very different from slum school dropouts—Negro, Mexican-American, rural white—just as in each group individuals differ widely one from another. Yet no one who has any familiarity with their problems can avoid being struck by certain parallels, both between groups and individuals.

In slum schools and Pine Ridge schools scholastic achievement is low, and the dropout rate is high; the children's primary loyalties go to friends and peers, not schools or educators; and all of them are confronted by teachers who see them as inadequately prepared, uncultured offspring of alien and ignorant folk. They are classified as "culturally deprived." All such schools serve as the custodial, constabulary, and reformative arm of one element of society directed against another.

Otherwise well-informed people, including educators themselves, assume on the basis of spurious evidence that dropouts dislike and voluntarily reject school, that they all leave it for much the same reasons, and that they are really much alike. But dropouts leave high school under strikingly different situations and for quite different reasons.

Many explicitly state that they do not wish to leave and are really "pushouts" or "kickouts" rather than "dropouts." As a Sioux youth in our sample put it, "I quit, but I never did *want* to quit!" Perhaps the fact that educators consider all dropouts to be similar tells us more about educators and their schools than about dropouts.

ON THE RESERVATION

The process that alienates many country Indian boys from the high schools they are obliged to attend begins early in childhood and reflects the basic Sioux social structure. Sioux boys are reared to be physically reckless and impetuous. One that does not perform an occasional brash act may be accepted as "quiet" or "bashful," but he is not considered a desirable son, brother, or sweetheart. Sioux boys are reared to be proud and feisty and are expected to resent public censure. They have some obligations to relatives; but the major social controls after infancy are exerted by their fellows—their "peer group."

From about the age of seven or eight, they spend alomst the entire day without adult supervision, running or riding about with friends of their age and returning home only for food and sleep. Even we (my husband, Dr. Murray L. Wax, and I), who had lived with Indian families from other tribal groups, were startled when we heard a responsible and respected Sioux matron dismiss a lad of six or seven for the entire day with the statement "Go play with Larry and John." Similarly, at a ceremonial gathering in a strange community with hundreds of people, boys of nine or ten often take off and stay away until late at night as a matter of course. Elders pay little attention. There is much prairie and many creeks for roaming and playing in ways that bother nobody. The only delinquencies we have heard Sioux elders complain about are chasing stock, teasing bulls, or occasionally some petty theft.

Among Sioux males this kind of peer-group raising leads to a highly efficient yet unverbalized system of intra-group discipline and powerful intro-group loyalties and dependencies. During our seven-month stay in a reservation community, we were impressed by how rarely the children quarreled with one another. This behavior was not imposed by elders but by the children themselves.

For example, our office contained some items very attractive to them, especially a typewriter. We were astonished to see how quietly they handled this prize that only one could enjoy at a time. A well-defined status system existed so that a child using the typewriter at once gave way and left the machine if one higher in the hierarchy appeared. A half-dozen of these shifts might take place within an hour; yet, all this occurred without a blow or often even a word.

Sioux boys have intense loyalties and dependencies. They almost never tattle on each other. But when forced to live with strangers, they tend to become inarticulate, psychologically disorganized, or withdrawn.

With most children the peer group reaches the zenith of its power in school. In middle class neighborhoods, independent children can usually seek and secure support from parents, teachers, or adult society as a whole. But when, as in an urban slum or Indian reservation, the teachers stay aloof from parents, and parents feel that teachers are a breed apart, the peer group may become so powerful that the children literally take over the school. Then group activities are carried on in class—jokes, notes, intrigues, teasing, mock-combat, comic book reading, courtship—all without the teacher's knowledge and often without grossly interfering with the learning process.

Competent and experienced teachers can come to terms with the peer group and manage to teach a fair amount of reading, writing, and arithmetic. But teachers who are incompetent, overwhelmed by large classes, or sometimes merely inexperienced may be faced with groups of children who refuse even to listen.

We marveled at the variety and efficiency of the devices developed by Indian children to frustrate formal learning—unanimous inattention, refusal to go to the board, writing on the board in letters less than an inch high, inarticulate responses, and whispered or pantomime teasing of victims called on to recite. In some seventh and eighth grade classes there was a withdrawal so uncompromising that no voice could be heard for hours except the teacher's, plaintively asking questions or giving instructions.

Most Sioux children insist they like school, and most Sioux parents corroborate this. Once the power and depth of their social life within the school is appreciated, it is not difficult to see why they like it. Indeed, the only unpleasant aspects of school for them are the disciplinary regulations (which they soon learn to tolerate or evade), an occasional "mean" teacher, bullies, or feuds with members of other groups. Significantly, we found that notorious truants had usually been rejected by classmates and also had no older relatives in school to protect them from bullies. But the child who has a few friends or an older brother or sister to stand by him, or who "really likes to play basketball," almost always finds school agreeable.

DAY SCHOOL GRADUATES

By the time he has finished the eighth grade, the country Indian boy has many fine qualities: zest for life, curiosity, pride, physical courage, sensibility to human relationships, experience with the elemental facts of life, and intense group loyalty and integrity. His experiences in day school have done nothing to diminish or tarnish his ideal—the physically reckless and impetuous youth, who is admired by all.

But, on the other hand, the country Indian boy is almost completely lacking in the traits most highly valued by the school authorities: a narrow and absolute respect for "regulations," "government property," routine, discipline, and diligence. He is also deficient in other skills apparently essential to rapid and easy passage through high school and boarding school—especially the abilities to make short-term superficial social adjustments with strangers. Nor can he easily adjust to a system which demands, on the one hand, that he study competitively as an individual, and, on the other, that he live in barrack-type dormitories where this kind of study is impossible.

Finally, his English is inadequate for high school work. Despite eight or more years of formal training in reading and writing, many day school graduates cannot converse fluently in English even among themselves. In contrast, most of the students with whom they will compete in higher schools have spoken English since childhood.

To leave home and the familiar and pleasant day school for boarding life at the distant and formidable high school is a prospect both fascinating and frightening. To many young country Indians the agency town of Pine Ridge is a center of sophistication. It has blocks of Indian

Bureau homes with lawns and fences, a barber shop, big grocery stores, churches, gas stations, a drive-in confectionary, and even a restaurant with a juke box. While older siblings or cousins may have reported that at high school "they make you study harder," that "they just make you move every minute," or that the "mixed-bloods" or "children of bureau employees" are "mean" or "snotty," there are the compensatory highlights of movies, basketball games, and the social (white man's) dances.

For the young men there is the chance to play high school basketball, baseball, or football; for the young women there is the increased distance from over-watchful, conservative parents. For both, there is the freedom, taken or not, to hitchhike to White Clay, with its beer joints, bowling hall, and archaic aura of Western wickedness. If, then, a young man's close friends or relatives decide to go to high school, he will usually want to go too rather than remain at home, circumscribed, "living off his folks." Also, every year, more elders coax, tease, bribe, or otherwise pressure the young men into "making a try" because "nowadays only high school graduates get the good jobs."

THE STUDENT BODY: TOWN INDIANS, COUNTRY INDIANS

The student body of the Oglala Community High School is very varied. First, there are the children of the town dwellers, who range from well-paid white and Indian government employees who live in neat government housing developments to desperately poor people who live in tar paper shacks. Second, there is the large number of institutionalized children who have been attending the Oglala Community School as boarders for the greater part of their lives. Some are orphans, others come from isolated sections of the reservation where there are no day schools, others come from different tribal areas.

But these town dwellers and boarders share an advantage—for them entry into high school is little more than a shift from eighth to ninth grade. They possess an intimate knowledge of their classmates and a great deal of local know-how. In marked contrast, the country Indian freshman enters an alien environment. Not only is he ignorant of how to buck the rules, he doesn't even know the rules. Nor does he know anybody to put him wise.

Many country Indians drop out of high school before they have any clear idea what high school is all about. In our sample, 35 percent dropped out before the end of the ninth grade and many of these left during the first semester. Our first interviews with them were tantalizingly contradictory—about half the young men seemed to have found high school so painful they could scarcely talk about it; the other half were also laconic, but insisted that they had liked school. In time, those who had found school unbearable confided that they had left school because they were lonely or because they were abused by more experienced boarders. Only rarely did they mention that they had trouble with their studies.

The following statement, made by a mild and pleasant boy, conveys some idea of the agony of loneliness, embarrassment, and inadequacy that a country Indian newcomer may suffer when he enters high school:

> At day school it was kind of easy for me. But high school was really hard, and I can't figure out even simple questions that they ask me . . . . Besides I'm so quiet [modest and unaggresive] that the boys really took advantage of me. They borrow money from me every Sunday night and they don't even care to pay it back . . . . I can't talk English very good, and I'm really bashful and shy, and I get scared when I talk to white people. I usually just stay quiet in the [day school] classroom, and the teachers will leave me alone. But at boarding school they wanted me to get up and talk or say something . . . . I quit and I never went back. . . . I can't seem to get along with different people, and I'm so shy I can't even make friends . . . . [Translated from Lakota by interviewer.]

Most of the newcomers seem to have a difficult time getting along with the experienced boarders and claim that the latter not only strip them of essentials like soap, paper, and underwear, but also take the treasured gifts of proud and encouraging relatives, wrist watches and transistor radios.

> Some of the kids—especially the boarders—are really mean. All they want to do is steal—and they don't want to study. They'll steal your school work off you and they'll copy it . . . . Sometimes they'll break into our suitcase. Or if we have money in our pockets they'll take off our overalls and search our pockets and get our money . . . . So finally I just came home. If I could be a day scholar I think I'll stay in. But if they want me to board I don't want to go back. I think I'll just quit.

Interviews with the dropouts who asserted that school was "all right" —and that they had not wished to quit—suggest that many had been almost as wretched during their first weeks at high school as the bashful young men who quit because they "couldn't make friends." But they managed to find some friends and, with this peer support and protection, they were able to cope with and (probably) strike back at other boarders. In any case, the painful and degrading aspects of school became endurable. As one lad put it: "Once you *learn* to be a boarder, it's not so bad."

But for these young men, an essential part of having friends was "raising Cain"—that is, engaging in daring and defiant deeds forbidden by the school authorities. The spirit of these escapades is difficult to portray to members of a society where most people no longer seem capable of thinking about the modern equivalents of Tom Sawyer, Huckleberry Finn, or Kim, except as juvenile delinquents. We ourselves, burdened by sober professional interest in dropouts, at first found it hard to recognize that these able and encouraging young men were taking pride and joy in doing exactly what the school authorities thought most reprehensible; and they were not confessing, but boasting, although their stunts had propelled them out of school.

For instance, this story from one bright lad of 15 who had run away from high school. Shortly after entering ninth grade he and his friends had appropriated a government car. (The usual pattern in such adventures is to drive off the reservation until the gas gives out.) For this offense (according to the respondent) they were restricted for the rest of the term—they were forbidden to leave the high school campus or attend any of the school recreational events, games, dances, or movies. (In effect, this meant doing nothing but going to class, performing work chores, and sitting in the dormitory.) Even then our respondent seems to have kept up with his class work and did not play hookey except in reading class:

It was after we stole that car Mrs. Bluger [pseudonym for reading teacher] would keep asking who stole the car in class. So I just quit going there . . . . One night we were the only ones up in the older boys' dorm. We said, "Hell with this noise. We're not going to be the only ones here." So we snuck out and went over to the dining hall. I pried this one window open about this far and then it started to crack, so I let it go . . . . We heard someone so we took off. It was show that night I think. [Motion picture was being shown in school auditorium] . . . All the rest of the guys was sneaking in and getting something. So I said I was going to get my share too. We had a case of apples and a case of oranges. Then I think is was the night watchman was coming, so we ran around and hid behind those steps. He shined that light on us. So I thought right then I was going to keep on going. That was around Christmas time. We walked back to Oglala [about 15 miles] and we were eating this stuff all the way back.

This young man implied that after this escapade he simply did not have the nerve to try to return to the high school. He insisted, however, that he would like to try another high school:

I'd like to finish [high school] and get a good job some place. If I don't I'll probably just be a bum around here or something.

YOUNG MEN WHO STAY IN SCHOOL

Roughly half the young Sioux who leave high school very early claim they left because they were unable to conform to school regulations. What happens to the country boys who remain? Do they "shape-up" and obey the regulations? Do they, even, come to "believe" in them? We found that most of these older and more experienced youths were, if anything, even *more* inclined to boast of triumphs over the rules than the younger fellows who had left. Indeed, all but one assured us that they were adept at hookey, and food and car stealing, and that they had frequent surreptitious beer parties and other outlaw enjoyments. We do not know whether they (especially the star athletes) actually disobey the school regulations as frequently and flagrantly as they claim. But there can be no doubt that most Sioux young men above 12 wish to be regarded as hellions in school. For them, it would be unmanly to have any other attitude.

An eleventh grader in good standing explained his private technique for playing hookey and added proudly: "They never caught me yet." A twelfth grader and first-string basketball player told how he and some other students "stole" a jeep from the high school machine shop and drove it all over town. When asked why, he patiently explained: "To see if we can get away with it. It's for the enjoyment . . . to see if we can take the car without getting caught." Another senior told our male staff worker: "You can always get out and booze it up."

The impulse to boast of the virile achievements of youth seems to maintain itself into middle and even into old age. Country Indians with college training zestfully told how they and a group of proctors had stolen large amounts of food from the high school kitchen and were never apprehended, or how they and their friends drank three fifths of whiskey in one night and did not pass out.

Clearly, the activities school administrators and teachers denounce as immature and delinquent are regarded as part of youthful daring, excitement, manly honor, and contests of skill and wits by the Sioux young men and many of their elders.

They are also, we suspect, an integral part of the world of competitive sports. "I like to play basketball" one of the most frequent responses of young men to the question: "What do you like most about school?" Indeed, several ninth and tenth graders stated that the opportunity to play basketball was the main reason they kept going to school. One eighth grader who had run away several times stated:

When I was in the seventh grade I made the B team on the basketball squad. And I made the A team when I was in the eighth grade. So I stayed and finished school without running away anymore.

The unselfconscious devotion and ardor with which many of these young men participate in sports must be witnessed to be appreciated even mildly. They cannot communicate their joy and pride in words, though one 17-year-old member of the team that won the state championship tried, by telling how a team member wearing a war bonnet "led us onto the playing floor and this really gave them a cheer."

Unfortunately, we have seen little evidence that school administrators and teachers recognize the opportunity to use sports as a bridge to school.

By the eleventh and twelfth grades many country Indians have left the reservation or gone into the armed services, and it is not always easy to tell which are actual dropouts. However, we did reach some. Their reasons for dropping out varied. One pled boredom: "I was just sitting there doing anything to pass the time." Another said he didn't know what made him quit: "I just didn't fit in anymore. . . . I just wasn't like the other guys anymore." Another refused to attend a class in which he felt the teacher had insulted Indians. When the principal told him that he must attend this class or be "restricted," he left. Significantly, his best friend dropped out with him, even though he was on the way to becoming a first-class basketball player.

Different as they appear at first, these statements have a common undertone. They are the expressions not of immature deliquents, but of relatively mature young men who find the atmosphere of the high school stultifying and childish.

THE DILEMMA OF SIOUX YOUTH

Any intense cross-cultural study is likely to reveal as many tragi-comic situations as social scientific insights. Thus, on the Pine Ridge reservation, a majority of the young men arrive at adolescence valuing *élan,* bravery, generosity, passion, and luck, and admiring outstanding talent in athletics, singing, and dancing. While capable of wider relations and reciprocities, they function at their social best as members of small groups of peers or relatives. Yet to obtain even modest employment in the greater society, they must graduate from high school. And in order to graduate from high school, they are told that they must develop exactly opposite qualities to those they possess: a respect for humdrum diligence and routine, for "discipline" (in the sense of not smoking in toilets, not cutting classes, and not getting drunk), and for government property. In addition, they are expected to compete scholastically on a highly privatized and individualistic level, while living in large dormitories, surrounded by strangers who make privacy of any type impossible.

If we were dealing with the schools of a generation or two ago, then the situation might be bettered by democratization—involving the Sioux parents in control of the schools. This system of local control was not perfect, but it worked pretty well. Today the problem is more complicated and tricky; educators have become professionalized, and educational systems have become complex bureaucracies, inextricably involved with universities, education associations, foundations, and federal crash programs. Even suburban middle class parents, some of whom are highly educated and sophisticated, find it difficult to cope with the bureaucratic barriers and mazes of the schools their children attend. It is difficult to see how Sioux parents could accomplish much unless, in some way, their own school system were kept artificially small and isolated and accessible to their understanding and control.

WORKING CLASS YOUTH

How does our study of the Sioux relate to the problems of city dropouts? A specific comparison of the Sioux dropouts with dropouts from the urban working class—Negroes, Puerto Ricans, or whites—would, no doubt, reveal many salient differences in cultural background and world view. Nevertheless, investigations so far undertaken suggest that the attitudes held by these peoples *toward education and the schools* are startlingly similar.

Both Sioux and working class parents wish their children to continue in school because they believe that graduating from high school is a guarantee of employment. Though some teachers would not believe it, many working class dropouts, like the Sioux dropouts, express a generally favorable attitude toward school, stating that teachers are generally fair and that the worst thing about dropping out of school is missing one's friends. Most important, many working class dropouts assert that they were pushed out of school and frequently add that the push was fairly direct. The Sioux boys put the matter more delicately, implying that the school authorities would not really welcome them back.

These similarities should not be seized on as evidence that all disprivileged children are alike and that they will respond as one to the single, ideal, educational policy. What it does mean is that the schools and their administrators are so monotonously alike that the boy brought up in a minority social or ethnic community can only look at and react to them in the same way. Despite their differences, they are all in much the same boat as they face the great monolith of middle-class society and its one-track education escalator.

An even more important—if often unrecognized—point is that not only does the school pose a dilemma for the working-class or Sioux, Negro, or Puerto Rican boy—he also poses one for the school. In many traditional or ethnic cultures boys are encouraged to be virile adolescents and become "real men." But our schools try to deprive youth of adolescence—and they demand that high school students behave like "mature people"—which, in our culture often seems to mean in a pretty dull, conformist fashion.

Those who submit and succeed in school can often fit into the bureaucratic requirements of employers, but they are also likely to lack independence of thought and creativity. The dropouts are failures—they have failed to become what the school demands. But the school has failed also—failed to offer what the boys from even the most "deprived" and "under-developed" peoples take as a matter of course—the opportunity to become whole men.

S. M. Miller and Ira E. Harrison, studying working class youth, assert that individuals who do poorly in school are handicapped or disfavored for the remainder of their lives, because "the schools have become the occupational gatekeepers" and "the level of education affects the kind and level of job that can be attained." On the other hand, the investigations of Edgar Z. Friedenberg and Jules Henry suggest that the youths who perform creditably in high school according to the views of the authorities are disfavored in that they emerge from this experience as permanently crippled persons or human beings.

In a curious way our researchers among the Sioux may be viewed as supporting both of these contentions, for they suggest that some young people leave high school because they are too vital and independent to submit to a dehumanizing situation.

A NOTE ON THE STUDY

In studying the adolescents on Pine Ridge we concentrated on two areas, the high school and a particular day school community with a country Indian population of about 1,000. We interviewed somewhat less than half the young people then enrolled in the high school plus a random sample of 48 young country Indians. Subsequently, we obtained basic socio-economic and educational data from all the young people who had graduated from the day school in 1961, 1962, and 1963. We interviewed 153 young people between the ages of 13 and 21, about 50 of whom were high school dropouts. We used many approaches and several types of questionnaires, but our most illuminating and reliable data were obtained from interviews conducted by Indian college students who were able to associate with the Sioux adolescents and participate in some of their activities.

While "country Sioux" or "country Indian" might loosely be considered a synonym for "full-blood," I have avoided the latter term as connoting a traditional Indian culture which vanished long ago and whose unchanging qualities were a mythology of white observers rather than a social reality of Indian participants. In any case, I use "country Indian" to refer to the people raised and living "out on the reservation (prairie)" who participate in the social and ceremonial activities of their local rural communities, as opposed to those persons, also known as Indians, who live in Pine Ridge town and make a point of avoiding these backwoods activities.

■ THERE SHE IS . . . MISS AMERICA

Judith Martin

"Anybody here over 35?" shouted Bert Parks.

"Yaaay" came back the answer from the crowd gathered in Atlantic City's Convention Hall last weekend to watch the Miss America Pageant. They had come to cheer their idea of what youth should be like and

50 girls had tried all week to personify that idea. Miss America girls do not smoke, drink, date, discuss controversial topics or go around unchaperoned during the pageant—the winner agrees to behave that way for a year—and they are very polite to their elders.

They support their government, condemn dissent, and set their goals on spending a year or two in traditional female occupations—modeling or elementary school teaching—until the right man comes along.

Miss America of 1970, Pamela Anne Eldred of Detroit, gave a press conference in which she said she was a spokesman for her generation and she made a statement about the Establishment:

"I feel that the people who were voted into office must have the intelligence to know what to do and that everybody should have faith in them."

She said she did not object when pageant officials refused to let her speak on certain subjects. "I feel that they are older and wiser than I am and I can always learn something, especially from someone who is older. If I am told I can't do something, I am told for a reason and I don't challenge it."

"God love you," said a state pageant official from Michigan.

Other pageant officials, the audience, and the judges all talked about how comforting it was to see this girl and the others like her. They called them "true representatives of American youth."

For a few magic days the drug scene, the sexual revolution, and the civil right, antiwar, female liberation, and student protest movements seemed to them to have been just bad dreams populated by "a tiny minority of kooks."

Miss America told her admirers that the war was right because otherwise the government never would have gotten into it. Miss Minnesota, Judith Claire Mendenhall, a runner-up to the title told them that women shouldn't try to run things "because they are more emotional and men can overcome their emotions with logic."

Miss Virginia, Sydney Lee Lewis, won a talent award for a speech in which she condemned student reform movements but lauded her generation for things like "conceiving the Rally for Decency."

The theme of this year's pageant was "the sound of youth." There was much talk in it about the new sound and then one talent winner sang "Get Happy" and another played "Bumble Boogie" on the piano.

"Each generation has its own translation of young, and this generation's is a search for the golden rainbow of peace and understanding," said Parks to introduce Miss America 1969, Judi Ford who wore a Ginger Rogers white pleated chiffon dress and danced the kind of number which used to be the finale of motion picture musical comedies of the '40s.

The pastel chiffon dresses with sequined tops, which the girls wore with 18-button length white cotton gloves in the evening dress competition, had to be specially made. So did the one-piece, solid-color, no-cutouts bathing suits, which are no longer stocked commercially. Spiked-heeled, pointed-toes shoes dyed to match were worn with the bathing suits.

Evening culottes were permitted during the talent competition, but most girls favored the sequined, drum majorette type of costume. Several chose mid-knee cocktail dresses just a shade longer than the new habits of a group of nuns who attended the preliminary competition one night.

Make-up was used in the shows to create the kewpie doll look of decades ago—bright red lipstick, blue eye shadow, and hair teased into beehives with wiglets or curls added.

Offstage, however, the girls were more contemporary, with shoulder-length hairstyles and little wool dresses which gave them the look of 50 Tricia Nixons.

The judges said they were gratified at what they saw and had a hard time picking a winner.

"It renews my faith in youth," said Hollywood make-up man Bud Westmore, a judge, whose wife was Miss California of 1952.

"We have a complete misconception of what is going on when we see the New York hippies who don't wash," said Leon Leonidoff, another judge, who has been staging Radio City Music Hall spectaculars since 1932. "This country is wholesome and healthy." His wife is a former Miss New Jersey, and he had been going around all week offering contracts to his favorite contestants.

"We really haven't got a thing to worry about," said judge Jane Pickens Langley, who describes herself as "singer, artist, and philanthropist."

"These aren't the girls you hear about, because there is never any scandal attached to them," said judge Zelma George, executive director of the Cleveland Job Corps Center for Women. "Someone should do a master's thesis on them."

"You don't hear about them later because basically they are not ambitious," said writer John Crosby, a judge. "They want to be good wives and mothers."

No one seemed to know, however, why most of the past Miss Americas have been divorced at least once.

The pageant officials expressed their delight with the way Miss America 1970 handled reporters' questions.

Topics on which she smiled and said "I really couldn't voice an opinion—I don't know enough about that" included drugs, nudity in the theater, unisex fashions, student unrest, what the priorities of America should be, and whether 18-year-olds should have the vote. She also said that she was happy about the moon shot "which proves that the United States is a great country" and that her goal in life is "to be a nice person."

Her mother, Mrs. William B. Eldred, who broke in once just after the crowning to tell Miss America, "You are no expert," said that she and her daughter feel alike on all topics. "There is no generation gap," said Mrs. Eldred.

Miss America's one moment of confusion was when she was asked where her father works. He is an employee of Chrysler, and loyalty to the pageant's sponsors, one of which is Oldsmobile, is an important quality of Miss America.

Miss America 1969 said that, during her year, love of Toni hair products, Pepsi-Cola, and Oldsmobile became a spontaneous part of her.

The past and present Miss Americas looked very much alike—both with blond hairdos, green eyes, pale skin, and wide smiles. They are both, said Bert Parks, "composites of positive wonders. All Miss Americas are," he said.

■ ADOLESCENCE, MARRIAGE, AND SEX

Cora DuBois

TATTOOING FOR GIRLS

The time for girls to be tattooed is on the first day of the four-day communal pig hunt at the end of the dry season, when most of the boys and men leave the village. There is no implied sex segregation in the choice of this time, since any man who has failed to go hunting may be present during the tattooing process. In fact, men also may be tattooed, but this is done casually by some friend at any time during the year, and later in young manhood. Tattooing is rarer among men than among women. Almost all women are tattooed, whereas only an occasional man is.

The men set off for the hunt shortly after dawn, accompanied by a group of women who may not go beyond the crest of the hill. The women then return and are required to be quiet and avoid unduly vigorous activity until the men come back. Girls whose breasts are beginning to develop take this opportunity to be tattooed, but they must wait until a black column of smoke rises from the grass fired by the men for the pig drives. If they do not wait, the tattoo designs will be light and impermanent. Each girl herself expresses the wish and collects the necessary materials. These are a thorn and finely pounded coconut-shell charcoal mixed with the juice of banana bark. Some grown woman who feels that she has a certain skill in the matter will volunteer to perform the operation. The girl lays her head in the operator's lap; a design is first traced on her forehead or cheek and is then pricked in with a thorn dipped in charcoal. The procedure usually draws a number of girls and adult women, all of whom discuss animatedly which of a limited number of simple designs will be used. Often a little girl who has taken no initiative in the matter will be urged by a friend or adult to undergo the operation. Beauty is the only objective.

It is a tradition to insist that the operation does not hurt, and when I asked a girl who had just had the task completed whether it was painful, older women answered before she was able to, assuring me that it was not. On one occasion some older women, by way of teasing the child's grandmother, urged a little girl of seven to let herself be tattooed. The grandmother arrived just in time to prevent the scheme from being carried out. She was very indignant that her grandchild should have been cajoled into it when she was obviously so young. In relation to a discussion of skills and craftsmanship, it should be stated that the tattooing process is often very crude and usually impermanent, so that traces of designs are rarely distinguishable on the faces of middle-aged women.

GROWING UP FOR BOYS

Whereas girls are tattooed from approximately ten to fourteen, the comparable badge of adulthood for boys, i.e., long hair, does not come until somewhat later, at ages I should estimate from sixteen to eighteen. When boys begin to let their hair grow long, they also begin borrowing or acquiring male accouterments. These are dwelt upon in loving detail in many myths and consist of a sword, a front shield, a back shield, a parrying shield, a bow, a wide belt of woven rattan that serves as a quiver, an areca basket with bells, and the tubular, areca-bark hair cylinder with the accompanying combs and head plumes. Naturally, a young man rarely succeeds in borrowing or acquiring all these articles at first, but he gets as many as he can and struts about in them, often followed by the half-admiring, half-derisive comments of older women and girls. There is a special expression for the type of laughter that women direct toward a young man, which I can translate only by our word *hoot*. Its character is as unmistakable as the laughter that accompanies the telling of smutty jokes in our culture. A young man of about twenty himself described in the following words this attitude and the associated courting interests of both boys and girls.

"When a lot of women get together to work in the fields or to fetch water, they talk and talk. When you hear them hoot, that means they are talking about a man. Maybe one girl says she likes a certain man and intends to sleep with him. When a young man ties up his long hair and walks with bells on his basket, women watch until he has passed by, and then they say, 'Isn't that a fine man!' and begin to hoot. If he wears a big white shawl from the coast, women will say, 'There goes my white chicken!' and then they hoot. The young man feels glad but also a little ashamed. Also, when a young man begins to versify at a dance and his voice rings out clear and strong, the next day the women will say, 'Don't we have a fine man in our village!' and then they will hoot. When there is a dance, the young man will hunt for areca and betel the day before so as to fill up his basket. When he reaches the dance place on the night of the dance, all the young women will crowd around him and hold out their hands for areca. If one woman comes back again and again for more areca, it is a sign that they already want each other, and soon they will go off and make an agreement. Then the girl says he must go find her bride-price."

This comment sets, better than any outsider could, the pattern of masculine vanity, which often persists through life and which is recognized as a male trait. Consistent with this newly developed swagger, other changes occur in young men's lives. In the course of a few months they break away from the irresponsible free-roving play groups of growing boys and become far more solitary and sedentary. They imitate the indolence of older wealthy men. At the same time, they begin to speculate about the possibilities and the means for entering the financial system of the adults and about ways of ingratiating themselves with men of influence who may be of assistance to them.

One significant detail concerning food should be noted in connection with the coming of age in boys. The picture so far of the development of masculine vanity and the good-natured teasing that it involves is thoroughly familiar to us. There is another and comparable source of teasing. Boys who are beginning to show open interest in girls and to visit the village of someone they find attractive will be teased by older people with comments like the following, "Padama has gone to visit his wife in Karieta. When boys grow up, the food their mother cooks no longer tastes good. They have to go to the house of a young woman to eat." This kind of teasing makes the younger boys squirm with embarrassment much as it would in our society. A few years later a young man will insist on a midday meal, even if he has to cook it himself, as a symbol of the adult status he is struggling to acquire. The extent to which food and courting ideas can be linked is also exemplified in the following instance. Langmai, who was courting Kolmani by helping her with the storage of her harvest, suggested that they had better marry, by saying, "Who will eat this corn I am stacking? I had better come and eat it myself."

TOOTH BLACKENING

It is during this period of adolescence that both boys and girls have their teeth blackened and filed. Again the matter is optional, but since shiny black teeth are much admired and long uneven ones are considered very ugly, practically every young person has his blackened and probably half have them filed. The process is more or less in the nature of a prolonged picnic, free from adult supervision. It is without doubt also a period of license for many of the young people, although adults vigorously contradicted my phrasing it so.

The best indication of the sexual liberty current at this time is that stricter parents forbid their daughters to remain in remote field houses overnight and insist upon their staying at home or near by in the house of some responsible elder kin. Further, when I visited such a group one evening at sundown just as the strips of dye were being passed out, the young man in charge of procuring and mixing the paste used to darken the teeth said sternly to the children, "Now, no intercourse tonight"—a comment that produced a ripple of giggling among the boys and girls.

The actual procedure is as follows: In July or August some young unmarried man, perhaps in his early twenties, announces that he will blacken teeth for the children of the community and designates the field house where it will be done. This is the slack season agriculturally, so that girls can be spared from the fields. He purchases from some friend in the village of Bakudatang a particular type of soil found there. This investment rarely exceeds five cents. With the earth he mixes a fruit resembling a small green fig. The resulting paste is smeared on a strip of banana bark which each child cuts to fit the size of his mouth. The preparation of each day's supply takes the better part of an afternoon. For at least seven nights, and often ten, the children sleep together in a field house, with the paste held against their teeth by the flexible bark strips. During the day boys assiduously hunt rats, and girls go to their fields to collect vegetable foods. The children all eat together, being careful to place small bits of food far back in their mouths in order not to spoil the dye. With the same objective a length of thin bamboo is used as a drinking tube during the period. Surplus rats are smoked to preserve them for a feast on the last day.

The whole procedure reminds one very much of "playing house." It is a carefree time for all the young people. There are no taboos associated with the period except that attending a dance will interfere with proper dyeing and that if small children loiter too near the older group they will fail to grow up rapidly. For his services the young man is paid a nominal sum of an arrow, or nowadays a penny, per child. He seldom makes more than twenty or thirty cents for a week's work. When I asked why a young man undertook such a task when the reward was so small, the answer was, "Because he likes to be near young girls."

On the last day or two of the period those who are to have their teeth filed go through the ordeal. The same person who prepared the dye usually does the tooth filing. The subject's head is laid on the thigh of the operator and wedged against his side with his elbow. The jaws are propped open with a piece of corncob. The six upper and six lower front teeth are then filed to half their length with an ordinary knife blade which has been nicked to resemble a saw. Apparently experience makes it possible to avoid the root canal, which occupies only the upper half of the incisors. The whole operation takes about two or three hours, and for this the operator is paid the equivalent of about five cents. It is undoubtedly painful but, as in tattooing, it is bad form to admit it. The result of this filing means that even when the back teeth are occluded, the tongue will show pinkly between the gaping front teeth when a person smiles. This is considered definitely attractive.

The complete informality of this ceremony is manifest by the fact that some of the young people return two or three years in succession if the first attempt at blackening was not successful. Also, anyone, at any time, may have his teeth filed down to a straight, even line for appearance's sake. The range of ages is also wide. Boys may be from about fourteen to twenty and girls from twelve to eighteen. There is no regulation against young married people joining the group. The married people, however, are most likely to be girls, since marriage comes early for them.

Tattooing, the beginning of masculine vanity, courting, and tooth blackening are all preliminaries to marriage for young people.

■ MARRIAGE IN SICILY

Charlotte Gower Chapman

It is taken for granted that every Sicilian, when he reaches the age of maturity, will marry and establish a household of his own. In so doing he establishes the only socially approved basis for his sexual life and the only proper arrangement of his economic existence. Any unmarried adult male, even a priest, is regarded as a menace to the honor of the women of his neighborhood. Moreover, since a woman is necessary for the management of his domestic affairs, if he does not marry he must remain dependent on the women of his parental family, and in his old age on possibly more remote relatives, unless he is able to arrange some extra-legal connection with a woman who fills the role of a wife, without enjoying the security of a wife's position. Either of these solutions is condemned by society, although the offender is subject to no formal punishments (except by the Church, which may refuse the sacraments to unrepenting sinners; as far as I know, this punishment was not inflicted in Milocca). The disapproval is expressed informally, and is usually limited to critical remarks made about the person, rather than addressed to him. On the whole, the criticism of Old Peppi Cassenti, who had been too miserly to accept the responsibilities of marriage, was more sharply expressed than that directed toward Doctor Callari, who maintained four women as servant-consorts. The doctor had treated his concubines well and at his death had divided his land between them, thus providing each with a dowry that enabled her to make a respectable marriage. His conduct was not correct, but he was rich and a man, and after all, none of them, since they were his social inferiors, could expect to marry him. Masru Peppi *Narisi's* irregular household was even less criticized, for it followed the normal pattern of domesticity in every respect except in the observance of the legal and religious rites. It was further recognized that these formalities were omitted through no fault of his, since his legal wife had left him and was believed to be still alive.

Except for the house-nuns, who have taken vows of chastity, unmarried women are regarded as not responsible for their condition and are not blamed. Donna Gilorma was very homely, and possibly for that reason never found a husband, although her family should have been able to provide her with a dowry that would cover any defect. Doctor Callari's Rose, the first girl he took to live with him, refused to accept any offer of marriage after his death, because she was already past forty and did not care to take a husband who was interested only in her money. Other women, whose reputations for loose conduct had prevented their marriage, were reproached for their improper behavior, but their failure to marry was taken for granted. The initiative in marriage is quite definitely left to the man. The house-nuns are condemned overtly, not for avoiding domestic responsibilities, but for affecting an unnatural virtue.

Marriage is thus represented as a duty for a man. It brings him certain advantages, especially if he has a good wife: "He who finds a good wife has discovered a fortune." Many proverbs, however, tend to emphasize the disadvantage of marriage.

> If you are too happy, get married.
> You ate the hen (got married)? You put on a chain.
> You got married? Now you'll have to carry wood on your back.

On the other hand, marriage is represented as the ardent desire of every woman. This appears in popular songs, in proverbs, and in legends. Sometimes the girl is represented as having a special interest in a certain young man, but more frequently she is merely interested in having a husband, any husband. "Let me have a man, though he be of rags." In a popular song a girl addresses her mother: "Mamma mine, I must marry!" "My daughter, to whom shall I give you?" "Mamma, you look out for that." Similarly in the legend, the sister of Saint Peter came to her brother and said, "I want to get married." Saint Peter discussed the matter with the Lord, who said, "Very well, let us find her a husband," and it was done. When the first husband died, she again wanted to marry, but this time the Lord said, "All right, you find her a husband." His disapproval of the second marriage was so evident to his disciple that when the sister, widowed again, asked for a third husband, Saint Peter did not even consult his Master, but replied, "Go find yourself a husband." The moral of this tale is that while widows may remarry, Christ looks with favor only on the first union; but it is cited here as an illustration of the attitude that women are more interested in the married state than in any particular man. This seems to be the case in actual life. While it was politely admitted that certain young women were still unmarried, although past thirty, because a pleasing partner had not yet appeared, the girls themselves said that it would be better to put up with a bad husband than to have none at all.

One of the reasons for the girls' enthusiasm for marriage is probably a definite sexual desire. The moral code for women permits them no gratification of their sexual impulses outside of marriage. At the same time, they are surrounded by allusions to the pleasures of love. Salacious riddles are common, and the familiar conversation of their elders may be definitely licentious. The board for kneading bread, with its heavy lever which is pressed down on the dough, is openly compared to a woman and a man engaged in intercourse. In the same way the act of grating cheese is also given a sexual significance. Much of the ordinary joking is heavily laden with double meanings of this sort. Moreover, the close quarters in which most poor families live makes it almost inevitable that the children see something of the sexual behavior of their parents. The interest in sexual matters is great, and even children so small that they still play in mixed groups may amuse themselves by attempts to counterfeit sexual intercourse. This type of play is indulged in only when they feel free from the observation of older people, for however free may be the allusions to sexual activity in general, the attitude toward specific instances of it is distinctly prudish. A woman never speaks of her own physical relations with her husband, and the love songs content themselves, as a rule, with requests for kisses.

Thus the young girls in Milocca grow up in the knowledge that sexual relations are a source of pleasure which they may experience only when they have been married, unless they wish to run the risk of being left with a ruined reputation and possibly a baby as well. The knowledge of the connection between intercourse and the bearing of children does not seem to be acquired nearly as early as is the interest in the former. It is usual to say that a woman "buys" a baby, and to tell children that the midwife brings it in her little black case. Children of nine or ten years of age seem to take this literally, and it is difficult to say at what age they become aware of the realities of birth. This would depend largely on the family's ability to keep them out of the way when a parturition is due. The desire for children is never given as a reason for wishing to get married.

An idea well fixed in the minds of Sicilian girls is that men are superior and rather fascinating beings. Even their brothers and their fathers live in a world sufficiently removed from their own to be faintly glamorous. The glamour is particularly strong about young men who might be possible mates, and predisposes the girls to fall in love rather readily. This is helped by the attitude of the parents, who seem to believe that any young people not of the same household who see much of each other are apt to form an attachment for each other. However, the girls are not without discrimination of a sort. They are more likely to fix their affections on a youth who is tall, good-looking or well dressed. Moreover, any show of interest on the part of a young man tends to awaken a response in the girl, unless she has for some reason already decided that he is stupid or unattractive. In Formisano's play *Matri-monii e Viscucati,* a young girl tells her mother about how she happened to fall in love with the young man she has set her heart on marrying.

> I got to know him at church. He was there beside the main altar, and by chance I happened to raise my eyes and I saw he was looking at me. After a while, always by accident, I raised my eyes again and saw that he was still look-ing at me. After another while I just happened to look up again, and he was still looking at me! When mass was over, he followed me. After I got home, I looked out of the window, and there he was, beside the lamp-post. When he saw me he took out his handkerchief and pretended to blow his nose, and I smoothed my hair. From then on he has been under the window every day! And the other day when we went to church he was just behind us, and while I was taking holy water I felt something touch my other hand, and he gave me a letter. A letter, mamma, that would break your heart! I answered it, and we have been writing to each other ever since.

While even this amount of initiative on the part of the young people is contrary to the pattern of parentally arranged marriages, the picture given is that of a typical courtship. One young man told me of falling in love with an American-born girl who had returned to Sicily to visit rela-tives. He had met her in the home of mutual friends, but they had had no conversation, for she knew no Italian and he no English. Later she went to Palermo, and he found an excuse for following her. There he spent his days under her window. She saw him, and twice dropped small articles into the street. His intentions were honorable, however, and he sent the things back to her by the doorman. I was entrusted with the translation of his first letter to her, and with its delivery. He was very serious in his desire to marry her.

This was virtually a case of love at first sight, as was that of Ange-lidda, who first became enamoured of 'Gnaziu when she heard him pass-ing through her *robba* singing. Later she wrote him letters, and they found occasions to talk when both were gathering almonds for the same proprietor. She considered herself engaged to him, although his attach-ment for a married woman was notorious and seemed likely to inter-fere with any marriage to Angelidda. In the meantime, Angelidda had acquired a rather dubious reputation on account of the letters and con-versations.

It is recognized that repeated contacts may permit the development of love. This might occur between members of families which were on intimate terms, or who live as close neighbors. A case of this sort, that of the doctor's daughter mentioned below, had in recent years ended tragically. In another instance a young man said, "I shall avoid seeing Maricchia, because if I don't, something may happen." Maricchia was a girl whom it would not have been suitable to marry, and with whom he wished to avoid having illicit relations; she was supposed to be a vir-gin, and it might have gone hard with him had she become pregnant.

At the time his cousin was in prison for refusing to marry his child's mother.

This belief that young people fall in love easily is given as the justification for the segregation of women, the purpose of which is to prevent any attachment from being formed until a suitable mate has been selected by the parents and introduced as a proper object of the affections. On the whole, it appears to be a fairly efficacious device, especially among the classes who can afford to keep their daughters at home or properly chaperoned. Young men are allowed greater freedom, possibly on the theory that they can satisfy their normal desires without forming any sentimental attachments. It would be an exceptional case where a prenuptial relationship might end in marriage, for the girl who permits herself to be seduced before her marriage reveals herself as a dishonest woman who would not make a good wife. Moreover, the fear of being involved in court proceedings leads the young men to seek out girls who already have a reputation for loose conduct, or married women whose pregnancy would cause no scandal. There are no real prostitutes in Milocca. Payments for favors are in the form of gifts and entertainment. The girls are expected to follow the pattern of monogamy, and take only one lover at a time.

When an unmarried man forms a strong attachment for a girl with whom he has had sexual connections, it is considered most unfortunate, and may be attributed to some spell which she has cast over him. Any woman with the reputation of a witch is believed to know how to make love potions. Maria *la Scrunchia* was offered one of these compounds to help her gain the affections of one of the young men in her *robba*. Being vowed to chastity, she was not interested. In her case the charm was supposed to make the man seek her in marriage. In another case, one of my male informants believed himself to have been the victim of such a charm. "I followed her around like a little dog and could never bear to leave her. She could make me do anything she wished." When his family heard about it, they hired another witch to remove the charm. Part of her treatment was the confinement of the man in his home for a considerable period. The cure was effective. When a woman seems to have a great power over her lover, she is said to have him enchained. It is she, as a rule, who is blamed for the situation. It is common to refer to her as a witch, but I am not certain that there is always the implication that she has actually made use of magic to gain his affections.

The attachment a man feels for his mistress is seldom spoken of as love, although it is not clearly distinguished from similar states of mind which are so designated. It certainly is not accepted as an excuse for the irregularity of his union, which is attributed to the sexual propensities of the male in general, rather than to any especial sentiment for the particular girl. Romantic love appears to be an entirely different matter. It is the state of mind reflected in the love songs which men sing as they ride about the countryside. The lover is ill with his love; he would go to the inferno for his lady, like whom there is none on earth. "I would put you in a frame of gold and give you more adoration than a saint; I would not care if I should die, for I would take out my heart and give it to you." She alone can soothe his pain, and if she will not, there is for him only "an open grave in the cemetery."

Sicilians pride themselves not only on the intensity of their passion, but also on their faithfulness. "The first love is never forgotten." They feel that in these respects they are superior to all other peoples. Girls in Milocca derive great satisfaction from the tragic story of the doctor's daughter who killed herself for love. The object of her affections belonged to a family with whom her parents were on terms of intimacy, and the two households usually took their evening strolls together. However, it was seen that the young people were more interested in each other than was desirable, since both were considered too young to marry. Consequently the doctor decided to take his wife and daughters walking somewhat earlier than usual, so as to avoid the company of the young man's family. The girl understood the meaning of the change, and drank corrosive sublimate. Her behavior was deplored, but at the same time admired as an example of the true Sicilian love. The young man's conduct was equally admirable from the romantic point of view. He watched her during her prolonged and painful death, and was too grieved to read the funeral address, an office which he usually performed at the burial of any person of a prominent family. Every year he took flowers to her grave on All Soul's Day. Even the girl's parents had behaved according to the proper code, for they were acting only for their daughter's good. In actual life such tragedies are rare, and as a rule the romantic ideal receives its only expression in love songs and in the few novels which may reach town. The popular legends are more concerned with the marvelous and supernatural than with purely human tragedies.

While some of the love affairs which have their beginnings before marriage may lead to the establishment of a household after the proper civil and religious formalities, love or even acquaintance before marriage is considered quite unnecessary. In fact, a marriage based on love is proverbially unsuccessful. "He who marries for love suffers all his life." Economic or social considerations are more important, and it is the parents' role to think of them. Their choice of a mate may be a person whom the child has never seen before, but objection is not expected, and is only occasionally made. As for love, that is expected to develop after the wedding. If it does not (and it required suggestion on my part to bring up this possibility), patience is necessary.

In one case a girl objected to the husband chosen for her by her parents. Antonietta's family was poor, and they were very glad when a relative of the mother who had recently returned from America asked for Antonietta in marriage. He offered to give the girl a dowry of twenty thousand *lire,* to be deposited in the Postal Savings, and to make out a will leaving his house in Montedoro to her in the case of his death. This was very generous, but he was an old man, over sixty years of age. All seemed to be going well; the future bridegroom had made the customary presents to his fiancee, when suddenly she eloped with the son of a goatherd who lived across the street. It was said that she wore her newly acquired finery when she fled, and that her brother followed her and made her give it up. After a day or so the elopers returned home, and to the scandalization of the village the aged bridegroom said that he would still be glad to marry Antonietta, for what she had done was simply a child's trick. Here was certainly something that he had picked up in America! Antonietta's parents tried to force her consent to the marriage with the man they had selected, using all the means at their disposal, even threatening her with a knife. She eloped a second time. This time she did not return home, but her brother went to stay with her and to support her. This left his parents in financial straits, for his blind father was unable to work, so that a reconciliation was soon affected, and the children returned home. All hope of the arranged marriage had now vanished, and the goatherd refused to allow his son to marry Antonietta. Consequently the matter was taken into court, for the girl was with child. This was all a great source of gossip. On the whole, public opinion was on the side of Antonietta on account of the age of the man she refused to marry, and her parents' behavior was criticized. They, however, were grieved by the family dishonor, and surprised that Antonietta should have behaved so after their careful training. Her mother said, "I kept her as carefully as a flower in a vase. I never let her go out at all, I was that jealous. It isn't as if I had other daughters."

■ LIM A-POU: A WIFE AND A SISTER

Margery Wolf

Lim A-pou was born into a family living on the far edge of the Hotien district near the town of Tapu, but only the earliest days of her life were spent in this home. When she was eight or nine months old, the Lim family adopted her to bring her up as a wife for their eldest son. As the Lims were still poor tenant farmers at the time, one of their motives must have been a desire to ensure a wife for their son. They could not be certain that they would be able to afford the bride price if they waited to acquire a wife for him when he reached marriageable age. The marriage of foster siblings has less prestige than that in which an adult bride is brought into the family, but there is some compensation in the knowledge that a girl raised in the family usually makes a more willing daughter-in-law. Even the wealthy who can easily afford the more prestigious marriage sometimes choose to adopt their sons' wives as infants for the sake of future domestic harmony. The introduction of a young woman into a family almost inevitably results in a competitive and often openly hostile relationship between mother-in-law and daughter-in-law; the girl who enters the house as a child is socialized in the ways of the house and bound to her husband's mother by all the ties of parental affection. She is both daughter-in-law and daughter. The adult bride is forever comparing her present life with that in her natal home, but the bride who grows up in her husband's family has no standards for comparison. She accepts her life because she knows no other.

As a girl and as a young woman, Lim A-pou evinced all the behavior hoped for by families who adopt daughters. She accepted reprimands and punishments without becoming sullen, she did not complain, and she worked at whatever job was at hand with a diligence that must have been impressive to satisfy such a hard taskmaster as Lim Han-ci. Several people told me that the old man was particularly fond of his adopted daughter and often said of her, "Where can you find another person who works as hard as A-pou?" His words are as apt today as they were then. She is always busy, and her activities are always productive. Whether in the fields or in the kitchen, her movements are efficient and purposeful. She can easily manage to cook for their family of fourteen, help her bewildered daughter-in-law care for a sick baby, and still have time to rake over a yard of drying rice every hour. The extent to which the family depends upon her was amusingly, if frustratingly, illustrated on one of the rare days she was away. Lim A-ki, her daughter-in-law, proved incapable of both cooking and attending to the needs of her two small children, and the smell of scorching food brought laughing neighbors in to help and to further the confusion. It was truly a memorable occasion in that Lim Chui-ieng was ordered by her husband to assist by washing down the pig pens, a daily task that takes A-pou a half hour and took the appalled Chui-ieng the better part of an afternoon.

I tried many times, without success, to get A-pou to reminisce about her childhood. She was very helpful in providing me with general information about the customs of adoption and the treatment of adopted daughters, but when I attempted to turn the conversation to her own experiences, I never got beyond a proverb. Once I twisted one of her proverbs into a question and asked, "Is it better to be a daughter or an adopted daughter?" It was a foolish question, but she didn't laugh. She just looked away and answered quietly, "I don't know. I have never been a daughter."

A-pou's fate as an adult was to marry her foster brother, Lim Hue-lieng. If she objected, and it must have been obvious that Lim Hue-lieng would be something less than a husband to her, she kept her objections to herself. There was little to be gained by a peace and much to be lost. Her foster father looked upon the marriage as a formal public statement of his eldest son's return to the status of son. A-pou was fond of her foster parents and saddened by the pain Lim Hue-lieng's desertion had caused them. If she refused the marriage, she would not only add to their pain but would also bring to an end the family's obligation to provide for her. To remain in their house under such circumstances would be unthinkable, but for a young woman of A-pou's temperament, the alternatives were too grim to be considered seriously. Where could she go, and how could she support herself and the daughter they had adopted for her—if indeed they allowed her to take the child with her? There were, after all, many advantages to the marriage. The simple ceremony making her a wife as well as a daughter-in-law would greatly improve her status both in the village and in the family itself. And, as the wife of the eldest son, she would have some control over her own future, particularly as the elder generations began to turn over their authority. Lim Hue-lieng's obvious indifference to her might even be an advantage since he would not be likely to remove her from his parents' home and protection. The abhorrence many adopted daughters feel toward coitus with their foster brothers may not have been as pronounced in A-pou's case. Lim Hue-lieng's long absence and the many romantic rumors circulating about his amorous exploits may have given him enough glamour to cloak if not destroy the familiarity that gives rise to feelings of incest. The security of being the eldest daughter-in-law in an increasingly prosperous family could make up for a great deal of what was lacking in the conjugal relationship.

Whether or not Lim A-pou weighed all these advantages and disadvantages, we have no way of knowing. Her decision may have been far simpler. The only respectable thing for a young woman to do in the first quarter of this century was to obey her parents, and A-pou's desire for respectability was, and still is, intense. It is the key to many of her present attitudes and was undoubtedly the motivation for much of her childhood docility. During my first few weeks in the Lim household, there were so many unfamiliar names to be attached to unfamiliar faces that I resorted to descriptive nicknames in conversations with my husband and staff. Lim A-pou was dubbed "the old lady." When I finally sorted out ages and names and relationships, I was amazed to find that she was not quite fifty years old. Unlike every other village woman her age, Lim A-pou wears the old-fashioned Chinese costume and hair style only seen now on Taiwanese women over 70. Around the village she wears dark cotton pants, hemmed to a clumsy level between ankle and knee, and a white Mandarin smock, sleeveless in summer and long-sleeved in winter. For her infrequent trips to Tapu or nearby temples, she wears dark Mandarin-collared dresses cut so loosely and with such decorous side slits that their generic relationship with the fashionable, clinging cheong-sam of Hongkong is questionable. Her hair is parted in the middle and pulled tightly back into a neat knot low on her neck. It is rarely disordered even in the roughest of farm work because (much to the horror of my modern minded interpreter) she keeps a heavy coating of fat on it.

Lim A-pou's extraordinary old-fashionedness, or devotion to tradition, is not limited to her dress. I found her, as do many of her neighbors, an excellent informant on ancient home remedies, rituals for placating household gods and ghosts, techniques for protecting pregnant women, and for purifying rooms following childbirth. Part of her conflict with her late husband's younger brother, Lim Chieng-cua, results from his introduction of more economical practices in the ceremonies honoring the ancestors. Many families on Taiwan now combine the ceremonies celebrating their more distant ancestors' birth and death days, presenting the expensive offerings of meat and fowl to them all on the same day, rather than repeating the expense for each on their specific anniversary. Besides this, Lim Chieng-cua also abolished the bi-monthly offerings to Tu Ti Kung—a less expensive ceremony but one that has not been celebrated in many households for decades. A-pou bitterly resented these omissions and continued to offer an apologetic bit of incense each night and morning to preserve what to her was at least a semblance of propriety. When Lim Chieng-cua installed the new pump in the house without consulting the almanac, A-pou was angry for days. According to the almanac, the Placenta God was resting in that particular room on that particular day. Through Lim Chieng-cua's negligence, the little god was disturbed or injured, and he took his vengeance on A-pou's grandson in the form of a high fever. Before the fever was finally controlled with an injection of penicillin, Lim Chieng-cua and his nephew, the father of the child, had to endure a week of foul humor, both of them alarmed by the illness and neither of them believing in A-pou's theory of causation.

Due to the indiscretion of the only other person who knew of the event, I learned of Lim A-pou's one lapse from rigid respectability. This lapse undoubtedly colored, if it did not start, the rift between her and her foster brother, Lim Chieng-cua. One evening before the death of either his father or his elder brother, Lim Chieng-cua walked into a thatch tool shelter in one of the family's distant fields and found A-pou and a hired man in compromising circumstances. He soundly thrashed the hired man who has never been seen in the area since, and then administered the same treatment to A-pou. Exercising his usual good judgement, Lim Chieng-cua did not mention the incident to anyone, other than my informant, thereby saving his foster sister's reputation and his father's peace of mind. The effect this strange incident had on whatever relationship had prevailed between Lim Chieng-cua and his foster sister can only be imagined.

A-pou's marriage, if it may be called that, seemed to change her very little. She chose to ignore her rival. When I asked one of her neighbors how it was that she allowed her husband to bring his second wife into the Lim family home, I was answered with laughter. "He was a *lo mua*. How could she dare to say anything about what he did? You have heard about his temper. When he stamped his foot the noise was like thunder. She wouldn't dare say anything to him."

It has been said that A-pou didn't make life easy for Lim So-lan when she lived in the house but I doubt that her displeasure was ever voiced. However, after the death of her husband and then of her father, people began to notice a change in A-pou, particularly people in the family. Chui-ieng, her sister-in-law, told me bluntly, "Before they died she was quiet, minded her own business, and didn't say anything. Now she is exactly the opposite." Obviously, this is an overstatement, but it comes closer to the Lim A-pou I knew than to the one described to me. She is still quiet and she still minds her own business, but her opinion as to what is her business seems to have broadened. To mind it requires that she speak up, if not herself, at least through her son. As long as her foster father was alive, she was confident that she and her sons would share the family's fortune, good or bad, in the same way as other family members, but many things changed with the death of this strong-willed man. As the eldest adult male, Lim Chieng-cua is the head of the family now, but his foster sister is the widow of the man who would have occupied this status had he lived. When Lim Chieng-cua makes a decision affecting the welfare of the family, he is obliged to consult her. Aside from the personal animosity between them, they speak across a barrier of misunderstandings. She is an uneducated woman who rarely ventures beyond the village world of her childhood; he is a sophisticated man who must compete in a business world that is becoming less and less tolerant of small family enterprises.

Before her foster father's death, A-pou accepted the division of labor in the family without questioning its fairness. Now she does not. One day while I helped her prepare some radishes for market, she talked to me with unusual bitterness: "The money in our family is all handled by Lim Chieng-cua and his wife. We work ourselves to death, and they take the profits. Except for the money we make by selling a *jin* of this or that to a neighbor, we give them every cent of the money. If Lim Chieng-cua doesn't see us take out the scales to sell something, his wife does and tells him about it. Last night Chui-ieng saw me selling fifty *jin* of radishes and right away she went into the house and told her husband who came out to see what I was doing. I knew he came out to see what I was going to get and so even though I had intended to give him the money, I purposely did not give it to him.

"When A-bok and I used to take vegetables to Lungyen to sell, we gave all of the money to Lim Chieng-cua except for our train fare and a few dollars we spent to buy bean curd for our lunch. Chui-ieng hires someone to wash her children's clothes. We work hard so that she can take it easy.

"When my father was alive, it wasn't like this. We had fish and meat on the table every day, and we even had to tell him not to buy so much food. We bought all of our vegetables. Now we have to eat what we raise. We used to have three people working for us in the fields, now we have none. At that time our family could save a little money each year, but now Lim Chieng-cua always says we haven't enough money to live on and even has to borrow money. My father gave me NT$200 every time we sold pigs because I was the one who raised the pigs. Since my father died, we have sold pigs seven or eight times, earning NT$17,000 to NT$18,000, and Lim Chieng-cua has not given me even one dollar. Last time we sold pigs, I told him I wasn't going to raise them anymore. So I want to see where he will get this much money now. This year we will make about NT$10,000 on the peanuts, but it will all go to Lim Chieng-cua. When my father was alive, he gave me a little money each time we made a sale, saying, 'You have worked very hard so take this money and spend it on yourself.' Now I can't plan on getting even a dollar for my own use. When I have to buy something, I have to go and ask Lim Chieng-cua for it."

Lim A-pou is not one of the village "wanderers," but she is less constrained now about airing her grievances to one or two sympathetic neighbors than she once was. She is always careful as to what she says, touching only on disparities that are apparent to all. The extent to which she exploits the villagers' general lack of sympathy with Lim Chieng-cua's wife is adroit. One of my favorite "wanderers," always eager to tell me about Lim family affairs, reflects the none too subtle influence of A-pou in her views: "In the Lim family, the work is divided between two brothers, but now that one brother is dead, that half of the family has it very hard. They take care of the fields but have to give all of the money they earn to Lim Chieng-cua. There is a lot of bad feeling between the two wives, Chui-ieng and A-pou. Chui-ieng always wants to manage everything. When Lim So-lan lived in the house she often suffered from that woman. Sometimes when So-lan was cooking, Chui-ieng would purposely drop sweepings into the food so that the old man would scold poor So-lan. Even A-pou felt sorry for So-lan. Chui-ieng never talks to A-pou if she can help it, and she never faces her fully when she does have to tell her something.

"They ought to divide the family and I don't see why they don't. Maybe there aren't any relatives who can do it for them [i.e., act as arbiters on the division of the property]. Lim A-pou's people work very hard in the fields and give all the money to the family. Lim Chieng-cua manages the cement bag factory. Who knows whether or not he gives the money the factory earns to the family? He had to borrow a lot of money and now the family is deeply in debt. He ought to let A-pou manage the family money and see if she can't do better."

The debts to which this woman refers illustrate Lim A-pou's misunderstanding of the management of the family factory. When Lim Chieng-cua is so fortunate as to receive a large order from one of his contracting companies, he is not paid until the order is filled. Since this might mean two or three months work and his factory workers cannot go unpaid longer than a week without suffering real hardships, he uses both factory accounts and family accounts to pay wages. On occasion he is forced to borrow from relatives to meet any large expenses that might arise in his own family. All too frequently the gossips note the borrowing but not the repaying.

According to their relatives and neighbors, the Lim family could solve all their troubles by simply dividing their property and becoming separate independent family units. The large, extended family living together under one roof and contributing their incomes to a common purse is accepted by all Taiwanese as an ideal toward which every family should strive, but few have been able to maintain this form of family for any period of time. The fact that the Lims have done so makes them uneasy and watchful. Lim A-pou, with her devotion to the old traditions, has until recently been quite proud of this further accomplishment of her family, but as my stay in the village lengthened, it was obvious that she now wished a division of the family, no matter what it cost her principles and pride. Her growing dissatisfaction with Lim Chieng-cua's management of the family is not entirely emotional. She remembers poverty more vividly than the younger members of the family and in her mind it is intimately connected with tenant farming. Land, for her, is the only stable unit in an economy that changes as often and as disastrously as Taiwan's. When she sees income from the land going to pay factory workers, she imagines a day when pieces of land may be sold to enlarge the factory or pay its debts. Recent years seem less prosperous than past years. Better that the property be divided now, while it is still in the form of land, than later, when it may be an intangible piece of the factory. Lim A-pou does not understand nor trust the world in which her foster brother operates.

In her quiet campaign for division A-pou first made sure that she had the sympathy of her neighbors, for the opinions of neighbors have no small influence on arbiters in the settlement of family differences. Then, she began to urge her eldest son to be less compliant in his dealings with his uncle.

How successful she is in exacerbating the tensions already existing between uncle and nephew can be seen in a quarrel I had no choice but to witness. Lim A-bok walked into the dining room, grumbling to himself as he read a letter. "This man! He should be embarrassed to write a letter begging me for cucumbers. If he scorns people so much, why should I pay any attention to him."

Lim Chieng-cua looked up and asked, "What letter is that? Who is it from?" A-bok handed him the letter which he quickly read. "What's wrong with this? What's the matter?"

Lim A-pou came in carrying some buckets and said, "We never let him feed us three meals. How can he do this?"

Lim Chieng-cua, looking confused and a little irritated since the letter was from one of his business associates, demanded, "What do you mean you never let him feed you three meals? Why do you say that? What's the trouble?"

Lim A-pou shrugged and said, "I don't know anything about it. Ask my son."

Lim Chieng-cua gave his nephew a questioning look. A-bok answered it unwillingly. "The last time I went to Lungyen to a festival [to represent the family] I missed the last bus. Even though I was in his house, he didn't say a word, so I had to walk all the way home [a distance of several miles]."

Lim Chieng-cua, impatient and rather disgusted, answered, "Is that all? Did it ever occur to you how he felt at that time? His house was full of guests and his mind full of obligations. Why didn't you just explain the problem to him? I'm sure he would have asked you to spend the night."

A-bok snorted, "Huh! Explain! He is so suspicious of people that he thought I'd steal all his possessions if I stayed there one night. Have I ever neglected to treat him well when he comes here? This kind of person we can ignore."

Lim Chieng-cua, clearly trying to be patient, explained, "Now how can you ignore him? It is in these little things that you make errors. I am the one that has to be in contact with him all the time and do business with him. You have to think of my relations, too. I am the one that bears our family's responsibility to him. The cucumbers are unimportant things. Obviously, he has the money to buy them anywhere. The letter is just a joke and a way of complimenting us on the quality of our cucumbers. He is not so poor that he has to write a letter begging cucumbers from us."

A-bok said nothing more, but as he followed his mother out of the room, his face was sullen and unconvinced.

That evening when we were sitting in the kitchen, the subject of the letter came up again. Lim Chieng-cua said, "Look at it this way. You have given people presents and people sometimes give you presents, too."

Lim A-pou, immediately on the defensive, interrupted him. "We only gave Ong A-giok cucumbers because she often helps us in the fields. We never gave them to anyone else."

Lim Chieng-cua answered patiently, "I'm not suggesting that you shouldn't give things to people. You can give things to your friends, and I can give things to mine. Didn't this man ever give things to us? He nearly always brings us a big bag of taste powder when he comes. I didn't ever hear him say it was only for me, did you? A person who wants to run a business outside can't be like this.

"Think about it this way for a minute. Suppose this person really had been very bad to you. And now here he is asking you for something, not you asking him. It is he who would be bringing shame on himself by asking, not on you. You can bring shame on yourself only by not giving it to him.

"You say he would not invite you to stay in his house for one night, but did you explain to him what the situation amounted to? No, you just said you had missed your bus. How was he to know it was the last bus or that there was no late train? He is my friend. If your friend came and asked for something and I wouldn't let you give it to him, how would you feel?"

A-bok had had all the lecturing on proper behavior that he could take for one evening, and he said rather loudly, "All right. All right. Don't just stand there and oppress me about it all night."

This bit of disrespect caused Lim Chieng-cua to drop the tight rein he had been holding on his infamous temper. He yelled at A-bok, "you accuse me of oppressing you! You are the one who is doing the oppressing. Haven't I explained anything to you?"

Evidently the expression on A-bok's face (which I couldn't see) angered Lim Chieng-cua even more, and he moved as if to strike him. A-bok jumped up and ran out of the room. A good friend of the family who had been sitting with us immediately pulled on Lim Chieng-cua's arm and began talking to him in a soothing manner. "All right. All right. This is just a little thing. There is no good in it for anyone in quarreling over it."

Lim Chieng-cua calmed down a little and the friend continued to talk to him softly and unemotionally—a trick this man has that makes him much called upon in the village to settle family disputes. "Don't argue with the boy anymore. He is young yet and still doesn't understand the 'affairs of the World.' You are of an older generation and must not lose dignity by arguing with him. If he cannot understand, just forget it for now."

After a bit, the friend in his role as peace-maker went in to talk to Lim A-bok and his mother. A-pou was scolding her son. "If he wants to hit you, just let him hit you. Why do you run? Let the others see how he treats us."

The friend cut her off and began to speak to A-bok as if his mother were not in the room. "Oh, cucumbers, Cucumbers are nothing special. You grow them yourself. It won't cost you any money. Just give them to him. Why argue over these unimportant matters?"

Lim A-pou muttered angrily, "My son is afraid of Chieng-cua just like a shrimp. Even if he doesn't want to give them away, he will have to."

I asked Lim A-pou later if she thought Lim Chieng-cua would really have struck her son. She scowled and said, "Why not? Last August he hit him." When I probed for more details, she said, "uh! That wife's slave!" and ended the conversation with her usual response of "I don't know anything about it."

A relative of the family did know something about it and was happy to discuss a topic of seemingly endless village interest. Lim Chieng-cua bought a fancy radio for the family. A-bok came in one afternoon to find it blaring loudly for the pleasure of Le-cu, Lim Chieng-cua's twelve-year-old daughter. Besides telling her it was far too loud, A-bok also pointed out that the broadcast was in Mandarin, a language with which none of them are too familiar, and that she should not listen to Mandarin broadcasts for fear that she pick up something from a mainland station and get them in serious political trouble. Le-cu felt saucy and told him it was none of his business because her father had bought the radio. This made A-bok angry and he said some things about Le-cu's mother and maternal ancestors (i.e., cursed in the familiar fashion.) Lim Chui-ieng overheard this, as she does nearly everything, and reported it to her husband. Lim Chieng-cua did not bring the matter up with his nephew until the family confidante and arbiter was present. He explained the exchange to him, in A-bok's presence, asking for a statement as to whose behavior had been remiss. One thing led to another, and A-bok got a sharp clip on the head. The friend told me sadly, "From the time he was a child, Lim Chieng-cua has been very fond of A-bok. The only reason they don't get along anymore is the women between them. A woman's heart is always narrower."

Although the quarrel over the cucumbers seems ridiculous and seemed to flare with little provocation, when viewed in a fuller context, it shows some of the finer qualities of both men. Lim Chieng-cua, though he might have suffered from A-pou's ill humor, would have been well within his rights as head of the family to simply order the cucumbers sent to his friend and business associate. Instead, he chose to reason with his nephew about the situation and to educate him in some of the subtle details of social relations, a subject the Chinese classify with their other art forms. He failed because of his own temper and because he was not aware of the real reason for A-bok's anger with the man. A-bok's younger brother, Masa, who is frantic to get out of the village and into a white-collar job, was sent to work in this man's pharmacy, a business concern in which the Lim family has invested a small amount of money. Masa often slept in the shop and one night, after obtaining the permission of the owner, three of his friends spent the night there with him. Sometime during that twenty-four hour period, a small sum of money was stolen from the shop. None of the boys were out of Masa's sight during their stay, and he knew them well enough to vouch for their complete honesty. The owner accepted his statement, but commented tactlessly, "When no one is here to guard, I don't lose money, but when I have four guards, the money disappears." This made Masa furious. He went out, borrowed the small sum that was missing, and presented it to the man who was graceless enough to accept it, still however agreeing to Masa's innocence in the matter. A-bok has never forgiven the man for this insult, but he cannot explain his anger to his uncle because relations between Lim Chieng-cua and his youngest nephew, Masa, are good only when they are out of each other's sight.

■ MARRIAGE AS A WRETCHED INSTITUTION

Mervyn Cadwallader

Our society expects us all to get married. With only rare exceptions we all do just that. Getting married is a rather complicated business. It involves mastering certain complex hustling and courtship games, the rituals and the ceremonies that celebrate the act of marriage, and finally the difficult requirements of domestic life with a husband or wife. It is an enormously elaborate round of activity, much more so than finding a job, and yet while many resolutely remain unemployed few remain unmarried.

Now all this would be particularly remarkable if there were no question about the advantages, the joys, and the rewards of married life, but most Americans, even young Americans, know or have heard that marriage is a hazardous affair. Of course, for all the increase in divorce, there are still young marriages that work, unions made by young men and women intelligent or fortunate enough to find the kind of mates they want, who know that they want children and how to love them when they come, or who find the artful blend between giving and receiving. It is not these marriages that concern us here, and that is not the trend in America today. We are concerned with the increasing number of others who, with mixed intentions and varied illusions, grope or fling themselves into marital disaster. They talk solemnly and sincerely about working to make their marriage succeed, but they are very aware of the countless marriages they have seen fail. But young people in particular do not seem to be able to relate the awesome divorce statistics to the probability of failure of their own marrige. And they rush into it, in increasing numbers, without any clear idea of the reality that underlies the myth.

Parents, teachers, and concerned adults all counsel against premature marrige. But they rarely speak the truth about marriage as it really is in modern middle-class America. The truth as I see it is that contemporary marriage is a wretched institution. It spells the end of voluntary affection, of love freely given and joyously received. Beautiful romances are transmuted into dull marriages, and eventually the relationship becomes constricting, corrosive, grinding, and destructive. The beautiful love affair becomes a bitter contract.

The basic reason for this sad state of affairs is that marriage was not designed to bear the burdens now being asked of it by the urban American middle class. It is an institution that evolved over centuries to meet some very specific functional needs of a nonindustrial society. Romantic love was viewed as tragic, or merely irrelevant. Today it is the titillating prelude to domestic tragedy, or, perhaps more frequently, to domestic grotesqueries that are only pathetic.

Marriage was not designed as a mechanism for providing friendship, erotic experience, romantic love, personal fulfillment, continuous lay psychotherapy, or recreation. The Western European family was not designed to carry a lifelong load of highly emotional romantic freight. Given its present structure, it simply has to fail when asked to do so. The very idea of an irrevocable contract obligating the parties concerned to a lifetime of romantic effort is utterly absurd.

Other pressures of the present era have tended to overburden marriage with expectations it cannot fulfill. Industrialized, urbanized America is a society which has lost the sense of community. Our ties to our society, to the bustling multitudes that make up this dazzling kaleidoscope of contemporary America, are as formal and superficial as they are numerous. We all search for community, and yet we know that the search is futile. Cut off from the support and satisfactions that flow from community, the confused and searching young American can do little but place all of his bets on creating a community in microcosm, his own marriage.

And so the ideal we struggle to reach in our love relationship is that of complete candor, total honesty. Out there all is phony, but within the romantic family there are to be no dishonest games, no hypocrisy, no misunderstanding. Here we have a painful paradox, for I submit that total exposure is probably always mutually destructive in the long run. What starts out as a tender coming together to share one's whole person with the beloved is transmuted by too much togetherness into attack and counterattack, doubt, disillusionment, and ambivalence. The moment the once-upon-a-time lover catches a glimpse of his own hatred, something precious and fragile is shattered. And soon another brave marriage will end.

The purposes of marriage have changed radically, yet we cling desperately to the outmoded structures of the past. Adult Americans behave as though the more obvious the contradiction between the old and the new, the more sentimental and irrational should be their advice to young people who are going steady or are engaged. Our schools, both high schools and colleges, teach sentimental rubbish in their marriage and family courses. The texts make much of a posture of hard-nosed objectivity that is neither objective nor hard-nosed. The basic structure of Western marriage is never questioned, alternatives are not proposed or discussed. Instead, the prospective young bride and bridegroom are offered housekeeping advice and told to work hard at making their marriage succeed. The chapter on sex, complete with ugly diagrams of the male and female genitals, is probably wedged in between a chapter on budgets and life insurance. The message is that if your marriage fails, you have been weighed in the domestic balance and found wanting. Perhaps you did not master the fifth position for sexual intercourse, or maybe you bought cheap term life rather than a preferred policy with income protection and retirement benefits. If taught honestly, these courses would alert the teen-ager and young adult to the realities of matrimonial life in the United States and try to advise them on how to survive marriage if they insist on that hazardous venture.

But teen-agers and young adults do insist upon it in greater and greater numbers with each passing year. And one of the reasons they do get married with such astonishing certainty is because they find themselves immersed in a culture that is preoccupied with and schizophrenic about sex. Advertising, entertainment, and fashion are all designed to produce and then to exploit sexual tension. Sexually aroused at an early age and asked to postpone marriage until they become adults, they have no recourse but to fill the intervening years with courtship rituals and games that are supposed to be sexy but sexless. Dating is expected to culminate in going steady, and that is the beginning of the end. The dating game hinges on an important exchange. The male wants sexual intimacy, and the female wants social commitment. The game involves bartering sex for security amid the sweet and heady agitations of a romantic entanglement. Once the game reaches the going-steady stage, marriage is virtually inevitable. The teen-ager finds himself driven into a corner, and the one way to legitimize his sex play and assuage the guilt is to plan marriage.

Another reason for the upsurge in young marriages is the real cultural break between teen-agers and adults in our society. This is a recent phenomenon. In my generation there was no teen culture. Adolescents wanted to become adults as soon as possible. The teen-age years were a time of impatient waiting, as teen-age boys tried to dress and act like little men. Adolescents sang the adults' songs ("South of the Border," "The Music Goes Round and Round," "Mairzy Doats"—notice I didn't say anything about the quality of the music), saw their movies, listened to their radios, and waited confidently to be allowed in. We had no money, and so there was no teen-age market. There was nothing to do then but get it over with. The boundary line was sharp, and you crossed it when you took your first serious job, when you passed the employment test.

Now there is a very definite adolescent culture, which is in many ways hostile to the dreary culture of the adult world. In its most extreme form it borrows from the beats and turns the middle-class value system inside out. The hip teen-ager on Macdougal Street or Telegraph Avenue can buy a costume and go to a freak show. It's fun to be an Indian, a prankster, a beat, or a swinging troubadour. He can get stoned. That particular trip leads to instant mysticism.

Even in less extreme forms, teen culture is weighted against the adult world of responsibility. I recently asked a roomful of eighteen-year-olds to tell me what an adult is. Their deliberate answer, after hours of discussion, was that an adult is someone who no longer plays, who is no longer playful. Is Bob Dylan an adult? No, never! Of course they did not want to remain children, or teens, or adolescents; but they did want to remain youthful, playful, free of squares, and free of responsibility. The teen-ager wants to be old enough to drive, drink, screw, and travel. He does not want to get pushed into square maturity. He wants to drag the main, be a surf bum, a ski bum, or dream of being a bum. He doesn't want to go to Vietnam, or to IBM, or to buy a split-level house in Knotty Pines Estates.

This swing away from responsibility quite predictably produces frictions between the adolescent and his parents. The clash of cultures is likely to drive the adolescent from the home, to persuade him to leave the dead world of his parents and strike out on his own. And here we find the central paradox of young marriages. For the only way the young person can escape from his parents is to assume many of the responsibilities that he so reviles in the life-style of his parents. He needs a job and an apartment. And he needs some kind of emotional substitute, some means of filling the emotional vacuum that leaving home has caused. And so he goes steady, and sooner rather than later, gets married to a girl with similar inclinations.

When he does this, he crosses the dividing line between the cultures.

Though he seldom realizes it at the time, he has taken the first step to adulthood. Our society does not have a conventional "rite of passage." In Africa the Masai adolescent takes a lion test. He becomes an adult the first time he kills a lion with a spear. Our adolescents take the domesticity test. When they get married they have to come to terms with the system in one way or another. Some brave individuals continue to fight it. But most simply capitulate.

The cool adolescent finishing high school or starting college has a skeptical view of virtually every institutional sector of his society. He knows that government is corrupt, the military dehumanizing, the corporations rapacious, the churches organized hypocrisy, and the schools dishonest. But the one area that seems to be exempt from his cynicism is romantic love and marriage. When I talk to teen-agers about marriage, that cool skepticism turns to sentimental dreams right out of *Ladies' Home Journal* or the hard-hitting pages of *Reader's Digest*. They all mouth the same vapid platitudes about finding happiness through sharing and personal fulfillment through giving (each is to give 51 percent). They have all heard about divorce, and most of them have been touched by it in some way or another. Yet they insist that their marriage will be different.

So, clutching their illusions, young girls with ecstatic screams of joy lead their awkward brooding boys through the portals of the church into the land of the Mustang, Apartment 24, Macy's, Sears, and the ubiquitous drive-in. They have become members in good standing of the adult world.

The end of most of these sentimental marriages is quite predictable. They progress, in most cases, to varying stages of marital ennui, depending on the ability of the couple to adjust to reality; most common are (1) a lackluster standoff, (2) a bitter business carried on for the children, church, or neighbors, or (3) separation and divorce, followed by another search to find the right person.

Divorce rates have been rising in all Western countries. In many countries the rates are rising even faster than in the United States. In 1910 the divorce rate for the United States was 87 per 1000 marriages. In 1965 the rate had risen to an estimated figure of well over 300 per 1000 in many parts of the country. At the present time some 40 percent of all brides are between the ages of fifteen and eighteen; half of these marriages break up within five years. As our population becomes younger and the age of marriage continues to drop, the divorce rate will rise to significantly higher levels.

What do we do, what can we do, about this wretched and disappointing institution? In terms of the immediate generation, the answer probably is, not much. Even when subjected to the enormous strains I have described, the habits, customs, traditions, and taboos that make up our courtship and marriage cycle are uncommonly resistant to change. Here and there creative and courageous individuals can and do work out their own unique solutions to the problem of marriage. Most of us simply suffer without understanding and thrash around blindly in an attempt to reduce the acute pain of a romance gone sour. In time, all of these individual actions will show up as a trend away from the old and toward the new, and the bulk of sluggish moderates in the population will slowly come to accept this trend as part of social evolution. Clearly, in middle-class America, the trend is ever toward more romantic courtship and marriage, earlier premarital sexual intercourse, earlier first marriages, more extamarital affairs, earlier first divorces, more frequent divorces and remarriages. The trend is away from stable lifelong monogamous relationships toward some form of polygamous malefemale relationship. Perhaps we should identify it as serial or consecutive polygamy, simply because Americans in significant numbers are going to have more than one husband or more than one wife. Attitudes and laws that make multiple marriages (in sequence, of course) difficult for the romantic and sentimental among us are archaic obstacles that one learns to circumvent with the aid of weary judges and clever attorneys.

Now, the absurdity of much of this lies in the fact that we pretend that marriages of short duration must be contracted for life. Why not permit a flexible contract perhaps for one to two or more years, with periodic options to renew? If a couple grew disenchanted with their life together, they would not feel trapped for life. They would not have to anticipate and then go through the destructive agonies of divorce. They would not have to carry about the stigma of marital failure, like the mark of Cain on their foreheads. Instead of a declaration of war, they could simply let their contract lapse, and while still friendly, be free to continue their romantic quest. Sexualized romanticism is now so fundamental to American life—and is bound to become even more so—that marriage will simply have to accommodate itself to it in one way or another. For a great proportion of us it already has.

What of the children in a society that is moving inexorably toward consecutive plural marriages? Under present arrangements in which marriages are ostensibly lifetime contracts and then are dissolved through hypocritical collusions or messy battles in court, the children do suffer. Marriage and divorce turn lovers into enemies, and the child is left to thread his way through the emotional wreckage of his parents' lives. Financial support of the children, mere subsistence, is not really a problem in a society as affluent as ours. Enduring emotional support of children by loving, healthy, and friendly adults is a serious problem in America, and it is a desperately urgent problem in many families where divorce is unthinkable. If the bitter and poisonous denouement of divorce could be avoided by a frank acceptance of short-term marriages, both adults and children would benefit. Any time husbands and wives and ex-husbands and ex-wives treat each other decently, generously, and respectfully, their children will benefit.

The braver and more critical among our teen-agers and youthful adults will still ask, But if the institution is so bad, why get married at all? This is a tough one to deal with. The social pressures pushing any couple who live together into marriage are difficult to ignore even by the most resolute rebel. It can be done, and many should be encouraged to carry out their own creative experiments in living together in a relationship that is wholly voluntary. If the demands of society to conform seem overwhelming, the couple should know that simply to be defined by others as married will elicit married-like behavior in themselves, and that is precisely what they want to avoid.

How do you marry and yet live like gentle lovers, or at least like friendly roommates? Quite frankly, I do not know the answer to that question.

■ SEX ANTAGONISM IN GUSII SOCIETY

Robert A. LeVine

The Gusii are a Bantu-speaking people practicing agriculture and animal husbandry in the Kenya highlands just east of Lake Victoria. They are strongly patrilineal and have a segmentary lineage system with a high degree of congruence between lineages and territorial groups. Before the onset of British administration in 1907, clans were the most significant political units and carried on blood feuds. Each of the seven Gusii tribes consisted of one or more large, dominant clans and a number of smaller clans and clan fragments. Clans of the same tribe united for war efforts against other tribes, but feuded among themselves at other times.

Each clan, although an independent military and territorial unit, was exogamous and patrilocal, so that wives had to be imported from clans against which feuds had been conducted. The Gusii recognize this in their proverb, "Those whom we marry are those whom we fight." Marriages did not mitigate the hostilities between clans on a permanent basis; in fact, women were used by their husbands' clans to aid in military operations against their natal clans. A captive from an enemy clan might be tortured in a pillory-like device while a married woman originally from his clan would be sent to relate tearfully to her kinsmen, "Our brother is being killed!" and to urge them to save his life by a ransom in cattle. Marriage among the Gusii was thus a relationship between hostile groups and it continues to be nowadays although blood feuds are prohibited. Clan territories in some areas have been broken up into discontinuous fragments, but local communities are homogeneous with respect to clan membership. Social relations between adjacent communities of different clans are minimal, whereas neighboring communities of the same clan have a considerable common social life. Marriages are still contracted with the aid of an intermediary (*esigani*) between members of alien and unfriendly groups.

The clearest expression of the interclan hostility involved in marriage can be found in the *enyangi* ceremonial. Enyangi is the final ceremony in a Gusii marriage and can be performed either shortly after the start of cohabitation or any number of years later, even after the children have grown up. During the ceremony, iron rings (*ebitinge*) are attached to the wife's ankles and are never removed until the death of her husband or her wilful desertion of him. The practice of enyangi is rapidly disappearing in many areas of Gusiiland, partly because of its expense and partly because many girls become nominal Christians to escape the indignities described below. However, the attitudes and emotions expressed in the traditional rite persist in the contemporary situation. Mayer, who witnessed the ceremony on several occasions, has described its setting as follows:

> *Enyangi* opens with formal contests between the two groups of affines—a wrestling match for the men and a dancing competition for the women. Afterwards, a strictly obligatory seating arrangement separates bride's from groom's people, who must face each other across the space occupied by the sacred beer pots—the groom's party under the surveillance of the "watcher" whose special task is to avert quarrels.[1]

On the following day the groom in his finery returns to the bride's family where he is stopped by a crowd of women who deprecate his physical appearance. Once he is in the house of the bride's mother and a sacrifice has been performed by the marriage priest, the women begin again, accusing the groom of impotence on the wedding night and claiming that his penis is too small to be effective. He attempts to refute their insults. The next day bride and groom go to the latter's home. The groom enters the door of his mother's house but when the bride attempts to follow she is met by a bellicose crowd of women who keep her at the door for a long time. They scream insults at her, mock her, pinch her, sometimes even smear dung on her lips. Throughout it all she must remain silent. Some brides have been kept at the door for so many hours that they have given up and returned home. Usually, however, the bride is allowed in and treated with kindness thereafter. Other examples of hostile interaction between affines at enyangi could be given, but Mayer has described them in great detail.

The enyangi ceremony allows the expression of hostility which inlaws must never give vent to under ordinary circumstances and is indicative of the interclan tensions which are involved in every Gusii marriage. Inevitably, it is the bride who experiences this tension in its most acute form. She must move from her childhood home into the enemy camp; she must sever allegiance to her native group and develop loyalty

[1] Philip Mayer, "Privileged Obstruction of Marriage Rites Among Gusii," *Africa*, 20 (1950), p. 123.

to an opposing group. It is not surprising, then, that girls are ambivalent toward marriage. On the one hand, they yearn for it because women can only achieve security and prestige in Gusii society through legitimate motherhood and especially through bearing numerous sons. On the other hand, they have heard the folk tale in which the innocent bride discovers her parents-in-law to be cannibalistic ogres, and other similar tales; they all know of girls who have returned to their parents claiming that their in-laws were witches who tried to lure them into witchcraft. They are thus as frightened by the prospect of marriage as they are attracted to it.

The fears of the bride are institutionalized in her traditional resistance to being taken to the home of the groom. Among the adjacent Luo and other East African tribes, it is customary for kinsmen of the bride to fight with kinsmen of the groom and attempt to prevent her departure. With the Gusii, however, it is the bride herself who resists, or who hides herself in a nearby house, and her father, having received the bridewealth cattle by this time, may even help persuade her to go if her reluctance appears to be sincere. Five young clansmen of the groom come to take the bride; two immediately find the girl and post themselves at her side to prevent her escape, while the others receive the final permission of her parents. When it has been granted, the bride holds onto the house posts and must be dragged outside. Finally she goes, crying and with her hands on her head. Her resistance is token and not really intended to break off the marriage, but it expresses the real fears of every Gusii bride.

When the reluctant bride arrives at the groom's house, the matter of first importance is the wedding night sexual performance. This is a trial for both parties, in that the impotence of the groom may cause the bride to break off the marriage, and the discovery of scars or deformities on the bride's body (including vaginal obstruction) may induce the groom to send her home and request a return of the bridewealth. The bride is determined to put her new husband's sexual competence to the most severe test possible. She may take magical measures which are believed to result in his failure in intercourse. These include chewing a piece of charcoal or a phallic pod commonly found in pastures, putting either of these or a knotted piece of grass under the marriage bed, and twisting the phallic flower of the banana tree. The groom is determined to be successful in the face of her expected resistance; he fortifies himself by being well fed, which is believed to favor potency, by eating bitter herbs, and nowadays by eating large quantities of coffee beans, valued as an aphrodisiac. His brothers and paternal male cousins give him encouragement and take a great interest in his prospects for success. Numerous young clansmen of the groom gather at the homestead in a festive mood; chickens are killed for them to eat and they entertain themselves by singing and dancing while waiting for the major events of the wedding night.

The bride usually refuses to get onto the bed; if she did not resist the groom's advances she would be thought sexually promiscuous. At this point some of the young men may forcibly disrobe her and put her on the bed. The groom examines the bride's mouth for pods or other magical devices designed to render him impotent. As he proceeds toward sexual intercourse she continues to resist and he must force her into position. Ordinarily she performs the practice known as *ogolega*, allowing him between her thighs but keeping the vaginal muscles so tense that penetration is impossible. If the groom is young (by traditional standards, under 25), the young men intervene, reprimand the bride, and hold her in position so that penetration can be achieved on the first night. An older groom, however, is considered strong enough to take care of himself, and the young men wait outside the door of the house, looking in occasionally to check on his progress. It is said that in such cases a "fierce" girl in the old days could prevent the groom from achieving full penetration as long as a week. Brides are said to take pride in the length of time they can hold off their mates. In 1957, a girl succeeded in resisting the initial attempts of her bridegroom. His brothers threatened and manhandled her until she confessed to having knotted her pubic hair across the vaginal orifice. They cut the knot with a razor blade and stayed to watch the first performance of marital coitus by the light of a kerosene pressure lamp.

Once penetration has been achieved, the young men sing in jubilation and retire from the house to allow the groom to complete the nuptial sexual relations. They are keenly interested in how many times he will be able to perform coitus on the first night, as this is a matter of prestige and invidious comparison. He will be asked about it by all male relatives of his generation, and the bride will also be questioned on this score when she returns to visit her own family. It is said that the groom's clansmen also question the bride, in order to check on the groom's account of his attainment. Six is considered a minimally respectable number of times and twelve is the maximum of which informants had heard. They claimed that it was traditional to achieve orgasm twelve times but that performances were lower in recent years.

The explicit object of such prodigious feats is to hurt the bride. When a bride is unable to walk on the day following the wedding night, the young men consider the groom "a real man" and he is able to boast of his exploits, particularly the fact that he made her cry. One informant quoted some relevant conversation from the *enyangi* ceremony which is performed at a later time. At the bride's home the insulting women say to the groom:

> You are not strong, you can't do anything to our daughter. When you slept with her you didn't do it like a man. You have a small penis which can do nothing. You should grab our daughter and she should be hurt and scream —then you're a man.

He answers boastfully:

> I am a man! If you were to see my penis you would run away. When I grabbed her she screamed. I am not a man to be joked with. Didn't she tell you? She cried—ask her!

The conception of coitus as an act in which a man overcomes the resistance of a woman and causes her pain is not limited to the wedding night; it continues to be important in marital relations. Wives in monogamous homesteads never initiate sexual intercourse with their husbands, and they customarily make a token objection before yielding to the husbands' advances. The wife does not take an active role in the foreplay or coitus and will not remove her clothes herself if she has not already done so for sleeping. Most importantly, it is universally reported that wives cry during coitus, moaning quietly, "You're hurting me, you bad man" and other such admonitions. Gusii men find this practice sexually arousing. The following statement by a 36-year-old husband epitomizes the attitude of the Gusii male toward his wife's sexuality.

> During coitus the husband asks her, "What do you feel? Don't you think it's good?" The wife says, "Don't ask me that." She will never say yes. When the woman cries and protests during intercourse you are very excited . . . . We are always mystified as to whether women enjoy it. But the wives in polygynous homesteads complain when their husbands neglect them, so they must like it.

There is good reason to believe that the reluctant sexual pose of Gusii wives is not feigned in all cases. Young husbands claim to desire coitus at least twice a night, once early and once toward dawn. In a number of monogamous marriages, however, this rate is not achieved, primarily due to the stubborn resistance of wives. Every community contains some married women with reputations for refusing to have intercourse with their husbands for up to a week at a time. Such husbands are eventually moved to beat their wives and even send them back to their parents. I knew of one case of this kind in which the wife's distaste for coitus was the only major source of conflict between husband and wife. Among monogamous wives who do not have anti-sexual reputations, refusal to have intercourse with their husbands usually occurs when they have quarreled over something else. Since family modesty prescribes the performance of intercourse in the dark after the children have fallen asleep, wives enforce their refusal by pinching a child awake if the husband is insistent. Such evidence suggests that for some Gusii wives the resistant and pained behavior in marital intercourse does not represent a conventional pose or an attempt to arouse their husbands but a sincere desire to avoid coitus.

On the basis of the Gusii case alone, it is difficult to arrive at a satisfactory solution to the problem of whether the sado-masochistic aspect of Gusii nuptial and marital sexuality is inexorably connected with, and a reflection of, the antagonism of intermarrying clans. Many of the above facts point to such a connection, but it is noteworthy that there is at least one culturally patterned form of expressing heterosexual antagonism within the clan. This is the practice of "arousing desire" (*ogosonia*) which Mayer has described in some detail. When Gusii boys undergoing initiation are recuperating from their circumcision operation, adolescent girls of the same clan come to the seclusion huts, disrobe, dance around the novices in provocative attitudes, challenge them to have intercourse, and make disparaging remarks about the genitals of the boys. The latter are of course incapable of coitus, and the girls are well aware of this. According to Mayer, "Most Gusii think that the purpose of *ogosonia* is to cause pain. The girls have their triumph if a resulting erection causes the partly-healed wound to burst open, with acute pain to the novice." Here, then, is the use of sexuality to inflict pain occurring between girls and boys of the same exogamous clan. It could be argued that the adolescent girls have already developed the attitudes appropriate to the wedding night and apply them to the nearest males whom they know to be in a uniquely vulnerable sexual condition. In any event, the practice of ogosonia indicates that the antagonism of Gusii females toward male sexuality and their view of sexual intercourse in aggressive terms are components of a general pattern of behavior not limited to the marital relationship.

■ THE FUNERAL TRANSACTION

Jessica Mitford

A funeral is not an occasion for a display of cheapness. It is, in fact, an opportunity for the display of a status symbol which, by bolstering family pride, does much to assuage grief. A funeral is also an occasion when feelings of guilt and remorse are satisfied to a large extent by the purchase of a fine funeral. It seems highly probable that the most satisfactory funeral service for the average family is one in which the cost has necessitated some degree of sacrifice. This permits the survivors to atone for any real or fancied neglect of the deceased prior to his death. . . .

—*National Funeral Service Journal*
August 1961

The seller of funeral service has, one gathers, a preconceived, stereotyped view of his customers. To him, the bereaved person who enters his establishment is a bundle of guilt feelings, a snob and a status seeker. The funeral director feels that by steering his customer to the higher-priced caskets, he is giving him his first dose of grief therapy. In the words of the *National Funeral Service Journal*: "The focus of the buyer's interest must be the casket, vault, clothing, funeral cars, etc.—the only tangible evidence of how much has been invested in the funeral— the only real status symbol associated with a funeral service."

Whether or not one agrees with this rather unflattering appraisal of the average person who has suffered a death in the family, it is never-theless true that the funeral transaction is generally influenced by a combination of circumstances which bear upon the buyer as in no other type of business dealing: the disorientation caused by bereavement, the lack of standards by which to judge the value of the commodity offered by the seller, the need to make an on-the-spot decision, general igno-rance of the law as it affects disposal of the dead, the ready availability of insurance money to finance the transaction. These factors predeter-mine to a large extent the outcome of the transaction.

The funeral seller, like any other merchant, is preoccupied with price, profit, selling techniques. As Mr. Leon S. Utter, dean of the San Fran-cisco College of Mortuary Science, writes in *Mortuary Management's Idea Kit:* "Your selling plan should go into operation as soon as the telephone rings and you are requested to serve a bereaved family . . . . Never preconceive as to what any family will purchase. You cannot possibly measure the intensity of their emotions, undisclosed insurance or funds that may have been set aside for funeral expenses."

The selling plan should be subtle rather than high-pressure, for the obvious "hard sell" is considered inappropriate and self-defeating by modern industry leaders. Two examples of what *not* to say to a customer are given in the *Successful Mortuary Operation & Service Manual:* "I can tell by the fine suit you're wearing, that you appreciate the finer things, and will want a fine casket for your Mother," and "Think of the beautiful memory picture you will have of your dear Father in this beautiful casket."

At the same time nothing else must be left to chance. The trade con-siders that the most important element of funeral salesmanship is the proper arrangement of caskets in the Selection Room (where the cus-tomer is taken to make his purchase). The sales talk, while preferably dignified and restrained, must be designed to take maximum advantage of this arrangement.

The uninitiated, entering a casket selection room for the first time, may think he is looking at a random grouping of variously priced mer-chandise. Actually, endless thought and care are lavished on the develop-ment of new and better selection room arrangements, for it has been found that the placing of the caskets materially affects the amount of the sale. There are available to the trade a number of texts devoted to the subject, supplemented by frequent symposiums, seminars, study courses, visual aids, scale model selection rooms complete with miniature caskets that can be moved around experimentally. All stress the desired goal: selling consistently in a "bracket that is above average."

The relationship between casket arrangement and sales psychology is discussed quite fully by Mr. W. M. Krieger, managing director of the influential National Selected Morticians Association, in his book *Suc-cessful Funeral Management.* He analyzes the blunder of placing the caskets in order of price, from the cheapest to most expensive, which he calls the "stairstep method" of arrangement. As he points out, this plan "makes direct dollar comparisons very easy." Or, if the caskets are so arranged that the most expensive are the first ones the buyer sees, he may be shocked into buying a very cheap one. A mistake to be avoided is an unbalanced line with too many caskets in a low price range: "The unbalanced line with its heavy concentration of units under $300 made it very easy for the client to buy in this area with complete satisfaction."

In developing his method of display, Mr. Krieger divides the stock of caskets for convenience into four "quartiles," two above and two below the median price, which in his example is $400. The objective is to sell in the third, or just above median, quartile. To this end the purchaser is first led to a unit in this third quartile—about $125 to $150 *above* the median sale, in the range of $525 to $550. Should the buyer balk at this price, he should next be led to a unit providing "strong contrast, both in price and quality," this time something below the median, say in the $375 to $395 range. The psychological reasons for this are explained. They are twofold. While the difference in quality is demonstrable, the price is not *so* low as to make the buyer feel belittled. At the same time, if the buyer turns his nose up and indicates that he didn't want to go *that* low, now is the time to show him the "rebound unit"—one priced from $5 to $25 *above* the median, in the $405 to $425 bracket.

Mr. Krieger calls all this the "Keystone Approach," and supplies a diagram showing units 1, 2, and 3, scattered with apparent artless abandon about the floor. The customer, who has been bounced from third to second quartile and back again on the rebound to the third, might think the "Human Tennis Ball Approach" a more appropriate term.

Should the prospect show no reaction either way on seeing the first unit—or should he ask to see something better—the rebound gambit is, of course, "out." "In" is the Avenue of Approach. It seems that a Canadian Royal Mountie once told Mr. Krieger that people who get lost in the wilds always turn in a great circle to their right. Probably, surmises Mr. Krieger, because 85 percent of us are right-handed? In any event, the Avenue of Approach is a main, wide aisle leading to the right in the selection room. Here are the better-quality third- and fourth-quartile caskets.

For that underprivileged, or stubborn, member of society who insists on purchasing below the median (but who should nevertheless be served "graciously and with just as much courtesy and attention as you would give to the buyer without a limit on what he can spend") there is a narrow aisle leading to the *left*, which Mr. Krieger calls "Resistance Lane." There is unfortunately no discussion of two possible hazards: what if an extremely affluent prospect should prove to be among the 15 per cent of *left*-handed persons, and should therefore turn automatically into Resistance Lane? How to extricate him? Conversely, if one of the poor or stubborn, possibly having at some time in his past been lost in Canada, should instinctively turn to the broad, right-hand Avenue of Approach?

The Comprehensive Sales Program offered by Successful Mortuary Operation to its particapating members is designed along the same lines as Mr. Krieger's plan, only it is even more complicated. Everything is, however, most carefully spelled out, beginning with the injunction to greet the clients with a warm and friendly handshake, and a suggested opening statement, which should be "spoken slowly and with real sincerity: 'I want to assure you that I'm going to do everything I can to be helpful to you!' "

Having made this good beginning, the funeral director is to proceed with the Arrangement Conference, at each stage of which he should "weave in the service story"—in other words, impress upon the family that they will be entitled to all sorts of extras, such as ushers, cars, pall-bearers, a lady attendant for hairdressing and cosmetics, and the like—all of which will be included in the price of the casket which it is now their duty to select. These preliminaries are very important for "the Arrangement Conference can *make* or *break* the sale."

The diagram of the selection room in this manual resembles one of those mazes set up for experiments designed to muddle rats. It is here that we are introduced to the Triangle Plan, under which the buyer is led around in a triangle, or rather in a series of triangles. He is started off at position A, a casket costing $587, which he is told is "in the $500 range"—although, as the manual points out, it is actually only $13 short of $600. He is informed that the average family buys in the $500 range—a statement designed to reassure him, explain the authors, because "most of the people believe themselves to be *above* average." Supposing the client does not react either way to the $587 casket. He is now led to position B on the diagram—a better casket priced at $647. However, this price is not to be mentioned. Rather the words "sixty dollars additional" are to be used. Should the prospect still remain silent, this is the cue to continue *upward* to the most expensive unit.

Conversely, should the client demur at the price of $587, he is to be taken to position C—and told that "he can *save* $100" by choosing this one. Again, the figure of $487 is not to be mentioned. If he now says nothing, he is led to position D. Here he is told that "at sixty dollars additional, we could use this finer type, and all of the services will be just exactly the same." This is the crux of the triangle plan; the recalcitrant buyer has now gone around a triangle to end up unwittingly within forty dollars of the starting point. It will be noted that the prices all end in the number seven, "purposely styled to allow you to quote as: 'sixty dollars additional' or 'save a hundred dollars.' "

The buyer is not likely to have caught the significance of this guided tour. As a customer he finds himself in an unusual situation, trapped in a set of circumstances peculiar to the funeral transaction. His frame of mind will vary, obviously, according to the circumstances which led him to the funeral establishment. He may be dazed and bewildered, his young wife having just been killed in an accident; he may be rather relieved because a crotchety old relative has finally died after a long and painful illness. The great majority of funeral buyers, as they are led through their paces at the mortuary—whether shaken and grief-stricken or merely looking forward with pleasurable anticipation to the reading of the will —are assailed by many a nagging question: What's the *right* thing to do? I am arranging this funeral, but surely this is no time to indulge my own preferences in taste and style; I feel I know what she would have preferred, but what will her family and friends expect? How can I avoid criticism for inadvertently doing the wrong thing? And, above all, it should be a nice, decent funeral—but what *is* a nice, decent funeral?

Which leads us to the second special aspect of the funeral transaction: the buyer's almost total ignorance of what to expect when he enters the undertaker's parlor. What to look for, what to avoid, how much to spend. The funeral industry estimates that the average individual has to arrange for a funeral only once in fifteen years. The cost of the funeral is the third largest expenditure, after a house and a car, in the life of an ordinary American family. Yet even in the case of the old relative, whose death may have been fully expected and even welcomed, it is most unlikely that the buyer will have discussed the funeral with anybody in advance. It just would not seem right to go round saying, "By the way, my uncle is very ill and he's not expected to live; do you happen to know a good, reliable undertaker?"

Because of the nature of funerals, the buyer is in a quite different position from one who is, for example, in the market for a car. Visualize the approach. The man of prudence and common sense who is about to buy a car consults a Consumers' Research bulletin or seeks the advice of his friends; he knows in advance the dangers of rushing into a deal blindly.

In the funeral home, the man of prudence is completely at sea without a recognizable landmark or bearing to guide him. It would be an unusual person who would examine the various offerings and then inquire around about the relative advantages of the Monaco casket by Merit and the Valley Forge by Boyertown. In the matter of cost, a like difference is manifest. The funeral buyer is generally not in the mood to compare prices here, examine and appraise quality there. He is anxious to get the whole thing over with—not only is he anxious for this, but the exigencies of the situation demand it.

The third unusual factor which confronts the buyer is the need to make an on-the-spot decision. Impulse buying, which should, he knows, be avoided in everyday life, is here a built-in necessity. The convenient equivocations of commerce—"I'll look around a little, and let you know," "Maybe, I'll call you in a couple of weeks if I decide to take it," "My partner is going to Detroit next month, he may pick one up for me there"—simply do not apply in this situation. Unlike most purchases, this one cannot be returned in fifteen days and your money refunded in full if not completely satisfied.

Not only is the funeral buyer barred by circumstances from shopping around in a number of establishments; he is also barred by convention and his own feelings from complaining afterwards if he thinks he was overcharged or otherwise shabbily treated. The reputation of the TV repairman, the lawyer, the plumber is public property and their short-

comings are often the subject of dinner party conversation. The reputation of the undertaker is relatively safe in this respect. A friend, knowing
I was writing on the subject, reluctantly told me of her experience in
arranging the funeral of a brother-in-law. She went to a long-established,
"reputable" undertaker. Seeking to save the widow expense, she chose
the cheapest redwood casket in the establishment and was quoted a low
price. Later, the salesman called her back to say the brother-in-law was
too tall to fit into this casket, she would have to take one that cost $100
more. When my friend objected, the salesman said, "Oh, all right, we'll
use the redwood one, but we'll have to cut off his feet." My friend was
so shocked and disturbed by the nightmare quality of this conversation
that she never mentioned it to anybody for two years.

Popular ignorance about the law as it relates to the disposal of the
dead is a factor that sometimes affects the funeral transaction. People are
often astonished to learn that in no state is embalming required by law
except in certain special circumstances, such as when the body is to be
shipped by common carrier.

The funeral men foster these misconceptions, sometimes by coolly
misstating the law to the funeral buyer and sometimes by inferentially
investing with the authority of law certain trade practices which they
find it convenient or profitable to follow. This free and easy attitude to
the law is even to be found in those institutes of higher learning, the
Colleges of Mortuary Science, where the fledgling undertaker receives
his training. For example, it is the law in most states that when a decedent bequeaths his body for use in medical research, his survivors are
bound to carry out his directions. Nonetheless an embalming textbook,
Modern Mortuary Science, disposes of the whole distasteful subject in a
few misleading words: "Q: Will the provisions in the will of a decedent
that his body be given to a medical college for dissection be upheld over
his widow? A: No . . . No-one owns or controls his own body to the
extent that he may dispose of the same in a manner which would bring
humiliation and grief to the immediate members of his family."

I had been told so often that funeral men tend to invent the law as
they go along (for there is a fat financial reward at stake) that I decided
to investigate this situation at first hand. Armed with a copy of the
California code, I telephoned a leading undertaker in my community
with a concocted story: my aged aunt, living in my home, was seriously
ill—not expected to live more than a few days. Her daughter was coming here directly; but I felt I ought to have some suggestions, some
arrangements to propose in the event that . . . Sympathetic monosyllables
from my interlocutor. The family would want something very simple, I
went on, just cremation. Of course, we can arrange all that, I was assured.
And since we want only cremation, and there will be no service, we
should prefer not to buy a coffin. The undertaker's voice at the other
end of the phone was now alert, although smooth. He told me, calmly
and authoritatively, that it would be "illegal" for him to enter into such
an arrangement. "You mean, it would be against the law?" I asked. Yes,
indeed. "In that case, perhaps we could take the body straight to the

crematorium in our station wagon?" A shocked silence, followed by an explosive outburst: "Madam, the average lady has neither the facilities nor the inclination to be hauling dead bodies around!" (Which was actually a good point, I thought.)

I tried two more funeral establishments, and was told substantially the same thing: cremation of an uncoffined body is prohibited under California law. This was said, in all three cases, with such a ring of conviction that I began to doubt the evidence before my eyes in the state code. I reread the sections on cremation, on health requirements; finally I read the whole thing from cover to cover. Finding nothing, I checked with an officer of the Board of Health, who told me there is no law in California requiring that a coffin be used when a body is cremated. He added that indigents are cremated by some county welfare agencies without benefit of coffin.

It is, however, true that most privately owned crematoria have their own privately established rule that they will not cremate without a coffin. After all, why not? Many are in the casket-selling business themselves, and those that are not depend for their livelihood on the good will of funeral directors who are.

Cemetery salesmen are also prone to confuse fact with fiction to their own advantage in discussing the law. Cemeteries derive a substantial income from the sale of "vaults." The vault, a cement enclosure for the casket, is not only a money-maker; it facilitates upkeep of the cemetery by preventing the eventual subsidence of the grave as the casket disintegrates. In response to my inquiry, a cemetery salesman (identified on his card as a "memorial counselor") called at my house to sell me what he was pleased to call a "pre-need memorial estate," in other words, a grave for future occupancy. After he had quoted the prices of the various graves, the salesman explained that a minimum of $120 must be added for a vault, which, he said, is "required by law."

"Why is it required by law?"

"To prevent the ground from caving in."

"But suppose I should be buried in one of those Eternal caskets made of solid bronze?"

"Those things are not as solid as they look. You'd be surprised how soon they fall apart."

"Are you *sure* it is required by law?"

"I've been in this business fifteen years; I should know."

"Then would you be willing to sign this?" (I had been writing on a sheet of paper, "California State Law requires a vault for ground burial.")

The memorial counselor gathered up his colored photographs of memorial estates and walked out of the house.

The fifth unusual factor present in the funeral transaction is the availability to the buyer of relatively large sums of cash. The family accustomed to buying every major item on time—car, television set, furniture—and to spending to the limit of the weekly paycheck, suddenly finds itself in possession of insurance funds and death benefit payments, often from a number of sources. It is usually unnecessary for the undertaker to resort to crude means to ascertain the extent of insurance coverage. A few simple and perfectly natural questions put to the family while he is completing the vital statistics forms will serve to elicit all he needs to know. For example, "Occupation of the deceased?" "Shall we bill the insurance company directly?"

The undertaker knows, better than a schoolboy knows the standings of the major league baseball teams, the death benefit payments of every trade union in the community, the social security and workmen's compensation scale of death benefits, the veterans' and servicemen's death benefits: social security payment, up to $255; if the deceased was a veteran, $250 more and free burial in a national cemetery; burial allowance of $400 and up for military personnel, $700 for retired railroad workers; additional funeral allowance of $300 to $800 under various state workmen's compensation laws if the death was occupationally connected, and so on and on.

The undertaker has all the information he needs to proceed with the sale. The widow, for the first time in possession of a large amount of ready cash, is likely to welcome his suggestions. He is, after all, the expert, the one who knows how these things should be arranged, who will steer her through the unfamiliar routines and ceremonies ahead, who will see that all goes as it should.

At the lowest end of the scale is the old-age pensioner, most of whose savings have long since been spent. He is among the poorest of the poor. Nevertheless, most state and county welfare agencies permit him to have up to $1,000 in cash; in some states he may own a modest home as well, without jeopardizing his pension. The funeral director knows that under the law of virtually every state the funeral bill is entitled to preference in payment as the first charge against the estate. (Efforts in some states to pass legislation limiting the amount of the priority for burial costs to, say, $500 have been frustrated by the funeral lobby.) There is every likelihood that the poor old chap will be sent out in high style unless his widow is a very, very cool customer indeed.

The situation that generally obtains in the funeral transaction was summed up by former Surrogate's Court Judge Fowler of New York in passing upon the reasonableness of a bill which had come before him: "One of the practical difficulties in such proceedings is that contracts for funerals are ordinarily made by persons differently situated. On the one side is generally a person greatly agitated or overwhelmed by vain regrets or deep sorrow, and on the other side persons whose business it is to minister to the dead for profit. One side is, therefore, often unbusinesslike, vague and forgetful, while the other is ordinarily alert, knowing and careful."

There are people, however, who know their own minds perfectly well and who approach the purchase of a funeral much as they would any other transaction. They are, by the nature of things, very much in the minority. Most frequently they are not in the immediate family of the deceased but are friends or representatives of the family. Their experiences are interesting because to some extent they throw into relief the irrational quality of the funeral transaction.

Mr. Rufus Rhoades, a retired manufacturer of San Rafael, California, was charged with arranging for the cremation of a ninety-two-year-old friend who died in a rest home in 1961. He telephoned the crematorium, and was quoted the price of $75 for cremation plus $15 for shipping the ashes to Santa Monica, where his friend's family had cemetery space. He suggested hiring an ambulance to pick up the body, but this idea was quickly vetoed by the crematorium. He was told that he would have to deal through an undertaker, that the body could not be touched by anyone but a licensed funeral director, that a "container" would have to be provided. This he was unaware of; and no wonder, for these are "regulations" of the crematorium, not requirements of California law.

Mr. Rhodes looked in the San Rafael telephone directory, and found five funeral establishments listed. He picked one at random, called, and was told that under no circumstances could price be discussed over the telephone as it was "too private a matter"; that he should come down to the funeral home. There he found that the cheapest price, including "a low priced casket and the complete services" was $480. Mr. Rhoades protested that he did not *wish* the complete services, that there was to be no embalming, that he did not want to see the coffin. He merely wanted the body removed from the rest home and taken to the crematorium, some five miles away. Balking at the $480, Mr. Rhoades returned home and telephoned the other four funeral establishments. The lowest quotation he could obtain was $250.

Not unnaturally, Mr. Rhoades feels that he paid a fee of $50 a mile to have his friend's body removed from the rest home to the crematorium. The undertaker no doubt felt, for his part, that he had furnished a service well below his "break even" point, or, in his own terminology, "below the cost at which we are fully compensated."

There was the case of a young widow whose husband died of cancer in 1950 after a long illness in Oakland, California. His death was fully expected by both of them, and they had discussed the matter of his funeral. The day he died, the widow left town to stay with her mother, leaving the funeral arrangements in the hands of their attorney, who was also a close friend. There was to be no religious service, just cremation and disposal of the ashes. Cremation, the attorney learned, would cost $60. The body had already been moved from the hospital to a nearby funeral establishment, so the attorney telephoned the undertaker to instruct him to deliver it to the crematorium. To his astonishment, he was told the minimum price for this would be $350—"including our complete services." There ensued a long conversation full of cross-purposes; for what "service" could now possibly be rendered to the dead man, to his widow who was thousands of miles away, or indeed to anybody? The funeral director insisted that this was the lowest price at which he would be fully compensated. Compensated for what? demanded the attorney. For the complete services . . . and so it went, until the attorney blew up and threatened to complain to the hospital that they had recommended an unscrupulous funeral establishment. At that point, the undertaker reduced his price to $150.

The point of view of the funeral director must here be explored. I talked with Mr. Robert MacNeur, owner of the largest funeral establishment in the Oakland area, with a volume of 1,000 funerals a year. Their cheapest offering is the standard service with redwood casket, at $485. "My firm has never knowingly subjected a person to financial hardship," Mr. MacNeur declared. "We will render a complete funeral service for nothing if the circumstances warrant it. The service is just the same at no charge as it is for a $1,000 funeral."

Mr. MacNeur produced a copy of the "Grant Miller Cooperative Plan," in which this philosophy is spelled out, and is here quoted in full: "Grant Miller Mortuaries have served the families of this community for over sixty years. It has always been their policy to provide funeral service regardless of financial circumstances. If a family finds the First Standard Arrangement including the finer type Redwood Casket at $485 to be beyond their present means or wishes, Grant Miller Mortuaries stand ready to reduce costs in accordance with the following cooperative plan chart, rather than use one or a series of cheap or inferior caskets."

The price chart which accompanies this shows the buyer that if he cannot afford to pay $485 for the cheapest casket in the house, he can have it, with the complete service, for $422.50. If he cannot afford that, he can pay $360, or $297.50, or $235, or $117.50, and so on down the line to "$0" for "persons in Distress Circumstances." It is the undertaker, of course, who decides who is eligible for these dispensations.

The retired manufacturer and the young widow happened to be extremely well off financially. They were not entitled to, neither did they solicit, any sort of charitable contribution from the funeral establishments or any reduction of the charges because of "distress circumstances." But as business people they were astonished that the undertakers should expect them to pay several hundred dollars for merchandise and services they wanted no part of, as a kind of assessment or contribution to the operation of the funeral establishment. The undertakers, it should be added, were equally incredulous, and possibly hurt, that these people should question their method of doing business.

The guiding rule in funeral pricing appears to be "from each according to his means," regardless of the actual wishes of the family. A funeral director in San Francisco says, "If a person drives a Cadillac, why should he have a Pontiac funeral?" The Cadillac symbol figures prominently in the funeral men's thinking. There is a funeral director in Los Angeles who says his rock-bottom minimum price is $200. But he reserves to himself the right to determine who is eligible for his minimum-priced service. "I won't sell it to some guy who drives up in a Cadillac." This kind of reasoning is peculiar to the funeral industry. A person can drive up to an expensive restaurant in a Cadillac and can order, rather than the $10 dinner, a 25-cent cup of tea and he will be served. It is unlikely that the proprietor will point to his elegant furnishings and staff, and will demand that the Cadillac owner should order something more commensurate with his ability to pay so as to help defray the overhead of the restaurant.

There is, however, one major difference between the restaurant transaction and the funeral transaction. It is clear that while the Cadillac owner may return to the restaurant tomorrow with a party of six and order $10 dinners all around, this will not be true of his dealings with the undertaker. In the funeral business it's strictly one to a customer.

■ BURIAL ON ALOR

Cora DuBois

When a person dies, the male lineal kin set out immediately to secure the shroud and as many contributions as possible in mokos, gongs, pigs, and food. The shroud will be worn after death by the deceased. This is part of his postmortem prestige, but since cloth is at a premium, this debt will have to be repaid at high interest rates, and around the shroud in future years will center most of the haggling for repayment. Forehanded kinsmen of the proper category see to it that they are prepared with a shroud of high value. Their eyes are on future profit. As a result the best pieces of cloth in the community are being continually put out of circulation. With the onset of death the female kin begin to prepare rice and corn. Not more than one or two women stay near the corpse to wail.

The spouse of the deceased is felt to be in so much danger from the dead that he leaves the immediate vicinity and stands guard with unsheathed knife, to prevent the ghost from carrying him off. For the following night and day he should not sleep. (These precautions are observed by both sexes.) Burial usually occurs not more than twenty-four to thirty-six hours after death, and it is courteous of friends to rush the procedure by urging the family on with comments about the stench of the body. Delays are usually caused by financial dickerings between lineal kin and the Male Houses.

Once the actual burial gets under way there is an outburst of wailing and a din of beaten gongs. This lasts for the half-hour to an hour that it takes four or six buriers to dig the grave, flex and wrap the corpse, and toss it hastily into the grave, which they fill rapidly. The whole procedure is carried out in an atmosphere of excited tension. Burials accompanied by large financial displays are among the rare events from which children are chased away (often quite ineffectually) because such displays are considered something deleterious and contaminating. When the body is dropped into the grave, the spouse, standing off at some distance, chops a string in two. This symbolically severs their relationship and prevents the ghost's returning for him. The rite, however, is not immediately reassuring since for two or three months after burial the spouse will still carry an unsheathed knife wherever he goes. "They do this until they forget"—which is a measure, perhaps, of the duration of grief.

I do not wish to imply that there is no grief, or even that it is slight. I have seen genuine and undoubtedly deeply felt grief at death; but my impression, gathered from a considerable range of material, is in agreement with that from quite other realms of human relationship—that there is no premium on cherishing sentimental ties once they are irrelevant. Expediency and realism are the determinants. People will be concerned over the illness of a kinsman but, once he is dead, they go on to other things. A woman, well-liked in the community, died and her "sisters" wept two hours for her, but then became engrossed in other duties. A mother who lost her third infant in succession was deeply grieved but in twenty-four hours was preoccupied once more by her quarrels with her husband and by her field work. When I bought the crop of the field on which my house was to be built, the woman who owned the field wept. A year later I had the opportunity to ask her about it, and she said in a matter-of-fact fashion, "My twelve-year-old daughter planted that field, and she died just two or three months before you came. When I saw her crop being pulled up, my heart remembered and I cried. But now I don't think of it any more." The expediency and realism in human relationships is basically a shallowness of positive affect.

Balanced against this, enough has been said in other connections to make it clear that the dead are sources of malignant power, i.e., negative affect. That death feasts may be delayed so long is perhaps a sign that negative affect is also shallow. Certainly by comparison with some Melanesians the Atimelangers cannot be considered ghost-ridden. The interesting point is that these potentially malignant dead are always one's most immediate kin. People have two souls. At death one goes to a village below if the death has not been violent. If it has been, the soul goes above (adiy hong), and a spirit-bird ceremony must be given for it. The second soul is the one that loiters about the village boundary and against which precautions are taken at the time of burial.

It is at this time that the soul is particularly dangerous because the deceased wishes company. To placate it in this early and more potent phase of malignancy and to relegate it to the village boundary there are special feasts, the Hevelaberka held on the fourth day after death and the Hevelakang on the ninth day after death. During these nine days a few minor restrictions are observed by the family, including taboos on salt, bathing, and sexual intercourse. During that time there may be also one or two all-night gong-playing memorials (sinewai), including the feeding of the guests who attend. It is during these nine days that there occurs all the ostentatious use of pigs and the incurrence of debts, which must be repaid in subsequent years, or even generations, in a series of feasts called Rolik, Baleti, and Tila (also called Ato in its final phase). The first two of these feasts are named, significantly enough, after two ways of preparing rice; the first refers to rice rolls, the second to small woven containers in which raw rice is boiled.

The third feast can really be broken down into a number of ceremonies. To the whole series I have given the name of the first ceremony, (*Tila*), which means *string* and refers to the purchase of either a sheep or a carabao for the final and supreme death feast after which the soul of the dead is banished from the village boundary and thus from interference in human affairs. The pressure of creditors, prestige, and, perhaps most often, illness of descendants lead to these final ceremonies. The dead become impatient and annoyed at the lack of postmortem prestige and manifest their displeasure by making trouble for the living.

As soon as an illness is diagnosed as the manifestation of a displeased soul, a small quantity of rice is offered it in a bamboo container raised on a pole. From here on, plans for a payoff feast should get under way; but frequently long delays occur, and it is hoped that meanwhile the small original offering will stave off the soul. In addition, the dead may withhold good crops if the smaller garden feasts are not made in the fields they have worked or if they are not named and fed at a series of new corn rituals owned by various lineages. All this placation of the dead involves saying their names as small quantities of food are set aside for them. Death feasts are given primarily for parents or grandparents. Such feasts, which may be precipitated by illness but nevertheless give prestige, may reproduce for the individual the positive and negative emotions that cluster around child training and are reinforced by the financial organization.

8

APPLIED ANTHROPOLOGY

Applied anthropology is the use of anthropological knowledge to help solve real human problems. From what we know about how different cultures react to certain changes, we can attempt to make social and cultural change less painful than it would otherwise be. This is by no means an easy task, and the ethical responsibilities of applied social science, or social engineering, are very stiff. Nevertheless, many anthropoligists believe that it is more immoral to ignore social-problem solving as a branch of social science than to make mistakes trying.

There have been many mistakes, but fortunately they are usually not translated into action. For the most part anthropologists, like other scientists, act as advisors to those who make political decisions rather than as decision-makers themselves. A lot of very bad advice gets filtered out by the political process. On the other hand, a lot of good advice gets filtered out, too. I recently did a study of communications between scientists and political decision-makers. The overwhelming result was that these two groups find it frustrating to deal with each other.

Every once in a while a scientist becomes a key decision-maker or an agent for change. This was the case with the late Professor Alan Holmberg from Cornell University, who actually leased a hacienda in Peru and became its landlord. The hacienda was called Vicos and between 1952 and 1957 he made some basic changes there. He abolished the feudal system of land tenure and set up a share system; each resident shared in the land holding and in the profits of production. He persuaded the Peruvian government to allow the peons to buy the land back from the government agency that held the lease on all haciendas in Peru. He established a city council style government; developed market-oriented farming, which produced monetary income for the Vicosinos; he helped to raise the productivity from $100 worth of potatoes per hectare (one hectare = 2.5 acres) to about $600 per hectare; he established a school system and a health clinic with resident teachers and medical personnel. In short, Alan Holmberg changed Vicos. He did not advise the government on a plan to make social changes; he *made* the social changes.

From the Vicos experience we learned a great deal in anthropology about applied social science. We learned that *people* do not change in a hurry, even though their external way of life changes drastically. In 1962, ten years after Holmberg went to Vicos, the people still lived in adobe huts, they still weaved their own clothes, and they still had no bathrooms. One reason for this, according to Holmberg, was that the change project was not designed to put on a show to the outside world. They learned quickly to let people make change decisions for themselves as much as possible. In the general scheme of priorities whitewashed houses with sanitary facilities was just not number one.

There are very few examples of applied anthropology like the Cornell project at Vicos. The people who worked there over the years admit to making many mistakes and causing pain as well as joy, and the basic lesson of Vicos is that we have a very long way to go before we can be sure of what we are doing. In fact, given the complexity of even the most primitive society, it is unlikely that we will ever have any guarantees that our advice is correct on a particular social issue.

The five selections that follow show some of the things we can do in applied anthropology. It will be clear in each of them that anthropological study of the population involved in culture change can only be an asset. Educators, agronomists, medical and paramedical teams, architects, and many other experts in technical fields will be increasingly involved in governmental programs throughout the world to change and upgrade living conditions. Industrializing countries everywhere in the world are developing their own programs of social change as well as programs for economic growth. Anthropologists from many countries can and probably will play a significant role in shaping these programs. Many anthropologists are doing directly applied work in the U.S. Some medical anthropologists, for example, are trying to understand why people do not use health care facilities even when they are available to them. Some educational anthropologists are studying the social structure of schools in an attempt to improve communications between administrators and teachers, and between teachers and students. All these efforts are part of the science of anthropology. As we try to apply our knowledge, we study what goes right and what goes wrong;

why people accept certain changes and why they reject
others. As we learn more about social change, we learn
more about the basic dynamic quality of culture; and we
learn more about what it means to be human.

■ THE MONKEY AND THE FISH

Don Adams

There is an old oriental story that accurately depicts the plight of an
unwary foreign educational adviser: Once upon a time there was a great
flood, and involved in this flood were two creatures, a monkey and a fish.
The monkey, being agile and experienced, was lucky enough to scramble
up a tree and escape the raging waters. As he looked down from his safe
perch, he saw the poor fish struggling against the swift current. With the
very best of intentions, he reached down and lifted the fish from the
water. The result was inevitable.

The educational adviser, unless he is a careful student of his own
culture and the culture in which he works, will be acting much like the
monkey; and, with the most laudable intentions, he may make decisions
equally disastrous. Using Korea as a case in point, I shall describe some
of the cultural pitfalls facing an American working in that country. The
description will involve examining some of the basic assumptions, or
"unconscious canons of choice" as the distinguished anthropologist Ruth
Benedict called them, of the Korean people. This analysis will be made
in terms of the behavior promoted by such assumptions in order to
indicate how such behavior may appear to be illogical or even unintelligible to a Western adviser. Many of the value orientations described
here also appear in other East Asian countries where similar cultural
roots may be found. Japan and Korea, for example, were both greatly
influenced by a variety of cultural forces emanating from China, the
most profound of which has been called Confucianism. But sharply
contrasting twentieth century forces of militarism, communism, and
democracy have brought elements of noticeable dissimilarity among
Asian countries that make extensive generalizations dangerous.

TIME ORIENTATION

The first obvious cultural difference noted by the American in Korea
is regarded by some to be an especially important element in differentiat-
ing cultures. This is *time orientation,* the perspective with which a

nation views the process of time. All peoples must examine problems rooted in the present or past and yet must try to anticipate the future. The differences in the view of time pointed out here are related to the degree of precedence given.

The American, for example, has historically looked with pleasant anticipation toward the future. Tomorrow is expected to be brighter than today, and, with minor exceptions, only things bigger and better can be envisioned for the future. History itself is often viewed as a continuum of progress, with each succeeding generation more advanced than the former. American schools consider that one of their major functions is the examination of the present so that their products may better plan the future.

Contrast this with the Korean culture, which historically has been oriented to the past; where the Good Life has been defined completely in terms of past living; where history has largely been viewed as cyclical, with the future regarded as a mere repetition of some portion of the past; and where innovations in terms of things bigger and better may be disrespectful to one's ancestors. The American technical adviser, geared to "getting things done" and "getting things moving," is often frustrated by situations in which his Korean colleagues appear to be acting too slowly or even stalling. Conversely, the American may by his direct approach appear exceedingly rude to the Korean, who sees no reason to be upset over current ills since the good times of the past are bound to reappear.

Historically, then, Korea has not viewed its institutions as developmental to the same degree as is done in the USA. While not adept at operation thinking, however, Korean students often pursue with skill the more purely academic and aesthetic interests. In so doing they exhibit characteristics that make the current-and-future-oriented American often seem superficial, even at times crude. Education in this cloistered setting could not be expected to be dynamic or experimental, and until the Japanese introduced colonial-flavored modern education in the twentieth century, the Korean school system was designed only to perpetuate the best of the past in an unaltered form. From ancient times the prescribed curriculum was the written wisdom of the Chinese sages and constituted what might be called a series of Asian Great Books. From the tender age when he memorized his first Chinese character until many years later when, if exceptionally able, he might pass the royal examination and become a government official the curriculum of the scholar was the literature of the past. He studied not only the ideas involved but the author's phraseology and his technique of calligraphy. As the ancient texts assumed the proportions of canons, he studied to imitate rather than to exceed, to conform rather than to create. Education that was prized was divorced entirely from the social, economic, and scientific problems of the present.

THE MAN-NATURE ORIENTATION

A second cultural difference lies in the relation of man and nature or what might be called *man-nature orientation*. In America man has increasingly expected to gain mastery over nature and he has watched his wildest expectations come true. Mountains he crossed, tunneled through, or even pulverized. Rivers proved no obstacle to his energy, for these were easily dammed or bridged. In the East Asian culture, man typically has not been so concerned with gaining mastery over his environment as he has been in living in harmony with it. Mountains that might obstruct travel and rivers that might be impassable during certain seasons have not been viewed as merely frustrating inconveniences. Rather, these are historical facts to which man must discipline himself. The challenge lies not in constructing new weapons for mastery but in developing a higher degree of resignation.

As with time orientation the traditional view held by Koreans with respect to nature has not contributed to a dynamic educational system. If man does not seek mastery over nature, there is little need for the schools to be concerned with the tools and skills for manipulating the physical universe. Rather, schools should be concerned with developing not the active but the passive person, one who seeks to avoid the common, tedious, daily environment by finding and developing problems in a more aesthetic realm. The educated man is the man of contemplation who carries about him at all times an air of peace and tranquillity. His view toward the natural environment is shown in many and diverse ways but perhaps is best expressed in his works of art, in which he so often chooses as his subject the essential harmoniousness of the universe and avoids portraying the raucous world of change and discord.

This view of man's relation to nature coupled with his orientation to time has created what Thorstein Veblen once called "a poverty of wants." Until recent years little need was felt among the great bulk of the population of Korea for the fruits of an educational system geared to produce the wide variety of skills and understandings needed to revamp and improve the existing mode of life. This does not mean that the less sophisticated people lack educational drive. On the contrary, individual families willingly make tremendous sacrifice to obtain schooling for their children. Yet these same families exert no pressure toward making the school an economically oriented institution capable of teaching functional knowledge. The urgency of keeping up to date lest history leave you behind or nature overwhelm you is not present to the same extent in the Korean culture as in the American. The goal of Korean education was, until the recent impact of Western culture, adjustment rather than improvement.

THE POWER AND STATUS
ORIENTATION

A third cultural difference could be called *power and status orienta-tion*. The USA has been proud of its decentralization of political and educational responsibilities. Under a system where considerable power is exercised at the state and local levels, every citizen becomes a leader, inasmuch as he has the right to share in decision-making. The town meeting, the school board, and all the trappings of direct and repre-sentative democracy have been widely eulogized. Because of these op-portunities the American citizen, it has been said, is a more sophisticated voter than his foreign brother, and the American student a more inde-pendent learner, as well as a better team man. Obviously there is more than a little jingoism mixed in these interpretations. Nevertheless, the fact remains that Americans are still committed largely to the belief in shared decision-making.

A power structure has existed in Korea that has equated position with authority while social custom has further equated authority with validity. This hierarchal structure and manner of decision-making are also re-flected in the classroom and in the family. The teacher and the father both occupy positions of ultimate trust, respect, power. Their word is law. The obvious difficulty of using modern educational methods within this framework is readily seen. The school in both fostering cooperation and stressing at the same time reliance on the individual's ability to solve his own problems runs into conflict with family and societal tradi-tion. Moreover, it is difficult to break down the school's authoritarian structure because of the fear that the teacher may lose the traditional respect felt for him.

The organization and administration of Korean education reflects the power structure found elsewhere in Korean society. Until 1948 and to a gradually modifying degree since then, Korean education has operated within a framework that was highly centralized. Major decisions ema-nated from the Ministry of Education. Even though opportunities for local control have been provided, they have not been taken advantage of, and lesser educational officials invariably refuse to take responsibility for decisions clearly within their jurisdiction but prefer the decisions to be made "higher up." The danger, in addition to the perpetuation of authoritarian procedures, is that the bases for determining professional action are largely founded on judgmental evidence as represented by the expressions of a status person rather than on factual evidence.

There are further and widespread educational implications of this lineally organized society. As with individuals in an organization, the schools have a definite order of rank, as do the courses of study within the school. Since academic subjects carry the most prestige, the technical and vocational schools, in attempting to gain recognition, tend to deempha-size the applied parts of their curriculum. There is so much status value attached to abstract and difficult works that Korean students enjoy being immersed in little understood concepts and often rebel in studying subjects within their comprehension.

Language is another major curriculum problem which is rooted partly in status factors. Although a simple phonetic alphabet, Hangul, had been developed in Korea in the fifteenth century, it had never been widely accepted by scholars. Government officials historically have used a written script based on Chinese characters, which has served to create and perpetuate the gulf between the Korean people and their culture. During the latter part of the Japanese annexation, to further complicate matters, the Koreans were required to use the Japanese language on all occasions. After being freed from colonial status, Korea erased most traces of the Japanese language, and the vernacular was not only re-introduced into the schools but also increasingly stressed in all literature.

The net result of this complex language situation is that Korea in 1959 finds itself with very little professional literature appropriate for students at the secondary school and college levels. There are few modern technical or professional books written in Chinese, and the children entering school after 1945 have been receiving only limited work with Chinese characters anyway. Most of the books written in Japanese (and all educated Korean adults are fluent in this language) have been destroyed. Moreover, the generation of Koreans now in school have no familiarity with the Japanese language. And at the present time, in spite of official government urgings, newspapers and most professional periodicals are being made incomprehensible to a major part of the Korean population by the inclusion of a large number of Chinese characters rather than relying on the vernacular. (It is interesting to note that under communism North Korea has made great strides in eliminating the use of Chinese characters, simplifying and refining the pure Korean. It appears that all literature being published in North Korea uses only the simple, practical Hangul script.)

The indirect influences of the West through Japanese colonialism and the direct contacts since 1945 have forced a re-examination of Korean value orientations. The sincere if awkward attempts to industrialize and democratize a nation with a long agrarian and authoritarian heritage have produced a considerable number of inconsistencies within the Korean society. For example, the political party in power one day exalts democratic freedoms, yet on the next may order all students to participate in "spontaneous demonstration" to promote a particular party bias. Police in one section of the country initiate youth clubs to combat delinquency yet themselves may at times use extremely harsh methods. The government through all avenues of propaganda promotes moral education, yet, as in older times, the bribe may often be the easiest recourse for the Korean citizen who attempts to get action through official channels. Such discrepancies indicate not only policy incongruities and personal confusion but also identify a major obstacle to a smooth cultural transition. Unity, loyalty, and morality are well defined and practiced in the family, making this an institution long admired in the West, but these qualities are yet to be raised to the societal level.

THE ADVISER AS CATALYST

The role of the foreign educational adviser in this setting is, then, both sensitive and difficult. His own knowledge and skills are to a certain extent culture-bound and unintelligible or incongruous in new surroundings. Yet it may be precisely his new perspective that is badly needed. The task of technical assistance can obviously not be defined as "teaching them to do it our way." But neither is the counter alternative, "helping them to do what they wish to do better," completely satisfactory. The former runs the danger of technical inapplicability or of cultural resistance while the latter may involve no substantial progress toward the newer and only partially defined goals. The adviser by his increased technical knowledge sheds light on possible alternatives, but neither through coercion nor through persuasion does he determine the direction of change.

Perhaps the adviser can best be likened to a catalyst. By bringing his knowledge and experience and points of view to the new situation, his role is to speed desirable change. To fulfill this role adequately the adviser must be a student of the culture and metaculture. He must establish guidelines that will determine in broad outline educational priorities acceptable to the host nation. He must face up to the enigmatic problem of focusing attention on grassroots education—for example, increasing literacy, helping the farmer to eke out a slightly bigger yield per acre—or striking out on a broad scale to teach the highly developed skills and understandings needed by a nation moving toward industrialization. Since it is extremely difficult or impossible to change a cultural pattern by attacking its isolated parts, he must answer the question whether the establishment of a few model projects can be justified in hopes that their influence will spread.

Korea is a nation in the throes of a rapid but uneven cultural change. While members of the older generation may still cling to the belief that "the scholar should neither shoulder a carrying pole nor lift a basket," young students are beginning to seek the skills requisite for nudging an ancient culture toward new directions. In Korea, as in any developing country, cultural modification depends primarily on the initiative and drive of the people. Through his minor but vital role, the adviser, by participating from the beginning with the people whose lives are being affected, may be able to lessen the traumatic effects of such change.

■ HEALING WAYS

Lyle Saunders

FOLK MEDICINE AND SCIENTIFIC MEDICINE

Anglo practice and village practice with regard to childbirth differ in several important respects. Anglo physicians, who are in a position to advise practicing midwives, recommend that the patient be delivered in bed to lessen the possibility of postpartum hemorrhage.[1] They advise that the mother should remove her clothing, that the *partera* should scrub her hands and arms with strong soap before approaching the mother, that the scissors used for severing the cord be washed in soapy water, that the mother be given a sponge bath soon after delivery. There has been a strong tendency, however, for many of the *parteras* to look upon Anglo medical ways as different from but not appreciably better than their traditional medicine and to continue to use their own more familiar methods. Or, if the Anglo methods are adopted, their efficacy may be reduced by the failure of the *partera* to grasp the reasons behind their use. The scissors, after being washed with soap, may be dried with an unsterile cloth or placed on a table that has not been cleaned. Water that has been boiled may be poured when cool into an unsterile container. The acceptance of Anglo ways may represent merely the adoption of new elements into an old pattern in which the new procedures are not understood in terms of the Anglo reasons for their use, but instead are fitted into the already existing pattern of understanding with respect to causation and healing of illness and disease. Just as Anglo medical personnel tend to see many of the Spanish-American folk practices as either worthless or dangerous, so Spanish-Americans are inclined to be skeptical about the efficacy, necessity, and safety of some of the Anglo healing practices, and may be at times reluctant to accept them. Surgical procedures, in particular, are frequently regarded as harmful, dangerous, and unnecessary, and many villagers can tell of someone who was done irreparable damage by an operation or who, being advised by an Anglo physician that an operation was absolutely necessary, was thereafter cured by some folk procedure.

The transition from Spanish-American folkways to the acceptance and use of Anglo scientific medicine is complicated by the fact that folk medical knowledge is widely disseminated, so that anyone giving medical care is subject to the critical attention of relatives and friends of the

---

[1] Anglo physicians advise first of all that women be delivered in hospitals rather than homes. However, in northern New Mexico there are frequently many reasons why hospital delivery is either not possible or not preferred by the expectant mother and her family.

patient, who are always ready to step in and insist on changes in treatment or to add to what is being done if they feel that proper care is not being given. Thus, the *partera* who has learned some new techniques from a physician or from the training program of the State Department of Public Health may find herself constrained by the pressure of family opinion to forgo her new knowledge and to continue with old ways. Knowing as well as she what herbs may be used to hasten delivery or check postpartum bleeding, the family have provided them, and they are likely to interpret the failure of the *partera* to use them as resulting from ignorance or indifference to the welfare of the patient. They *know* these traditional remedies assure comfort and safety for the patient, and they are likely to feel that no treatment process can be good which withholds them.

Among many Spanish-American villagers, Anglo medicine is regarded as something to be used chiefly as a last resort when all other known procedures have failed. Consequently, for a long time, the Anglo record of successful treatment was less good than it need have been because too frequently Anglo practitioners were not consulted until the case was practically hopeless. Most of the successes in treatment were thus credited to folk practices; many of the failures were charged to Anglo medicine. As a result, another barrier to the acceptance of Anglo medicine was raised through the development of the belief, which could be supported by reference to known cases, that Anglo medical institutions were places where people went to die.

The continued use of their own medical practices by Spanish-Americans sometimes leads the Anglo, who knows his ways are better, to characterize Spanish-Americans as ignorant or superstitious, to accuse them of being indifferent to the well-being of their families and friends, and to become impatient and annoyed at their failure to see the obvious benefits of Anglo procedures. What such Anglos fail to appreciate is that Spanish-Americans also *know* that their ways are superior and that their use, far from constituting neglect of or indifference to the needs of sick relatives and friends, actually constitutes the provision of first-rate medical care. The Anglo may argue that by the pragmatic test of results his *is* the best medicine and that the Spanish-American ought to have enough sense to see it. But the evidence of the superiority of Anglo medicine is not always available to the Spanish-American in a form that has meaning to him and, in any case, what is or is not "good sense" is relative to culture. In utilizing his own knowledge and that of his friends, relatives, and neighbors, and when that fails, in calling in a *médica* or *curandera* or even a *bruja,* the Spanish-American villager is acting in a way that is eminently sensible in the light of his convictions about the nature of disease and the proper ways to deal with it. To behave otherwise, to disregard what he knows and subject himself or a member of his family to a course of treatment that may bear no particular relationship to his understanding of disease, simply because some Anglos say that it is what he should do, would constitute a very strange kind of behavior indeed.

Sickness, particularly if it be serious, is likely to be viewed as a crisis, and in situations of crisis people in all cultures tend to resort to those patterns of thinking and acting that have been most deeply ingrained in them as a result of their cultural experiences. To meet a crisis with the resources of one's culture, whatever they may be, is to behave in a manner that is both sensible and sound; it is, in fact, to behave in the only way that most human beings can under such circumstances. The Spanish-American, in utilizing the medical ways of his culture is neither ignorant nor indifferent. If he knew no way of dealing with illness, he might be called ignorant. But he does know something to do, frequently many things. If he did nothing, he might be called indifferent. But he does something, and continues to do something while his resources remain undepleted or until he achieves results. The sequence in which he does things is determined by the differential value he places on the various procedures as they apply to the particular situation. If the seeking of Anglo medical care is, for a given illness, well down on the list, it is because this is the way he sees the particular procedure in relation to the others that are available to him. That an Anglo, in a similar situation, might have a different set of resources and a different order of importance for them, cannot be expected to have any considerable influence on his behavior.

FOLK PRACTITIONERS

Although folk medicine is in general known by all members of a cultural group, some persons, because of age, experience, or special interest, may have a more extensive knowledge than their neighbors and friends and thus acquire a somewhat specialized status. The *partera,* or midwife, is an example of such a person. In the field of general medicine, *médicas* and *curanderas,* whose knowledge of herbs and household remedies is somewhat greater than that of the general population, perform a similar function, being called upon for assistance when a medical problem gets beyond the competence of the patient or his relatives. None of them, of course, is a specialist in the Anglo sense of having a specialized kind of training and being given distinctive formal recognition (licensure) for their skill. But they are specialists in the sense that they are considered to have a greater knowledge of medical matters than other people in the population and perform a specialized function. Like *parteras, médicas* and *curanderas* expect to be paid for their services, either in goods or in cash, and, like Anglo practitioners, they are called upon to do a certain amount of "charity" work for which they are not paid. In most instances, the commercial part of the transaction is definitely subordinated, although in urban areas where close village relationships are no longer possible, *médicas* and *curanderas* are likely to regard themselves and to be regarded as impersonal purveyors of medicines and services, and the commercial element in the relationship is quite prominent.

One type of "specialist" with no exact counterpart in Anglo folk or scientific medicine is the *bruja* or witch, whose extensive command of both the malevolent and benevolent techniques of witchcraft makes her a person both sought after and feared. Although a belief in magical powers is becoming less and less respectable, there are few Spanish-speaking communities in the Southwest that do not include among their inhabitants one or more persons known to be witches. Their continued activity has made possible the rise of another "specialty," that of the *albolaria* whose particular skill is the ability to thwart or render harmless the evil powers of *brujas*. Not many Spanish-speaking will admit a belief in witches any more, but nearly everyone can tell about someone else who believes in them, and it can be noted that the services of *albolarias* continue to be in demand.

The general patterns of behavior of both rural and urban Spanish-Americans with respect to illness and therapy are almost always a mixture of elements from their own and Anglo culture. A number of Spanish-Americans interviewed in the San Luis Valley of Colorado in 1952 indicated that in general they utilized the services of both folk and Anglo scientific medical practitioners, and that their knowledge of remedies for various conditions included items drawn from both cultures. One *médica,* who also performs as a *partera,* serves patients from many surrounding communities and works closely with an Anglo physician in caring for her maternity cases. When pregnant women come to her, they are sent to the doctor for a blood test and a "check-up" after which, if everything seems normal, they return to her for the actual delivery. Most of the deliveries take place in her home. Difficult cases are delivered by the doctor and in a hospital. For the treatment of other than maternity cases the *médica* uses remedies that she obtains by mail from supply houses in San Antonio and Trinidad.[2]

Nearly everyone interviewed knew of *médicas* and *curanderas* practicing in the vicinity, and many made no particular distinction between the services they offered and those available from Anglo physicians. The *médica* mentioned above thinks that many people do not like doctors and hospitals because they are afraid of both. Many women who come to see her, she said, refuse to go to the physician for a check-up and can be persuaded to do so only when she threatens to withhold her assistance. A man who was interviewed said that he does not consult a doctor until he is "about dead." He and his wife have four children, two of whom were delivered by *parteras* and two by physicians. He knows a good deal about folk remedies and uses them for himself and his family when indicated. A large proportion of his acquaintances use folk remedies, and a few have told him that they would not go to a doctor under any circumstances. One woman reported that a physician who came

2 The catalogue of the Trinidad "laboratory" gives a long list of "yerbas and medicinales," priced at from 25 cents to $3.00, including (using the catalogue spelling) Raiz de Immortal, Yerba De El Manzo Raiz, Chuchupaste, Gobernadora, Alusema, Flor de Mansanilla, Polello, Yerba Buena, Oregano, Valeriana, Alumbre, Romero, Gardenias, Yerba Mora, Culiantrillo, and Flor de Asufre Mexicano, as well as syrup of onions, green oil liniment, an eye wash made of "el manzo herb," and a preparation advertised as a cockroach chaser.

into the area just before the turn of the century used to take her mother, a *médica,* with him on his calls. By allowing her to make diagnoses and prescribe treatments, the mother said, he was able to learn the value of her *remedios* and later to use them in his own practice.

In cities, as well as in rural areas, the medical practices of Spanish-Americans continue to be a mixture of elements of both cultures, although because of greater availability of Anglo medicine, the somewhat better financial status of many Spanish-speaking persons, and a higher level of acculturation, Anglo medicine is used proportionately more in cities than in the country. *Remedios,* including both Anglo patent preparations and medicinal herbs, are sold in the "Mexican" sections of cities and large towns, and one who has need of the services of a *médica* or *curandera* does not have far to look for them. In addition to giving service, they will also prescribe and sell medicine.

No precise studies have been made of the extent to which Spanish-speaking people of the Southwest use one or another of the several types of medical aid available to them for particular kinds of illness. One small survey of a group of families living in Fort Collins, Colorado, showed a greater acceptance of Anglo practices by young people than by the older folk, but a rather large use of Anglo procedures by persons of all ages.[3] Another study of Colorado migrant families living in four agricultural areas of Colorado gives some evidence on the observed and reported use of Anglo medical personnel, facilities, and practices, but no comparative information on the use of folk medicine.[4] In this report a physician is quoted as saying, "We know that communicable diseases are present among the migrants. The fatalistic acceptance of the situation, plus their poverty, makes the problem of medical care a critical one. Tuberculosis, enteritis, smallpox, typhoid fever, dysentery, and venereal diseases have been more often detected by accident or search by public health officials than by patients voluntarily seeking medical assistance."[5] A conspicuous finding of this study was that health and medical care services were not widely used by the migrants observed. Of 1,098 persons from whom information was obtained, 947 had not seen a doctor during the preceding year, and 955 of 1,101 persons giving information had not visited a dentist during that period. Of those who had consulted a dentist, the majority wanted extractions or went to get relief for a toothache. Of the few who had gone for prophylactic reasons, all were persons who had served in the armed forces or were members of households where there were ex-army personnel. Just over 42 per cent of the

---

[3] Samora, Julian, *The Acculturation of the Spanish-Speaking People of Fort Collins, Colorado, in Selected Culture Areas,* Master's thesis, Colorado Agricultural and Mechanical College, 1947, pp. 120–125. It should perhaps be pointed out that there is no problem of availability of Anglo medical care in Fort Collins.

[4] Thomas, Howard E., and Florence Taylor, "Medical and Health Care" in *Migrant Farm Labor in Colorado:* A Study of Migratory Families, National Child Labor Committee, New York, 1951, chap. 4. Inasmuch as these were low-income families living in rural areas, both the availability and cost of Anglo medicine would be limiting factors.

[5] *Ibid.,* p. 55.

631 children reported on had been vaccinated for smallpox; only a fifth had been immunized against whooping cough, and about the same proportion against diphtheria. Nine out of ten migrants above seven years of age had not been hospitalized at any time during the previous five years, and only 15 per cent had undergone physical examinations during that period, the majority of these having occurred during an illness or as a requirement for a job.

REASONS FOR ANGLO MEDICINE NOT BEING MORE EXTENSIVELY USED

A number of explanations can be found for the failure of Spanish-speaking people in close contact with Anglo culture to adopt completely its medical ways. One such factor is certainly the extent to which Anglo medical services and facilities are available. Although the Spanish-speaking are rapidly becoming urbanized, many of them still live in rural areas where medical personnel and facilities are not readily available. Large numbers of Spanish-speaking people live in sparsely settled areas where one has to drive many miles to see a physician or enter a hospital. A map of health facilities in New Mexico, prepared in 1946 for the New Mexico Health Council, showed four counties to be completely without medical facilities and a large part of the state to lie outside a 30-mile radius from any type of health facility.[6] In parts of Colorado, Arizona, and Texas, similar conditions exist. The present widespread distribution of automobiles and recent improvements in rural roads have done much to make Anglo medicine more readily available to rural Spanish-speaking people and have undoubtedly contributed to its somewhat greater use. But there still remain many areas where, either because of sparseness of population or a high concentration of Spanish-speaking people among the residents of the areas, it would be quite difficult to get to an Anglo doctor or hospital even if one were highly motivated to do so.

Another factor related to availability is that of cost. Anglo medical care is expensive and the Spanish-speaking, as a group, are poor. In many instances they cannot afford, or do not feel that they can afford, the services of a physician or a sojourn in a hospital. Anglo medicine involves bills for home or office calls, some likelihood of being given an expensive prescription, and the possibility of surgery, or hospitalization for some other reason, which may be very costly. A *médica* usually does not charge much and under certain circumstances can be paid with products instead of cash, a definite advantage to those living in rural areas. Her medicines are not likely to cost much, and there is little likelihood that she will recommend hospitalization or an operation. Diagnosis and treatment by oneself and one's family cost little or nothing, and for many minor illnesses can be quite satisfactory. These differences in costs certainly constitute an influence in the readiness or

6 *New Mexico Health Council News-Letter*, November, 1946.

reluctance with which an individual or family makes the decision to seek any given type of medical care.

Lack of knowledge of Anglo medical ways is probably another factor in the extent to which Spanish-speaking people do or do not use Anglo practitioners and facilities. The simple matter of getting in touch with a doctor and putting oneself under his care can seem complicated to a person who is not at ease in either the English language or Anglo medical culture. How does one find a doctor? How can one be sure that the chosen doctor will be either competent or *simpatico?* How is a doctor approached? How can one know in advance how much the treatment will cost or what will be the expected manner of payment? What illnesses may properly be taken to a physician? These and other questions, the answers to which most of us take for granted, can be puzzling to persons not wholly familiar with Anglo culture, and can be effective barriers to the initiation of a doctor-patient relationship, particularly when the potential patient may not be highly motivated in the direction of wanting Anglo medicine.

Closely related to a lack of knowledge of Anglo medical ways as a deterrent to seeking Anglo medical care is the factor of fear. That which is strange or unknown is often feared, and there is much in Anglo medicine that is strange and fear inducing even to Anglo laymen. The instruments used, the pain that sometimes accompanies their use, and the unfamiliar surroundings of the office, clinic, or hospital in which they are used, all can arouse fear. So can the unfamiliar elements in the medical routine—the examination procedure, the invasion of one's physical and mental privacy, the uncertainty of the diagnostic procedure, the incomprehensible language that may be used. For a Spanish-speaking person, for example, a physical examination can be a very unpleasant experience, particularly if it involves the participation of persons of the opposite sex. The fear of being examined by a man is sometimes enough to keep Spanish-speaking women away from Anglo medical practitioners and to make traumatic for others the contact they have with Anglo medicine. Foster reports the failure of a considerable proportion of women coming to a prenatal clinic in Mexico City to return for a follow-up visit after their initial experience, which included an unexpected physical examination.[7] It is not without significance for the

7 Foster, George M., editor, *A Cross-Cultural Analysis of a Technical Aid Program,* July 25, 1951, p. 85. "The concept of modesty, closely allied to that of morality, is inculcated at an early age. Although an entire family may live in a single room, each turns to the wall when dressing and undressing. After childhood, individuals never see others, even of the same sex, unclothed. Intimacies between the parents do not occur until after all others are asleep. The subject of sex is not mentioned between husband and wife nor explained to the children. The young people are expected to observe life of farm animals and they are known to discuss between themselves the immoral conduct of certain villagers, especially those caught in the problems of what they conceive to be rapid Anglicization. But on the surface, modesty and morality are equally to be observed at all times. Even the use of better clothes and grooming than those of one's neighbors is considered immodest because it is believed to advertise a girl's intention of attracting

medical relations of Spanish-speaking and Anglos in the Southwest that most of the healing personnel in the culture of the Spanish-speaking are women, whereas proportionately more of those in the Anglo culture are men. Spanish-speaking men, too, are likely to have some reluctance to subjecting themselves to examination by Anglo physicians and to being placed in potentially embarrassing situations with Anglo nurses.

Another possible factor that may operate is resistance to being separated from one's family and being isolated for an indefinite time in an Anglo institution, where all relationships are likely to be impersonal. Good medical care, from the Anglo point of view, requires hospitalization for many conditions. Good medical care, as defined in the culture of the Spanish-Americans, requires that the patient be treated for almost any condition at home by relatives and friends, who are constantly in attendance and who provide emotional support as well as the technical skills required in treatment. In time of sickness one expects his family to surround and support him, and to supervise closely and critically, if not actually carry on, the treatment process. Members of the family, in turn, feel obligated to remain close to the patient, to take charge of his treatment, and to reassure him as to his place in and importance to the family group. The Anglo practice of hospitalization, with the treatment being taken over by professional strangers and the family relegated to the meager role permitted by the visiting regulations, runs counter to the expectation patterns of the Spanish-speaking and, thus, may be a factor in the reluctance of some members of the group to seek or accept Anglo medical care.

There are some illnesses for which Anglo medical care is not sought because, as has already been noted, the type of sickness is not ordinarily known to Anglo practitioners. A patient suffering from *mal ojo, susto,* and similar conditions seeks relief, if at all, from someone who is familiar with these diseases and who, therefore, may be expected to know something about the proper method of treatment. This difference between the two cultures in the conceptualization of disease serves to restrict the range of conditions for which Anglo medical assistance might be sought to those recognized by both cultural groups and gives to the folk practitioner almost exclusive influence in dealing with those conditions that are recognized only by the Spanish-speaking group.

A final factor that may be mentioned as possibly contributing to the hesitancy of Spanish-speaking people to use Anglo medicine is that such attempts as are made often do not provide the satisfactions that the Spanish-speaking expect. With the *curandera* and *médica* the whole process of diagnosis and treatment moves along in an atmosphere of informal cooperation and collaboration between patient, family, and the healer. Alternative procedures are discussed and courses of treatment agreed upon, with the opinions of patient and family frequently

men for immoral purposes." Hawley, Florence, and Donovan Senter, "Group-Designed Behavior Patterns in Two Acculturating Groups," *Southwestern Journal of Anthropology,* vol. 2, Summer, 1946, p. 139.

being given much weight in the final decisions. The folk practitioner works less as an independent specialist than as a consultant and technician who implements the therapeutic plans of the patient or his family, all of whom remain very much in the picture throughout the treatment period. All know what is going on and why. All are free to offer suggestions and criticisms. The diagnosis and treatment of illness thus involve active participation by the patient and members of his family in a situation in which the relationships are mainly personal and informal. Diagnosis is usually easy and swift, and treatment follows immediately.

By contrast, Anglo medicine is likely to be somewhat impersonal and formal. It is expected that the patient will be turned over to the physician, who will then direct the diagnostic and treatment procedures, largely without the benefit of advice or suggestion from either the patient or his family. Information may be sought from both, but usually only for the purpose of getting at the present complaints or learning the patient's medical history. Diagnosis may be slow and may involve techniques that are not understood by the patient or his family. Treatment may be delayed pending the establishment of a definite diagnosis and, when instituted, may involve hospitalization of the patient. The patient and his family are expected to be relatively passive participants in a situation in which most of the new relationships established are impersonal, businesslike, and, frequently, very unsatisfactory. In treatment by either folk practitioner or physician the possible range of outcomes is about the same. The patient may get better, may remain as he is, may get worse, may die. There being no conclusive evidence of the relatively greater frequency of desirable results when using Anglo medicine than when relying on folk healers, the amount of satisfaction that patient and family get in the medical relationship becomes an important factor in determining which of the two types of medicine they will select.

The most important differences between Spanish-American folk medicine and Anglo scientific medicine that influence the choice of one or the other are these: Anglo scientific medicine involves largely impersonal relations, procedures unfamiliar to laymen, a passive role for family members, hospital care, considerable control of the situation by professional healers, and high costs; by contrast the folk medicine of Spanish-American villagers is largely a matter of personal relations, familiar procedures, active family participation, home care, a large degree of control of the situation by the patient or his family, and relatively low costs. Given these differences, it is easy to understand why a considerable motivation would be necessary for a Spanish-American to have any strong preference for Anglo medicine over that which is not only more familiar and possibly psychologically more rewarding—or at least less punishing—but also less expensive.

Despite the many factors that operate to hinder the seeking and acceptance of Anglo medical care by Spanish-speaking people of the Southwest, however, Anglo medicine is rapidly coming to play an increasingly larger part in the total complex of attitudes and activities of the Spanish-speaking people with respect to illness and health. In cities where Anglo medical facilities and personnel are accessible, the use made of them by the Spanish-speaking probably is not greatly different in either amount or kind from that of Anglos of comparable social class status. In some rural areas, activities of private practitioners, medical groups, health cooperatives, local and state health departments, and, particularly, public health nurses have brought a considerable amount of Anglo medicine within the reach of Spanish-speaking people and have done much to develop the attitudes necessary to the acceptance and use of Anglo medical ways. If we think of the Spanish-speaking population as distributed along a continuum ranging from complete reliance on their own folk medicine at one pole to the complete acceptance of Anglo scientific medicine at the other, the greatest numbers would be concentrated near the center, with the highest proportion probably being found on the Anglo half of the continuum.

■ ABORTION AND DEPOPULATION ON A PACIFIC ISLAND

David M. Schneider

THE PROBLEM: THE PRACTICE OF SELF-INDUCED ABORTION

Before the coming of the first European explorers to the Pacific Island of Yap, its 39 square miles supported an estimated population of more than 50,000 people. By 1945, when American troops landed on Yap, the island's population had fallen to about 2,500. This spectacular decline in population has had far-reaching consequences for the people of Yap and their mode of life.

The people of Yap had developed a social system predicated on a relatively large population. While the population continued to decline, the form of their organized groupings changed but slowly. Today people bemoan the fact that there is a constant scarcity of individuals to hold the offices and perform the necessary jobs. Political organizations calling for a staff of 15 officials have only four or five men available to fill these posts. Present-day Yap society, with its several thousand people, is still geared to a population 20 times that large, and it is with deep regret that people contemplate the spectacle of unfilled positions and depleted organizations. As they express the situation, something should be done "to have more babies."

In the face of this dramatic population shrinkage and the keenly felt need to refill the thinned ranks of their society, Yap women engage in a practice that produces results exactly opposite to those desired. Evidence indicates that self-induced abortion is widely practiced by Yap women precisely during the years of maximum fecundity. This lowers the fertility rate in a situation where a higher rate is urgently desired. Moreover, the methods of inducing abortion are such as to expose women to the risk of infection. Abortion is widely condemned on moral grounds. A Yap woman will tell of other women who have induced abortion but never admit having done so herself. The admission would create serious trouble with her husband or, if she were single, it would impair her chances of making a good marriage.

In view of the unfavorable consequences of abortion, as well as the moral strictures against it, why do women persist in this practice? Could the very methods devised by the people of Yap to stabilize the population at the optimal level have produced results that defeat their own ends? The enigma of abortion has roots deep in the history of Yap and its people. It is not an isolated practice that can be understood by itself, but is bound up with the totality of Yap culture, its values, moral standards, social organization, and the aspirations of its people.

THE SITUATION: FERTILITY AND CULTURAL VALUES

As part of a four-man team of social scientists studying the problem of depopulation on Yap in 1947 and 1948, I became interested in cultural factors relating to the low birth rate. In the course of ethnographic research, I was particularly struck by the fact that 34 per cent of Yap women between the ages of twenty-six and fifty who were interviewed claimed that they had never given birth to a child. In seeking to account, at least in part, for this high incidence of infertility, I began to accumulate information pointing to the prevalence of self-induced abortion. It was next to impossible to get direct evidence. Morally disallowed, this practice was performed in secret. Women readily told about *other* women who had induced abortion. Their knowledge of the precise details of technique, however, left little doubt that this information was based on more than indirect experience. The facts that emerged on the illicit but widespread practice of self-induced abortion are these.

SELF-INDUCED ABORTION ON YAP

Abortion techniques fall into three classes. One consists in a series of magical manipulations with little apparent efficacy. These were universally recited to me as "ways to abort, but they don't always work." Doubtless they are tried from time to time, however. The other two techniques are empirically more effective. One of these is drinking boiled concentrated sea water. Women described the effect as a general feeling of illness accompanied by vomiting and severe cramps.

The other technique consists in introducing a thin rolled plug of hibiscus leaves (which expand when moist) into the mouth of the cervix and then injuring and scratching the mouth of the cervix with a bit of stick, stone, iron, fingernail, or other sharp object until blood is drawn. Women informants generally agreed that injuring the area about the mouth of the cervix was necessary in addition to inserting the plug; the plug without injury or injury without the plug was subject to failure. The boiled sea water technique was held to be less reliable than the plug-and-injury method, and therefore the less common of the two techniques. One technique common on the Pacific islands of Melanesia and Polynesia, that of massage, was never mentioned by Yap informants and is apparently unknown on Yap.

Induced abortion fits neatly into the Yap way of life, for a woman who knows how to induce abortion can usually do so without the fact ever being discovered. Yap women customarily repair to a special area during their menstrual periods. There they sit within a small but comfortable hut on their voluminous skirts of dry banana leaves and other grasses. When the peak of the flow is over, the woman is free to move around within the menstrual area, and she busies herself with making her new skirt, cleaning up the area, and such basketry work or other appropriate occupation as may come to hand. At the conclusion of her menstrual period, she places her soiled skirt in a place reserved for that purpose in the menstrual area; these old skirts are burned when the pile is great enough to warrant it. She is then free to return to the village and resume her daily life.

It is customary for a woman to keep pregnancy a secret for the first three months at least, for both she and her child are considered to be most vulnerable to sorcery at that time. So whether or not she is actually menstruating, she will repair to the menstrual area about the time she would normally have expected her period to begin. So far as the rest of the world can tell, she is not pregnant and is menstruating regularly. A young woman who becomes pregnant is thus in an excellent position to keep her condition secret and to induce abortion without discovery if she so wishes and knows how.

Contraception, in certain of its forms, is known on Yap but hardly ever used. Coitus interruptus was reported by some male informants to have been learned in relatively recent times from Japanese occupation personnel. It is something some women try once or twice but abandon quickly; men will not tolerate it, and a woman finds that it defeats her own ends in that it drives lovers away. Condoms were made familiar by the Japanese; they were known to be effective in preventing pregnancy, but Yap men were not motivated to use them for this purpose, preferring to make excellent slingshots out of them instead. Other forms of contraception are unknown.

Abortion induced by the plug-and-injury method is likely to produce infection, which in turn may possibly lead to some lasting impairment of a woman's reproductive capacity. On the other hand, it seems clear that more serious consequences of the plug-and-injury method are unlikely, though they may well occur in individual cases. Yap women live in their microbiological environment all their lives without the protection of antiseptics or the habits of cleanliness and hygiene common among us. Consequently, the resistance to infection on the part of those who survive is generally quite high. This does not mean that they never become infected. It only means that were an American woman to try to abort by the plug-and-injury method she would very likely incur a serious if not fatal infection, where the typical Yap woman probably incurs only a mild, localized infection. Medical experts have made actual observations of this sort.

As already mentioned, deliberate abortion is considered "wrong" and immoral on Yap. A husband who discovers that his wife has resorted to abortion may beat her or divorce her, or do both. A woman who becomes known among men as one who practices abortion jeopardizes her chances of a stable marriage. Men are interested in having children, and a woman who destroys her unborn child is viewed as a woman who "throws her child away."

Because Yap abortion techniques are in fact effective, the practice has a critical bearing on the fertility rate. However, the low rate cannot be attributed entirely to the practice of abortion. In all likelihood, there are additional important causes. Although the evidence remains inconclusive, there are good indications that gonorrhea or some other low-grade infection is present and contributes to the low fertility on Yap.

But the practice of abortion by itself is a problem of sufficient gravity to cause concern on the part of American officials charged with the responsibility of administration and on the part of natives themselves. The problem of devising effective means for dealing with abortion requires a searching look at the whole complex of circumstances that surround it. Only by understanding this problem can one hope to plan suitable countermeasures.

THE ISLAND OF YAP

Yap is a large, eroded mountain top of 38.7 square miles surrounded by a reef and rising to about 500 feet at its highest point. It lies 451 miles southwest of Guam; it is approximately 10° north of the equator and 138° east of Greenwich. Yap is a western member of the Caroline Islands, which in turn are part of a widespread group of small islands and island clusters known as Micronesia. In 1947 Yap had a population of 2,600 living in more than a hundred villages.

Although Yap was discovered by westerners in the sixteenth century, its contact with European and American peoples was sporadic until the last three decades of the nineteenth century, and even so the direct effects of foreign contact on Yap culture have been minimal. Nominal and ineffective administration of Yap by the Spanish lasted until 1899, when the whole Caroline Islands, from Ponape in the east to Palau in the west, were sold to Germany. In 1914 the Japanese took over the former German South Seas Colony in Micronesia and continued effective administration of Yap until 1945, when the American Navy gained control of the islands. Soon after, they became the Trust Territory of the Pacific Islands ultimately under United Nations control but administered first by the Navy Department and later by the United States Department of the Interior.

American administration of Yap since the fall of 1945 saw the introduction of health and sanitation measures, the erection of a hospital and dispensary for the natives, isolation of all known lepers, and the dramatic eradication of yaws. This last task alone, completed before my visit in 1947, went far toward enlisting native support for medical and hygienic suggestions emanating from the American administration.

Yap is known as one of the most conservative islands in Micronesia. After more than fifty years of occupation by a succession of foreign powers—Spain, Germany, Japan, and now the United States—the Yap way of life has altered very gradually, if at all. Missionary efforts are a good example. In the late 1800's, Spanish soldiers and missionaries alternately tried to establish stations on Yap. At first, they were treated with direct hostility, and some missionaries and soldiers were killed. Later Spanish forces were augmented and became sufficient to maintain their position, and fear of retaliation prevented violence from the Yaps. Toward the end of the period of German administration in the first decade of the twentieth century, there were some 60 Capuchin missionaries on Yap, and their published report lamented the fact that for all their work and for all their numbers, but 15 natives could be counted as converts. At the time of my visit in 1947 many natives felt it a gesture of friendliness toward the Americans to claim to be Christians, since in their view all Americans were Christians. In fact, however, the number of regular church-going Christians who had more than a vague notion of what Christianity was, did not far exceed the number cited by the German missionaries.

DEPOPULATION AND ITS BACKGROUND

One change of major importance that has taken place over the past hundred or more years is the severe depopulation of the island. Precisely when this depopulation started is unknown. The best guess is that it probably began sometime before 1850, although how long before is unknown. For the people of Yap, a whole series of alterations and adjustments have followed in the wake of the decrease in numbers. The reduction in available personnel simply prohibits certain activities and restricts others to a scale which distorts their meaning and function. Yet these activities of an older day are still thought to be the proper and good ways, while the restricted ways of today are seen as unavoidable compromises to be rectified at the earliest opportunity. It is in this latter sense that the Yap way of life has changed but little; the ideal patterns, so to speak, appear to be unchanged, while their necessarily inadequate realization is universally deplored.

The traditional table of organization for the government of a village lists so many political offices ranging from village chief down to the janitor of the old men's clubhouse that nowadays one man alone may hold four or five out of the 12 or 15 political offices in a given village, while in other villages the complaint is that "everybody is a chief." Such focusing of political function in the hands of one man and such diffusion of offices throughout the whole population distort the concept of evenly balanced political powers implicit in traditional Yap political organization. Furthermore, this situation defeats the traditional intent of restricting the governing function to a selected segment of the society. The Yaps are well aware of this and insist that the time-honored ideal pattern remains "right" but that the present undesirable arrangement is unavoidable because of the shortage of people.

Although the complete history of Yap depopulation is impossible to recover, certain inferences can be made with reasonable confidence. The depopulation trend started during a period of acute overpopulation. According to a careful estimate based on a study of abandoned house sites, the population at one time was in the neighborhood of 51,000 with a density of approximately 1,300 person per square mile, a figure 20 times that of the present, but no greater than the present density of some other Micronesian islands, according to official sources:

Island	Density per Square Mile
Nama	2,093
Losap	1,892
Eauripik	1,477
Yap (estimated)	(1,300)
Pingelap	914
Kapingamarangi	892

At no time during the depopulation of this island did genuine social disorganization take place. Yap is highly conservative with respect to change of any kind. It is even possible that conservatism increased precisely as depopulation progressed, since barrenness, death, and disease are essentially believed by the natives to be supernatural punishments for breaches of custom and taboo. The frequent occurrence of such departures might well have made the Yaps feel that compulsive observance of customary modes of action was essential to avoid these evil consequences. Associating misfortune with improper behavior is not uncommon elsewhere in the world. The combination of conservatism and absence of severe social disorganization helps to explain why Yap culture, as a blueprint for how life should be lived, remains today in many ways the same culture as obtained during the period of overpopulation. In brief, Yap culture is one that is geared not only to a large population, but in important respects to overpopulation.

If the practice of abortion began during a period of overpopulation, it was at that time a successful adaptation to a pressing problem. These circumstances could account for the origin of the practice of abortion on

Yap, and a simple explanation for its current prevalence in spite of a drastic change in population would be that it is a "survival," a custom that has lost its utility but persists of its own inertia. Such an explanation would fail to take account of the interrelated nature of the components that comprise a society's culture. The values and institutions that arose in past response to overpopulation became linked to form a fairly coherent cultural totality with powers of persistence greater than those of the constituent parts.

THE YAP WAY OF LIFE:
YOUTH AND LOVE AFFAIRS

Insight into the motives that impel abortion can be gained by examining the childhood and youth of Yap men and women. A man's life goes through a protracted period of childhood, lasting well into the late teens, without many responsibilities, without duties of any serious kind, and with a predominant interest in play. As a youth, he has begun to take love seriously, to learn the elaborate code and ritual of love affairs, and has perhaps had one lover and is going on to a second. He has learned that Yap girls are hard to get and harder to keep; they demand much and they are not constant. If he can talk the girl into coming to live with him, he has a firmer hold over her, though her affection is still likely to wander.

Even a married man with a wife and child, however, has few responsibilities. He will have built a house for himself on his father's land (but well apart from his parents' dwelling) when he was between fifteen and twenty. At that time plots for his yams and pits for his taro and trees for his coconuts will have been set aside from those of his mother and father, for he may not share with them food grown on the same land, cooked over the same fire, or in the same pot. He may share food only with men or women of his age-group. A man's wife cultivates and cooks his vegetable food, and the man should provide her with coconuts and fish, and betel nut for chewing; and these he provides as the need arises or as the spirit moves him. Beyond these duties he has but one other, to provide his father-in-law with fish or other gifts from time to time. Otherwise the care of the child, house, and garden falls almost entirely on his wife. She should help her mother-in-law in the house and in the garden and with any small children her mother-in-law may have.

A man's serious responsibilities and obligations do not begin until he is in his late forties or early fifties when, as head of his kin group, he takes part in the councils and the serious political affairs of his village.

A woman's life need be no different from a man's with regard to responsibilities and work. As a young girl she celebrates her first menses with a year-long residence in a specially designated area outside her village, usually near the inland grassy region. There her friends come to visit and play with her, and she begins her love affairs in earnest. According to the cultural rules, no man can have exclusive claim on her affections during this year, even if she is married, and she spreads her favors widely. After this year she returns to the village, living in a house her father builds for her not far from her parents' dwelling, unless she is married. Except for the fact that she has put on the black neck cord of a mature woman, she continues to lead the life she led as a girl. Her primary interests are in play, in love affairs, and in sociability.

If a woman comes to live with her lover, she is regarded as married, but except for the fact that she is expected to be faithful to him, her life is not radically altered. True, she should do his cooking eventually, but for months after arriving at her husband's house, his mother will still cook for him, and she will share his food. Properly the right to cook her husband's food should be ceremonially transferred from the man's mother to his wife, but since young women do not particularly like the chore, they postpone this ceremony. Often it is just as well, for the couple frequently decide, after a week or a month or a year, that they would rather terminate the marriage. Young people do not get married in the sense of solemnly undertaking the responsibilities of home and family; for them, marriage is in effect a special arrangement to make a love affair easier. When married, they no longer have to meet secretly at night.

The procrastination of the very few ceremonies which are supposed to attend a marriage reflects the instability of this period. There are only two ceremonies, and as often as not one or both are never performed. Besides the ceremonial transfer of cooking privileges, there is supposed to be a small gathering of the bride and groom's immediate families and an exchange of food between them. In this last ceremony the groom's father always makes a little speech which dwells on the hope that the couple will get along together and not fight, will stay together and have children.

There is nothing to prevent the separation (which is divorce) of a couple if they so desire, provided no children have been born. The girl simply goes back to her father's house, taking with her what property she brought—her skirt, her basket, and the knives and jewelry she carries in it. There is no ceremony marking this separation.

On the other hand, considerable social pressure is put on a woman to remain in the marriage if she has borne a child and if the child is alive, for on divorce a child remains with his father unless the child is still nursing, when he will go with his mother until weaned and then return to his father. The mother's parents, her husband's parents, and public opinion bring pressure to bear to keep her with her child. The whole burden of the appeal is laid squarely on her relationship with her child. She is not asked to stay with her husband. She is not appealed to on the ground that she owes her husband's kin group anything, either through her work or her fertility. She is only asked to stay with her child who needs her. It is considered the gravest misdeed for a mother to separate herself from her child and, indeed, the very few children whom I saw whose mothers had been divorced after the child's birth, suffered markedly from the sense of abandonment engendered in Yap in such a situation. A woman who does this is said to have "thrown her child away" and her reputation is badly damaged.

When there are no children divorce is simple, practically without repercussion and consequences; divorce after children are born is a very serious matter and occurs relatively rarely. Out of a group of 28 married women who had each borne one live child, nine had never been divorced at all, 15 had been divorced before the birth of their first child, while only four had been divorced after the birth of their first child.

Thus, when a woman bears a child, her position changes radically. She is primarily responsible for the care and feeding of the child, and she must be with him almost all the time. She will take him with her to the gardens and she will take him along when she goes visiting, but she must be with him. Although her husband shares most of the pregnancy taboos with her and helps with the actual delivery, his responsibility toward the child duplicates his responsibility toward his wife—providing coconuts, fish, and betel. He is not constantly tied to the child the way she is, and a husband's extramarital affairs are not sharply curtailed as are a woman's when she has a child. A woman with a child cannot go "playing about," with her husband or anyone else, at night or by day. A woman becomes tied to a man when she bears a child, and young women on Yap do not like to be tied to one man.

Women up to the age of thirty do not want children because they would no longer be free to fall in and out of love, to attract lovers, to have and break off affairs at will, to practice the elaborate games of love and sociability that appeal to young Yap men and women. They do not want to be tied to a child and to a husband when they are in the best position to gain and enjoy the rewards of being unattached. It is one thing to want to avoid having a child, and something else again to actually do so. Wishing alone will not suffice. On Yap the standard and available means of avoiding children is to induce abortion when pregnancy occurs.

The Yap Way of Life:
Adulthood and Prestige

When a woman is about thirty, her attitude changes. She begins to want children. Women say that they want children then because they are lonely and need someone to talk to. This is another way of saying that they find it hard to attract and keep lovers. At this time a woman will have a child if she can. If she cannot, she will resort to a host of magical aids, medicines, prayers, and whatever else promises to bring the child she now desires. If all of her efforts fail, she will try to adopt a child. Adoption is a common practice on Yap, but the supply of children for adoption is, of course, insufficient to meet the demand.

Although women over thirty give as their main reason for wanting babies that they are "lonely" and are tired of running around, it is significant that at this age a woman leaves the age category of "youth" by Yap standards and enters the status of "adulthood." This social transition has important consequences for the people of Yap. Different kinds of rewards are available to people in different age-groups. Older men and women are less dependent on the gratifications that arise from love affairs and sexual conquest and can turn instead to new activities that now become appropriate and available. The reasons for this shift are connected with the basic values of Yap culture.

The dominant value of Yap culture is prestige. People are ranked and assigned differential prestige in almost every conceivable way. Family groups are ranked within a village, and the villages themselves are ranked into a nine-class system divided into an upper and a lower group. This is crosscut by a formal "war organization" now oriented primarily to political ends. Districts are ranked within three major alliances, and these three alliances continually jockey in the political arena for temporary dominance. Organization within the family itself is conceived as a rank system with father taking precedence over mother, mother over children, and older children over younger. Each plot of land within the village has its inherent, almost inalienable rank, and the highest ranking piece of land validates its owner's position as village chief, while lower political statuses inhere in lower ranking plots of land.

Older people, men and women, have more prestige than younger, and the responsibilities which go with age are seen as privileges appropriate to the older people's prestige. It is the old men, the heads of family groups, who sit around in conference, planning large and ostentatious exchanges of valuable shells or exhibitions of dancing by the men or women of the village. Old men and heads of families achieve the available political statuses of chief, subchief, magician, messenger, and so forth. Owing to depopulation, chieftainships today are often inherited by young men and boys, and when this happens a trusted relative of advanced age is often called in to act as regent for them. In the past when population was at its peak, it was only the oldest who could hold such offices, who were admitted to the old men's clubhouse, who could sit with the council of family heads. The young men were the warriors and fishermen, with time on their hands and without important responsibilities.

Closely related to the fact that age, prestige, and responsibility go together is the conception that a man is still a "young man" until he is about forty or fifty years old. Technically a "young man" becomes a "man" when he succeeds to the head of his kin group. Since succession to the position of "leader of the kin group" goes from a man to his next oldest brother, through all brothers in order of descending age, and then to the oldest male among the sons of all the brothers, it was unlikely in the past that a man would succeed to that position until he was nearly fifty. Depopulation has now accelerated this progression, but it has not changed the rules of the system.

Although this elaborate system of ranking is stable, as far as its rules and regulations are concerned, it has a degree of flexibility in that the rank of any particular unit (family, village, district, alliance, plot of land) is not necessarily fixed permanently. Families, villages, districts, and alliances all vie with each other according to prescribed and orderly rules for legitimate improvement in their position; magic, sorcery, and pure chicanery are often used to hasten this necessarily slow process. But whatever the position held by any social unit, the aim is to increase its prestige and better its position.

Prestige on Yap is not correlated with such powers or privileges as make daily life precarious for some and easy for others, as in the United States. For all practical purposes food is now and was in the past equally accessible to all, regardless of rank. High prestige groups do not have the right to exploit the labor of low prestige groups except in ways which are primarily symbolic. Thus, certain families within the upper groups have the right to demand that their roofs be repaired by persons from lower groups. This amounts to a token expression of ranked relationship rather than a continuous work obligation of great magnitude. So far as can be discovered now, depopulation affected all social classes on Yap equally, for all social classes had equal access to the necessities of life and no social class was disadvantaged by being overworked or otherwise penalized in any but symbolic ways.

WHY ABORTION PERSISTS

I have shown that Yap women induce abortion because they do not want to be tied down with children during a time when they feel they would be better occupied in love affairs and in sociability. In terms of our own standards we might feel that such an attitude was morally "wrong," but they would insist that it was morally "right" and such indeed is the Yap cultural premise in terms of which they act. Young people *should* spend their time in love affairs and in nonresponsible pleasures. But Yap women also feel that they should have children and care for them. The problem is one of timing; after their period of love affairs is over, women want to have children and care for them, but they do not want the children earlier to interfere with the game of love. Yet it happens that children often come before they are wanted.

Yap standards of behavior for young men and women differ from our own standards. This is a matter of cultural relativity, but more than relativity is at issue. What is also involved is the fit between one part of culture and the rest of the cultural totality. Let us suppose that young Americans in their twenties emulated Yap and consistently preferred to engage in love affairs than to assume adult responsibilities. Quite apart from morality, such a shift would set in motion a series of other changes disrupting what we regard as our way of life. Conversely, if young men and women on Yap suddenly decided to settle down in their twenties and rear families, a host of other changes would ensue and the Yap way of life would similarly be disrupted.

I have said that the dominant values of Yap culture center around gaining and keeping prestige. Fundamental to any prestige system is the fact that a kind of scarce commodity (prestige) is differentially distributed; some have a lot and some have a little, but all cannot share equally. For such a system to work, there must be rules and regulations governing who has prestige and who has not, how it can be gained and how it can be lost. These rules must be obeyed if they are to prevent the chaos which would follow a disorderly scramble after the coveted values. One important consequence of such rules is that people must wait, often for long periods of time, before they can obtain the ultimate rewards, and in the nature of such a system some people will be destined never to achieve them. Waiting, along with the possibility of never gaining valued ends, is difficult for human beings. Accordingly, the prestige system of every society has built into it devices that will make waiting bearable and will make the fact that all cannot attain the highest goals a tolerable if not a happy situation. One such device is embodied in proximate rewards, rewards which can be achieved during the waiting period as substitutes for the ultimate goals.

It is likely that characteristic features of Yap culture—non-responsible early adulthood, love affairs during youth, and induced abortion—originated during a period of ample population. At that time these practices were undoubtedly effective in keeping down the birth rate. When young men and women spent their time avoiding the responsibilities of adulthood, they did not press closely on the high prestige statuses of the old people. When young women were strongly motivated to postpone reproduction until their later years by inducing abortion, they shortened the time span within which they could reproduce and thus limited the overall number of births on the island.

Today, however, underpopulation rather than overpopulation is the dominant problem, and shortening the reproductive span of a woman's life by inducing abortion during her younger years serves instead to aggravate the imbalance. Why, then, does abortion persist? Because they cannot become chiefs or heads of kin groups, women can never achieve the same rewards from the prestige system that the men do. For them, the pattern of repeated love affairs provides pleasure and reward; resort to abortion makes it easier to maintain this pattern of behavior. For men, who must still mark time before assuming positions of prestige and responsibility, protracted love-making offers interim rewards. These practices persist, not merely as useless holdovers from a past era of overpopulation, but as vehicles that continue to serve useful purposes and give psychological gratifications.

■ CHANDIGARH WAS PLANNED BY EXPERTS BUT SOMETHING HAS GONE WRONG

Brent C. Brolin

Cattle wander through shopping centers and lounge in the middle of the streets, even though it is illegal for most residents to own them. Sidewalk vending is outlawed, yet you can't walk on one without stumbling over peanut vendors, shoe repairmen and turban washers. There is an expansive park called Leisure Valley, yet hardly anyone takes his leisure there. This is the city of Chandigarh, in northwestern India, and it is a complex phenomenon.

Unlike other Indian cities, Chandigarh did not develop organically over the centuries, but sprang full-grown from the vision of post-independence India and the planning philosophy of the famous French architect Le Corbusier. After the partition of India and the loss of the old Punjab capital of Lahore to Pakistan in 1947, the Indian government decided to build a totally new capital city for the Punjab. In the words of Prime Minister Nehru, it was to be a city "unfettered by the traditions of the past."

The first expert called in was an American architect and planner, Albert Mayer, who prepared a master plan. He chose Mathew Nowicki to be the liaison architect at the site; before his death in a plane crash in 1950, Nowicki significantly revised Mayer's preliminary plan. Following Nowicki's death the Indians turned to Le Corbusier, who accepted and went to the Punjab in February of 1951. (Two English architects, Maxwell Fry and Jane Drew, were also employed, along with Le Corbusier's cousin, Pierre Jeanneret.)

Chandigarh's evolution was followed with great interest. Le Corbusier was then one of the world's foremost architects and planning theorists, and this was to be his most comprehensive work. Furthermore, he was able to implement his theories without interference, although within reasonable economic limitations. Given all this, Chandigarh came to be looked on as a primer of modern planning and an open laboratory for testing the planners' concepts.

Today, after more than 20 years, the people of Chandigarh appear to be happy. Almost to a man they boast about their closed sewers, flush toilets, hot and cold running water and other conveniences. But then they add: "In the old cities people are closer; in Chandigarh we do not share one another's joys and sorrows."

This confession shows a recurrent malaise that we recently encountered in Chandigarh. If you are given a house with plumbing and electricity, of course you will prefer it to one without them. But beyond the easy observation that all people enjoy the basic amenities, one must ask how well this city meets the subtler human needs. That is, do the planners' ideas about how people should live coincide with the way people really *do* live?

The population of Chandigarh is not typical. Eighty percent of all Indians are villagers, while Chandigarh's residents are primarily educated government workers who, at least superficially, are far more Westernized than most Indians. This was certainly in the minds of the Europeans who designed the city, and it must have made it easier for them to believe that their Western values would be readily accepted.

In the first planning phase a rectangular grid divided the city into 29 sectors one-half mile wide by three-quarters of a mile long. The main business center is near the geographic center of the city, while government buildings (the only ones actually designed by Le Corbusier himself) are located to the north near a man-made lake. Special sectors are devoted to industry and the university, but the typical sector is limited to housing, schools and a shopping center.

Le Corbusier is responsible for this plan, which gives the city its present form. Although the buildings in the commercial and housing areas were designed by his European associates and even by some Indians, these architects had to fit their designs into the overall concepts of Le Corbusier. When a designer comes from the same background as his clients, his needs and likes will probably be similar to theirs. The situation is not so simple when the designer, such as Le Corbusier, comes from a foreign culture.

For example, the perception of space differs considerably from culture to culture. Two Indian businessmen will normally stand about one and a half feet apart while talking, and might even hold hands if they are good friends; Americans in a similar situation would have to be twice as far apart to be comfortable and certainly wouldn't hold hands.

As the designer deals exclusively with the creation of spaces, the cultural difference may create a serious problem. What *he* perceives to be the proper relationship between the living room and the kitchen, for instance, may not be the right one for clients whose life-style is "foreign," or in some way different from his.

Most Americans do not want their guests to pass a messy kitchen on their way to a neat living room, as we can see from the majority of house plans in this country. Yet Puerto Rican families in East Harlem need exactly such a room arrangement if things are to run smoothly: The mother has to keep a close watch on who comes and goes, and since she spends most of her time in the kitchen, it must be by the front door.

Modern architects have often said that basic human needs are the same everywhere, but this is a misleading half-truth. Although the need may be the same, the means of satisfying it will differ from culture to culture. Thus, some form of privacy within the home is an almost universal need, but it can be achieved by closing doors, as in most Western cultures, or by closing your ears, as it is in India where openings are only curtained off.

Unfortunately, most architects today (including Indians) are educated in architectural schools that teach Western values, which they then apply in their own countries. The result is often conflict between the people's traditional life-style and their new surroundings.

In Chandigarh spacious living-dining areas, so popular in the West, are consistently cut in two by a curtain. Food is often stored on the counter-top stoves in the kitchens and the cooking done on the floor. Clothes are hung on wall pegs rather than in the closets. Beds are put in living rooms and living rooms made into bedrooms. These misuses remain riddles until one looks beyond the designer's intentions and into the people's way of life.

To do that, let us follow an Indian resident through a normal day in Chandigarh. Our friend's home was one of the first to be built. Its rooms are large compared with those of more recently built government houses; it has a front yard, living-dining room, two good-sized bedrooms, kitchen, bath, rear veranda and rear courtyard. He has a wife and three children, and his grandfather has come to live with them temporarily. He holds a white-collar job in the Secretariat building, and is thus a member of the middle class.

It is one of the colder months, and so the family sleeps inside rather than outdoors, as they do during the summer. The man and his wife and their six-year-old daughter sleep in one bed in the back bedroom; a son, aged nine, sleeps beside them on the floor. The grandfather and the oldest son, 13, sleep together on the large double bed in what was meant to be the living-dining room; besides the bed, it holds a dining table, six chairs and a side table with the family radio.

We can see that the room intended as a second bedroom has become the formal entertaining area, the drawing room. Our friend explains this by saying that when he invites friends to his house, they should not be able to see the family areas: the kitchen, bedrooms, rear veranda, court-yard and bath. These correspond to the areas that, a hundred years ago, would have been restricted to the women of the family. Our friend's guests must still be brought through the dining-sleeping room, but that inconvenience can be borne. Once the guests are in the drawing room, the family can move about discreetly out of their view.

In the majority of the homes we visited, even those of college-edu-cated professionals, the wife would not join the guests in the drawing room until her husband summoned her. This made it imperative for her to have some way of circulating through the family rooms without being seen. A manifestation of the need for separation between these two parts of the house is the curtain that is always hung between the living and dining areas.

AN ALTAR IN THE CLOTHES CLOSET

After bathing, our friend performs his morning *pujah,* or Hindu prayer ritual. The family altar is in a neat corner of the clothes closet, so that it can be kept in solitude between periods of worship. After praying, he closes the closet door and takes his day's change of clothes off the pegs he himself put up.

His wife has been up for some time. She began working on the rear veranda, picking stones out of the uncooked rice and lentils. It is brighter on the veranda than in the kitchen and, like most Indians, she prefers working in the fresh air. The cooking is done, however, on the kitchen floor over a portable kerosene stove.

The children are just finishing their breakfast on the floor. They like eating there because the *chapatis* (flat wheatcakes served with every meal) are only good when they are hot from the stove. It is a small kitchen, too small to hold the whole family at once, so it is a good thing that the children go off to school early. Unfortunately, in the evening, when they would all like to dine together, they have to eat in shifts. The dining table with its six chairs is seldom used; it is one of those things our friend uses only when he entertains Western guests or other people who he knows would think him "backward" if he invited them to eat on the kitchen floor.

The kitchen counter is not used for cooking as intended, even though the hood would help to carry off the fumes. The wife prefers cooking on the floor. A few "progressive" friends have said that it is unhygienic, but Indian kitchens are scrupulously clean and, anyway, she believes these friends are thinking more about status than hygiene.

After breakfast the wife folds up the bedding and puts it in large metal trunks which take up a fair amount of floor space. They hold all the family's off-season clothing, plus extra bedding. These things are not kept on the built-in shelves provided for them for fear of mice. "Box storage" represents a considerable investment, and so they don't feel safe in putting it on the rear veranda; although loft storage space was provided, it is too high for the women to reach easily. A lockable interior storeroom would have been ideal, but that wasn't planned for.

Our friend leaves home shortly and catches a government bus to travel the two and a half miles to the Secretariat. His wife has packed some lunch for him, but at noon he still goes to one of the unofficial "restaurants" outside the Secretariat for the hot sauces and condiments that accompany a traditional meal. Topping it off with a cup of tea from the *chai khan* or teahouse, also unauthorized, he lounges on the grass and chats with friends before going back to the office.

In the course of a normal day, our friend has encountered many situations where the designer misinterpreted his needs. The front bedroom of his house is turned into a drawing room because the intended drawing room offers too little privacy for the family. This misuse causes another, the bed in the dining area. No closable niche was provided for the family's altar, so a part of the clothes closet is given over to it, and the clothes are hung on wall pegs. The family is deprived of one part of its highly prized communal life, eating together, because their kitchen is too small.

Looking at this and other houses, we see more inconveniences. The façades often have grilles which cast attractive shadows in the sunlight, but many occupants see them as convenient steps for burglars to climb into the rear courtyard. In this early one-story house it was assumed that the courtyard would be used for warm-weather sleeping; the owners would actually prefer the extra security of sleeping on the roof, but no access was provided.

We often saw paper pasted over living room or bedroom windows that faced onto public areas such as a well-traveled walk or courtyard. The Indian house has always been an intensely private place for the family and a few guests; a window that lets passers-by catch a glimpse into this sanctum is very disagreeable. The openness which Westerners are accustomed to is unacceptable to any but the most thoroughly Westernized Indians, a tiny minority.

After seeing the narrow, winding streets of a traditional city like Amritsar, one is struck by the vast expanses of unused space in Chandigarh. Even though some of these areas are future building sites, there will be a tremendous amount of open space left. Fine, one might say—lots of parks. But there is no Indian tradition of park use. "The parks and clubs are the foreigner's invention" we were told by one political figure. The most frequent park visitors are old pensioners who sit in the sun playing cards and young men who, as single men of marriageable age, are in social limbo. These two groups have always gathered under the sacred pipal tree or at the village well.

Much lower-income housing is arranged around open spaces that are 60 or 70 feet square. Here people sit in front of their houses, sewing, knitting, playing cards and reading, but the action is always on the periphery: They can't make contact across the large central area.

Chandigarh's spaciousness makes it more of a suburb than a city. The "cityness" may come in time, but only if its density increases. Le Corbusier originally thought that the horizontal phase of development would be finished when the population reached 150,000; then the vertical phase would begin, and it is to this phase, one imagines, that he looked forward. Chandigarh would begin to look like the dream cities of his youth, where 80-story apartment blocks housed huge populations that would indeed have filled Chandigarh's parks. But this is still a dream on the sparsely settled Punjab plain.

BARGAINING FOR A BOOK OR A BANANA

Each of the city's sectors is cut into nearly equal halves by a shopping street. These commercial areas were supposed to have one of each kind of shop, so that people could buy their everyday necessities without leaving their own sector. But what has happened is that in many of the sectors the shops are all of the same kind: in one sector mostly hardware and plumbing stores, in another mostly auto and scooter repair establishments, in still another mainly dry-goods stores, and so on. As the head of the sociology department at the Punjab University explained: "Shopping customs are different in our country. People believe in bargaining, so they must have a lot of the same kind of stores in one place."

In the West we walk into a store, pick out what we want and pay the price stamped on the item, but the act of buying is not so simple or impersonal in India. The stated price, whether for a book or a banana or a sari, is seldom the final price if the shopper has his wits about him. What good is it, then, to have only one fruit seller to choose from, one sari shop? It is easier to get a lower price if you can go from one shop to the next and back again. The planned use of the commercial areas is being slowly, unofficially altered in line with traditional Indian bazaars.

The shopping streets were designed with shops on the south side only, to keep pedestrians from crossing the street and getting tangled up with car traffic as well as to keep the shopper in the shade. This sounds reasonable. But people still walk in the streets, and—if you are shopping in winter—the sun can be a very comfortable companion. Furthermore, when you walk or bicycle along the street looking at shop signs, you are always looking south into the glaring sun. But again the natural course of events is easing the situation: In all sectors shops have grown up illegally on the north side of the streets.

Dodging cattle on the sidewalks and streets turns out to be as common in Chandigarh as in other Indian cities, even though by statute cattle are supposed to be restricted to a few areas. Every foreigner knows that the cow is sacred in India, but few are aware that it has always been prestigious to own a buffalo. Buffalo are desirable because they give good, rich milk; people want absolutely fresh, high-quality milk and ghee (clarified butter) for cooking. In a country where the adulteration of food is not uncommon, you can only be certain the milk is pure if you see it leave the cow. Buffalo are kept openly in the rear courtyards of small row houses, even though they have to be brought in through the front door in plain view of the neighbors—and, presumably, the authorities.

The original plan was for garbage to be put in cans and collected daily. Actually, it is collected only once a week, but the fact that cattle wander about freely, combined with other Indian habits, makes the situation quite acceptable. Since it is a religious duty to feed the wandering cows, edible garbage (as well as garden trimmings) is left on a pile in front of the house for the cows to browse on. Other waste like paper is saved and sold by the pound to the "paper wallah" who comes round once a week and who, in turn, sells it to the food vendors. We often had peanuts sold to us in some child's day-old English lesson.

Tradition has short-circuited the original concept of Chandigarh in other, less obvious ways. The sector, the building block of the plan, grew out of the idea of the neighborhood unit, which was first introduced into city planning in the late 1920s and has enjoyed continued popularity with planners in the West. It is a self-contained unit surrounded by high-speed roads and focused on an elementary school, placed within walking distance of all the houses, and a small shopping center. It was a practical concept in the West, and particularly in middle-class America where the elementary school (at least until busing) really was a rallying point for the community. This is not the case in India because the schools are not locally run and parents may send their children to any school.

The government-built housing in Chandigarh is arranged according to a strict economic hierarchy and rented to government workers for ten percent of their salary. Those earning the most money live near Le Corbusier's buildings on the north edge of the city. The less you earn, the farther away you live. Consequently, people of similar incomes do live close together, and one might expect this to be a common bond within the community. Yet the sense of family is still so strong that friends are much more likely to come through family connections than through proximity. We were told of a merchant who had had an advertising poster printed showing an attractive young woman holding his product. He proudly showed the poster to his mother, who promptly asked: "Who is this girl's family?"

Except for the illegal bazaars and cattle, there is nothing Indian in the visual quality of Chandigarh; it could be any modern city in the world. Some residents already feel the lack of Indianness. They show it by nostalgia for traditional cities like Amritsar or, sadly, in resignation: "We thought it was horrible when we first came, all like little biscuit boxes and everyone so far apart. But we've got used to it."

Chandigarh is a classic example of what goes wrong when planners apply their own values indiscriminately. They assumed in this case that the architecture would form people in its own image. It hasn't. Where Chandigarh fails to meet the Indians' needs they are fighting to bend it to their accustomed way of life. It is an established fact that we can eradicate other cultures by imposing our own ways. We do not know what the future of Chandigarh will be, but we do know, from the experience of other countries whose cultures have been eroded through contact with the West, that little is gained by abandoning things that connect people with their past while a great deal of pride and cultural self-respect is lost. Perhaps the Indians can make a truly vital, *Indian* city out of Chandigarh—but it can only be at the expense of the original concept.

■ PLIGHT OF THE IK AND KAIADILT: A CHILLING POSSIBLE END FOR MAN

John B. Calhoun

The Mountain—how pervasive in the history of man. A still small voice on Horeb, mount of God, guided Elijah. There, earlier, Moses standing before God received the Word. And Zion: "I am the Lord your God dwelling in Zion, my holy mountain."

Then there was Atum, mountain, God and first man, one and all together. The mountain rose out of a primordial sea of nothingness—Nun. Atum, the spirit of life, existed within Nun. In creating himself, Atum became the evolving ancestor of the human race. So goes the Egyptian mythology of creation, in which the Judaic Adam has his roots.

And there is a last Atum, united in his youth with another mountain of God, Mt. Morungole in northeasternmost Uganda. His people are the Ik, pronounced eek. They are the subject of an important new book, *The Mountain People*, by Colin M. Turnbull (Simon and Schuster). They still speak Middle-Kingdom Egyptian, a language thought to be dead. But perhaps their persistence is not so strange. Egyptian mythology held that the waters of the life-giving Nile had their origin in Nun. Could this Nun have been the much more extensive Lake Victoria of 40 to 50 millennia ago when, near its borders, man groped upward to cloak his biological self with culture?

Well might the Ik have preserved the essence of this ancient tradition that affirms human beginnings. Isolated as they have been in their jagged mountain fastness, near the upper tributaries of the White Nile, the Ik have been protected from cultural evolution.

What a Shangri-la, this land of the Ik. In its center, the Kidepo Valley, 35 miles across, home of abundant game; to the south, mist-topped Mt. Morungole; to the west the Niangea range; to the north, bordering the Sudan, the Didinga range; to the east on the Kenya border, a sheer drop of 2,000 feet into the Turkanaland of cattle herdsmen. Through ages of dawning history few people must have been interested in encroaching on this rugged land. Until 1964 anthropologists knew little of the Ik's existence. Their very name, much less their language, remained a mystery until, quite by chance, anthropologist Colin M. Turnbull found himself among them. What an opportunity to study pristine man! Here one should encounter the basic qualities of humanity unmarred by war, technology, pollution, over-population.

Turnbull rested in his bright red Land Rover at an 8,000-foot-high pass. A bit beyond this only "navigable" pass into the Kidepo Valley, lay Pirre, a police outpost watching over a cluster of Ik villages. There to welcome him came Atum of the warm, open smile and gentle voice. Gray-haired at 40, appearing 65, he was the senior elder of the Ik, senior in authority if not quite so in age. Nattily attired in shorts and woolen sweater—in contrast to his mostly naked colleagues—Atum bounced forward with his ebony walking stick, greeted Turnbull in Swahili, and from that moment on took command as best he could of Turnbull's life. At Atum's village a plaintive woman's voice called out. Atum remarked that that was his wife—sick, too weak to work in the fields. Turnbull offered to bring her food and medicine. Atum suggested he handle Turnbull's gifts. As the weeks wore on Atum picked up the parcels that Turnbull was supplying for Atum's wife.

One day Atum's brother-in-law, Lomongin, laughingly asked Turnbull if he didn't know that Atum's wife had been dead for weeks. She had received no food or medicine. Atum had sold it. So she just died. All of this was revealed with no embarrassment. Atum joined the laughter over the joke played on Turnbull.

Another time Atum and Lojieri were guiding Turnbull over the mountains, and at one point induced him to push ahead through high grass until he broke through into a clearing. The clearing was a sheer 1,500-foot drop. The two Iks rolled on the ground, nearly bursting with laughter because Turnbull just managed to catch himself. What a lovable cherub this Atum! His laughter never ended.

NEW MEANING OF LAUGHTER

Laughter, hallmark of mankind, not shared with any other animal, not even primates, was an outstanding trait of the Ik. A whole village rushed to the edge of a low cliff and joined in communal laughter at blind old Lo'ono who lay thrashing on her back, near death after stumbling over. One evening Iks around a fire watched a child as it crawled toward the flames, then writhed back screaming after it grasped a gleaming coal. Laughter erupted. Quiet came to the child as its mother cuddled it in a kind of respect for the merriment it had caused. Then there was the laughter of innocent childhood as boys and girls gathered around a grandfather, too weak to walk, and drummed upon his head with sticks or pelted him with stones until he cried. There was the laughter that binds families together: Kimat, shrieking for joy as she dashed off with the mug of tea she had snatched from her dying brother Lomeja's hand an instant after Turnbull had given it to him as a last token of their friendship.

Laughter there had always been. A few old people remembered times, 25 to 30 years ago, when laughter mirrored love and joy and fullness of life, times when beliefs and rituals and traditions kept a bond with the "millions of years" ago when time began for the Ik. That was when their god, Didigwari, let the Ik down from heaven on a vine, one at a time. He gave them the digging stick with the instruction that they could not kill one another. He let down other people. To the Dodos and Turkana he gave cattle and spears to kill with. But the Ik remained true to their instruction and did not kill one another or neighboring tribesmen.

For them the bow, the net and the pitfall were for capturing game. For them the greatest sin was to overhunt. Mobility and cooperation ever were part of them. Often the netting of game required the collaboration of a whole band of 100 or more, some to hold the net and some to drive game into it. Between the big hunts, bands broke up into smaller groups to spread over their domain, then to gather again. The several bands would each settle for the best part of the year along the edge of the Kidepo Valley in the foothills of Mt. Morungole. There they were once again fully one with the mountain. "The Ik, without their mountains, would no longer be the Ik and similarly, they say, the mountains without the Ik would no longer be the same mountains, if indeed they continued to exist at all."

In this unity of people and place, rituals, traditions, beliefs and values molded and preserved a continuity of life. All rites of passage were marked by ceremony. Of these, the rituals surrounding death gave greatest meaning to life. Folded in a fetal position, the body was buried with favorite possessions, facing the rising sun to mark celestial rebirth. All accompanying rituals of fasting and feasting, of libations of beer sprinkled over the grave, of seeds of favorite foods planted on the grave to draw life from the dust of the dead, showed that death is merely another form of life, and reminded the living of the good things of life and of the good way to live. In so honoring the dead by creating goodness the Ik helped speed the soul, content, on its journey.

Such were the Ik until wildlife conservation intruded into their homeland. Uganda decided to make a national park out of the Kidepo Valley, the main hunting ground of the Ik. What then happened stands as an indictment of the myopia that science can generate. No one looked to the Ik to note that their hunter-gatherer way of life marked the epitome of conservation, that the continuance of their way of life would have added to the success of the park. Instead they were forbidden to hunt any longer in the Kidepo Valley. They were herded to the periphery of the park and encouraged to become farmers on dry mountain slopes so steep as to test the poise of a goat. As an example to the more remote villages, a number of villages were brought together in a tight little cluster below the southwest pass into the valley. Here the police post, which formed this settlement of Pirre, could watch over the Ik to see that they didn't revert to hunting.

These events contained two of the three strikes that knocked out the spirit of the Ik. *Strike No. 1:* The shift from a mobile hunter-gatherer way of life to a sedentary farming way of life made irrelevant the Ik's entire repertoire of beliefs, habits and traditions. Their guidelines for life were inappropriate to farming. They seemed to adapt, but at heart they remained hunters and gatherers. Their cultural templates fitted them for that one way of life.

Strike No. 2: They were suddenly crowded together at a density, intimacy and frequency of contact far greater than they had ever before been required to experience. Throughout their long past each band of 100 or so individuals only temporarily coalesced into a whole. The intervening breaking up into smaller groups permitted realignment of relationships that tempered conflicts from earlier associations. But at the resettlement, more than 450 individuals were forced to form a permanent cluster of villages within shouting distance of each other. Suppose the seven million or so inhabitants of Los Angeles County were forced to move and join the more than one million inhabitants of the more arid San Diego County. Then after they arrived all water, land and air communication to the rest of the world was cut off abruptly and completely. These eight million people would then have to seek survival completely on local resources without any communication with others. It would be a test of the ability of human beings to remain human.

Such a test is what Dr. Turnbull's book on the Mountain People is all about. The Ik failed to remain human. I have put mice to the same test and they failed to remain mice. Those of you who have been following *Smithsonian* may recall from the April 1970 and the January 1971 issues something about the projected demise of a mouse population experiencing the same two strikes against it as did the Ik.

FATE OF A MOUSE POPULATION

Last summer I spoke in London behind the lectern where Charles Darwin and Alfred Wallace had presented their papers on evolution—which during the next century caused a complete revision of our insight into what life is all about and what man is and may become. In summing up that session of 1858 the president remarked that nothing of importance had been presented before the Linnean Society at that year's meeting! I spoke behind this same lectern to a session of the Royal Society of Medicine during its symposium on "Man in His Place." At the end of my paper, "Death Squared: The Explosive Growth and Demise of a Mouse Population," the chairman admonished me to stick to my mice; the insights I had presented could have no implication for man. Wonderful if the chairman could be correct—but now I have read about the Mountain People, and I have a hollow feeling that perhaps we, too, are close to losing our "mountain."

Turnbull lived for 18 months as a member of the Ik tribe. His identity transfer became so strong that he acquired the Ik laughter. He laughed at seeing Atum suffer as they were completing an extremely arduous journey on foot back across the mountains and the Kidepo Valley from the Sudan. He felt pleasure at seeing Lokwam, local "Lord of the Flies," cry in agony from the beating given him by his two beautiful sisters.

Well, for five years I have identified with my mice, as they lived in their own "Kidepo Valley"—their contrived Utopia where resources are always abundant and all mortality factors except aging eliminated. I watched their population grow rapidly from the first few colonizers. I watched them fill their metal "universe" with organized social groups. I watched them bring up a host of young with loving maternal care and paternal territorial protection—all of these young well educated for mouse society. But then there were too many of these young mice, ready to become involved in all that mice can become, with nowhere to go, no physical escape from their closed environment, no opportunity to gain a niche where they could play a meaningful role. They tried, but being younger and less experienced they were nearly always rejected.

Rejecting so many of these probing youngsters over-taxed the territorial males. So defense then fell to lactating females. They became aggressive. They turned against their own young and ejected them before normal weaning and before adequate social bonds between mother and young had developed. During this time of social tension, rate of growth of the population was only one third of that during the earlier, more favorable phase.

Strike No. 1 against these mice: They lost the opportunity to express the capacities developed by older mice born during the rapid population growth. After a while they became so rejected that they were treated as so many sticks and stones by their still relatively well-adjusted elders. These rejected mice withdrew, physically and psychologically, to live packed tightly together in large pools. Amongst themselves they became vicious, lashing out and biting each other now and then with hardly any provocation.

Strike No. 2 against the mice: They reached great numbers despite reduced conceptions and increased deaths of newborn young resulting from the dissolution of maternal care. Many had early been rejected by their mothers and knew little about social bonds. Often their later attempts at interaction were interrupted by some other mouse intervening unintentionally as it passed between two potential actors.

I came to call such mice the "Beautiful Ones." They never learned such effective social interactions as courtship, mating and aggressive defense of territory. Never copulating, never fighting, they were unstressed and essentially unaware of their associates. They spent their time grooming themselves, eating and sleeping, totally individualistic, totally isolated socially except for a peculiar acquired need for simple proximity to others. This produced what I have called the "behavioral sink," the continual accentuation of aggregations to the point that much available space was unused despite a population increase to nearly 15 times the optimum.

All true "mousity" was lost. Though physically they still appeared to be mice, they had no essential capacities for survival and continuation of mouse society. Suddenly, population growth ceased. In what seemed an instant they passed over a threshold beyond which there was no likelihood of their ever recouping the capacity to become real mice again. No more young were born. From a peak population of 2,200 mice nearly three years ago, aging has gradually taken its toll until now there are only 46 sluggish near-cadavers comparable to people more than 100 years old.

It was just such a fading universe Colin Turnbull found in 1964. Just before he arrived, *Strike No. 3* had set in: starvation. Any such crisis could have added the coup de grace after the other two strikes. Normally the Ik could count on only making three crops every four years. At this time a two-year drought set in and destroyed almost all crops. Neighboring tribes survived with their cultures intact. Turkana herdsmen, facing starvation and death, kept their societies in contact with each other and continued to sing songs of praise to God for the goodness of life.

By the beginning of the long drought, "goodness" to the Ik simply meant to have food—to have food for one's self alone. Collaborative hunts were a thing of the past, long since stopped by the police and probably no longer possible as a social effort, anyway. Solitary hunting, now designated as poaching, became a necessity for sheer survival. But the solitary hunter took every precaution not to let others know of his success. He would gorge himself far off in the bush and bring the surplus back to sell to the police, who were not above profiting from this traffic. Withholding food from wife, children and aging parents became an accomplishment to brag and laugh about. It became a way of life, continuing after the government began providing famine relief. Those strong enough to go to the police station to get rations for themselves and their families would stop halfway home and gorge all the food, even though it caused them to vomit.

VILLAGE OF MUTUAL HATRED

The village reflected this reversal of humanity. Instead of open courtyards around each group of huts within the large compound, there was a maze of walls and tunnels booby trapped with spears to ward off intrusion by neighbors.

In Atum's village a whole band of more than 100 individuals was crowded together in mutual hostility and aloneness. They would gather at their sitting place and sit for hours in a kind of suspended animation, not looking directly at each other, yet scanning slowly all others who might be engaged in some solitary task, watching for someone to make a mistake that would elicit the symbolic violence of laughter and derision. They resembled my pools of rejected withdrawn mice. Homemaking deteriorated, feces littered doorsteps and courtyard. Universal adultery and incest replaced the old taboo. The beaded virgins' aprons of eight-to-twelve-year-old girls became symbols that these were proficient whores accustomed to selling their wares to passing herdsmen.

One ray of humanity left in this cesspool was 12-year-old, retarded Adupa. Because she believed that food was for sharing and savoring, her playmates beat her. She still believed that parents were for loving and to be loved by. They cured her madness by locking her in her hut until she died and decayed.

The six other villages were smaller and their people could retain a few glimmers of the goodness and fullness of life. There was Kuaur, devoted to Turnbull, hiking four days to deliver mail, taunted for bringing food home to share with his wife and child. There was Losiké, the potter, regarded as a witch. She offered water to visitors and made pots for others. When the famine got so bad that there was no need for pots to cook in, her husband left her. She was no longer bringing in any income. And then there was old Nangoli, still capable of mourning when her husband died. She went with her family and village across Kidepo and into the Sudan where their village life turned for a while back to normality. But it was not normal enough to keep them. Back to Pirre, to death, they returned.

All goodness was gone from the Ik, leaving merely emptiness, valuelessness, nothingness, the chaos of Nun. They reentered the womb of beginning time from which there is no return. Urination beside the partial graves of the dead marked the death of God, the final fading of Mount Morungole.

My poor words give only a shadowy image of the cold coffin of Ik humanity that Turnbull describes. His two years with the Ik left him in a slough of despondency from which he only extricated himself with difficulty, never wanting to see them again. Time and distance brought him comfort. He did return for a brief visit some months later. Rain had come in abundance. Gardens had sprung up untended from hidden seeds in the earth. Each Ik gleaned only for his immediate needs. Granaries stood empty, not refilled for inevitable scarcities ahead. The future had ceased to exist. Individual and social decay continued on its downward spiral. Sadly Turnbull departed again from this land of lost hope and faith.

Last summer in London I knew nothing about the Ik when I was so publicly and thoroughly chastised for having the temerity to suspect that the behavioral and spiritual death my mice had exhibited might also befall man. But a psychiatrist in the audience arose in defense of my suspicion. Dr. Geoffrey N. Bianchi remarked that an isolated tribe of Australian Aborigines mirrored the changes and kinds of pathology I had seen among mice. I did not know that Dr. Bianchi was a member of the team that had studied these people, the Kaiadilt, and that a book about them was in preparation, *Cruel, Poor and Brutal Nations* by John Cawte (The University Press of Hawaii). In galley proof I have read about the Kaiadilt and find it so shattering to my faith in humanity that I now sometimes wish I had never heard of it. Yet there is some glimmer of hope that the Kaiadilt may recover—not what they were but possibly some new life.

A frail, tenacious people, the Kaiadilt never numbered more than 150 souls where they lived on Bentinck Island in the Gulf of Carpentaria. So isolated were they that not even their nearest Aboriginal neighbors, 20 miles away, had any knowledge of their existence until in this century; so isolated were the Kaiadilt from their nearest neighbors that they differ from them in such heredity markers as blood type and fingerprints. Not until the early years of this century did an occasional visitor from the Queensland Government even note their existence.

For all practical purposes the first real contact the Kaiadilt had with Western "culture" came in 1916 when a man by the name of McKenzie came to Bentinck with a group of male mainland Aborigines to try to establish a lime kiln. McKenzie's favorite sport was to ride about shooting Kaiadilt. His helpers' sport was to commandeer as many women as they could, and take them to their headquarters on a neighboring island. In 1948 a tidal wave poisoned most of the freshwater sources. Small groups of Kaiadilt were rounded up and transported to larger Mornington Island where they were placed under the supervision of a Presbyterian mission. They were crowded into a dense cluster settlement just as the Ik had been at Pirre.

Here they still existed when the psychiatric field team came into their midst 15 years later. They were much like the Ik: dissolution of family life, total valuelessness, apathy. I could find no mention of laughter, normal or pathological. Perhaps the Kaiadilt didn't laugh. They had essentially ceased the singing that had been so much a part of their traditional way.

The spiritual decay of the Kaiadilt was marked by withdrawal, depression, suicide and tendency to engage in such self-mutilation as ripping out one's testes or chopping off one's nose. In their passiveness some of the anxiety ridden children are accepting the new mold of life forced upon them by a benevolent culture they do not understand. Survival with a new mold totally obliterating all past seems their only hope.

So the lesson comes clear, and Colin Turnbull sums it up in the final paragraph of his book: "The Ik teach us that our much vaunted human values are not inherent in humanity at all, but are associated only with a particular form of survival called society, and that all, even society itself, are luxuries that can be dispensed with. That does not make them any the less wonderful or desirable, and if man has any greatness it is surely in his ability to maintain these values, clinging to them to an often very bitter end, even shortening an already pitifully short life rather than sacrifice his humanity. But that too involves choice, and the Ik teach us that man can lose the will to make it."